EXPOUNDING THE CONSTITUTION

What does it mean to interpret the constitution? Does constitutional interpretation involve moral reasoning, or is legal reasoning something different? What does it mean to say that a limit on a right is justified? How does judicial review fit into a democratic constitutional order? Are attempts to limit its scope incoherent? How should a jurist with misgivings about the legitimacy of judicial review approach the task of judicial review? Is there a principled basis for judicial deference? Do constitutional rights depend on the protection of a written constitution, or is there a common law constitution that is enforceable by the courts? How are constitutional rights and unwritten constitutional principles to be reconciled? In this book, these and other questions are debated by some of the world's leading constitutional theorists and legal philosophers. Their essays are essential reading for anyone concerned with constitutional rights and legal theory.

Grant Huscroft is Professor and Associate Dean at the Faculty of Law at the University of Western Ontario in London. He has written extensively about constitutional rights and judicial review and his work has been published internationally. He is co-author of the leading treatise *The New Zealand Bill of Rights* and has co-edited four collections of essays.

Expounding the Constitution

Essays in Constitutional Theory

Edited by

GRANT HUSCROFT

Faculty of Law
University of Western Ontario

CAMBRIDGE
UNIVERSITY PRESS

CAMBRIDGE UNIVERSITY PRESS
Cambridge, New York, Melbourne, Madrid, Cape Town, Singapore,
São Paulo, Delhi, Dubai, Tokyo, Mexico City

Cambridge University Press
The Edinburgh Building, Cambridge CB2 8RU, UK

Published in the United States of America by Cambridge University Press, New York

www.cambridge.org
Information on this title: www.cambridge.org/9780521173346

First published 2008
First paperback edition 2010

A catalogue record for this publication is available from the British Library

Library of Congress Cataloging in Publication Data
Expounding the constitution : essays in constitutional theory / edited by Grant Huscroft.
p. cm.
Includes bibliographical references and index.
isbn 978-0-521-88741-0 (hardback)
1. Judicial review. 2. Constitutional law. I. Huscroft, Grant. II. Title
k3175.e967 2008
347'.012 – dc22 2007042586

ISBN 978-0-521-88741-0 Hardback
ISBN 978-0-521-17334-6 Paperback

Contents

Preface

This book arises out of a colloquium held at the Faculty of Law at the University of Western Ontario in October 2006. The idea was to bring together leading constitutional theorists and legal philosophers to discuss and debate issues of mutual interest – issues that transcend the doctrinal, country-specific interests that often dominate discussion of constitutional judicial review.

The result is a book of essays that addresses the key questions in constitutional rights theory today, not only in jurisdictions such as the United States and Canada, where judicial review and the power of the courts to strike down legislation are well established, but also in the UK and New Zealand, where rights protection comes in ordinary statute form and judges are denied the power to strike down legislation, and in Australia, which has no bill of rights at the federal level.

I am grateful to Craig Brown, who was Acting Dean at Western Law, and Associate Dean Tim Edgar, without whose enthusiastic support the colloquium could not have taken place.

Grant Huscroft
Faculty of Law
University of Western Ontario

Contributors

Larry Alexander, Warren Distinguished Professor of Law, University of San Diego

James Allan, Garrick Professor of Law, University of Queensland

T.R.S. Allan, Professor of Public Law and Jurisprudence, University of Cambridge

David Dyzenhaus, Professor of Law and Philosophy, University of Toronto

Jeffrey Goldsworthy, Professor of Law, Monash University

Grant Huscroft, Professor of Law, University of Western Ontario

Aileen Kavanagh, Reader in Law, University of Leicester

Bradley W. Miller, Assistant Professor of Law, University of Western Ontario

Steven D. Smith, Warren Distinguished Professor of Law, University of San Diego

Jeremy Waldron, University Professor, New York University

Mark D. Walters, Associate Professor of Law, Queen's University

W. J. Waluchow, Professor of Philosophy, McMaster University

EXPOUNDING THE CONSTITUTION

Introduction

Grant Huscroft

Constitutional interpretation is a serious matter in any political community committed to the rule of law. Widespread disagreement about the most fundamental moral issues is to be expected, and it is bound to play itself out in the interpretation of legal rights. The essays that make up this volume – contributed by some of the most accomplished legal philosophers and constitutional law scholars in the common law world – address three pressing issues in contemporary constitutional interpretation and constitutional theory: (1) the role of moral reasoning in constitutional interpretation; (2) the legitimacy and justification of judicial review; and (3) the place of unwritten constitutional principles in the constitutional order. Although these papers reflect the jurisdictional roots of their authors, they are theoretical works of wide application rather than doctrinal accounts of the workings of the constitution of any particular jurisdiction.

I

The essays in Part I are concerned with morality and its place in constitutional interpretation.

What does it mean to interpret the constitution? Are judges engaged in an enterprise of moral reasoning, or is legal reasoning about moral questions something different? What sort of morality informs legal reasoning? What does it mean to say that a limit on a right is justified?

The focus of constitutional law scholarship is often on interpretive methodology and the well-known schools of interpretation. But as Steven D. Smith argues, the *object* of constitutional interpretation is never made clear. What, exactly, is it that is interpreted under the rubric of constitutional interpretation? We assume that we are interpreting "the constitution" – which may be written and detailed or largely unwritten – and get right into the substantive question at hand. The focus of scholarship is usually not on what it is that we are trying to know, but on *how* we can know it.

All of the well-known schools of interpretation are vulnerable to the complaint that there is no consensus around their adoption, nor is there ever likely to be one. Each school has its proponents, but no school provides an accurate descriptive account of what is going on in constitutional interpretation; all of them are apt to some extent, but at the same time all of them are normative in nature. They are, Smith argues, best understood as prescriptions for reform. Intention-based originalists want the intention of the drafters to be the focus of constitutional interpretation; text-based originalists want the original meaning of the words of the constitution itself to be the focus; whereas nonoriginalists insist that the focus should be on the principles they suppose to be inherent in the constitution.

In light of this, how is it possible to engage in a practice of constitutional interpretation? The tentative answer from Smith is that "the constitution" is a placeholder – a "facilitative equivocation" – for a variety of interpretive purposes, one that obscures the lack of agreement about what exactly is being interpreted, and deliberately so, in order to let the interpretive enterprise proceed. The importance of the enterprise to the community is contestable, but there is no doubt that it goes on and that its consequences are often momentous.

It is often supposed that, in interpreting the constitution, judges are engaged in moral reasoning. As Jeremy Waldron argues, this gives rise to a number of questions, given that people disagree in good faith about moral issues (including rights) and there is no way in which to determine the truth in these matters – at least, no way that is, itself, beyond dispute.

Waldron notes that philosophers ascribe a wider meaning to the term moral reasoning than do legal philosophers and lawyers. Philosophers are concerned with morality as a subset of ethical reasoning, normative reasoning, or practical reasoning, whereas legal philosophers and lawyers may simply use the term to refer to anything other than black-letter legal reasoning. Waldron thinks the distinction between wider philosophical and narrower legal senses of morality may be important. Judges operate in the realm of government and in the context of political issues; they decide for society rather than simply as individuals. The question, then, is whether the philosopher's conception of moral reasoning is appropriate for the sort of practical reasoning with which judges must be concerned.

The need for judges to pay attention to institutional factors often comes at the expense of their ability to engage with the primary moral issue before them, as litigation over assisted suicide demonstrates. No one doubts that assisted suicide has a moral dimension, but the legal questions it raises concern institutional roles – normative questions about institutional responsibility in a constitutional democracy rather than a moral question of the sort over which philosophers have relevant expertise.

Waldron thinks that conceptions of adjudication wrongly assume that the component parts of the judicial task – understanding and applying the law, on one hand, and engaging in moral reasoning on the other – can be separated cleanly. What if, he asks, the task of moral reasoning is always "contaminated" by the legal processes such as applying rules, deferring to text, and following precedent? If this is so, the more pervasive the involvement of moral reasoning in the judge's task, the less relevant the philosophical ideals for moral reasoning will be. In other words, we should not assess judicial performance having regard to the standards of moral philosophy no matter how important moral reasoning appears to be in a particular context, because judges do not engage in *pure* moral reasoning. They engage in *legal* reasoning, and legal reasoning is neither pure moral reasoning nor is it like reasoning in Rawlsian reflective equilibrium. Judges are constrained in ways that the method of reflective equilibrium is not: They are constrained by precedent, doctrine, and other things that flow from authoritative legal text such as constitutions. Even accepting that legal reasoning may have a moral component, philosophical ideals are not apposite.

According to Waldron, if we think that moral reasoning about rights is important, then we may need a venue in which it can occur, uncompromised by the sorts of things with which legal reasoning is properly concerned. It matters whether the moral reasoning is purely personal or is done in the name of society, because each must be assessed according to different standards. Contrary to the argument W.J. Waluchow makes in his paper, however, it does not follow that judges are better at moral reasoning, even if we mean reasoning in the name of society, involving an attempt to keep faith with society's existing commitments. There are other ways of reasoning in the name of society and these must be compared.

Waldron asserts that everyone agrees that some morally important issues should be addressed by the legislature, even if its decisions are subject to judicial review. When legislatures address a problem, they, too, reason in the name of society. Unlike courts, however, they are not constrained by legalisms – text, doctrine, and precedent. They may consider the matter directly and, to the extent that legislators reason on their own behalf, they do so in the context of hundreds of others doing the same thing, all of whom are attempting to persuade the others to support their positions.

There are, then, two ideals of moral reasoning in the name of society on important moral issues: one legislative, and one judicial. Both are bound to operate imperfectly. Which ideal should be used to judge an institution's moral reasoning? And which institution should we choose to do the moral reasoning? It is usually argued that the decision to adopt a bill of rights presupposes that the judiciary should make the relevant decisions: We have decided to treat rights issues as legal issues, so judicial reasoning is required. But only in a formal sense do bills of rights govern the outcome of rights disputes. In practice, their text does not settle any of the relevant matters, usually because they were drafted in such a way as to finesse the major disagreements that are likely to arise. Bills of rights bear on these matters, to be sure, but they do not resolve them in a manner that is beyond reasonable dispute. To commit these matters to the judiciary is to discourage their confrontation by our legislators. Better, Waldron argues, to use the legislative model of moral reasoning than the judicial one to ensure that the issues are addressed on the merits, rather than get bogged down in interpretive disputes about the meaning of the constitution. From Waldron's perspective, if we want real moral deliberation on rights questions, our job is to make legislative debate the best it can be.

W.J. Waluchow takes a different tack, outlining a conception of morality that *ought* to be relevant to judges in interpreting a bills of rights – something between "Platonic morality," on one hand, and the morality of the community on the other, both of which he regards as problematic. The relevant conception of morality, which Waluchow dubs the "community's constitutional morality," includes the set of moral norms and considered judgment that are properly attributed to the community as a whole, as reflected in the community's constitutional law and institutions. Significantly, and contrary to Waldron, he argues that judges are better placed than legislators to reason from this morality.

Waluchow's argument depends on the existence of an "overlapping consensus" in the moralities of the communities in a multicultural society. In this case, the consensus concerns not particular judgments about rights, but, instead, broader premises – the sort of vague commitments that characterize agreement to bills of rights that include such things as equality, due process, and so on. This overlapping consensus may not be apparent; he stresses that it may be recognized only upon careful reflection. He invokes John Rawls' reflective equilibrium concept in arguing that responsible moral decision-making requires that we reconcile our general moral norms so that they are consistent, rather than in opposition to one another, and in harmony with our considered judgments about particular cases and types of cases.

This is a large task, and leads to what Waluchow considers the main problem: Having made commitments to constitutional morality, members of the community will, from time to time, embrace opinions that are at odds with their broader commitments, properly understood. He observes that this problem is uncontroversial when speaking of personal morality, yet it becomes controversial when moral rights acquire legal force in bills of rights. Judges are often criticized for making decisions at odds with the community's current moral views. It is forgotten that their decisions are designed to give effect not to the community's moral views or opinions, but instead to the larger commitment the community has made to its constitutional morality – something that Waluchow thinks should be clear if the requirements of reflective equilibrium are met.

Waluchow uses the controversial example of same-sex marriage to illustrate this point. In his view, opposition to same-sex marriage is tantamount to racial bigotry and sexism, practices that all agree are condemned by our bill of rights commitments. The problem is that opponents of same-sex marriage have failed to understand their own constitutional commitments. Judicial review is salutary, then, because judges are well placed to understand the community's constitutional commitments and to identify their implications, and may perform an important role in educating the community in the process.

Waluchow assumes that ascertaining the community's true moral commitments is not significantly different from what judges normally do in common-law cases and, in this regard, his views are quite different from those of Waldron. To the extent that Waluchow acknowledges a need to "fill the gaps," he is content to have judges do it because he regards common-law methodology as superior to legislative action. He suggests, again contrary to Waldron, that judicial decisions may well be more acceptable than legislative decisions to those who lose out, and concludes with a paradox: Not only may judicial review be consistent with democracy, it may well be one of its requirements.

Judicial review is all about assessing the nature and quality of the reasons proffered in support of state action. In many jurisdictions, there is a formal division between the tasks of defining rights and assessing justification for limiting them. A two-stage approach to rights protection is taken, and Bradley Miller argues that this is problematic for a number of reasons.

The separation of definition and justification in bills of rights such as the *Canadian Charter of Rights and Freedoms*, the *New Zealand Bill of Rights Act*, and the *South African Bill of Rights* renders the formal definition of rights far less important than the highest court's approach to the concept of reasonable limits on those rights. Freedom of expression is the best example of this: It is easy for courts to expound on the importance of expression and commit to expansive interpretations of it only to limit the extent of the *freedom of* expression at the second stage of the inquiry, when justification for limits on particular forms of expression is assessed.

The separation of definition and justification and the establishment of a presumption against limits on rights (and concomitant burden of justification on the state) is thought by many to be a virtue of two-stage bills of rights, but Miller argues that this is based on a clear misunderstanding. As American experience demonstrates, it is not the case that in the absence of a reasonable limits provision, bills of rights must protect rights absolutely. Moreover, the separation of definition and justification causes conceptual difficulty. It encourages the courts to define rights in such a way as to leave something for the justification clause to do, and causes courts to misdescribe the nature of reasoning with constitutional rights. It is commonly thought, for example, that reasonable limits provisions allow infringements on rights to be upheld, when what is really happening is that the claim of right is defeated in view of the nature and force of the reasons proffered in support of the state's action.

There are further problems. The separation of definition and justification may cause contextual factors that should be relevant to determining whether or not the right has been infringed to be excluded from consideration at the first stage of the inquiry. Alternatively, the concepts of definition and justification inquiries may collapse into each other. It would be one thing if there were a meaningful distinction between matters of principle and policy, as Ronald Dworkin has argued, but Miller eschews this distinction. Following John Finnis, he advances a nonaggregative account of interests in which legislating for the common good is a matter of securing the background conditions necessary for each person to pursue his own good, rather than securing the aggregate interests in the community. Thus, both sides in a dispute may be speaking the language of rights.

Using the Supreme Court of Canada as his example, Miller argues that "reasonable limits" jurisprudence should not be understood as simply a means of giving effect to majoritarian preferences. Properly understood, it is a means of establishing the common good for the community, which includes the rights claimant. It does not make sense, then, to approach rights as inherently more important than anything the state is pursuing, such that the state should always face a difficult burden of justification. Everything depends on whether or not the state is pursuing a collective interest that can be supported by a sound moral and political philosophy.

This leads Miller to consider the "dollars vs. rights" controversy. In the early days of the Canadian Charter, the Supreme Court of Canada incautiously suggested that fiscal concerns could never be a relevant reason for limiting rights. This was based on the hostility of the Court to aggregative interests when rights were at stake. But, Miller argues, a decision to spend or not spend money is not an end in itself; it is instrumental to some purpose, and this purpose must be considered in order to determine whether or not a limit on a right is justified. In order to do this, the moral evaluations behind the fiscal decision must be considered.

Having regard to the legislature's responsibility to legislate for the common good – understood as providing individuals with the conditions necessary for them to pursue their own good – on Miller's account, the question should be whether or not the reasons for legislating were strong, and the government has not treated any person or group wrongly in making its decision. If the reasons are strong, and the government has not acted improperly in the latter sense, its decision is justified and there is no reason to attempt to limit the impact of the decision by describing the province's fiscal situation as an "emergency." There may be no reason to grant automatic priority to Charter rights over the justificatory values inherent in the Charter's reasonable limits provision. Fiscal justification for limiting rights is inadequate per se, but an argument that situates a limit on a right in the context of the requirements of a free and democratic society is not, and fiscal consequences are not irrelevant to that context.

II

The essays in Part II are concerned with the perennial problems of legitimacy and justification where judicial review is concerned.

How does judicial review fit into a democratic constitutional order? Do the precepts of liberal constitutionalism demand it? If so, are attempts to limit its scope incoherent? How should a jurist with misgivings about the legitimacy of judicial review approach the task of judicial review? Is there a principled basis for judicial deference?

Larry Alexander attempts to separate the basic questions. Constitutions tend to be written, are generally understood as higher forms of law, and are usually entrenched against majoritarian amendment or repeal. But the line between constitutional and ordinary forms of law is not clear. The UK has no formal constitution, but appears to have a constitution nonetheless. The people accept as much, and this is what counts. Constitutions rest on acceptance, not formality; they are, on Alexander's account, not democratic but anarchic. The real question is not whether we should have one, but instead whether existing arrangements should be formalized such that they are removed from control by democratic majorities.

Alexander assumes that judicial review is a corollary of the decision to have a written constitution, and that judges are better equipped to interpret constitutions if interpretation involves discerning their intended meaning. To object to judicial review is, he suggests, to object to the decision to constitutionalize things in the first place. This is all controversial, but Alexander acknowledges that he is referring only to constitutions with determinate rules, rather than indeterminate standards. The latter call for evaluative judgments, and the case for judicial review in regard to these is weaker – yet may still be strong, in his view.

The case for including rights in a constitution depends on whether the relevant rights are legal rights or pre-existing moral rights. Legal rights must be embodied in a rule or standard, but a standard requires some moral reference point, and if there is no moral right, none may exist. It might be thought desirable to entrench specific rules, for example, as corollaries to the requirements of democratic government. Judicial review can work well for these, but if instrumental rights are protected in indeterminate standards, then evaluation will be required, and it will be controversial.

The case for including moral rights in a constitution, and determining the way in which they should be enforced, occupies the bulk of Alexander's attention. He identifies the problem from the outset: Moral rights have to be constrained by the institutional provisions of the constitution, lest they overwhelm them. The equal protection clause in the Fifth Amendment cannot be invoked, for example, to declare the Senate unconstitutional on the basis that it denies equality among voters by basing membership on states rather than population. For Alexander, it follows that moral rights can never be constitutionalized to their full extent, whatever might have been intended, and that our understanding of constitutionalized moral rights must be subordinated to the decisions of the body charged with interpreting them. If a court is to have the final say, then its decisions must be seen as constitutionally controlling even if they are thought wrong.

In short, there are real limits on our ability to constitutionalize moral rights. But, he notes, we are subject to real moral rights in any event. They are superordinate no matter how we purport to deal with them in our constitution. The question is not *whether* they should bind us, but *how* we should be bound by them. The debate about constitutionalizing moral rights is a debate about who should decide what those moral rights require.

The relative ease with which legislative decisions can be reversed is not an argument in support of legislative supremacy, in his view, unless it *should* be easier to reverse judicial decisions, and that is the very question in issue. But, as Alexander notes, if judges are better at settling moral questions – a point on which he remains agnostic – there is no reason why their decisions should be more easily overturned. On the contrary, there is every reason to make it difficult to do so.

If we assume that there are right answers to moral questions, and the judiciary is well placed to answer them, does a majority have a right to be morally wrong in any event? Alexander argues that democratic majorities aren't all that they are cracked up to be; they are, at best, a majority of legislative representatives, and their view may not reflect a real majority in the community in any event. But even assuming the superiority of the legislature's democratic credentials *vis a vis* the court, Alexander insists that they do not have a right to be wrong.

He concedes, as Waldron argues, that the U.S. Supreme Court's forays into moral questions constitute less-than-compelling reasons to prefer judicial resolution; that court, like most others, has a tendency to respond with legalistic reasoning rather than moral deliberation. But Alexander turns the point around, illustrating some of the matters that need to be resolved if legislatures are to be supreme in matters of moral deliberation.

How are legislatures to be constituted? More broadly, he asks why it should be assumed that democratic resolution of moral issues should take place at the national level. Given that legislatures are not the only bodies with democratic credentials, why favour them over other bodies – international or otherwise – with such credentials? And given that the franchise for electing a legislature is subject to extensive restrictions, how does this affect the case for legislative supremacy in any event? Given that moral decisions are not either/or propositions, how are problems of intransitivity to be avoided? Is it legitimate to vote based on self-interest or is a broader judgment required? Finally, how are process-related rights that are preconditions to democratic decision-making to be protected?

According to David Dyzenhaus, "constitutional positivists" like Jeremy Waldron and Jeffrey Goldsworthy – both of whom reject the notion that judges should have the final say on human rights matters, rather than the idea of human rights – are in an impossible position. Waldron's argument focuses on jurisdictions with strong-form judicial review, but Dyzenhaus notes that the distinction between strong and weak-form review depends upon the way in which the public perceives what the judges say. If legislators amend legislation to conform to judicial interpretations, there is no meaningful distinction. Additionally, Dyzenhaus notes that interpretive commands in weak bills of rights turn out to be tantamount to instructions not to apply inconsistent legislation – the very sort of power judges have in strong review models. So Waldron cannot assume that weak-form judicial review is not problematic. Moreover, his concession that judicial review of executive action is appropriate gives away too much.

On Dyzenhaus's account, Waldron's core case against judicial review of legislation amounts to the claim that, given the pluralism of society – given what

Waldron describes as good faith disagreement about the meaning of the rights we cherish – we should prefer legislative interpretations of rights to judicial interpretations because legislative interpretations have democratic credentials, and legislatures have the capacity to engage in the sort of deliberation that courts, confined by the circumstances of litigation, do not.

Dyzenhaus disagrees with this argument from top to bottom. In his view, the establishment of a human rights culture – or any culture of justification that subordinates majoritarian settlement – is problematic for constitutional positivists because it leads inevitably to the establishment of strong-form judicial review. All that remains is for them to counsel judicial restraint and, according to Dyzenhaus, there is no principled basis for doing so. In any event, by this point, the game has been lost; to argue about whether or not a judge has gone too far is to presuppose the legitimacy of judicial review.

Dyzenhaus then turns his sights on Jeffrey Goldsworthy, who has argued in favour of a moderate form of originalism. According to Dyzenhaus, no term in a constitution – not even a boilerplate term like "peace, order, and good government" in the Australian Constitution – cannot be given a new meaning by courts in the right circumstances. A judge could invoke the term "good government," he argues, to limit the power of the Australian Parliament if it were to attempt to change the system of government by installing a dictatorship.

Judges committed to constitutional positivism are, on Dyzenhaus's account, attempting to do the impossible. They are committed to recognizing a legislative monopoly on law-making, but they are operating in a common-law legal order. The best they can do is to attempt to curb judicial activism, which Dyzenhaus defines as the propensity of judges to affirm their interpretation of a bill of rights over the legislature's. Even here, however, they are unlikely to be successful. Indeed, to the extent that judges discover inconsistency between legislation and their understanding of a bill of rights, they will, themselves, be activists.

The problem, in short, is that constitutional positivists have been overtaken by events. As Dyzenhaus puts it, "their understanding of their obligation of fidelity to law is inconsistent with many of the pieces of constitutional furniture in place." In effect, he challenges them to acknowledge the need for the extensive legal reform he says is necessary to make their views tenable.

For her part, Aileen Kavanagh does not accept that exercises of restraint in judicial review are necessarily unprincipled. The concept of deference is under-theorized, however, and she asks not only why judges sometimes defer to the elected branch of government, but whether or not there are circumstances in which they should.

Deference, on Kavanagh's account, is a matter of the court assigning weight to the judgment of the elected branch when that judgment is at variance with its own, or when the court is uncertain about the correctness of its judgment.

The primary reason for deferring is when a court considers that the judgment of the elected branch is worthy of respect, perhaps because the elected branch possesses superior skill, expertise, or knowledge in regard to the matter at hand. But deference may also be accorded on the basis of respect for relationships. Judges, she argues, owe some amount of deference to the legislature simply because the branches of government owe each other respect as a matter of interinstitutional comity. Relatedly, deference may be accorded for prudential reasons. There are limits to what the courts can accomplish, and sometimes they should defer to the elected branch rather than take on a fight they may lose. They have an interest, in other words, in preserving judicial capital for future cases, and Kavanagh regards even deference of this sort as rooted in a judgment of political morality about appropriate institutional roles.

Deference is a matter of degree; it depends on how much weight a court assigns to the judgment of the elected branch. Minimal deference involves the attribution of some presumptive weight to the decision of an elected body and, on Kavanagh's account, is always owed by the judiciary by virtue of the elected branch's status *as* the elected branch. Substantial deference, on the other hand, has to be earned. Like Bradley Miller, Kavanagh rejects Ronald Dworkin's policy-principle dichotomy; the distinction is not so clear-cut. Substantial deference is only warranted where the courts *judge themselves* to be deficient in their ability to deal with the matter at hand, whether because of institutional competence, comparative expertise, or institutional legitimacy.

Judicial review is not a positive or a negative thing on Kavanagh's account; everything depends on the circumstances of its use. Deference does not require judges to adopt any particular course of action. In particular, they need not choose between striking down and upholding legislation. Courts may impose interpretive solutions by reading-down legislation or reading-in provisions to make it consistent with a bill of rights – solutions that may be more invasive than deferential. Alternatively, they may simply issue declarations of inconsistency with a bill of rights. However, even in the context of an ostensibly weak judicial review model – one in which the courts are precluded from invalidating or striking down legislation – the courts' declarations are likely to have tremendous impact, if not be determinative of the subsequent legislative outcome. Like David Dyzenhaus, she accepts that weak judicial review may well morph into strong.

James Allan considers how someone concerned about judicial review should approach the practice of it by means of a thought experiment: What, he asks, would Jeremy Waldron do if he were appointed to a country's highest court?

Allan tracks Waldron's argument from "The Core of the Case Against Judicial Review," asking first whether or not the democratic institutions are in reasonably good working order. Nothing is perfect, of course, and democracy is understood differently in different contexts, but it is fair to say that the UK, Australia, New Zealand, the United States, and Canada are countries that enjoy well-functioning democratic institutions. This is a problem for Justice Waldron because, on Professor Waldron's account, well-functioning democratic institutions are one of the assumptions that render judicial review illegitimate. Thus, Justice Waldron would have at his disposal the very power that Professor Waldron thinks judges should not have. Worse, Allan thinks there is a risk that Justice Waldron might rationalize the exercise of this power, regardless of his principled opposition to judicial review.

In principle, the vagueness of the sorts of guarantees found in bills of rights would force judges to eschew textualism: Plain meanings of things like freedom of expression, due process, and equality do not exist. At the same time, however, progressive or "living tree" interpretation is equally problematic because it appears to afford open-ended discretion to judges, rendering judicial review more powerful than Professor Waldron would like. Perhaps Justice Waldron could revamp Hercules' mission, interpreting the bill of rights in light of society's commitment to majority rules rather than a Dworkinian "right answer." Alternatively, he could adopt a variant of Justice Holmes' "puke test," adopting a general standard of deference but holding out the possibility that, in exceptional cases, he may exercise the power he thinks, in general, is illegitimate.

Allan queries whether it is possible to have a more robust approach to judicial review for some rights than others, but he finds that this is not a principled option, and it is one that Professor Waldron has rejected in any event. Nor could judicial review be rationalized in situations in which the legislature had not yet dealt with a matter: Whether judges get to the matter after the legislature has dealt it or before it has had the chance to do so, judicial decisions under constitutional bills of rights foreclose legislative options.

At this point, then, the task for Justice Waldron looks daunting. Allan asks whether a Canadian-style "notwithstanding" clause changes anything. If the judges' decisions are not final – if they can be overcome with ordinary legislation in the democratic processes – should judges otherwise concerned with the legitimacy of judicial review be put at ease?

Allan notes that the particular features of the Canadian notwithstanding clause render this question hypothetical. As Professor Waldron has argued, in order to use the notwithstanding clause in Canada, legislatures are forced into the position of appearing to override the *Canadian Charter of Rights and Freedoms* itself, rather than simply expressing disagreement with a judicial decision interpreting it. But what if, as Jeffrey Goldsworthy has asked, the notwithstanding clause were worded to avoid this objection? Allan thinks that even an acceptably worded notwithstanding clause would not resolve the problem, but he suggests that Justice Waldron might find judicial review legitimate were such a clause to exist.

III

Part III addresses the debate about unwritten constitutional principles and their relevance in the constitutional order.

The enterprise of constitutional interpretation usually focuses on the written constitution. What is the place, if any, for unwritten constitutional principles in a written constitutional order? Are bills of rights merely examples of the moral content immanent in a common law constitution, or are they exhaustive of the state's legal obligations? What if a bill of rights contains things that conflict with the common law constitution, or the people amend their bill of rights to overcome some aspect of the common law constitution. What are courts to do?

T.R.S. Allan argues that law presupposes substantive content that respects human dignity and individual autonomy, and that the integrity of the judicial process is integral to the law. But this, too, has a substantive content; the integrity of the judicial process is intimately connected to the nature of the legal rules judges are asked to enforce. He parts company, at the outset of his paper, from the views recently expressed by the Supreme Court of Canada, which has insisted upon the primacy of the written constitution. A written constitution, on Allan's account, is simply an articulation of the *main* components of the rule of law. Courts, he argues, cannot avoid making judgments about the justice or fairness of the legislation they are asked to apply, whether or not a bill of rights is in place.

These are significant claims, and they are built on a conception of the rule of law that extends beyond formal equality to embrace a form of substantive equality: Distinctions drawn between persons must be capable of rational justification. Laws must serve legitimate public purposes – purposes compatible with a "plausible conception" of the common good. This leads Allan to find much implicit in the rule of law: natural justice; due process; the right to a fair trial; protection from abuse of process, double jeopardy, and bills of attainder; a right to counsel; prohibition of cruel and unusual punishments and retrospective legislation; and so on. These things flow from the separation of powers and the rule of law, and so do not depend on the protection of a bill of rights.

The rule of law does not require that any *particular* conception of substantive justice be adopted; Allan purports to be content to leave the detailed implementation to individual jurisdictions. Thus, variation in the way in which particular rights are understood is not problematic. Judicial decisions appeal to shared standards and traditions, but they also reflect the judge's view of the moral basis of those standards and the grounds of the legitimacy of that tradition. Allan regards the task of adjudication as creative in part, and makes a number of claims as to the primacy of moral reasoning. Legal rules are, he says, only guides; they are not binding where they would cause injustice. Allan's views are not directed simply to judges; citizens are the ultimate arbiters of the law, and must decide as a matter of moral conviction whether or not the law deserves their obedience.

On Allan's account, the nature of a judge's power in a particular constitutional order is not significant. It does not follow from a judge's obligation to the rule of law that he has the authority to strike down legislation; Allan assumes, however, that a judge can simply decline to give effect to a provision in circumstances in which it would be unjust to do so. In other words, legislation has only provisional or inchoate authority; its fate is in the hands of its legitimate interpreters, which include judges, officials, and private citizens.

Allan allows judicial interpreters considerable leeway; judicial decisions are at best "partial insights," the use of which may be limited by the circumstances in which they arose. Thus, Allan counsels that lower courts must try to distinguish erroneous decisions of higher courts, "matching the ingenuity of [their] reasoning to the level of [their] repugnance." In difficult cases, judges must rely on their own moral compass. Ultimately, however, they must ask whether or not a prohibition on individual conduct "can be defended by recourse to reasons that the autonomous citizen, duly respectful of other people's interests and concerns, could fairly be expected to acknowledge."

Mark Walters traces the historical lineage of unwritten constitutions in English law, to the point at which written law became a metaphor for law made by a lawmaker using a formula considered canonical by judges. Unwritten law represents the sort of law reached through a discourse of reason: All legal propositions already established are examined not as exhaustive, canonical statements but instead as examples of more general principles from which specific legal propositions may be derived.

Walters is at pains to distinguish his conception of unwritten constitutionalism from other forms that have been proffered. His approach concerns engagement in a normative analysis unrelated to the search for rules of recognition that occupies positivists. It is not about interpreting written text and deducing legal propositions to make sense of abstract concepts, or "filling in gaps." Nor is unwritten constitutionalism about interpreting common law concepts that become incorporated into constitutional text, or about accumulated layers of case law that come to provide canonical expressions of the text.

Unwritten constitutionalism describes the "discourse of reason" used to identify not only the substance of a legal principle but also its status as part of the supreme law constitution. It is, Walters argues, about the spirit of legality that pervades the form of constitutionalism. In considering what he calls the structuralist account, Walters observes that the approaches taken by American, Australian, and Canadian judges are remarkably similar. American and Australian judges insist that inferences from the written constitution form part of the written constitution itself, whereas Canadian judges describe the relevant principles as unwritten. But courts in all three jurisdictions are engaged in the same thing: the articulation of an unwritten constitution. The extent to which a constitution is comprehensive does not depend upon choices made by those who drafted it; instead, it must be recognized that choices made by those who draft constitutions may not be uniform or consistent, and that it is for courts to conclude that what was drafted is merely an elaboration of an unwritten principle, rather than an exhaustive code. Thus, structural reasoning fits within the traditional common-law conception of unwritten law.

Walters acknowledges that there are arguments to be made against unwritten constitutionalism as he conceives it: When judges treat written constitutions as simply evidence of deeper commitments, they may develop the law in ways that deviate from choices made by those who wrote the constitution, as Jeffrey Goldsworthy argues. Walters thinks there is an answer to arguments of this sort: In many ways written constitutions are shaped by accident and force rather than reflection and choice, and the choice made by one set of people may have coerced another. Here, he asserts, objections to interpretation from abstract principles behind the text lose force.

Following Lon Fuller, Walters suggests that "made law" is inadequate; it cannot accommodate all of the requirements of individual difference essential to the values of legality and the rule of law. A just legal system depends on reconciliation of the general and the particular by judges, so unwritten constitutionalism is inevitable. "Equality of reason" is an unwritten value of constitutionalism that informs the value we place on written constitutionalism.

Jeffrey Goldsworthy examines the three main claims that are made about unwritten constitutional principles, and finds each of them wanting. The first sort of claim is a conceptual claim made by natural lawyers designed to establish that the law is infused with moral content. The problem with this sort of claim is that it overlooks the fact that some legal systems include components like parliamentary sovereignty that positively assert that even unjust laws are legally valid. Goldsworthy argues that our ancestors were well aware of the importance of limits to legislative authority, but classified these limits as moral rather than legal because they did not want to promote unjustified resistance to legal authority.

Goldsworthy agrees with T.R.S. Allan that judges should disobey truly wicked legislation, but his reasons for counseling disobedience are starkly different. Goldsworthy regards it as a moral obligation that overrides other moral reasons for complying with legal obligations, whereas Allan conceives of disobedience as not only a moral but also a legal obligation. Their positions are, ultimately, motivated by opposite concerns. Whereas Allan fears that the separation of law and morality might lead to an abdication of responsibility by the judiciary, Goldsworthy is concerned that the judiciary might take on too much authority. As he puts it, "It is unwise to claim on behalf of the judiciary an authority that will undermine democratic decision-making in many cases that are certain to arise, in order to provide a remedy for extreme situations that are very unlikely to arise, and which would probably useless if they did . . ."

The second sort of claim about unwritten constitutional principles is often referred to as common-law constitutionalism, which, in general, describes theories that attribute constitutional status to the common law as the ultimate source of authority in a state. In its strong form, common-law constitutionalism posits that the common law is superior to statute law. Common to most conceptions of common-law constitutionalism is the idea that the unwritten constitution is the preserve of the courts. Goldsworthy finds little historical support for this conception of the common law and suggests that, in its modern form, common-law constitutionalism is a bootstraps operation. If judges' authority derives from the common law, and the common law consists of judicially posited rules and customs, then the judges have conferred constitutional authority upon themselves. A shift to a Dworkin-inspired defence based on principles of political morality runs into the same objection. Given disagreement on matters of political morality, judges would be left to determine the relevant principles themselves, hence the scope of their authority. Goldsworthy argues that common-law constitutionalism can only be sustained if it is based on the notion that the common law is based on the customs or conventions of the community, or perhaps the legal elite – something the judges did not create, and are precluded from changing unilaterally. But this notion is problematic for a number of reasons.

The third version of the claim about unwritten constitutional principles is based on the idea that a constitution is an attempt to convey meaning, and that meaning is informed by numerous unspoken assumptions. Goldsworthy considers that common-law interpretive presumptions are consistent with parliamentary supremacy. They may, of course, cause legislation to be interpreted more narrowly than parliament intended and frustrate its purpose, and, as a result, their use can be endorsed only in the face of genuine uncertainty about legislative intentions. He rejects the notion that common-law interpretive presumptions give effect to constitutional principles that can be invoked to control legislation regardless of legislative intention.

For Goldsworthy, the fact that judges have sometimes thought it necessary to lie about their intentions rather than assert superiority over legislation is telling of the illegitimacy of their actions. Finally, he argues that the notion that common-law interpretive presumptions are really constitutional principles should be resisted because the theory may prove difficult to confine. The weak version of common-law constitutionalism may collapse into a stronger model: Once it is accepted that the common law authorizes partial disapplication of legislation, it is a short step to full invalidation.

Goldsworthy accepts that implications can properly be drawn from a written constitution, but this does not compel acceptance of broader claims. The problem lies in containing the ability to draw implications. Particularly problematic is the notion that implications can be made on the basis that they are "necessary" to make the constitution achieve its purpose. Coupled with a nonoriginalist conception of purpose, this would establish a unlimited power for the judiciary to change the constitution, bypassing cumbersome amendment procedures. Contrary to Mark Walters, Goldsworthy insists that judges are bound not only by the purposes of those who draft a constitution but the means they used to achieve those purposes. There is room for implication on the basis of necessity only if something is so obvious as to go without saying, a test familiar from contract law. The distinction is between recognizing what is implicit in the constitution, and inserting something into the constitution to rectify it. Goldsworthy is aware that the difficulty in amending a constitution might be a reason for judicial creativity in interpreting it, but abhors the idea that it is for judges to presume to correct constitutions they regard as deficient.

PART ONE

MORALITY AND THE ENTERPRISE OF INTERPRETATION

1 What Does Constitutional Interpretation Interpret?

Steven D. Smith*

Suppose that for a literature class, you and I are assigned to present and debate our interpretations of the novel *Invisible Man*. Our exchange starts promisingly with what appears to be a spirited clash of views. Later, though, and to our mutual mortification, it becomes apparent that you are offering an interpretation of the *Invisible Man* written by Ralph Ellison, while I am talking about a similarly named novel by H. G. Wells. What would happen at this point?

Well, I suppose that, overcoming the initial awkwardness, we might just proceed to offer our respective interpretations of the different books we have read. But we would no longer be engaged in a debate, and we would no longer be agreeing or disagreeing with each other. That is because in order to debate, and to agree or disagree, we must be talking about the same thing.

Fortunately, this sort of embarrassment could not arise with constitutional interpretation. Or could it? It is obvious, someone might observe, that when lawyers and judges and scholars and even citizens engage in constitutional interpretation, they are all talking about, and interpreting, the same thing – namely, "the constitution." The observation is correct, I think, and also crucially important, and I will return to it later in this essay. But it is also true that this name or label – "the constitution" – might be variously used to refer to different things.

In legal systems with a written constitution, as in Canada or the United States, invocations of "the constitution" often appear to refer to something other than, or at least in addition to, the document.[1] Even when people are self-consciously

* I thank Larry Alexander, Michael Perry, Sai Prakash, George Wright, and, of course, the participants in the colloquium for helpful comments on an earlier draft.

[1] See H. Jefferson Powell, *A Community Built on Words: The Constitution in History and Politics* (2002) at 2 [Powell, *A Community Built on Words*]:

> When people talk about "the Constitution," ... they sometimes have in mind neither the document nor our practice of abiding by its housekeeping details. What is in view,

talking about the document, moreover, it has been persuasively argued that although the words – or perhaps more accurately, the *marks* – may remain the same, insofar as we do not treat those marks as the expression of a particular author or collection of authors, we are in reality dealing with different texts.[2] And of course there can be legal systems (the English, for example) featuring "constitutions" that are not identified with any specific document at all.

So it is worth asking directly: What is the object of constitutional interpretation? The question is one we typically skip past in our haste to address particular concrete questions ("Is the death penalty unconstitutional?") or, at a somewhat more "meta" level, general approaches to or prescriptions about constitutional interpretation (Intentionalism vs. textualism vs. . . .). Not "*What* are we interpreting?" but rather "*How* should we go about interpreting it?" This preference for "How?" over "What?" is typical of much modern thought that, leery of what look like intractable metaphysical questions, tries to shift as much discussion as possible into a more epistemological domain – not "What is it that we are trying to know?" but rather "How can we know it?" However, the "What?" deserves attention as well, in part because, as in the *Invisible Man* example, we might think we are engaging with each other – agreeing and disagreeing – when, in fact, we are not even talking about the same thing.

So: When we interpret "the constitution," *what* exactly are we interpreting?

CONSTITUTIONAL INTERPRETATION AS AN ACTUAL, PRACTICAL ACTIVITY

Before pursuing the question, we need to try to clarify it in several respects. To begin with, we need to acknowledge that constitutional interpretation, as we are using the term here, refers to a practical human activity that actually occurs. The point may seem obvious but it is important, for more than one reason.

First, the fact that the term refers to something that actually occurs would seem to preclude the conclusion that constitutional interpretation is impossible. As our discussion proceeds, that conclusion may sometimes seem inviting, even unavoidable. But whenever it makes its appeal we need to resist with the

more often than not, is constitutional law, and by that Americans usually mean a political practice they associate with the courts, and especially the Supreme Court of the United States.

[2] See Paul F. Campos, "Against Constitutional Interpretation," in Paul F. Campos, Pierre Schlag, and Steven D. Smith, *Against the Law* (1996) at 116.

recollection that (as with baptism by immersion, in the old joke[3]) we've "seen it done." Of course (also as with baptism by immersion), we might be confused, or deceived, about the properties and powers of what we've seen done. But *something* going under the description of constitutional interpretation happens all the time, and anything that *is* done *can* be done.

Second, however, the fact that we are asking about a practice that actually occurs suggests that our question (What does constitutional interpretation interpret?) is essentially a descriptive question, not a normative one – not initially, at least. We are not, at the moment, asking what constitutional interpretation *should* take as its object. We are asking what it *does* take as its object. Our immediate goal, in this inquiry anyway, is not to prescribe, but to give an account of what's going on.

To be sure, constitutional interpretation is a practical activity with a heavily normative character, so normative factors and concerns will enter into our inquiry. If, in our descriptive quest, we declined to pay attention to constitutional interpretation's normative dimension, we would likely misunderstand – and hence misdescribe – the practice. Even so, any answer we give will need to "fit" the practice as it occurs.[4] So suppose that someone struts before us an object of interpretation that is irresistibly attractive, and that any red-blooded lawyer would love to embrace for interpretive purposes. If the people who engage in the practice we call constitutional interpretation do not, in fact, understand themselves to be interpreting that object, then it cannot supply the answer to our question[5]: What *does* constitutional interpretation interpret?

INTERPRETATION WITHOUT AN OBJECT?

One other preliminary question demands attention. Someone might object that our question is presumptuous: It presumes that if we are interpreting, then there must be *something* – some text, some object, perhaps some historical

[3] The one about the farmer who, asked whether he believes in baptism by immersion, responds, "Believe in it? Hell, I've seen it done."

[4] It is possible in principle – though not, I will argue, true in fact – that more than one answer would "fit" the facts, and we might then feel free to choose the most attractive answer – the one that would make constitutional interpretation "the best it can be." So you may, if you like, regard our question, "What does constitutional interpretation interpret?" as an "interpretive" question rather than a purely descriptive one. See Ronald Dworkin, *Law's Empire* (1986); Ronald Dworkin, *Justice in Robes* (2006) at 51–72.

[5] Unless, that is, someone could supply a convincing demonstration of what seems *prima facie* improbable – namely, that judges and lawyers are, in fact, interpreting some particular object even though they do not think they are doing so. In that case, the assertion in the text would need to be qualified.

tradition – that we are interpreting. But is this assumption warranted? From time to time, theorists suggest that constitutional interpretation – or at least constitutional argumentation, which seems to refer to the same basic activity – needs no object: It need not be about anything outside itself. Thus, Jefferson Powell notes that when Americans refer to "the Constitution" they usually mean to refer not so much to the document as to constitutional law,[6] and he answers the obvious ensuing question ("Okay, then, what sort of thing is 'constitutional law'?") by asserting that "[c]onstitutional law is an historically extended tradition of argument, a means . . . by which this political society has debated an ever shifting set of political issues."[7]

I am not sure how much Powell intends by this assertion, but he at least seems to be gesturing toward the sort of position self-consciously articulated by Philip Bobbitt and Dennis Patterson, who maintain that constitutional argument (and, in Patterson's case, legal argument generally) is not *about* anything outside itself. A constitutional argument, Bobbitt and Patterson think, can be advanced, opposed, and evaluated in terms of the modalities of constitutional argumentation (of which Bobbitt gives a learned and perceptive account).[8] But "legal propositions are not propositions about the world."[9] Rather, "the practice of constitutional argument . . . *is* constitutional law."[10] There is nothing outside the argument that can serve as a measure of the correctness of the argument: "There is only the practice and nothing more."[11]

If constitutional argumentation or interpretation were a self-sufficient activity that needed no object outside itself, then the question I have posed ("What does constitutional interpretation interpret?") would seem to be misconceived. But I think the "objectless interpretation" position is untenable.[12] In the first place, the position pays insufficient attention – gives insufficient respect – to the very practice that it otherwise so carefully studies and seeks to elevate to self-sufficiency. That is because constitutional argumentation or interpretation does *not* purport to be self-sufficient or merely self-referential. Rather, constitutional interpreters always purport to be interpreting *something* – the constitution (whatever that is).

Nor is this commitment to interpreting *something* a merely contingent feature – one that might be discarded if, say, enough constitutionalists read

[6] Powell, *A Community Built on Words*, *supra* note 1.
[7] *Ibid.* at 5–6.
[8] Philip Bobbitt, *Constitutional Fate: Theory of the Constitution* (1982).
[9] Dennis Patterson, *Law and Truth* (1996) at 135 (explaining and endorsing Bobbitt's view).
[10] *Ibid.* at 136 note 39 (quoting Bobbitt) (emphasis added, deleted).
[11] *Ibid.* at 142.
[12] These criticisms are developed at greater length in Steven D. Smith, *Law's Quandary* (2004) at 70–4 [Smith, *Law's Quandary*].

Patterson and Bobbitt. Rather, "interpret" seems by its nature to be a transitive verb: It requires (at least implicitly) an object. In this respect, interpreting is like, say, eating. The point is substantive, not grammatical. You can, to be sure, form a sentence using "eat" or "interpret" without an explicit direct object. But you cannot actually engage in interpreting or eating without an object. So suppose that after observing your pallid countenance I urge you to eat. "Eat *what*?" you ask, "A hamburger? A burrito? A candy bar?" and I explain, "Oh, you misunderstand. I don't want you to eat *something*, or *anything*. I just want you to eat. Eat, period, full stop, *tout court*." My directive would be nonsensical. How could you possibly follow it? By sitting there, chewing on air? The same holds, it seems, for "interpreting."

But suppose these doubts could be overcome: "Interpret" somehow becomes an intransitive verb, so that it is somehow possible to engage in constitutional interpretation without having anything to interpret. What would be the practical sense of engaging in that activity in the way we do? Remember that constitutional interpretation is not just an amusing little game that a few academics engage in to distract themselves (like punning, for instance, or post-tenure performance evaluations). Enormous real world consequences turn on the results of our efforts in constitutional interpretation. The enterprise proceeds, as Robert Cover noted, "in a field of pain and death."[13] People are committed to or released from jail (or the electric chair), laws are struck down, and cherished traditions are obliterated with the invocation of "The constitution requires. . . ." or "The constitution forbids. . . ." If these ominous phrases are understood to refer to nothing more than the discursive permutations of some byzantine and wholly self-referential "language game," what sense would it make to attribute such crushing authority to that game?

In short, for the practice of constitutional interpretation to make sense, conceptually and practically, those who engage in it necessarily suppose that interpretation is interpreting *something* – something worthy of the weight they place on it. But what *is* that something?

FAMILIAR ANSWERS, AND OBJECTIONS

There are, of course, some familiar positions about constitutional interpretation. These positions typically appear to be offering prescriptions about *how*

[13] Cover went on to suggest that this violent dimension of law is one that "the growing literature that argues for the centrality of interpretive practices in law blithely ignores." Robert Cover, "Violence and the Word," reprinted in Martha Minow, Michael Ryan, and Austin Sarat, eds., *Narrative, Violence, and the Law: The Essays of Robert Cover* (1992) at 203.

to interpret the constitution, but they also offer views – or at least reflect presuppositions – about *what* constitutional interpretation interprets. Not surprisingly, each of these positions has its appealing features. But each also provokes objections that are so well known that it would be tedious to rehearse them here at length: A simple allusion should usually be sufficient. Some of these objections are specific to particular positions, but at least one – we can call it the "no consensus" objection – is common to all, and is especially significant for the present inquiry.

Enactors' Intentions

One familiar position, often called "originalist," supposes that what we are interpreting is the intentions of the enactors of a constitutional provision, as expressed in that provision. So the object of interpretation would be a particular kind of mental state (intentions or perhaps, more narrowly, semantic intentions) that existed in a body of persons – those who occupied seats in the convention or Congress that drafted the provision in question, or in the conventions or legislatures that ratified the provision, or both.

This "enactors' intentions" answer appeals to our democratic commitments. Why interpret and treat ourselves as governed by the intentions of long-dead enactors? Because they spoke for "We the People," the intentionalist suggests: Hence, constitutional interpretation is a process by which we (in an admittedly loose and temporally extended sense of "we") govern ourselves. In addition, if we happen to think that the enactors were a particularly wise or prescient bunch, then interpreting and carrying out their intentions might be a way of importing wisdom into our community's governance.

Of course, this answer provokes well-rehearsed objections. Particularly if the group of enactors is held to include ratifiers, then enactors' intentions provides a pretty diffuse object of interpretation, and this quality leads to objections both epistemic (How can we really know what the enactors intended?) and ontological (Is there really even such a thing as a collective intention to know?). A different sort of complaint (the "dead hand" objection) rebels against subjecting ourselves to the authority of long-dead framers – particularly if, as contemporary critics of the United States Constitution do not tire of pointing out, those framers were a group of privileged white males.

Volumes have been (and will be) written pro and con about these objections, but what appears to be beyond controversy – and most germane to our purposes here – is that there is no consensus that enactors' intentions provide the proper object of constitutional interpretation. Some constitutionalists think so; others disagree. Some constitutional decisions at least purport to rest on this sort of interpretation; others do not. For example, decisions interpreting the nonestablishment clause of the United States Constitution have often pretended (plausibly or not) to be interpreting the enactors' intentions,[14] whereas free speech decisions typically make no such representation – and even committed "originalists" may concede that speech decisions cannot or should not rest on interpretations of original intentions or understandings.[15]

These divergences indicate that, whatever its virtues or deficiencies, the enactors' intentions answer cannot provide a satisfactory overall *descriptive* account of constitutional interpretation as we know and practice it. Instead, intention-emphasizing originalists are best interpreted as offering a sort of reform proposal: *Some* constitutional interpretation takes enactors' intentions as its object of interpretation, or at least pretends to, and more or even all such interpretation *should* accept that object. For present purposes, we can remain agnostic regarding those normative claims. *Our* question is "What *does* constitutional interpretation interpret?," and it seems that enactors' intentions do not provide a satisfactory answer to that question.

The Words (in Historical Context)

A related answer, also often dubbed "originalist," suggests that what constitutional interpretation interprets is not the subjective mental states of the enactors, but rather the objective meaning of *the words* themselves in their historical context. The assumption here is that words have meanings, given by something like "the rules of language," apart from the semantic intentions of their authors, and those meanings are what constitutional interpretation aims to interpret. Hence, if the enactors intended A but used words that (according to the rules of language) *meant* B, it is B that governs.[16]

This "textualist" answer appeals to our commitment to "rule of law, not of men." Even though elected, enactors do not get to rule us, exactly; their authority is limited to making law, and *that* is what rules us – namely, the law. Constitutional law is something that, by pulling out our pocket copy, we can

[14] The seminal instance is *Everson v. Board of Education*, 330 U.S. 1 (1947).

[15] See, *e.g.*, Robert Bork, "Neutral Principles and Some First Amendment Problems," 47 Ind. L.J. 1 at 22 (1971) ("We are . . . forced to construct our own theory of the constitutional protection of speech. We cannot solve our problems simply by reference to the text or to its history.").

[16] See Robert H. Bork, *The Tempting of America: The Political Seduction of the Law* (1990) at 144:

> If someone found a letter from George Washington to Martha telling her that what he meant by the power to lay taxes was not what other people meant, that would not change our reading of the Constitution in the slightest. Nor would the subjective intentions of all the members of a ratifying convention alter anything.

all read; it is thus not demanded of us that we somehow discern the private, subjective intentions of a distant and diffuse collection of enactors.

Like its intentionalist cousin, the textualist position has been subjected to wide-ranging debate and criticism. Perhaps the most devastating criticism, if sound, is ontological; it holds that textual meaning is the sort of thing (like "the present king of France") that, alas, possesses the unhappy property of not existing. Severed from the intentions of authors, texts do not "mean" at all, and, indeed, are not truly even "texts," but rather mere marks.[17] If this thrust is parried with the explanation that textual meaning is equivalent to what English-speaking readers of the time would have understood the words to mean, then the "diffuseness" objection returns in force: If the mental states of a few hundred enactors was an amorphous object for interpretation, how much more amorphous is an object composed of the mental states of thousands or millions of citizen-readers? The "dead hand" objection revives as well: Long since buried "English speakers" are not obviously better qualified to govern us than are long since dead enactors. Sometimes the textualist position is elaborated in terms of some fictional author or reader – the "average" or "ordinary" English speaker – but the problem of authority persists. It may be irksome to be ruled by people who died generations ago, but isn't it an even greater indignity to be bossed around by a purely fictional character who never actually lived at all?[18]

Or the textualist may stick to his guns and insist that rules of language *can* give meaning to words independent of the semantic intentions of speakers. This response, if plausible, may seem to escape the "dead hand" objection: Rules of language are not exactly dead, perhaps, since they were never exactly alive" to begin with. But the essential objection remains and, indeed, grows stronger: Why would we want to submit to the authority of *words* – marks on a page – divorced from the intentions of their human authors and instead generated by a set of impersonal rules of language? At least the enactors had minds *once*; divorced from speakers, the rules of language never did.[19]

We need not consider here, however, whether these objections can be answered persuasively. Rightly or wrongly, the objections plainly persuade *some* people, and for our purposes, that is what proves decisive. It seems clear, that is, that although some people, including some judges (Justice Scalia of the U.S. Supreme Court is probably the most conspicuous), believe that words have

[17] See, *e.g.*, Stanley Fish, "There is No Textualist Position," 42 San Diego L. Rev. 629 (2005); Steven Knapp and Walter Benn Michaels, "Not a Matter of Interpretation," 42 San Diego L. Rev. 651 (2005).

[18] These and related criticisms are developed at greater length in Smith, *Law's Quandary*, *supra* note 12 at 105–22, 132–4, and 142–9.

[19] See generally Steven D. Smith, "Law Without Mind," 88 Mich. L. Rev. 104 (1989).

objective meanings and that those history-bound meanings are the appropriate object of constitutional interpretation, other people and other judges disagree. So there is plainly no consensus embracing textual meaning as the proper object of constitutional interpretation.

As with the enactors' intention view, therefore, the textualist view is best understood as a reform proposal. Textual meanings *should be* the object of constitutional interpretation, the argument goes, but in a good deal of constitutional decision-making that object is not, in fact, what is being interpreted. Textualists can admit this point; indeed, they often insist upon it.[20]

But then what is the object that constitutional interpretation as we know it *does* seek to interpret?

Principles

Possibly the most popular answer, favored in one form or another both by many originalists and by many who are wary of the label, is that constitutional interpretation seeks to ascertain or elaborate the meanings of the "principles" or "norms" that are, in some sense, embodied or referred to in the constitution.[21] The constitution is, as Bruce Ackerman says, "a rich lode of principle";[22] and it is those principles (and not the enactors' imperfect understanding of the principles) that constitutional interpretation interprets.[23]

Those who favor this position typically leave the nature of these principles or norms obscure – and for good reason, because an attempt to elaborate on that nature encounters daunting problems. Whatever they are, these principles evidently have the quality of being able to carry content or meaning different from the content or meaning ascribed to them by the enactors of the constitutional

[20] See, *e.g.*, Antonin Scalia, "Review of Steven D. Smith's Law's Quandary," 55 Cath. U.L. Rev. 687 at 692–3 (2006).

[21] See, *e.g.*, Michael J. Perry, *We the People: The Fourteenth Amendment and the Supreme Court* (1999) at 15–16 [Perry, *We the People*]. Perry often describes the content of constitutional provisions as "directives," but the basic position seems unchanged: The directive is evidently viewed by Perry as a directive to honor or adhere to some principle or norm.

[22] Bruce A. Ackerman, "Constitutional Politics/Constitutional Law," 99 Yale L.J. 453 at 525 (1989).

[23] This statement passes over a complication. It would seem that, in reality, the adoption of "constitutional principles" as the object of interpretation would require a two-step process containing interpretation at both steps. At step one, the interpreter would need to figure out which principles are contained in the constitution, and this would presumably require the interpreter to turn to enactors' intentions or textual meaning or something of the sort. Once the principles have been identified, however, and at stage two, the interpreter would interpret the principles, not the enactors' intentions or the textual meaning or whatever. Given the generality of the principles typically attributed to constitutions – liberty, equality, property, and so forth – it seems that most of the interpretive work would occur at stage two.

provisions in which they are supposedly embodied. For example, proponents of this sort of position typically hold (a) that the enactors of the Fourteenth Amendment to the United States Constitution constitutionalized some sort of principle or norm of equality; (b) that those enactors did not believe that this principle forbade racially segregated schools, or that it had anything to say about legal distinctions between men and women; but (c) that, in fact (as we now understand), the principle or norm of equality *does* prohibit virtually all state-supported racial segregation as well as many legal distinctions between the sexes.[24] For the principle to be able to have this quality and do this work, it seems that it must be some sort of reality or fact independent of the beliefs or mental states of the people who chose to ensconce the principle in the Fourteenth Amendment. Thus, it seems most plausible to understand proponents of the "constitution-as-principles" position to be contending that the object of constitutional interpretation is a set of political-moral facts that the constitution somehow embodies or references.

Like the other answers to the "What are we interpreting?" question, this answer has its appeal. It aspires to introduce goodness – morality or justice – into constitutional law. As we have seen, a familiar challenge to the enactors' intentions and textualist views asks, in essence, "Why would we submit to being governed by *that*?" The constitution-as-principles position supplies a more attractive response to that challenge. At least it appears to. After all, who can complain about being ruled by goodness, or justice, or morality?

Even so, the suggestion that the object of constitutional interpretation is a set of moral-political facts provokes troubling objections.[25] An initial but powerful doubt wonders whether facts of this kind exist at all. It would seem that we need to be moral realists in order to accept this answer. Even if we are moral realists, however, that would not be enough: We might still be skeptical that moral reality takes the form of *these sorts* of facts – entities such as the principle of equality or the principle of humane punishment, hovering spookily in some sort of ethereal Platonic realm, only dimly perceptible to our view. Perhaps it is not so hard to imagine that, say, the principle of equality is some kind of Platonic fact – "equality" seems sufficiently august for the honor, or

[24] See, *e.g.*, Perry, *We the People, supra* note 21 at 48–131.

[25] I have discussed some of these objections at greater length in Steven D. Smith, "Moral Realism, Pluralistic Community, and the Judicial Imposition of Principle: A Comment on Perry," 88 Nw. U.L. Rev. 183 (1993). For a thoughtful critical assessment of some of the difficulties, see Jeffrey Goldsworthy's contribution to this volume, "Unwritten Constitutional Principles." For an analysis of the relation of constitutional principles to relevant policy considerations, see Bradley Miller, "Justification and Rights Limitations," also in this volume.

maybe sufficiently elemental – but what about more complex and seemingly artificial constructions such as the principles of "federalism," or "separation of powers," or "church-state separation"? Is it really plausible to conceive of these things as political-moral facts that constitution-makers could incorporate into a constitution even while only imperfectly understanding their content and implications, so that later interpreters who depart from the enactors' concrete understandings of separation of powers or church-state separation can, nonetheless, be said to be acting on *the same* principle or fact?

Additional questions arise. Suppose we take seriously (and not just expediently, for rhetorical purposes) the reality of political-moral facts, of the sort that this account of constitutional interpretation seems to presuppose. Do we have any warrant to suppose that these political-moral facts are necessarily good? Or, as with angels, could there also be fallen or rebellious principles that sometimes seduce us by posing as pristinely virtuous – a principle of oppressive regimentation that calls itself something like "order" or "uniformity" or "equality," maybe, or a principle of "rule of law," a.k.a. judicial supremacy, a.k.a. judicial usurpation? If so, how can we be sure the enactors did not put some perverse or mischievous principles into the constitution – no doubt by mistake? And if they did, would we really want the courts to interpret, elaborate, and enforce these principles to their fullest extent?

Maybe, like humans, principles can be a mixture of good and bad. And maybe the enactors understood this, and intended to constitutionalize only the good parts: but if the courts interpret and enforce *the principles* rather than *the enactors' intentions*, we will find ourselves stuck with the obnoxious parts as well. Or maybe, like virtues in Aristotle's presentation, principles are good when employed in moderation, so as to achieve a "golden mean..." And maybe even unqualifiedly good-hearted principles sometimes compete and conflict with each other (liberty versus equality, for example, or free speech versus fair trial), so that, once again, by interpreting and enforcing a principle for all it is worth rather than the more truncated commitment to the principle contemplated by the enactors, we will displace or distort or diminish other worthy principles – and thereby throw a delicate constitutional equilibrium out of whack.

A different sort of objection to the constitution-as-principles position asserts a mismatch between principles as an *object* of interpretation and constitutional argumentation as a method of *understanding* that object. If we really want to be governed by political-moral facts rather than by enactors' intentions or legalistic textual meanings, isn't our method of arguing over text and historical context and precedents and such a manifestly dubious means of securing such governance?[26] Wouldn't it be better just to do political-moral philosophy in an open, honest, straightforward way?[27]

These are complicated questions, no doubt, not to be answered quickly – or by me. But the questions at least help explain why, although many constitutionalists enthusiastically endorse principles or norms as the proper object of constitutional interpretation, others remain skeptical. So once again, the one thing that seems incontestable is that there is no consensus (among either theorists or judges) accepting principles, or political-moral facts, as the proper object of constitutional interpretation. It follows, once again, that the "principles" answer is more in the nature of a reform proposal than an explanation of what is actually happening in constitutional interpretation as we know and practice it.

Other Objects?

The discussion thus far has considered the answers to the "What are we interpreting?" question suggested by three of the most common approaches to constitutional law, and, without pretending to assess or adjudicate the pro and con arguments, the discussion has suggested that although each has its appeal (so that it is understandable why some people would favor it), each also provokes serious objections (so that it is understandable why other people would reject it). As a result, there appears to be no consensus, either current or imminent, embracing any of the objects of interpretation proposed by the different positions.

Nor does it seem likely that this impasse could be avoided by any other theory or possible object of interpretation. Other theories are available, of course. For example, a familiar view suggests that what constitutional interpretation interprets (or at least *should* interpret) is not the enactors' intentions, or the original textual meaning, or the abstract principles or norms in some fashion embodied in the constitution, but rather something more like an ongoing tradition,[28] or

[26] See Jeremy Waldron, "The Core of the Case Against Judicial Review," 115 Yale L.J. 1346 at 1380–6 (2006). Waldron's appraisal in the present volume seems considerably more sanguine. See Jeremy Waldron, "Do Judges Reason Morally?"

[27] See, *e.g.*, Larry Alexander and Ken Kress, "Against Legal Principles," 82 Iowa L. Rev. 739 at 753–4 (1997); Edward B. Foley, "Interpretation and Philosophy: Dworkin's Constitution," 14 Const. Comm. 151 (1997).

[28] David Strauss, "Common Law Constitutional Interpretation," 63 U. Chi. L. Rev. 877 (1996). I have advocated something like this approach for the establishment clause. See Steven D. Smith, "Separation as a Tradition," 18 J. Law & Politics 215 (2002). Mark Walters's contribution to this volume, "Written Constitutions and Unwritten Constitutionalism," is a learned and insightful exploration of the connections between written and unwritten constitutionalism.

the "traditions and conscience of our people."[29] This view might be especially attractive in legal regimes without a written constitution. Or, where a written constitution is present, someone might argue that constitutional interpreters should interpret the words, but abstracted from their historical context: so we might do what Alexander Aleinikoff suggests we should do with statutes – that is, regard ourselves as bound by the meanings of the words while treating those words "as if [they] had been enacted yesterday."[30]

Presumably, any object of interpretation that anyone proposes will have some appeal (why else would anyone propose it?) and will also generate objections similar to those brought against the objects of interpretation already considered – objections based on diffuseness or unknowability or unworthiness to wield authority over the democratic processes. But the inescapable fact is that there does not seem to be any consensus among judges or scholars adopting any particular object as the object of constitutional interpretation. There are arguments, in short, about what we *should* interpret, but there is no agreement about what we *are* interpreting.

So, should this lack of consensus worry us?

"THE CONSTITUTION" AS PLACEHOLDER

Lack of consensus about what we are interpreting presents no barrier to *normative* arguments advocating one or another approach to constitutional interpretation; indeed, it is precisely the lack of consensus that provides the occasion and motivation for such arguments. But in the meantime, the fact of fundamental disagreement among the participants might seem to present a serious embarrassment to the practical enterprise of constitutional interpretation. How can we join together in a common interpretive enterprise if we do not even agree on what we are interpreting?

So it seems we are back to the pseudo-debate over different novels having the common title of *Invisible Man*. In that case, we said that no actual debate among interpretations – and no genuine agreement and disagreement – was possible. A similar conclusion would seem to be indicated here.

And yet . . . we've seen it done. There *is* a practice, involving thousands or even millions of judges, lawyers, scholars, and citizens, that we call "constitutional interpretation." Though these people do not seem to agree on exactly

[29] *Griswold v. Connecticut*, 381 U.S. 479 at 493–4 (1965) (Goldberg, J., concurring, quoting Cardozo J. in *Snyder v. Commonwealth of Massachusetts*, 291 U.S. 97 at 105 (1934).

[30] T. Alexander Aleinikoff, "Updating Statutory Interpretation," 87 Mich. L. Rev. 20 at 49 (1988) (emphasis deleted).

what they are interpreting, they do propose and criticize competing interpretations on the assumption that they are carrying on a debate – that they are agreeing and disagreeing and basically engaging with each other. It would be possible, no doubt, to reinterpret the discussion itself as an argument about *what the proper object of interpretation is*. But that is not how the participants typically talk; they talk as if they are disagreeing about *what 'the constitution' means*. Justice Scalia does not write opinions that say, "On a different subject (and one that *I* happen to find more within our job description), the textual meaning suggests that. . . ." He writes opinions that say, fiercely, "I *dissent*. The majority has *misinterpreted* the Constitution."

So, what is going on?

It seems that the phrase "the constitution" must be serving as a sort of placeholder for a variety of different objects, and that some people use the phrase to refer to one sort of object while others use it to refer to another sort of object. (Of course, many of us may use the phrase without having any clear notion of what in the world we are referring to.)

But this observation raises other questions. How does this practice manage to continue? Why does it not quickly become obvious that the various partisans are not talking about the same thing, so that genuine agreement and disagreement are impossible (at least on the level of *constitutional interpretation* on which we purport to be talking)? Should we find this whole affair embarrassing, maybe intolerable, or does it serve a useful purpose?

NOBLE EQUIVOCATIONS?

Obviously, I cannot supply any confident answers to these questions, but some tentative suggestions may provide matter for thought. Plato famously suggested that a republic might be founded on "noble lies." Respectable people may recoil from Plato's suggestion,[31] but perhaps a marginally more scrupulous society can persist and even flourish on the basis of "noble equivocations." Indeed, one need not be unusually cynical to suppose that there are many such equivocations that do yeoman's work; in a society marked by pluralism, suspicious of religious or metaphysical truth, and confounded by claims of authority,[32] these pervasive equivocations may do rhetorical or diplomatic work that nothing and no one else could do.

[31] In his contribution to his volume, however, James Allan suggests (ironically, perhaps) that we should give thought to "when it is justifiable and defensible to . . . lie about what [the constitution] requires." See James Allan, "The Travails of Justice Waldron," at 182.

[32] See Steven D. Smith, "Hart's Onion: The Peeling Away of Legal Authority," 16 S. Cal. Interdisc. L.J. 97 (2006).

"Equality" is, perhaps, the leading example. It has been persuasively maintained that the notion is wholly innocent of definite substantive content;[33] nonetheless, advocates both popular and academic routinely appeal to equality, with varying degrees of sophistication, to argue for concrete conclusions.[34] How do they manage to do this? In part, it seems, by equivocation: By using the vocabulary of equality, advocates think they are appealing to a common ethical principle when, in fact, they are not.[35] It would not be difficult, perhaps, to observe similar deployments of other mincing terms, such as "neutrality," or "harm,"[36] or "law" (as in "rule of law"[37]).

Or take "morality." Everyone – high or low, sophisticated or innocent – routinely uses the vocabulary of morality. It is morally right – or morally obligatory – to do such-and-such. Conversely, this policy or that practice or that other state of affairs is "wrong" or "immoral." But what *is* morality, exactly?[38] When theorists reflect on that question, they give wildly different answers.

33 See Peter Westen, "The Empty Idea of Equality," 95 Harv. L. Rev. 537 (1982).

34 For a recent elaborate and sophisticated example, see Christopher L. Eisgruber and Lawrence G. Sager, *Religious Freedom and the Constitution* (2007).

35 For an exposition of how this tactic of equivocation operates in Rawls, see Michael P. Zuckert, "Is Modern Liberalism Compatible with Limited Government? The Case of Rawls," in Robert P. George ed., *Natural Law, Liberalism, and Morality* 49 at 77–8 (1996). Zuckert argues that although there may be a cultural consensus favoring the *concept* of equality, "there is also a wide range of disagreement over what about persons makes them equal, and over what the claim of equality entitles them to." But "when Rawls brings the agreement on the *concept* of equality into his system he treats it as if it were an agreement on a *conception*" (emphasis added). No such agreement exists, however, so the "shift from concept to conception is simply arbitrary and illegitimate within the terms of Rawls's own thought."

A confession is perhaps called for here. To me, the common concept/conception distinction, so often appealed to in these sorts of discussions, does little to clarify what is going on in these debates: That is because the ontological status of both "concepts" and "conceptions" seems to me mysterious. What sort of thing *is* a concept? Is it a mental state, existing in the brain or mind of the person who holds or thinks about the concept? A Platonic idea or form? A more sociological sort of fact? Maybe just a word? And what does it mean to say that conceptions that are different and perhaps at odds with each other are, nonetheless, variations on – or versions of, or instantiations of – the same concept? Given my uncertainty, to me the assertion that "Well, although we disagree, at least we're interpreting the same concept" is approximately as unilluminating as the assertion that "At least we're all interpreting the same constitution." I acknowledge that for those who *do* confidently grasp the nature of concepts and conceptions, this confession may tend to discredit much of the discussion in this essay, because the various possible objects of interpretation noted here presumably might stand to "the constitution" in the same relation as different "conceptions" supposedly stand to their common "concept."

36 See Steven D. Smith, "Is the Harm Principle Illiberal?," 51 Amer. J. Juris. 1 (2006).

37 T. R. S. Allan's contribution to this symposium provides an impressive example of how much can be squeezed out of the basic concept of rule of law. See T. R. S. Allan, "Constitutional Justice and the Concept of Law."

38 Wil Waluchow's contribution to this volume struggles valiantly with this question, offering some useful distinctions but not, I think, any fully satisfying overall account. See W.J Waluchow, "Constitutional Morality and Bills of Rights."

Some emphasize consequences, preferences, wants and desires; others protest that these things are not the stuff of morality at all, and instead direct our gaze to a mistier realm of duties and obligations and rights. Still others refer to altogether different desiderata – the will of God, for example. The divergences are so great that one might be tempted to conclude that until the matter is resolved, people who refer to morality or who make moral arguments will just not be talking about the same thing,[39] so that genuine debate and engagement could not occur. But far from submitting to this chastening and inconvenient appraisal, for the most part, we simply bracket the problem – banish it to the academic, largely inscrutable, and hence practically irrelevant domain of meta-ethics – and forge ahead cheerfully as before, arguing zestfully about whether abortion or same-sex marriage or the current distribution of wealth are or are not immoral (whatever that might mean).

"The constitution," I humbly submit, seems to be another in this family of facilitative modern equivocations. The label is a placeholder, and we do not know (or at least do not agree on) just what it is a placeholder for. Nonetheless, we manage to suppress that uncertainty and dissensus in order to carry on the enterprise of "constitutional interpretation," acting for all the world as though we know what we are doing. We manage to do this, perhaps, in part because, as we have seen, the various objects for which the placeholder might stand resonate with dulcet tones of democracy, wisdom, rule of law, morality and justice, and venerable tradition. And we manage to do it, also, maybe, because the happy illusion of being genuinely engaged in a momentous common project is one of the blessed ties that serve to bind us into a community. Communities, after all, are "imagined" entities – so we are told[40] – and nationhood evidently can be built on myths,[41] so it should probably not be surprising if our own communities are founded on the myth that there is some venerated object ("the constitution"), the common acceptance and interpretation of which serve to unite us as a people.

To be clear: Nothing in the preceding discussion is intended as a *justification* for the enterprise of "constitutional interpretation" as we currently practice it. For myself, I am loathe to commend (though no doubt I sometimes descend to) dishonesty or equivocation – not even for noble purposes. And I

[39] See Michael Smith, *The Moral Problem* (1994) at 3: "For if one thing becomes clear by reading what philosophers writing in meta-ethics today have to say, it is surely that enormous gulfs exist between them, gulfs so wide that we must wonder whether they are talking about a common subject matter."

[40] See Benedict Anderson, *Imagined Communities: Reflections on the Origin and Spread of Nationalism* (rev. edn. 1991).

[41] See, generally, Eric Hobsbawm and Terence Ranger eds., *The Invention of Tradition* (1984).

am deeply skeptical of at least some of the more grandiose claims sometimes made about constitutional interpretation as a requisite of national unity.[42] Still, it seems undeniable, first, that there is no consensus about *what* we are interpreting when we do constitutional interpretation and, second, that the practice of constitutional interpretation rolls along anyway – rolls along exuberantly, confidently, and sometimes with exalting or devastating consequences for the various institutions and individuals who find or place themselves in its path. The conjectures offered here are intended as a modest and tentative attempt not to glorify or even defend that practice, but only to understand what on earth is going on.

[42] Perhaps the most ambitious such claims are in the Joint Opinion in *Planned Parenthood v. Casey*, 505 U.S. 833 (1992). Robert Nagel has aptly described the plurality's claims as "an extravagant expression of . . . hubris." See Robert F. Nagel, *Judicial Power and American Character: Censoring Ourselves in an Anxious Age* (1994) at 138.

2 Do Judges Reason Morally?

Jeremy Waldron

Legal philosophers have devoted a lot of attention to the following questions: Do judges engage in moral reasoning? Should they engage in moral reasoning? Are they good at moral reasoning? Are they better at moral reasoning than other official decision-makers? Is the quality of their moral reasoning a reason for assigning final decisions about issues of rights to the judiciary rather than to legislatures?

The last couple of questions are particularly important for constitutional jurisprudence. In the debate about judicial review of legislation, it is often suggested that because courts are better at moral reasoning than legislatures are, we should entrust them with final authority over the essentially moral issues of individual and minority rights.[1] Now, this is a quite specific claim about institutional competence, and I suspect it is often put forward on a flimsy basis. We catch a glimpse of what goes on in legislatures, and it sounds like a cacophony. (We ignore Machiavelli's warning not to "consider the noises and the cries that . . . arise in such tumults more than the good effects that they engender."[2])

[1] Matthew Adler, "Popular Constitutionalism And The Rule Of Recognition: Whose Practices Ground U.S. Law?" 100 Nw. U. L. Rev. 719 (2006) at note 96, states the view this way (without necessarily endorsing it): "Differential judicial moral expertise would support nondeferential constitutional adjudication either because constitutional adjudication at many junctures reduces to straight moral reasoning, or simply because, like all legal decision-making, it is appropriately 'interpretive' at some point and therefore responds to considerations of moral 'justification' as well as 'fit.' In short, if judges do indeed possess special moral expertise, then Dworkin can plausibly conclude that the best 'interpretation' of U.S. practice – the constructed rule of recognition for our system – requires . . . judicial supremacy."

[2] Nicciolo Machiavelli, *The Discourses*, Bernard Crick ed. (1983) at 113 (Book I, ch. 4): "To me it appears that those who damn the tumults between the nobles and the plebs blame those things that were the first cause of keeping Rome free, and that they consider the noises and the cries that would arise in such tumults more than the good effects that they engendered."

We read a few Supreme Court opinions and they appear to be careful analytic treatments of important issues of rights. Certainly they seem to be talking about the issues in the measured tones and with the articulate arguments that *we* would expect to use when we discuss them in our seminars and workshops. And so, because they seem to reason as we do when we consider moral issues in our workshops and colloquia – because they reason in the careful, measured, deliberative, and analytic way that moral philosophers think moral reasoners should reason[3] – we conclude that judges are pretty good at morality. They define their terms, they separate different lines of reasoning, they pay attention to the logical force of the arguments they consider, they distinguish issues and discuss them in a certain order, they entertain objections to their own lines of reasoning and try to respond to them, and so on. They treat matters of principle as matters of principle; they do not try to reduce them to dollars and cents or to tendentious and oversimplified popular slogans or to the bargaining and vote trading that characterize electoral politics. In short, judges seem to take moral issues seriously, in a way that does not seem to be true of the noisy, smelly, common, and tumultuous majoritarian proceedings of our legislatures.

Well, as you would expect, I have a number of interrogatories to put to those who rest their faith on this touchingly optimistic account. In this chapter I will pose them as questions that need to be considered by anyone who expects judges to engage in high-quality moral reasoning about rights. I hope my questions will be considered on all sides of this debate. I think we need a clearer picture of what we mean by "moral reasoning" and how it relates to other things that we expect judges to do. Here are my questions:

1. What distinguishes *moral* reasoning from other forms of practical reasoning? Does the claim that judges are moral reasoners (or good at moral reasoning) survive such a distinction?
2. Is there an important difference between morality and *political* morality? If so, is political morality not what judges should be doing? Are judges good at political morality?
3. How does a judge's responsibility to find and apply the law affect his moral reasoning? Does he have two jobs to perform – moral reasoning and legal reasoning? Or are they inseparable?

[3] There is a considerable literature on ideals of moral reasoning. See, for example, John Rawls, "Outline of a Decision-Procedure for Ethics" (1951), in John Rawls, *Collected Papers*, Sam Freeman ed. (1999) 1; Kurt Baier, *The Moral Point of View: A Rational Basis for Ethics* (1965); R. M. Hare, *Moral Thinking: its Levels, Method, and Point* (1981); T.M. Scanlon, *What We Owe to Each Other* (1998), etc.

4. Is there an important difference between reasoning morally on one's own account and reasoning morally in the name of a whole society? What is it like for a whole society to reason morally?

In amplifying these questions, my remarks will have a skeptical tone, but only about the claims that are made on behalf of judges. My arguments in this paper are about judicial tasks and comparative institutional competence. I rest nothing on any general skepticism about morality. Some have suggested that anti-realism in moral philosophy undermines the case for judicial review.[4] I have argued elsewhere that it makes no difference.[5] My argument in this paper is not about moral objectivity. All I assume is the following: Moral issues – including issues about rights – are issues on which people of good faith can disagree and many such disagreements are intractable. (If there is moral truth on these matters it does not disclose itself in ways that are beyond dispute.) Moral reasoning and moral argument are possible as much for an anti-realist (or even noncognitivist) as for a realist.[6] And it is possible for us to make, discuss, and sometimes agree upon judgments about the competence of a person's moral reasoning, even when we disagree about the moral positions that are the subject of his reasoning, and even if we think there is no objective fact of the issue. These assumptions are, all of them, controversial. But I set them out here both because I believe them to be true and because, in the rest of the chapter, I would like not to be distracted by the question of moral objectivity.[7]

[4] Michael S. Moore, "Moral Reality Revisited," 90 Mich. L. Rev. 2424 (1992) at 2469–70:

> "[C]onstitutional interpretation . . . includes moral reasoning by judges, in part because the U.S. Constitution seems to invite such reasoning by its value-laden phrases. . . . In light of this fusion of constitutional and moral reasoning, my thesis has been that what status one accords moral reasoning matters. If one is an anti-realist about morality . . . one will allow for only two possible statuses for moral reasoning: (1) the moral conventionalists' sort, where all moral reasoning is no more than teasing out the implications of established social convention; and (2) the moral skeptic's sort, where all moral reasoning is no more than the assertion of one's individual will. Each of these meta-ethical possibilities should increase our discomfort with the idea of judges' having the power of judicial review. A moral realist will glimpse a third possibility: . . . when judges decide what process is due a citizen, or what equality requires, or when a punishment is cruel, they judge a moral fact capable of being true or false."

[5] See Jeremy Waldron, "Moral Truth and Judicial Review," 43 Am. J. Juris. 75 (1998) and "The Irrelevance of Moral Objectivity" in Robert George ed. *Natural Law Theory: Contemporary Essays* (1992) 158.

[6] The locus classicus of this position is R.M. Hare, *The Language of Morals* (1952) and R.M. Hare, *Freedom and Reason* (1963). For a modern defense of the possibility of moral argument on anti-realist assumptions, see Simon Blackburn, *Essays in Quasi-Realism* (1983).

[7] Accordingly, although I will devote considerable attention to Richard Posner's attack on the infiltration of academic moralizing into legal theory and constitutional jurisprudence – see

1. WHAT DISTINGUISHES MORAL REASONING FROM OTHER FORMS OF PRACTICAL REASONING?

Legal philosophers sometimes use the term "moral" casually to describe any mode of reasoning that is not simply the citation and exposition of black-letter law. But "moral" and "morality" are not always used so casually. The phrase "moral reasoning" is used by various philosophers to identify a subset of ethical reasoning, normative reasoning, or practical reasoning. When we talk about moral reasoning by judges, are we buying into any of these distinctions? And, if so, does the claim that judges ought to be moral reasoners (or the claim that they are good at moral reasoning) survive such a distinction?

Seventy years ago, Felix Cohen – a realist who thought all legal questions were ethical questions – warned his readers against confusing the ethics of public policy with an otherworldly "Sunday School morality."[8] Presumably those who defend the role of judges as moral reasoners do not want to find their judges on the "morality" side of that distinction. This may be a trite example, but there are many other things that the word "morality" connotes with which we would not want judges to meddle. Consider Immanuel Kant's suggestion that whereas legality has to do with "[t]he mere conformity or non-conformity of an action with law, irrespective of the incentive of it," morality focuses on "that conformity in which the idea of duty is also the incentive to the action."[9] Or consider Bernard Williams's suggestion that "morality" operates as a very "peculiar institution" in the realm of the ethical.[10] Or consider John Rawls's contrast between a political conception of justice and more comprehensive moral views.[11] Or consider the contrast drawn recently in Richard Posner's Holmes Lectures between moral reasoning, which was something he thought judges for the most part should eschew, and normative reasoning, which, as he acknowledged, was something they could not and should not avoid.[12]

Richard A. Posner, *The Problematics of Moral and Legal Theory* (1999) [Posner, *Problematics*] – I will not discuss his moral skepticism.

[8] Felix S. Cohen, "Transcendental Nonsense and the Functional Approach," 35 Colum. L. Rev. 809 at 840 (1935). But elsewhere – in "Modern Ethics and the Law," 4 Brook. L. Rev. 33 at 36 (1934) – Cohen contrasted "Sunday School ethics" with "an ethics that squarely faces the problems which modern commerce and modern science have brought into our world."

[9] Immanuel Kant, "The Metaphysics of Morals," in Mary J. Gregor ed., *Immanuel Kant: Practical Philosophy* (1996) at 383 (6: 219 of Prussian Academy edition of *Kant's Werke*) [Kant, "Metaphysics of Morals"].

[10] Bernard Williams, *Ethics and the Limits of Philosophy* (1985) at 174–96.

[11] John Rawls, *Political Liberalism* (1996) at xviii and 13 [Rawls, *Political Liberalism*].

[12] Posner, *Problematics*, *supra* note 7 at 112–13.

In each of these cases, morality is contrasted with something else, and in each case I think we should be nervous about any suggestion that judges preoccupy themselves with what "morality" refers to in these contrasts, as opposed to the "something else." The extent of our nervousness might vary from case to case. For example, we might be much more worried by the idea of judges' concerning themselves with the Kantian question of whether duty is its own incentive than we are with their getting involved in Bernard Williams's peculiar institution, partly because what critics such as Williams think is distinctive and perhaps objectionable about morality is the imported *legalism* of its obsession with obligation.[13]

The proposition that judges should not be involved in morality in Kant's narrow sense may seem obvious to us. But actually it is not an uncontested position. When Ronald Dworkin, Thomas Nagel, and several other eminent philosophers produced their "Philosophers' Brief" for the U.S. Supreme Court in a case about assisted suicide,[14] much of their argument had to do with subtleties of the distinction between actions and omissions, subtleties that often turned on issues of the nature of the agent's willing involvement in the decision about assisted suicide. These subtleties are much more at home in Kant's theory of morality, in the narrow sense, than in his theory of legality. And it is certainly an open question whether attention to them is either necessary or appropriate for the making of good positive law on the matter.[15]

On the other hand, the positions of Kant, Williams, Rawls, and Posner on the distinctiveness of morality are hardly uncontested. There are those who draw a distinction between morality and other elements of ethics which points in the opposite direction: P. F. Strawson, for example, distinguished between social morality and individual ethical ideals, and plainly judges ought to be concerned with the former, not the latter (if they are to be working in this area at all).[16] (Strawson's paper was one of a number of pieces that appeared in the 1960s, debating the definition of morality and whether it was to be distinguished from other forms of normative reasoning by its form, its content, or its

[13] Of course the more that distinctively moral reasoning is thought to imitate legalistic reasoning, the less interest there is for us in the claim that judges should reason morally.

[14] Ronald Dworkin, Thomas Nagel, Robert Nozick, John Rawls, Thomas Scanlon, and Judith Jarvis Thomson, Amici Curiae Brief for Respondents in *Washington v. Glucksberg* 521 U.S. 702 (1997). See Ronald Dworkin *et al.*, "Assisted Suicide: The Philosophers' Brief," *New York Review of Books*, March 27, 1997, at 41.

[15] See the discussion in Posner, *Problematics*, *supra* note 7 at 132–3. See also Jeremy Waldron, "Ego-Bloated Hovel (reviewing Richard A. Posner's *The Problematics of Moral and Legal Theory*)," 94 Nw. U. L. Rev. 597 at 603–9 (2000) [Waldron, "Ego-Bloated Hovel"].

[16] P. F. Strawson, "Social Morality and Individual Ideal," in *Freedom and Resentment and other Essays* (1974) 26.

subject-matter.)[17] Even Kant seems to use "morality" in a wide sense as well as the narrower sense that I indicated a couple of paragraphs ago. His *Metaphysics of Morals* includes both a theory of virtue, which concerns itself with the nature of people's motivation to duty (which is morality in the narrower sense), and a theory of right, which, being concerned with external action, is much closer to matters that we would call political and legal.[18]

With all this terminological disagreement and indeterminacy, a fair response might be that these finicky distinctions between different parts of practical reasoning are all very interesting for moral philosophers in their native habitat, but they need not bother the legal philosopher. When he talks about judges' moral reasoning, the legal philosopher means any reasoning about values and principles, rights and duties, and reasons for action generally – or at least any reasoning about these matters that is not directly dictated by existing black-letter law.

This view sounds unsophisticated, but it need not be. Joseph Raz, I think, holds a sophisticated version of this view. Raz notes that some philosophers have distinguished between a wider and a narrower concept of morality, and he acknowledges that such distinctions may be helpful in certain contexts. But he, himself, thinks that all such distinctions are superficial, and that morality in the narrower sense is not a deeply distinctive and distinctively coherent idea.[19] Mainly, he wants to say that moral reasons are just reasons, and we reason morally whenever we reason practically, paying attention to all the reasons that apply to us and according them the weight that they actually do have.[20] (And moral, as opposed to legal, reasoning is simply ordinary reasoning that positive law has not preempted or displaced.[21])

My own view is that, in the context of constitutional theory, there is more to the relevance of this issue of the narrower and wider senses of morality than meets the eye. In what follows, I want to explore a couple of ideas.

One is that (a) first-order normative questions about the rightness and wrongness of (say) abortion or euthanasia can be distinguished from (b) normative questions about the politics of banning or permitting these practices. We often associate "morality" and "moral reasoning" with (a) rather than (b). That is not always true. We do sometimes say that the following is an interesting moral

[17] See, *e.g.*, the papers in G. Wallace and A.D.M. Walker eds. *The Definition of Morality* (1970).

[18] Kant, "Metaphysics of Morals," *supra* note 9.

[19] See Joseph Raz, *The Morality of Freedom* (1986) at 213–16.

[20] See also Joseph Raz, *Engaging Reason: On the Theory of Value and Action* (1999), especially chapters 11 and 13.

[21] Joseph Raz, "Incorporation by Law," 10 Legal Theory 1 at 14 (2004): "Judges are humans, and they are subject to morality without any special incorporation of morality, as are we all. What appear as incorporation are various instances of nonexclusion."

question: "Is it permissible to punish conduct simply because it is wrong or immoral?", and that is a question of type (b). But type (b) also comprises questions such as "Is there any reason for decisions about abortion law to be taken by the central government rather than by individual states in a federation?", and that would not ordinarily be described by most people as a moral question. I will explore this under heading (2).

The other idea I want to explore concerns what happens to the moral character of an argument [at any of these levels, (a) or (b)], when it is also affected, permeated, and to a large part dominated by legal texts and doctrine. Does moral reasoning remain intact when certain moves in argument (or certain lines of argument, or certain ways of pursuing the implications of a position one has adopted) are blocked by a precedent or by the contrary implications of a statute? Is it possible to pick apart the moral element and the positive law or doctrinal element in judicial reasoning? Or do they merge together to make something that, though it has a certain moralizing flavor, is not really moral argument at all? I will pursue this under heading (3).

2. IS THERE AN IMPORTANT DIFFERENCE BETWEEN MORALITY AND POLITICAL MORALITY?

As we consider the nature and quality of judges' moral reasoning, we need to bear in mind that judges operate as government officials, in the context of political institutions, and so their reasoning is in the realm of the political rather than the straightforwardly ethical or moral. They are not deciding what to do as individuals; they are making decisions for and about a whole society. On abortion, for example, the judge is not in the moral position of (say) a woman who is wrestling with the question of whether it is right or wrong to procure an abortion for herself. The judge is participating in the setting of national abortion policy. Even if the issues the judge confronts are, at bottom, moral issues, they are posed for the judge in a certain institutional setting.

Now Joseph Raz points out quite correctly that a change of context does not necessarily mean that decisions are not moral. The application of morality is always affected to some extent by institutional role.[22] The question, though, is not about whether the word moral is the appropriate word to use to describe the questions that have to be faced in a given institutional setting. Instead, the question is whether what we know as moral theory gives a good account of what ought to go on in that setting and whether the process we philosophers

[22] *Ibid.* at 9.

idealize as moral reasoning is an appropriate ideal for practical reasoning in that context. If Raz is right, then moral theory, our theory of moral reasoning, *ought* to be oriented to cases of this kind. But of course that is no guarantee that it has been.

In fact, given the level at which the judge is operating when he considers his decisions, it is not at all clear that *moral* theory gives us the sort of account we would want of his decision-making, nor is it clear that philosophical models or ideals of moral decision-making are appropriate for characterizing or illuminating the task that he faces. What we need, in order to characterize and illuminate the sort of reasoning in which the judge should be engaging, is *political* philosophy. It is an open question – heavily contested in political philosophy – how far normative political philosophy should be understood simply as applied moral philosophy or how far moralism or the construction of moral systems and ideals is the appropriate way to get a normative grip on political decision-making. (To take just one aspect of this, political decision-making is very heavily burdened by issues about the legitimacy of the threat or use of force in a way that individual moral decision-making is not. And it is not clear that we can treat that issue about the use of force in society as just another moral issue; it may be that this issue requires a mode of argument that is quite different from, as it were, all-purpose moral argumentation.[23])

I have said that judges operate in a particular political and institutional context. Some aspects of this we shall postpone until heading (4), when we consider the implications of the fact that judges make their "moral" decisions not on their own account, but in the name of a whole society. But there is also a question about how far their political and institutional context should, itself, be a subject to which their reasoning is addressed. An intriguing debate between Richard Posner and Ronald Dworkin arose over this issue.[24]

In his Holmes Lectures, Richard Posner argued that judges often have to direct their attention to institutional factors, and such attention is often – and (he thinks) quite rightly – at the expense of any direct engagement with the primary moral issue involved in the case before them. For example, according to Posner, the issue that confronted the U.S. Supreme Court in the 1997 case of *Washington v. Glucksberg*[25] was not the morality of suicide or the morality of physicians' assisting patients to commit suicide. The sole issue the court was

[23] For an attack on moralism in political philosophy, see Bernard Williams, "Realism and Moralism in Political Theory," in his posthumous collection, *In the Beginning Was the Deed* (2005) 1.
[24] The following paragraphs are adapted from Waldron, "Ego-Bloated Hovel," *supra* note 15.
[25] *Washington v. Glucksberg*, 521 U.S. 702 (1997).

called upon to decide was whether state laws that already banned or limited such assistance violated the U.S. Constitution. Now let us assume, as Posner and Dworkin both assume, that this cannot be answered by simply reading from the text of the U.S. Constitution. It requires reasoning and both jurists say it requires normative reasoning on the following question: Should this issue be taken out of the hands of state legislatures and entrusted to the federal judiciary? But the fact that *normative* reasoning is called for does not mean that the Court has to engage in *moral* reasoning. According to Posner, it is a characteristic mistake of legal philosophers on all sides of the jurisprudential debate to divide "the judicial function into applying rules and doing moral theory." A better division, he says, is between applying rules and making rules. He continues: "Of all the aids to making rules, moral theory is one of the least promising."[26]

> Adjudication is a normative activity, and any time a judge is doing more than just applying positive law . . . the problem of getting from "is" to "ought" rears its troublesome head and it may seem that the judge is plunged into the domain of moral theory. But ethics and practical reason are not identical with moral theory unless the term is to be used unhelpfully to denote all normative reasoning on social questions.[27]

So, on Posner's account, the need for normative reasoning in a case like *Glucksberg* does not turn the constitutional issue into a debate about the morality of the practice that the statute forbids. The constitutional issue is a normative question about the allocation of institutional responsibility between the democratic institutions of the states and the nondemocratic institution of the federal judiciary. To answer this normative question, the Court had to confront a number of subordinate political and institutional issues. The issue of physician-assisted suicide is highly charged, involving questions about the sanctity of life, the morality of suicide generally, the ethics of the medical profession, the imperative of alleviating suffering, the meaning and importance of individual autonomy, and the need for assurance against the possibility of abuse. We know that posing it as a general question – for example, "Is it right for a doctor to accede to a patient's wish to have his or her death accelerated?" – is likely to reveal deep disagreement among the citizens of a pluralistic society like ours. In the face of such highly charged disagreement, where in our political structure is it best for a decision about permitting physician-assisted suicide to be made? Is there any reason to think it cannot be made through the ordinary mechanisms of majoritarian legislative institutions? In the particular case, Posner did not see any obstacles:

[26] Posner, *Problematics*, *supra* note 7 at 97–8. [27] *Ibid.* at 112.

> The issue was on the legislative front burner in a number of states, and the people favoring the status quo – the legal prohibition of all forms of euthanasia – had the strength of inertia and intense conviction behind them, while the people favoring change were by and large the wealthier and better educated, who usually get their way in the political process as elsewhere. The political struggle not being one-sided, the case for judicial intervention was attenuated.[28]

Whichever institution decides such issues, it will need access to a great amount of empirical information about social effects, the operation of various regulatory regimes, and the interaction among the professions (legal, regulatory, medical). In Posner's view, it is more difficult for courts than for legislatures to get hold of this information and put it to good use.[29] Some may disagree, or they may deny that the courts have to do everything themselves if they decide to address the basic issue of rights. Still, one way or another, whether this *is* more difficult for courts than legislatures is in large part an empirical issue – an issue about institutional resources, institutional competence, and relations between institutions. And it is pretty clear that that question is, of all the questions that arise in and around *Glucksberg*, the one least amenable to the skills and methods of moral philosophy.

Ronald Dworkin, at whom much of this argument by Posner was directed, disputed this way of carving up the terrain. Posner said this: "Dworkin famously believes that judges should engage in moral reasoning, at least in difficult cases.... His proposal would fall completely flat if he substituted 'political' for 'moral.'"[30] But Dworkin protested:

> That is baffling: most of my examples of the kind of moral theory judges need, particularly in my work in constitutional law, are principles that, on Posner's apparent suggestion, would be political... Of course, moral theory of the kind under discussion doesn't include strategic or instrumental "reasoning on social questions." But why doesn't it include reasoning on social questions that is normative not in these senses, but in the categorical sense of moral reasoning? What sense would any definition of moral theory make if it left moral issues about politics out? On another occasion, Posner says of his argument that on a proper understanding of democracy, euthanasia should be left to the political process: "That is not a moral point unless morality is a synonym for policy." [Citation omitted] "Morality" is, indeed, not a synonym for "policy" if the latter term is used to refer to instrumental or strategic considerations. But Posner's argument about democracy is not strategic

[28] *Ibid.* at 131.

[29] *Ibid.* at 132.

[30] Posner, *Problematics*, *supra* note 7 at 267.

> or instrumental; it states a controversial position about how democracy is best understood and administered, and that is – what else could it be? – an argument of political morality.[31]

Dworkin might have the better of the argument so far as the use of the term moral is concerned. His distinction between categorical and instrumental forms of normative reasoning seems much more helpful than Posner's distinction between "moral" and "normative." And Posner actually concedes that a very broad use of "moral" would locate all these institutional questions in the realm of morality and moral reasoning:

> In favoring resolution of the issue by the democratic process, I may seem to be smuggling into the analysis a moral theory about the goodness of self-government. I would be if moral theory equaled social theory, so that every claim about the political or judicial process was necessarily a moral claim. But such a confusing equation should be avoided . . . [I]t is a moral point only if morality is a synonym for sound policy.[32]

However, I do not think it is necessary to decide what morality is or is not a synonym for. As I said in the paragraph on Raz at the beginning of this section,[33] for us, the question is not what we *call* the issue, but whether the issue is one to which moral theory of the sort with which philosophers are familiar is particularly germane, and whether moral reasoning, of the sort that moral philosophers idealize, is appropriate. In my view, Posner gives some good reasons for thinking it is not and Dworkin does little to rebut that part of his argument (as opposed to the argument about terminology).

[31] Ronald Dworkin, "Darwin's New Bulldog," 111 Harvard L. Rev. 1718 at note 46 (1998). Dworkin also says (*ibid.* at 1730–1):

> "Of course, Posner must hide his appeal to moral theory, and he does so in a breathtaking way. He declares that convictions about political morality, including his own convictions about the proper workings of a democracy, are not moral judgments at all: they are only, he says, claims "about the political or judicial process." (Similar statements about the difference between "moral" and "political" claims are sprinkled throughout his essay.) But these convictions are not "political" in any descriptive sense. They are normative claims about how political and judicial institutions should work. Nor are they normative in the strategic sense, as Posner sometimes suggests: they are not judgments about how best to achieve a stipulated goal, but rather highly controversial claims about what goals should be pursued. They are moral judgments about how the powers of government should be distributed and exercised, and when, if at all, these powers should be limited out of respect for individual moral rights."

[32] *Ibid.* at 131–2.

[33] See text accompanying note 22.

3. HOW DOES THE JUDGE'S RESPONSIBILITY TO APPLY THE LAW AFFECT HIS MORAL REASONING?

Some people do not think judges should be reasoning morally at all. They think judges just should be finding the law and applying it to the cases that come before them, in a way that is independent of their own values and principles. Even those who think that judges do and should engage in moral reasoning believe it is *also* important for them to find and apply existing law, which often means discovering the results of *other people's moral reasoning* – the moral reasoning of the framers or the moral reasoning of legislators or the moral reasoning of earlier generations of judges – and applying those results to the cases that come before them.

Maybe judges have two kinds of task to perform: (i) they must be alert to and familiar with existing legal sources and able to interpret and apply them to the cases that come before them; and (ii) they must be capable of engaging in moral reasoning about some or all of those cases. So here is our third question: What is supposed to be the relation between these two tasks, according to those who idealize the moral side of judicial reasoning? Does it make a difference to the sort of moral reasoning in which the judge engages, that he also has this other responsibility to find and apply the law, whether or not he agrees with it morally?

Can the two tasks be kept separate so that the judge can engage different skills, a different quality of reasoning, at different times of the day or in different parts of the opinions he writes? Legal positivists have sometimes encouraged this picture: They suggest that the judge operates as a law-detector (using the rule of recognition) and law-applier most of the time but occasionally, when he runs out of law or when the law is found to be indeterminate, he has to switch to a different role – that of a legislator – and begin making the moral judgments (or normative judgments, or judgments of policy, or whatever you want to call them) that responsible law-making involves. The descriptive implausibility of this picture is well known, and is, indeed, conceded by its most distinguished proponent.[34]

Others have suggested that judges sometimes have to switch between applying rules and applying standards, and that the latter task involves moral reasoning in a way that the former task does not.[35] Versions of what is known

[34] H.L.A. Hart, *The Concept of Law*, 2nd edn., Penelope Bulloch and Joseph Raz, eds. (1994), "Postscript," at 274: "It is true that when particular statutes or precedents prove indeterminate, or when the explicit law is silent, judges do not just push away their law books and start to legislate without further guidance from the law."

[35] See Emily Sherwin, "Rule-Oriented Realism," 103 Mich. L. Rev. 1578 at 1591 (2005).

as "inclusive positivism"[36] observe that sometimes the law that the judge is supposed to apply actually instructs him to engage in moral reasoning – the Eighth Amendment to the U.S. Constitution instructs him to make judgments about the excessiveness of bail and the cruelty of punishments – and when he is given these instructions to reason morally he has no choice but to obey. He certainly should not flinch from this task and substitute the sort of historical judgment that the originalists favor – what did *the framers* think was cruel – for the moral judgments that the law requires *him* to make.[37]

The idea would then be that *in these instances*, moral judgments have to be made. Such instances, it is thought, are particularly common in constitutional law, where we often use standards rather than rules to protect minority rights and place limits on the legislation that majorities can enact. Now, in principle, legislators as well as judges can pay attention to these standards and try to apply them, try to engage in the moral reasoning that their application requires. We hope that legislators will engage in moral reasoning of this kind. But for cases in which the reasoning they have engaged in yields conclusions that are at odds with the results of the reasoning that the courts have engaged in, we have to settle on some rule of institutional finality. And so the issue about judicial review of legislation is presumably this: The final say about the constitutionality of legislation should be assigned to that institution which is better at doing the moral reasoning that determinations of constitutionality often involve. If judges are better than legislators at this part of their task (that is, at making moral determinations about rights), then judges should keep this as part of their mission and have the last word on it, even though they also have this other mission of finding and applying the law.

I believe that this rests on too simple a picture of adjudication. It separates out one part of the judicial task – moral reasoning, *e.g.*, in the application of constitutional standards – and it considers how good judges are in discharging that part of their assignment. But what if the two parts of the judicial task cannot be separated so clearly? What if they are thoroughly mixed up with and pervade one another? What if the task of reasoning morally in the application of constitutional standards is always contaminated by the process of applying rules, deferring to texts, and following precedents?

I put it that way because I want to resist a common view that holds that the more *pervasive* the role of moral reasoning in the judge's overall task, the greater the importance of evaluating the judge's performance by the standards and ideals for moral reasoning that we develop in moral philosophy. *I think the*

36 See W.J. Waluchow, *Inclusive Legal Positivism* (1994).

37 See Ronald Dworkin, *Freedom's Law: The Moral Reading of the American Constitution* (1996).

truth is exactly the opposite: The more the judge's moral reasoning pervades and is pervaded by his other tasks, the less relevant to the assessment of his overall performance are the philosophical ideals that we develop for moral reasoning in its pure form.[38]

So – think about some sophisticated alternatives to the simple dual-task theory of judicial functioning that we have been pursuing so far. Suppose it is the case that applying a standard always involves rocking back and forth between rule-like reasoning and something more like moral reasoning. Suppose there is always a question of deference to earlier applications of the same standard, under whatever strong or weak principle of *stare decisis* is appropriate in these matters. Suppose that finding, interpreting, and applying the law always has a moral element to it, as we reject interpretations that seem absurd or choose among eligible interpretations those that show the law in a good light, subject always, of course, to more or less determinate constraints of precedent. Suppose that in applying precedents, we always have to make determinations of what counts as *relevant similarity*, and that those determinations always have a moral element to them; suppose also that in determining whether case D is relevantly like case C, for the purposes of the application of a precedent, we have to subject the moral judgment we make about important commonalities and differences to the approach (to matters like this) that was laid down when C was judged relevantly similar by another court to case B and B relevantly similar to case A. Suppose all this is true. Then, on the one hand, we have something like moral judgment popping up everywhere and at every stage of judicial reasoning. On the other hand, however, we have all such instances of moral judgment being constrained, influenced, and, on occasion, even deflected from their proper course by operation of other sources of law. Then what we have, overall, is not pervasive moral reasoning by the standards of moral theory, but a *mélange* of reasoning – across the board – which, in its richness and texture, differs considerably from pure moral reasoning.

What I have just described is a version of Ronald Dworkin's theory of legal reasoning. Dworkin believes that moral reasoning is involved at almost every stage of legal reasoning. Some commentators try to render Dworkin's theory of interpretation as though it involved two distinct kinds or stages of judgment: When we are choosing between possible interpretations of a text or a doctrine, we make judgments about *fit* (which are technical legal judgments of a familiar

[38] *Cf.* Michael S. Moore, "Do we have an Unwritten Constitution?," 63 S. Cal. L. Rev. 107 at 112 (1989): "The value judgments made in the application of statutes are restricted by the existence of an authoritative text, a restriction not found in ordinary moral reasoning."

kind) and we make judgments about *moral appeal*; and (according to Dworkin, or so these commentators say) we engage in the latter only to break ties that exist with regard to the former. Dworkin may have encouraged this misreading in the way that he expounded his theory in *Law's Empire*.[39] But I think he made it clear enough that this distinction of types of judgment is expository only, and not supposed to represent distinct and independent styles of reasoning that judges engage in.[40]

With this account of what legal reasoning involves, the undeniable fact that there are important moral elements involved does not entitle us to judge legal reasoning by the standards of ordinary moral reasoning. Superficially, it may resemble our ideal of moral reasoning in some of its structural features – defining terms, distinguishing separate lines of reasoning, addressing issues in a certain order, entertaining and responding to objections, and so on. Substantially, it will be quite different. Basic premises will be set sometimes by referring to fundamental values, sometimes by referring to texts. Lines of argument will be sometimes followed through, sometimes stopped in their tracks by contrary precedents. What appear to be moral considerations will vary in their strength depending as much on the use that has been made of them in the past as on their inherent normativity. By the standards that philosophers tout for moral reasoning, this will all seem very exasperating – technical, at best, and flawed and heteronomous, at worst. But by its own standards, it is quite appropriate.[41]

I can imagine two objections to the line I have been following about the mixed nature of the moral reasoning that judges engage in and about its inseparability from the legalistic part of their mission.

One objection will say that moral reasoning is actually more like legal reasoning than I have suggested. In particular – it will be said – the method of reflective equilibrium, recommended by Rawls and others as a way of addressing moral issues, is very much like legal reasoning in its rocking back-and-forth between particular judgments and general principles.[42] In my view, this is a wholly superficial analogy. Reflective equilibrium is compatible with the autonomy and integrity of moral argument because we think of ourselves as free to give up any particular considered judgment or to modify any particular

[39] Ronald Dworkin, *Law's Empire* (1986) at 238–58 [Dworkin, *Law's Empire*].

[40] See, *e.g.*, *ibid.* at 256.

[41] See also the excellent account in John Finnis, "Natural Law And Legal Reasoning," in Robert P. George ed., *Natural Law Theory: Contemporary Essays* 134 (1992) at 141–2, where Finnis associates the technicality, the distinctiveness and the peculiar elusiveness of legal reasoning with the distinct moral task that law has to perform in a pluralistic society.

[42] John Rawls, "Outline of a Decision Procedure for Ethics," 60 The Philosophical Review 177 (1951) and John Rawls, *A Theory of Justice* (1971).

abstract formulation of principle; but in law we are not free in that way either to drop inconvenient precedents or modify doctrines or abstract propositions embodied in authoritative texts at will. The character of and the constraints upon the two kinds of argument – reflective equilibrium and legal reasoning – are quite different.

The other objection is more subtle. It will insist that although moral argument in the legal case has to entangle itself with deference to texts and precedents and so on, those later elements also have standing as moral considerations. After all, even when they are just finding and applying clear law – clear statutes, the clear provisions of a constitution, or clear precedents obviously on point – judges are not machines. They do these things for reasons: There are reasons they regard themselves as (sometimes) governed by statutes or by constitutional texts; and there are reasons for their deferring to precedents. And in the last resort, these are *moral* reasons – reasons of concern for established expectations, reasons of deference to democratic institutions, and reasons associated with integrity and the moral value of treating like cases alike. So – according to this objection – judges never really leave moral reasoning behind in *anything* they do, not even in the most technical and legalistic reasoning with which they entangle the more recognizably moral elements of their argumentation. Engaging in that sort of entangled reasoning is also one of the things that morality requires (of persons in their situation).[43]

I have a lot of sympathy for this objection, and I suspect that it is right in roughly the way that Dworkin's complaint about Posner in the previous section was right. In some sense, reasons of deference and reasons of integrity are as much moral reasons as the reasons of institutional allocation that we considered in that section. On the other hand, they are such importantly complicated moral reasons as to create – in a sense – a normative world of their own, and their distinctiveness may render any operational comparison with our familiar ideals of moral reasoning inapposite.

I have pursued a complex line of argument. Let us pause now to see where we stand. I considered two views of legal reasoning.

One view is that legal reasoning divides in two types: (i) finding, applying and interpreting the law; and (ii) moral reasoning. Type (ii), it was said, is particularly important when we are determining constitutional issues about whether individual and minority rights are being properly protected. Because judges are very good at type (ii) reasoning – better than legislators – they should have the final say on moral issues about rights.

43 Thus Dworkin, for example, regards the duty of integrity as one important part of morality, not as something separate from morality: See Dworkin, *Law's Empire*, *supra* note 39 at 164–78.

The other view is that (i) and (ii) cannot be separated. They are mixed up together and they pervade one another. This means that although moral elements are involved in all adjudication, they are mingled in a way that makes legal reasoning quite unrecognizable by the standards of moral reasoning. I think this is the better view of what law and legal reasoning are like.

Now, suppose we hang on to the proposition that it is very important for moral issues concerning individual and minority rights to be addressed directly *as moral issues*. Then, we may well *not* think that courts are the proper institutional forum for final and fundamental decisions about these matters. We need judicial reasoning about rights, of course, and courts are indispensable. Maybe not for the fundamental moral phase, however: Perhaps that is better conducted in a setting where it will *not* be compromised by the doctrines, precedents, texts, and interpretations with which legal reasoning is necessarily preoccupied, and which inevitably and quite properly compromise all such moral reasoning in which courts are able to engage. That, at least, is a possibility.

4. IS THERE AN IMPORTANT DIFFERENCE BETWEEN REASONING MORALLY ON ONE'S OWN ACCOUNT AND REASONING MORALLY IN THE NAME OF A WHOLE SOCIETY?

Before we accept that conclusion, however, there is an important adjustment we have to make in our ideal of moral reasoning. The image of moral reasoning that we use in philosophy is one that places a considerable premium on autonomy – on each reasoner thinking things through for himself and taking personal responsibility for the upshot of his actions. Now, is this the way we expect judges to reason? Does it not make a difference that judges operate, not on their own account, but in the name of a whole society of millions of individuals?

Some have argued that it makes an immense difference to the real and perceived legitimacy of judicial decision-making. Commenting on what his liberal brethren on the bench regarded as the distressing tendency of American citizens to hold demonstrations on the steps of the Supreme Court, Justice Antonin Scalia once said:

> As long as this Court thought (and the people thought) that we Justices were doing essentially lawyers' work up here – reading text and discerning our society's traditional understanding of that text – the public pretty much left us alone.... But if in reality, our process of constitutional adjudication consists primarily of making value judgments... then a free and intelligent people's attitude towards us can be expected to be (ought to be) quite different. The

> people know that their value judgments are quite as good as those taught in any law school – maybe better. If, indeed, the "liberties" protected by the Constitution are, as the Court says, undefined and unbounded, then the people should demonstrate, to protest that we do not implement their values instead of ours.[44]

It is all too easy to forget the point about legitimacy – "their values instead of ours" – that Justice Scalia entangles here with a more tendentious point about competence – "The people know that their value judgments are quite as good as those taught in any law school." There are some matters on which comparative institutional competence is not conclusive. Various philosophers I know might be more adept at setting tax rates than the "queer and cowardly rabble" elected for that purpose to Congress.[45] But given that we believe there should be no taxation without representation, we are stuck with tax rates determined by our representatives rather than by fiscal experts. Still, that does not mean the issue of comparative competence is uninteresting. And it comes together with the legitimacy issue when we ask whether judicial moral reasoning is really superior to legislative moral reasoning when considered as *moral reasoning in the name of a whole society*. The judges' reasoning may look more like good individual moral reasoning than the legislature's, but that will not be conclusive if individual moral reasoning is not what we ought to be modeling.

There is a line of thought associated with Robert Cover's argument in *Justice Accused*, which suggests that it is precisely conscientious individual moral reasoning that we want from our judges, and that something goes wrong when that is suppressed by or subordinated to a formalistic obligation to apply positive law. Cover told the story of nineteenth-century American judges who applied the Fugitive Slave Clause and *Fugitive Slave Act* according to their terms rather than following through on their own personal convictions that slavery was morally abhorrent. "As a citizen and as a man," said one such judge, "I may admit the injustice and immorality of slavery.... But as a jurist, I must look

[44] *Casey v. Planned Parenthood of S. E. Pennsylvania* 505 U.S. 833 at 1000–1 (1992) (Scalia J. dissenting in part).

[45] *Cf.* A.P Herbert, "*Sparrow v. Pipp*: The Lords Rebel," in *Uncommon Law: Being Sixty-Six Misleading Cases* (1969). Responding to the argument that judges never make law, only discover it "in the inexhaustible womb of the Common Law," Herbert has his Lord Chancellor say:

> "My Lords, as you know, this is nonsense. The judges of our land are constantly making law, and have always done so. The pity is that there is not more judge-made law. For most of His Majesty's judges are much better fitted for the making of laws than the queer and cowardly rabble who are elected to Parliament for that purpose by the fantastic machinery of universal suffrage."

at that standard of morality, which the law prescribes."[46] When I teach this chapter of Cover's work, many of my students immediately condemn the judges who took this line. They regard the subordination of personal conscience as an evil; they see the judges as reasoning in bad faith; they are outraged that the judges are hiding behind black-letter law to avoid the difficult choices that conscience and morality dictate; and they see this as a prime example of the way legal practice tends to suppress and deaden the better, moral angels of our nature. A number of scholarly commentators take this line too, claiming that it would have been better if Cover's judges had just reasoned morally rather than distracting themselves with texts and precedents and doctrines.[47]

I think this is a clear case of result-driven jurisprudence. I suspect that the view that judges ought to reason autonomously rather than follow the legal texts, precedents, and doctrines that appear to bind them is most persuasive to a modern commentator when the judge's conscience, if indulged, would point to a conclusion that the commentator regards as morally congenial. When it is a case of a judge indulging personal moral convictions with which the commentator disagrees – a pro-life judge refusing to apply *Roe v. Wade*, for example, or a racist judge standing on his own conscientious views about the importance of separate facilities rather than the Fourteenth Amendment or the *Civil Rights Act* – enthusiasm for this sort of moral reasoning tends to wane a little.

Be that as it may, one can concede that judges ought not to close down their own consciences altogether in cases like this and that they should be willing occasionally to take a stand against what they figure is the most heinous injustice – one can concede all that, but *still* acknowledge that it ought to make a difference to the way one exercises one's conscience whether one is taking a moral stand purely on one's own account – like Henry David Thoreau, for example[48] – or whether one is acting in and for a group, which comprises a great many others with a diversity of views on the matter at hand. It simply cannot be the case that these circumstances make no difference. We must be sure, when we judge the way a given official grapples with such a problem, that we do not apply to the one set of circumstances standards or ideals for moral reasoning that are best suited for the other.[49]

[46] *Jackson v. Bullock*, 12 Conn. 39 (1837) (Bissell J. dissenting) – cited by Robert Cover, *Justice Accused: Antislavery and the Judicial Process* (1975) at 120 [Cover, *Justice Accused*].

[47] See, *e.g.*, Rudolph J. Gerber, "On Dispensing Injustice," 43 Ariz. L. Rev. 135 at 168 (2001) and Benjamin Zipursky, "Conflicts of Integrity," 72 Fordham L. Rev. 395 at 397 (2003).

[48] See "Civil Disobedience" in Henry David Thoreau, *Walden and Civil Disobedience* (1983) at 383.

[49] Incidentally, Cover himself did not condemn out of hand the slavery judges whose evasions he described. He did say that "[t]he judicial conscience is an artful dodger" and that "[b]efore it will

Here's another way of reaching a similarly shaped conclusion. Earlier, I mentioned John Rawls's distinction between political conceptions and comprehensive moral conceptions.[50] Modern societies exhibit a plurality of incompatible and incommensurable comprehensive moral conceptions, and Rawls believes – this is his doctrine of public reason – that it is not appropriate for any official to appeal to moral arguments rooted in or premised upon any particular comprehensive conception when justifying public decisions (at least when they are decisions about constitutional essentials or basic justice). In circumstances of moral dissensus, says Rawls, it is incumbent on those who exercise power to justify what they do in terms that they can reasonably expect others to grasp and follow. Reasoning that proceeds from the premises of a particular comprehensive moral conception may not be intelligible to, let alone have a reasonable prospect of convincing, citizens who hold to a different comprehensive view. So, Rawls argues, official justification must go forward on the basis of a more limited set of moral ideas and constructions that everyone can reasonably be expected to grasp, if not endorse. Once again, therefore, we see a gap between the kind of moral reasoning appropriate for someone ordering his own affairs and the kind of moral reasoning appropriate for public decisions. On Rawls's view, if we were to judge the latter in terms appropriate for judging the former – saying, for example, that the decision-maker did not sufficiently explore the deep foundations of his starting points – we would be making a serious mistake.

Intriguingly, Rawls associates this doctrine of public reason with the reasoning of courts. He titles the penultimate section of the chapter on public reason "The Supreme Court as Exemplar of Public Reason."[51] He says that the application of the constraints of public reason is clearer in the judicial setting – "the

concede that a case is one that presents a moral dilemma, it will hide in the nooks and crannies of the professional ethics, run to the cave of role limits, [and] seek the shelter of separation of powers" (Cover, *Justice Accused, supra* note 46 at 201). But Cover's main criticism of the judges he described was that they were insufficiently inventive legally, less resourceful than they could have been in the ways of the law, neglectful of various sources of law that might have taken them in another direction, not that they failed to switch from legal reasoning to individual moral reasoning. That said, Cover also acknowledged the complexity of the judges' position, including its moral complexity, denying that deference to existing statutes and constitutional provisions is a formalistic or amoral position. There were, he argued, good moral reasons which a responsible moral agent would have to grasp why it might be inappropriate for a judge to follow his own conscience in these matters. These moral considerations range from straightforward points about role-morality and public expectations all the way through to major considerations about the fragility and preservation of the Union. (This last point is analogous to the argument considered towards the end of section 3 about the moral reasons behind following precedent and deferring to other bodies' enactments etc.; see text accompanying note 44.)

[50] Rawls, *Political Liberalism, supra* note 11 at 212–54.

[51] *Ibid.* at 213.

discourse of judges in their decisions, and especially the judges of a supreme court"[52] – than in any other setting:

> [P]ublic reason is the sole reason the court exercises. It is the only branch of government that is visibly on its face the creature of that reason and that reason alone. . . . The justices cannot, of course, invoke their own personal morality, nor the ideals and virtues of morality generally.[53]

Although he mainly associates public reason with the abstract features of his own conception set out in *Political Liberalism*, when he talks about the court, he associates their exemplary use of public reason with following precedent and deferring to legislative and constitutional texts.[54] If Rawls is right about this,[55] then the conclusion we reached at the end of section (3) is premature. The fact that judges compromise their autonomous moral reasoning in some of the ways discussed in section (3) may not be a disqualifier at all. On the contrary, it may just show that they are reasoning morally in accordance with the constraints of public reason that apply to them, *reasoning morally just as they should if they are reasoning not on their own individual accounts but in the name of the whole society*. This ought to hearten those who think not only that judges reason well from a moral point of view but also that they have what it takes to figure out the style of moral reasoning appropriate to their station.

Even if one does not work from Rawlsian premises, it might seem that the legal reasoning described at the end of the previous section is exactly the sort of thing we want for reasoning (*e.g.*, by judges) in the name of a whole society. True, it may seem like an affront to the autonomy of moral reason when a judge proceeds from a given text rather than from fundamental moral axioms, or when he dresses up a legal doctrine in the garb of moral principle, or when

[52] John Rawls, *The Law of Peoples* (1999) at 133.

[53] Rawls, *Political Liberalism*, *supra* note 11 at 235–6.

[54] *Ibid.* at 215–16: "[T]he ideal of public reason . . . applies . . . in a special way to the judiciary and above all to a supreme court in a constitutional democracy with judicial review. This is because the justices have to explain and justify their decisions as based on their understanding of the constitution and relevant statutes and precedents. . . . [T]he court's special role makes it the exemplar of public reason."

[55] Personally, I don't actually agree with Rawls on either public reason itself or the courts as its exemplars or the idea of deference to legal texts as an example of it; I have a paper on this entitled "Public Reason and 'Justification' in the Courtroom," that I am happy to make available, and which, I am told, will appear shortly in the Catholic University of America's new *Journal of Law, Philosophy and Culture*, in the proceedings of a symposium of several years ago devoted to John Rawls's idea of public reason. But I cite Rawls's argument to exemplify the popularity and depth of the more general position – which I certainly do accept – that moral reasoning in the name of a whole society is different in character from, and must not be judged by the standards appropriate to an individual's moral reasoning about some personal matter.

he stops a perfectly good moral argument in its tracks with some contrary precedent, or when he deflects the force of a moral consideration by some move that makes sense in the law but no sense in ethics. That may seem to compromise the integrity of moral argument. But if we look at it in another light, we see it as the judge participating in the elaborate construction of a moral argument put forward by, for, and in the name of a very large group – his society. Instead of following his own moral lights in a single-minded manner, he tries to reconcile what he is disposed to do about the problem that comes up before him with what others have done in the society's name with problems more or less like this. He does that not just with regard to the bottom line, but with regard to the stages and components of his moral reasoning, so that all the way through, one is conscious that it is not just him who is disposing morally of this case. To use a phrase of Dworkin's, the judge does not see it as his task "to plant the flag of his [own moral] convictions over as large a domain of power or rules as possible."[56] The litigants who come before him should not expect him to reason about their problem as though from a moral *tabula rasa*; they come to him for *society's* disposition of their problem and they should welcome the introduction into his reasoning of elements of earlier social decisions by other judges and other officials, and not regard that as an affront to the autonomy of morality or justice. Not that the judge simply cites and plonks down a bunch of texts and precedents. He weaves them into an argument that he gives in his own voice and takes responsibility for. He offers his argument not in the spirit of "Here's what I would do, morally, if I ruled the world," but, rather, "Here's the best way I can see of disposing properly of this case in a way that keeps faith with how other people in this society have been treated in similar circumstances." Judges are very good at doing this sort of thing. Legislators are not, not that they very often try. So – once again – it would seem that we have reached a position congenial to judicial review. Judges do show themselves to be better at moral reasoning if, by moral reasoning, we mean reasoning morally in this manner of keeping faith with the existing commitments of the society.

Before we get too excited about this, however, we need to ask whether this mode of reasoning is the only way of reasoning in the name of a whole society. And of course it is not. Everyone agrees that some morally important issues should be settled by legislation. (Most think that the legislature should have at least a first stab at even the issues upon which they think courts should have the final say.) Patently, legislatures do not reason as courts do, and most of us

[56] Dworkin, *Law's Empire*, *supra* note 39 at 211.

would say they should not attempt to imitate courts.[57] The ideal – let alone the reality – of legislative reasoning is quite different.

Legislative reasoning is a way of reasoning in the name of a whole society about important moral issues when it is appropriate that such reasoning *not* be constrained by existing texts, doctrines, or precedents. Legislators address the issue afresh, as though for the first time (even though it may be an issue that has come before them several times). Of course, it is important for them to figure out how the decision they come up with will fit with adjacent law on other issues.[58] But that is different from a court's obligation to reconcile its decision with previous decisions on the same and similar issues. Mostly legislatures are in a position to reason about moral issues directly, on the merits. Members of the legislature talk directly to the issues involved, in a way that is mostly undistracted by legal doctrine or precedents.

In a number of other writings, I have made a comparison between the sort of reasoning that was used to address the issue of abortion in the United Kingdom in the mid-1960s, where the issue was assigned to Parliament for final decision, and the sort of reasoning that was used to address the same issue a few years later in the United States, where the federal courts have, for the time being, the final say on this contentious moral question.[59] The contrast is stark and instructive. The second reading debate in the House of Commons debates on the *Medical Termination of Pregnancy Bill* in 1966 is as fine an example of a political institution grappling with moral issues as you could hope to find. It is a sustained debate – about 100 pages in *Hansard*[60] – and it involved pro-life Labour people and pro-choice Labour people, pro-life Conservatives and pro-choice Conservatives, talking through and focusing on all of the questions that need to be addressed when abortion is being debated. They debated the questions passionately, but also thoroughly and honorably, with attention to the rights, principles, and pragmatic issues on both sides. In the Supreme Court's fifty-page opinion in *Roe v. Wade*, by contrast, there are but a couple of paragraphs dealing with the moral importance of reproductive rights in relation to privacy, and the few paragraphs addressed to the other

[57] See Mark Tushnet, *Taking the Constitution Away from the Courts* (1999) at 63 *et passim*, arguing that we should not criticize legislators for failing to reason as judges do, because reasoning like judges may not be a smart way to address the issues at stake.

[58] See John Stuart Mill, *Considerations on Representative Government* (1991), c. 5, at 109, and Dworkin, *Law's Empire*, *supra* note 39 at 217–19 (on the principle of legislative integrity).

[59] See Jeremy Waldron, "The Core of the Case against Judicial Review," 155 Yale L.J 1346 at 1383–5 (2006) [Waldron, "The Core of the Case"] and "Legislating with Integrity," 72 Fordham L. Rev. 373 at 390–1 (2003).

[60] 732 Parl. Deb., H.C. (5th ser.) (1966) 1067–1166.

moral issue at stake – the rights-status of the fetus – are mostly taken up with showing the diversity of opinions on the issue.[61] A lot of the fifty pages is either a review of case law and doctrine or a review of the history of the issue. Now, if the argument I made in the first part of this section is correct, it is not fair to castigate the court for this lop-sided balance between legalistic argument and moral argument. That is, perhaps, how judges ought to proceed in moral argument when they are arguing in the name of a whole society. But the British legislative proceedings capture an alternative mode of moral reasoning, and that, too, is moral reasoning in the name of a whole society.

Now how can that be? If the moral issues are being addressed directly rather than through the filters of legal text, doctrine, and precedent, how can I say that the legislature is arguing in the name of the whole society? A contribution by a given legislator will sound like an ordinary individual grappling autonomously with a moral issue. (That was more or less what happened in the House of Commons; each legislator gave his or her own moral view on abortion and the issues surrounding it.) The crucial thing, however, is (first) that there are scores of such individuals participating in the debate and hundreds who are entitled to; and (secondly) that a given line of moral reasoning does not yield its practical conclusion directly, but is, rather, oriented towards a process of voting, in which the views of each representative are given equal weight. Lines of moral reasoning are presented but in a way that gives them an opportunity to test their persuasiveness in a setting in which they are arrayed against rival lines of reasoning, a setting in which (hopefully) all major lines of reasoning are arrayed. Then representatives of the whole society, elected on a basis that treats all individuals in the society as equals, vote as equals on the whole measure and on its parts. And that is how legislative institutions reason morally in the name of the whole society.

Of course the proceedings of any actual legislature may look a bit more ramshackle than this. But my point is that, even at the level of ideals, we now have *two ideals of moral reasoning in the name of a whole society on important moral issues*, – a legislative ideal and a judicial ideal. We have two ideals, of which we might use one or the other to judge how actual officials or actual institutions are operating. So here is a possibility we have to consider: An actual legislature may operate rather crudely compared with the legislative ideal, but it may be closer to that ideal than a court operating well by the standards of the judicial ideal.

[61] *Roe v. Wade*, 410 U.S. 113 (1973). The paragraphs on privacy and the importance of reproductive rights are at *ibid.* at 153–5, and the paragraphs arguing in moral terms about the alleged rights or personality of the fetus are at *ibid.* at 159–60.

When is it appropriate to use one or the other as the ideal by which we judge an institution's moral reasoning? We can answer this in terms of different institutions or we can answer it in terms of different kinds of decisions. I have called them legislative and judicial ideals, but that does not necessarily mean that courts should always be judged by the judicial ideal as a matter of definition.

One possibility is that courts should not be judged by the legislative ideal because they do not satisfy the legitimacy conditions that ideal presupposes. (For example, I said that moral reasoning by a legislature involves voting on equal terms by representatives and that is justified partly because the representatives are elected on a basis that treats citizens as equals. Given that judges are not elected, it may not be appropriate to assess their decision procedures according to the standard we use to assess legislative decision procedures.)[62]

Another possibility is that decision-making should be judged by one ideal or the other depending on whether what is called for is a fresh decision on the merits or a decision reconciled with existing texts, doctrines, and precedents. To figure this out, one would have to make a substantive judgment about what sort of decision-making is called for. If a fresh judgment on the merits is called for, then what we should look for is good moral reasoning on the legislative model; and if the courts cannot offer that, because it is not how they operate or because they cannot satisfy the legitimacy presuppositions, then we will have to assign the task of moral reasoning to an institution that can offer it. On the other hand, if an essentially legal decision is called for, then it will not be appropriate for the institution concerned to reason as legislatures do. What we need is judicial reasoning of a familiar type, and it is well known that legislators do not have the competence to reason in this way.

So, finally, we come back round to the issue of individual rights. If what is called for on issues of rights is moral reasoning in the name of a whole society, should we use the legislative model of moral reasoning or the judicial model of moral reasoning?

The case for using the judicial model in most societies is that these issues are already supposed to be covered by the provisions of a written constitution (a bill of rights) and so they should be treated as legal issues, and reasoned about in the way that courts are best at reasoning. Such reasoning, with all its legalisms, texts, case analyses, and so on, may not look much like moral reasoning, but (as we have seen) we should not judge it by the standards of individual moral reasoning and we should not judge it by the standards of reasoning legislatively in the name of a whole society.

[62] I argue this at greater length in Waldron, "The Core of the Case," *supra* note 59 at 1391–3.

The case for using the legislative model rejects the premise that important issues of individual and minority rights are covered, in the appropriate sense, by the provisions of a bill of rights. They may be covered in the formal sense that some of what is in a bill of rights can be made to seem relevant to the issues that they pose – as, for example, the First, Fourth, and Fourteenth Amendments to the U.S. Constitution can be made to seem relevant to the issue of abortion. But the text holds out no hope of really settling the matter, either because the issue was not contemplated in its drafting or because the Bill of Rights was drafted in a way that was supposed to finesse major disagreements about rights in the community.

The issues I have in mind are mainly not issues of interpretation in a narrow legalistic sense.[63] They may present themselves in the first instance as issues of interpretation, but everyone knows that they raise questions of considerable practical moment for the political community. Elsewhere, I have referred to these as "watershed" issues of rights.[64] They are major issues of political philosophy with significant ramifications for the lives of many people. Moreover, I assume that they are not idiosyncratic to the society in which they arise. They define major choices that *any* modern society must face, choices that are reasonably well understood in the context of existing moral and political debate, choices that are focal points of moral and political disagreement in many societies. Examples spring quickly to mind: abortion is one, also affirmative action, the legitimacy of government redistribution or interference in the marketplace, the rights of criminal suspects, the precise meaning of religious toleration, minority cultural rights, the regulation of speech and spending in electoral campaigns, and so on.

In the United States, it is indisputable *both* that the provisions of the Bill of Rights have a bearing on how each of these issues is to be resolved *and* that the provisions of the Bill of Rights do not, themselves, determine a resolution of the issue in a way that is beyond reasonable dispute. This is not to deny that arguments can be made that seem conclusive – at least to those who make them – as to the bearing of the Bill of Rights on the issue in question. If judicial review is set up in the society, then lawyers will argue about these issues of disagreement using both the text and the "gravitational force" of the text of the Bill of Rights. In fact, lawyers will have a field day. Each side to each of the disagreements will claim that its position can be read into the bland commitments of the

[63] The paragraphs that follow are adapted from Waldron, "The Core of the Case," *supra* note 59 at 1366–9.

[64] J. Waldron, "Judicial Power and Popular Sovereignty," in Mark Graber and Michael Perhac eds., *Marbury versus Madison: Documents and Commentary* (2002) 181 at 195.

Bill of Rights if only those texts are read generously (or narrowly) enough. Neither will be prepared to acknowledge what I think is obvious: The bland rhetoric of the Bill of Rights was designed simply to finesse the very real and reasonable disagreements that are inevitable among people who take rights seriously for long enough to see the Bill enacted. Instead of encouraging us to confront these disagreements directly, an institution of judicial review is likely to lead to their being framed as questions of interpretation of those bland formulations. Whether that is a desirable context in which to deliberate about the moral issues that they pose is exactly what we are considering.

My own view is that it is important for some or all of these watershed issues about individual rights to be debated, from time to time, freshly on their merits in a way that is relatively uncontaminated by interpretive disputes about the constitution. These, as I have said, are not primarily interpretive questions: They are well-known and major choices that all liberal societies face. It is important that they be debated in a morally responsible manner, and fairness demands that they be debated in a way that reflects the fact that a decision is being made, not just for an individual, but for a whole society. To address these issues in that manner, on their merits, we should use the legislative model of moral reasoning, not the judicial model. And if we think it appropriate to use the legislative model, we should probably not use the judicial model as a basis for reviewing the decision made in the legislative model. Instead, we should deploy the legislative model and make the ensuing moral debate the best it can be, by the standards of that model.

I suppose it is imaginable that courts could use this model of moral reasoning – addressing issues directly on their moral merits, undistracted by legalisms. We could try this if we distrusted representative democracy as much as most of the defenders of judicial review seem to distrust it. But we would have to remember that courts have little experience of this sort of moral reasoning and some of its presuppositions make little sense when applied to courts. Maybe the case could be made nevertheless. But what I hope to have established is this: If we pay proper attention to the sort of moral deliberation that is appropriate for major issues of individual and minority rights, the case that can be made for assigning those issues to courts is by no means compelling.

3 Constitutional Morality and Bills of Rights

W. J. Waluchow

TWO CONCEPTIONS OF MORALITY

To what kind of norms does a court refer in justifying its claim that a statute is constitutionally invalid because it unjustifiably infringes "equality before and under the law," or violates "the right to life, liberty and security of the person" in a manner that fails to comport with "the principles of fundamental justice?" Presumably, the norms in question are norms of political morality. But what exactly are these? Are they the norms moral philosophers often dispute – that is, norms that purport to be universal, valid, rationally justified, or maybe even "objectively true," much as Kant and Plato thought? Are they perhaps something more modest than this – for example, the norms of conventional or positive morality, rooted not in the fabric of the universe, but in the variable beliefs and convictions of a particular community? Or are they something else entirely? Debates about bills of rights and judicial review – as well as debates among legal philosophers concerning the various relations between law and morality – have been curiously silent on this important question. It is well past time to draw attention to it, however, if only because the answer one gives can seriously affect one's assessment of bills of rights and the various practices of judicial review to which they give rise.

In addressing this neglected question, I will use as my point of departure a popular complaint one often hears in both academic and popular discourse. Judicial review under a bill of rights is often said to be a bad thing because it renders the law far too dependent on the subjective moral opinions or predilections of judges. Although it need not be so based, the popular complaint is usually premised on the implicit assumption that the morality to which bills of rights purport to make reference, and which judges are foolishly expected to discover and apply, is the rationally justified and discoverable morality whose nature and content concerned Plato and Kant.[1] Because there is no such morality (it is claimed), or we cannot discover and agree on its requirements even if it does exist, the law ends up depending far too heavily on the subjective moral opinions of judges, and this cannot possibly be justified in any society that purports to respect the principles of democracy and the rule of law.

One obvious way round the popular complaint (aside from abandoning bills of rights altogether) is to suggest that a bill of rights need not be taken to refer to Platonic morality, but to the norms of conventional or positive morality – the morality actually accepted by the relevant population and the content of which we can (it might be thought) discover using largely empirical methods. But this option brings along its own set of difficulties. For instance, discerning the content of positive morality is surely not a matter of value-free, empirical discovery. It is risking trouble to suggest that value-free inquiry occurs within the realms of science; it is probably sheer foolishness to think that we could have "pure theory" when the object of discovery is not space, black holes, or public opinion on Afghanistan, but the content of their norms of positive morality. If all this is true, then "discovering" positive morality may depend as much on the moral predilections of an interpreter as on any neutral fact of the matter. And if that interpreter ends up being a judge, then we are right back to the popular complaint.

A second, equally troublesome, difficulty is the moral disagreement one encounters in pluralistic, multicultural communities such as the United States and Canada. If moral dissensus is a fact of life,[2] then it is far from clear that we could identify a set of norms properly ascribable to the community as a whole. If that is so, and if judges are supposed to ground their bill of rights judgments in the norms and beliefs of positive morality, then presumably they are going to have to pick and choose among the various options on offer. But this, too, will force them to rely on their own subjective, moral predilections and preferences – and we're back, once again, to the popular complaint.

A third objection is this: Positive morality is supposed to be the morality of the community. But what it really amounts to (when it exists) is a set of beliefs and norms of the prevailing group(s) within that community, that is, of *the majority*. By its very nature, however, a bill of rights is supposed to serve to protect vulnerable minorities and individuals against the errors, prejudices, and excesses of powerful majorities. To view the rights protected by a bill of

[1] For the sake of convenience, we will refer to this simply as Platonic morality.

[2] A large measure of disagreement on moral matters does seem to be the norm in western societies, as witnessed by recurring debates about topics such as abortion, the death penalty, and same-sex marriage.

rights as a function of the moral beliefs of the very majorities against whom protection is thought essential therefore threatens to undermine the very point of having them.

So whichever way we turn – Platonic or positive morality – we seem to run into a picture of bills of rights, judges, and judicial review, which leads to the popular complaint. And if one's philosophical and moral intuitions suggest that bills of rights are good things to have, then one is going to have to address the serious challenge posed by that complaint. This is what I hope to do in this chapter. My goal is to sketch a plausible, alternative picture of the morality to which bills of rights might sensibly be thought to make reference. This morality is not the Platonic morality of the philosophers, and though it is, in large measure, relative to the society to which it applies and therefore can be viewed as a kind of positive morality, it is, in no way, fully reducible to the moral beliefs and opinions currently shared by the majority and discoverable using standard methods of social science. Rather, it is a morality that lies somewhere between these two extremes, combining elements of what is normally thought of as positive morality with something like what H. L. A. Hart termed critical morality.

TWO FURTHER CONCEPTIONS

Recall the popular complaint: Judges engaged in judicial review under a bill of rights are granted far too much licence to impose their own subjective moral views on the community and its democratic representatives.[3] These are moral views that a judge personally prefers, prescribes, or which her moral utterances express, or to the truth or validity of which she is personally committed as an autonomous moral agent. So construed, it is obvious that a judge's personal moral views can diverge significantly from positive morality, understood as those moral beliefs and norms widely shared within the community. For this reason, it makes sense to refer to them as her own, subjective or personal moral opinions. Against personal morality so construed is pitted the community's morality, viewed, now, not as the morality of any particular person(s) but of the community as a whole. In saying that judicial review results in a judge substituting her own personal moral views for those of the community and/or

[3] Henceforth, I will use the phrase judicial review to mean judicial review *under a bill of rights*. I will also assume that the exercise in question is one in which the issue to be decided by the judges is whether otherwise valid law satisfies moral conditions of validity constituted by the moral provisions in a bill of rights, provisions such as sections 15 and 7 of the *Canadian Charter of Rights and Freedoms*.

its representatives, one implies that there is a morality (or at the very least a set of moral beliefs) that can be ascribed to the community and which the judge's decision displaces. The identity of the relevant community can, of course, be a notoriously difficult question – one that can arise in any number of different contexts, not just bill of rights cases. For example, criminal governing of indecency and obscenity has, historically, been interpreted in light of "community standards of tolerance." But these can vary tremendously depending on how one identifies the relevant community.[4] This difficulty is acute within multicultural, pluralistic societies. If community standards depend on culture, and such societies include a plurality of different cultures whose standards lead to significantly different judgments of tolerance, then it may be a serious mistake to assume that we could discover a single community with a single set of moral norms about indecency and obscenity which could be said to be recognized or reflected in obscenity law. If so, then what reason is there to think that things will be any different when one turns to bill of rights norms?

What reason indeed. But let us look at this all a bit more carefully. The assumption that there are discoverable norms, properly attributable to a pluralistic, multicultural community, may depend on whether or not there is a sufficiently rich overlap in the relevant moral beliefs and norms widely accepted within the various subcommunities in question. It may well be that on at least some of the moral issues addressed in bill of rights cases there is, in the relevant moralities of the relevant subcommunities, something like a Rawlsian "overlapping consensus."[5] Rawls explains what he means by this phrase in the following passage:

> There can, in fact, be considerable differences in citizens' conceptions of justice provided that these conceptions lead to similar political judgments. And this is possible, since different premises can yield the same conclusion. In this case there exists what we may refer to as overlapping rather than strict consensus.... Of course, this overlapping need not be perfect; it is enough that a condition of reciprocity is satisfied. Both sides must believe that however much their conceptions of justice differ, their views support the same judgment in the situation at hand, and would do so even should their respective positions be interchanged.[6]

[4] For Canadian examples, see *R. v. Butler*, [1992] 1 S.C.R. 452; *R. v. Jacob* (1996), 31 O.R. (3d) 350; and *Towne Cinema Theatres Ltd. v. The Queen*, [1985] 1 S.C.R. 494.

[5] I say 'something like' because Rawls' particular notion has been subject to much discussion and some dispute – and because I do not wish to become embroiled in the intricacies of Rawlsian exegesis.

[6] *A Theory of Justice* (1971) at 387–8 [Rawls, *Theory of Justice*]. It is not clear that this is the same notion of overlapping consensus as one finds in Rawls' more recent book, *Political Liberalism*

Rawls seems to envision a situation in which we agree on a range of particular conclusions but disagree about the general premises required to yield them. In this respect, the state of overlapping consensus is like the situation in which an appeal court is unanimous in its judgment – for example, the defendant does not have the right to the compensation he claims – but the judges disagree on their reasons for judgment. In other words, the judges agree on a result, but their concurring opinions reveal that they disagree on how that result is to be justified. Whether this is an accurate reading of Rawls need not concern us. The important point to stress at this juncture is that there is no reason to restrict overlapping consensus in the way the passage appears to suggest. The consensus can, indeed, be on particular judgments, with differing premises yielding shared conclusions. But it can also be on the premises, with differences of opinion emerging as to what these shared premises require in the way of particular judgments or rules. We often agree on abstract principles of justice, equality, and the like, but disagree on the implications of these principles – more particular rules, policies, and decisions – for the concrete circumstances of democratic politics. Everyone agrees that we should pursue equality – but there is considerable disagreement about whether, for example, this justifies affirmative action programs.

In any event, I hazard to suggest that on at least some questions of political morality that arise in cases under a bill of rights there is some measure of overlapping consensus within the relevant community on norms and/or judgments concerning justice, equality, and liberty that would emerge upon careful reflection. Lest I lose the reader instantly, I wish to stress the importance of the phrase "upon careful reflection," about which something will be said in a moment. There is no doubting the fact that, on many, many issues, we differ in ways often stressed by critics of judicial review. But sometimes these disagreements are not as deep as might appear at first blush. A society that differs in many of its surface moral opinions is often one in which there is considerably more agreement than initially meets the eye – even if these are agreements that are "incompletely theorized," and even if they emerge only after an attempt has been made to reconcile conflicting moral views.[7] I also suggest that on at

(rev. edn. 1996) [Rawls, *Political Liberalism*]. There, the object of the overlapping consensus appears to be a political conception of justice upon which all reasonable people, regardless of their acutely differing comprehensive doctrines, can be expected to agree. See *Political Liberalism*, 14–15. See especially note 17, where Rawls writes: "The idea of an overlapping consensus, or perhaps better, the term, was introduced in *Theory*, pp. 387f, as a way to weaken the conditions for the reasonableness of civil disobedience in a nearly just democratic society. Here and later in these lectures I use it in a different sense and in a far wider context."

[7] The term "incompletely theorized agreements" derives from the work of Cass Sunstein. See his *Legal Reasoning and Political Conflict* (1996), especially ch. 2.

least some occasions we can identify the relevant community – or "community of communities" – the moralities of which enjoy a significant, if imperfect, overlap and can, in virtue of this fact, be said to constitute a kind of shared morality. When I henceforth speak of the community's morality, whether this be in reference to constitutional morality or a community's positive morality understood in the more usual way discussed earlier, I mean my comments to apply to either possibility.

How one identifies the relevant community or communities is therefore an important question. Equally important, however, is the question of how one conceives of the relevant norms of the community once the latter has been identified. It is here, I believe, where things get very murky indeed. And this murkiness feeds the popular complaint, as well as many other associated objections put forward by critics of judicial review. So let us try to clear away some of the murkiness by introducing yet further distinctions.

ELEMENTS OF A MORALITY

To this point we have drawn a number of distinctions. First, there is the traditional distinction between positive and Platonic morality; that is, the morality commonly accepted within a community versus the morality sought by Kant and Plato. Next, we noted a distinction between personal morality and the morality ascribable to something other than a person – in this instance, a community or community of communities. In each instance, however, we have been talking about "a morality." But what exactly is a morality? What sorts of things make it up? Let us begin with a number of fairly uncontroversial observations.

Observation 1

Whether we attribute it to a person, a community, or perhaps an institution like an organized religion, a morality typically includes a range of different elements. It will usually include (a) a number of very general principles, values and ideals – or perhaps only one, as in some versions of utilitarianism; (b) more specific rules, principles, and maxims; and (c) opinions and judgments about particular cases and types of cases. It might even include (d) certain meta-ethical rules telling us how we are to go about making our moral decisions. Examples from the first category include Mill's Harm Principle,[8] the value of

[8] On many theories of political morality, Mill's Harm Principle functions more or less as a moral axiom. In such cases, the principle clearly belongs in our first category. But it is not so clear

autonomy, and the ideals of democracy. The second category might include the rule that the consent of a subject is necessary in any scientific study in which that subject's interests are at stake, or the rule that one may keep the truth from one's small children in order to spare them nightmares. The third category might include the belief that same-sex unions are immoral, that gays should not be allowed to adopt, or that a woman's provocative clothing serves as a mitigating factor in sexual harassment cases. As for (d), two prime examples are Kant's categorical imperative and Hare's universal prescriptivism, which, in each case, do not tell us directly how to act, but state the meta-ethical rule we must follow in determining the moral maxims or prescriptions upon which we should act.

Observation 2

It is a commonplace in moral philosophy that an individual's personal morality, understood as including elements of the aforementioned four kinds, can be internally inconsistent, based on false beliefs and prejudices, and otherwise subject to rational critique. None of us gets everything right. It is also a commonplace that it is an individual's moral responsibility to explore and adjust her personal morality so as to avoid as many of the aforementioned deficiencies as possible. This is true whether the agent in question is a utilitarian or a Kantian, a social contract theorist, a feminist, or one who believes that moral judgments express universalizable prescriptions. It is even true of one who thinks that his moral judgments are in some fundamental way subjective or merely expressive of the speaker's attitudes or emotions. A person who thinks in either of these last two ways will recognize the need to ensure that his subjective moral beliefs or noncognitive exhortations are based on true non-moral propositions and are relatively consistent with one another.[9] Whatever one's moral stripe, fresh cases, or old cases considered in a new light, lead a responsible moral agent to explore the elements of her morality and to adjust them accordingly. She typically strives, in so doing, to achieve something like

that it belongs there if what we have in mind is Mill's own theory. It is tempting, upon reading *On Liberty*, to think that Mill has posited the Harm Principle as a fundamental moral axiom. But Mill is very clear that the Harm Principle is justified by the Principle of Utility. Whether this means that the Harm Principle belongs in category 2, category 1 being reserved for the Principle of Utility alone, is a question that need not concern us, however.

[9] Various noncognitivists have developed theories according to which moral utterances, though not truth-bearing, are nonetheless subject to rational governance and critique. A prime example is R.M. Hare, whose theory of universal prescriptivism includes a logic governing imperative utterances, of which moral utterances are thought to be a species. See his *Freedom and Reason* (1965) and *Moral Thinking: Its Levels, Method, and Point* (1981).

a Rawlsian "reflective equilibrium," where her principles, rules, values, and maxims are internally consistent with one another, based on true beliefs and valid inferences, and in harmony with her "considered judgments" about particular cases and types of cases.[10] Reflective equilibrium is the state for which a responsible moral agent aims, and moral justification, whatever the nature of morality, partly rests upon how the set of general moral norms to which we subscribe "fits in with and organizes our considered judgments in reflective equilibrium."[11] Meeting this condition – which we will henceforth refer to as "the requirement of reflective equilibrium" or RRE – is a necessary condition of responsible moral decision-making.[12]

Our discussion of RRE brings to light a further distinction it would be useful to observe: between mere *moral opinions*, on the one hand, and our *true moral commitments*, on the other. The former phrase will be used to describe moral views that have not been critically examined (in pursuance of RRE) to some minimally adequate degree, and the latter to describe those that have been so examined. In calling the latter "true" I do not mean to imply that they are all true propositions or beliefs; only that they are ones to which we are truly committed. It is the commitments, not the beliefs, which are said to be true – although those who believe that moral sentences express propositions to which truth values can be assigned, will hope that at least most of their beliefs share this further property as well. With this distinction in hand, we are in position to offer what I hope will be a yet further uncontroversial observation.

Observation 3

Our moral opinions sometimes conflict with our true moral commitments. People's views on some contentious moral issues are sometimes mere opinions so construed, that is, their moral opinions do not reflect their true moral commitments. A person might, for example, believe that it is permissible to base a hiring decision on gender grounds only to discover, on reflection – that is, on fulfilling RRE – that this particular opinion is deeply inconsistent with general principles and judgments she is not prepared to relinquish. Perhaps more importantly for our purposes, people can differ in their moral opinions while sharing the same moral commitments, a source of common ground that

[10] Again, I say "something like" because I do not wish to become embroiled in the intricacies of Rawlsian scholarship.

[11] Rawls, *Theory of Justice*, *supra* note 6 at 579.

[12] It is an interesting question, which we will leave unexplored, whether and to what extent RRE is a requirement of all forms of rational decision-making, not just decision-making of the moral kind. But whatever its extent, I take it to be true that RRE is a requirement of responsible moral decision-making.

often emerges as the product of vigorous, open-ended debate. They discover that they agree on much more than they thought they did – and that they know more than they thought they knew. As we shall see shortly, this important observation, when applied at the communal level, has crucial implications for our understanding of judicial review, the popular complaint, and the nature of the morality to which judges are expected to repair in deciding bill of rights cases.

IDENTIFYING A COMMUNITY'S CONSTITUTIONAL MORALITY

Most of the observations made in the preceding section are relatively straightforward and uncontroversial when applied to personal morality. Of particular interest is Observation 2. Aside from moral nihilists and those who believe that foundational moral principles can be infallibly ascertained through pure reason, moral intuition, or the pronouncements of religious authorities, most individuals approach personal moral questions in the manner described.[13] We work things out as we go along, all the while cognizant of two important facts: (a) that our moral opinions almost never square exactly with our true moral commitments; and (b) that the latter are not always consistent with one another and can sometimes change over time as new facts and circumstances are brought to light. In short, we recognize that, for each of us, meeting the demands of RRE is an *ongoing* requirement of responsible moral decision-making.

As I said, most of this is uncontroversial when speaking of personal morality. What is surprising, however, is that these commonplace observations are almost completely ignored when the questions in play involve judges, judicial review, and the political morality to which bills of rights make reference. When bill of rights decisions are criticized for being out of sync with (and supplanting) the moral views of citizens, it always seems to be the case that the focus is on some widespread moral *opinions* that are at odds with the court's ruling. The focus is seldom on the general principles and values to which most citizens are actually committed – that is, their true commitments – or on moral judgments about the issue in question which could survive scrutiny under RRE when that requirement is applied to the community's morality. When judicial recognition of same-sex marriage, to take just one example, is criticised for being at odds with the received moral views of Canadians, the reference is more than likely to mere moral opinions. These are opinions that, upon careful reflection, contradict fundamental beliefs, principles, values, and considered

[13] For further discussion of the many ways in which our judgments can be inconsistent with our fundamental beliefs, values, commitments, and "authentic" wishes, see Chapter 3 of Waluchow, *A Common Law Theory of Judicial Review: The Living Tree* (2007) [Waluchow, *The Living Tree*].

judgments that enjoy widespread, if not universal, currency within the community – that is, with its true moral commitments. They are also – though the point cannot be argued here – opinions that are inconsistent with the most reasonable interpretation of the equality right in the *Canadian Charter of Rights and Freedoms* and the many judicial decisions made in its name, and in the name of the people whose fundamental commitments all this represents. The principles and considered judgments upon which reasonable Canadians, of whatever political and moral stripe, are keen to condemn racial bigotry and sexism, and which virtually all would agree are embodied in the *Charter* and the jurisprudence surrounding its interpretation, equally condemn prejudice against same-sex marriage.[14] This, despite the fact that many people have yet to recognize this connection, and may not do so for some time to come. Discovering, or being made to acknowledge, one's *true* commitments in reflective equilibrium is often a long and difficult process – indeed, it can sometimes be a painful, soul-wrenching experience. It is, nonetheless, one of the burdens of responsible decision-making in matters of morals – one that applies, I submit, when the morality in question is the community's morality just as much as it does when the morality in question is personal. But this vital point is often overlooked or ignored. It is simply assumed that the commitments of a community's morality on some issue are whatever widespread opinion says they are.[15]

[14] Many Canadian courts have held that the opposite-sex requirement for civil marriage violates the equality guarantee enshrined in s. 15(1) of the Charter. As a result, same-sex marriages gradually came to be viewed as legal and have been regularly taking place in British Columbia, Ontario, Quebec, the Yukon, Manitoba, Nova Scotia, and Saskatchewan. See *EGALE Canada Inc. v. Canada (Attorney General)* (2003), 225 D.L.R. (4th) 472; *Halpern v. Canada (Attorney General)* (2003), 65 O.R. (3d) 161 (C.A.); and *Hendricks v. Québec (Procureur général)*, [2002] R.J.Q. 2506 (Sup. Ct.); *Dunbar v. Yukon*, [2004] Y.J. No. 61 (QL), 2004 YKSC 54, *Vogel v. Canada (Attorney General)*, [2004] M.J. No. 418 (QL) (Q.B.), *Boutilier v. Nova Scotia (Attorney General)*, [2004] N.S.J. No. 357 (QL) (S.C.), and *N.W. v. Canada (Attorney General)*, [2004] S.J. No. 669 (QL), 2004 SKQB 434. In each of those instances, the court ruled that the common-law definition of marriage was inconsistent with s. 15(1) of the Charter and was not justifiable under s. 1, and publicly adopted the position that the opposite-sex requirement for marriage was unconstitutional. In *Reference re Same Sex Marriage*, [2004] 3 S.C.R. 698, the Supreme Court of Canada declined to rule on the constitutionality of the opposite-sex requirement, advising that the burden of establishing the requirements of marriage in Canada lay with Parliament. Following this decision, federal legislation changing the definition of marriage to include same-sex couples was passed.

[15] It is here that Hart's distinction between critical and positive morality comes into play and explains why I earlier characterized charter morality as lying somewhere between positive morality (as it is normally conceived) and critical morality. In pursuing RRE, we are, in effect, employing something like Hart's critical morality (with a Rawlsian spin) to assess personal and communal morality. As Hart makes plain, positive morality is no more immune than law to rational and moral critique.

But once we acknowledge that this assumption is false, that a community's true moral commitments on some issue can be very different from what, at the moment, members of that community believe them to be, a crucial question comes to the fore: Why should judges, in deciding moral questions under a system of judicial review, be required, for reasons of democracy, fairness, and the like, to respect the community's mere moral opinions on the matter in question – as opposed to its *true* moral commitments in reflective equilibrium?

Though the matter is far from incontestable, let us agree, for purposes of argument, that Platonic morality is not a good source upon which judges should draw in making bill of rights decisions. Because judges are clearly not philosopher kings with a pipeline to objective moral truth, we probably do not want them second-guessing the legislature on the basis of (what they believe to be) its elusive requirements. Some kind of positive morality is the only source consistent with democracy, the rule of law, our epistemic limitations, and so on. But (to repeat) why should we think that positive morality is nothing more than *the current moral opinions of most members of the community*? More specifically, why should we identify the positive morality to which judges should appeal in bill of rights cases with whatever the majority of people happen to think on some particular occasion about some particular moral issue? As we have already noted, individuals often get things wrong on moral questions, and are expected to adjust their thinking and their actions accordingly. Why should we expect anything less of communities? If our answer is that we should *not* expect anything less, then we will *not* want to identify positive morality with whatever most members of a community currently think about a moral question. We'll be more inclined to identify it with what most of them *would think* were they more fully to engage RRE and attempt to reconcile their current belief(s) with their (overlapping) true moral commitments. If individuals are expected, on an ongoing basis, to implement RRE in their moral thinking, I see no reason why we should let a community get off with anything less. Why should it, too, not be expected, on an ongoing basis, to take reasonable steps to implement RRE in its thinking and subsequent actions? If our answer is that ongoing commitment to RRE is exactly what one expects of a morally responsible community, then we are left with an important question: How is a community, best able to work towards compliance with RRE? Presumably, open, critical public debate, both inside and outside legislatures, is one such means, and a very important one at that. But this may not, for reasons to be explored later, be enough. Could it be that our judges are in a better position to determine the requirements of our true moral commitments in reflective equilibrium than our politicians, pundits, professors, priests and pub-crawlers? If they are, then we may have good reason to consider adopting judicial review as a means, not of ensuring compliance with Platonic morality or the received moral opinions of the community, but of holding the community to its true moral commitments. There may actually be nothing amiss in asking judges to enforce these elements of positive morality against the opinions of a public and its representatives when the latter have failed to meet the demands of RRE.

So, in considering the popular complaint, it is important to distinguish between true moral commitments and moral opinions, and between an individual's personal morality and the morality ascribed to a community, or a community of communities, of which she is a member.[16] It is also important to distinguish one further category: what we will, henceforth, call *the community's constitutional morality*. I should like to propose the hypothesis that the moral norms to which a bill of rights makes reference are not those of personal morality, Platonic morality, or even the community's positive morality broadly construed (and subject to the application of RRE), but only those of the community's *constitutional* morality. By this latter phrase I mean the set of moral norms and considered judgments, properly attributable to the community as a whole as representing its true moral commitments, but with the following additional property: They are in some way tied to its constitutional law and practices. Following Dworkin, we might say it is "the political morality presupposed by the laws and institutions of the community."[17]

[16] Other theorists who invoke a similar notion of community morality in explaining the processes of judicial review include Harry Wellington in "The Nature of Judicial Review," 91 Yale L.J. 486 (1982) and Christopher Eisgruber, *Constitutional Self Government* (2001). For a critique of the suggestion that community morality – or "conventional morality" – be invoked in interpreting a Charter, see A. Marmor, *Interpretation and Legal Theory* (rev. 2nd edn. 2005) at 160–2. I shall have something to say about Marmor's arguments later.

[17] Ronald Dworkin, *Taking Rights Seriously* (1977) at 126. In drawing upon Dworkin, my intention is not to signal acceptance of the particular theory of interpretation he recommends for ascertaining the positive morality presupposed by or imbedded in constitutional law. For reasons that lie well beyond the scope of this investigation, I do not believe that an interpretation of a body of law must, as Dworkin claims, be a full-blown, first-order Herculean moral theory of that object to which the theorist personally subscribes as the one closest to the ideal demands of Platonic morality. It can, instead, be something more like what Julie Dickson terms an "indirectly evaluative" theory of the sort outlined and defended by Dickson and, also, by Jules Coleman. It can be a theory that invokes moral norms, not to justify the law morally but to explain why it is the way it is, to show its relationships with other areas of the law, to reveal the coherent structure implicit in it, and so on. One could, with this understanding in mind, explain – *i.e.*, interpret – much of early twentieth-century South African law as presupposing racist moral norms and beliefs. Such norms and beliefs were part of that community's (deplorable) "constitutional morality." See Julie Dickson, *Evaluation and Legal Theory* (2001) and Jules Coleman, *The Practice of Principle: In Defence of a Pragmatist Approach to Legal Theory* (2001). For my critique of Dworkin's theory of interpretation, see *Inclusive Legal Positivism* (1994).

It is important to stress, once again, that a community's constitutional morality is not the personal morality of any particular person or institution. Nor is it the morality decreed by God, inherent in the fabric of the universe, or discernible via the exercise of pure practical reason. Rather, it consists of the moral norms and convictions to which the community has actually committed itself, and which have, in some way or other, been drawn into the law via the rule of recognition and the law it validates. It is the morality actually imbedded in social and legal practices in the way in which principles of corrective justice are, if Jules Coleman is correct, imbedded in our tort law. So construed, a community's constitutional morality is a subset of the wider community morality, which includes norms and convictions that lack legal recognition. Even if there are norms of positive morality governing friendship, gratitude, marital fidelity, and charitable giving within the community moralities of contemporary western societies, these are not, in the main, part of the constitutional moralities of those societies because they lack legal recognition. Distinct (and different) principles of equality and fundamental justice are, on the other hand, characteristic elements of the constitutional moralities of western societies. In the case of the United States and Canada, legal recognition of such principles includes (though is not limited to) enshrinement in the U.S. Bill of Rights and the Canadian Charter.

I have, admittedly, provided little more than a thumbnail sketch of a community's constitutional morality. I need, for example, to flesh out what it means to say that a norm of political morality enjoys legal recognition. I also need to say something about the relationship between legal judgments on matters of constitutional morality and the less formal "judgments of the community" outside courts and legislatures, judgments upon which judges sometimes draw and which they sometimes use to dislodge well-established precedents. I have also done little beyond raising the possibility that, a critic's scepticism notwithstanding, an overlapping consensus of true commitments might, indeed, be there to be discovered in a community's constitutional morality. But enough has been said, I hope, to warrant some tentative conclusions. First, it is far from clear that a form of judicial review that requires appeal to the community's constitutional morality is a complete nonstarter because we often disagree fundamentally when it comes to matters of morals. Individuals in pluralistic societies no doubt differ dramatically in their personal moral beliefs and convictions, a fact seized upon by critics of judicial review, especially those prone to lodge the popular complaint. Yet there is reason to believe that the constitutional morality imbedded in our shared social and legal practices – including our shared constitutional practices with their wealth of rules, principles, and precedents – can include an overlapping consensus of true commitments on many issues, a consensus which may be "incompletely theorized," but which can emerge, notwithstanding this fact, into explicit agreement once an attempt is made to fulfil RRE. Of course, it is almost certainly true that such an agreement will not always emerge. Indeed, on some deeply contestable questions – for example, questions concerning the morality of abortion – there may be no overlapping consensus, implicit or otherwise. If so, then the community's constitutional morality will fail to provide determinate answers in bill of rights cases, and judges may have to draw upon other resources, about which I will have to say something later. But there is little reason to think that this will *always* be so. Yet, if the community's constitutional morality can sometimes provide the answers we seek, then it can supply norms against which legal validity can sensibly be measured in at least some cases.

A second important conclusion brings us round to H. L. A. Hart's reflections on the dangers we face when, as a society, we choose to occupy a world governed by law. One such danger famously highlighted by Hart is the possibility of a significant gap between legal validity and community morality that inevitably accompanies the introduction of a rule of recognition. Without law, Hart notes, a community's norms will be restricted to its social rules. Such rules cannot exist absent their widespread acceptance; hence there will be no reason for the community to fear imposition of a norm that it finds unacceptable. If the community finds the norm unacceptable, the practice conditions of its existence will simply disappear. But along with the rule of recognition comes the distinct possibility of a binding norm of which the community disapproves morally. Conditions for legal validity can, after all, be limited to such bald criteria as proclamation by a king. In recognition of the dangers inherent in such possibilities, communities often take steps to protect themselves. One way to address the danger is to replace kings and queens with democratically elected legislators whose decisions can usually, though not always, be counted on to reflect widespread moral views within the community. This is, no doubt, a step in the right direction, one that liberal societies have all chosen to take. But there is reason to think that this step, though highly useful, might not be enough. Abuses, especially against minorities and individuals by powerful majorities, can still occur. This is one reason why some societies have opted for entrenched bills of rights – they are thought to serve as vital protections against such abuses. Yet, as Hart also stressed, even when abuse is not the motivating factor, things can still go wrong when legislatures seek to govern. No legislature, not even a democratically chosen one fully informed of all the relevant facts and competing considerations, can anticipate all the results to which its general legislation will inevitably lead. Some of these unanticipated results will be absurdities, others will merely be results we would have tried to avoid in advance had we known what we now know. An important subset of these unanticipated results, I submit, involves conflicts, in unforeseen future cases, with the community's very own moral commitments. Such conflicts, of which we often become aware only at the point of application of our legal rules, are as inevitable as they are unforeseeable. They are unforeseeable in the sense that no one can predict exactly when and in what particular contexts they will arise, and what they will look like when they are brought to our attention. What is confidently foreseeable, however, is that many such cases will, in fact, arise, despite any and all efforts to avoid them. If this is true, then a community might well ask itself an important question, one which will occupy us in the remainder of this chapter: Why should we not include conformity with the true commitments of our constitutional morality among our conditions of legal validity? And why should we not entrust our judges with the task of deciding whether and when the relevant norms of this morality have been compromised by particular laws and government actions in particular cases?

A RETURN TO JUDICIAL REVIEW AND THE POPULAR COMPLAINT

So there are some fairly understandable reasons why a community might choose to adopt a bill of rights that seeks to place moral conditions on law and government. And there are some other equally understandable reasons why it might wish those conditions to be conceived, not in terms of Platonic morality, personal morality, or mere moral opinions, but in terms of constitutional morality as I have described it. But of course good, understandable reasons do not always add up to compelling reasons. I have yet to address some of the major criticisms that have been levelled against judicial review by its foremost critics – and many of these seem to remain even when the practice is understood as invoking norms of a community's constitutional morality. Indeed, I have yet to address fully the popular complaint, the objection with which we began and which still might convince us to do away with bills of rights altogether. So let us turn to some of the more prevalent of the critics' objections and see how our proposal stacks up against them.

I would like to begin by revisiting the popular complaint that judges, in deciding cases under a bill of rights, too often end up replacing the moral views of the community and/or its legislative representatives with their own personal moral beliefs. Examples that prompt the complaint presumably include rulings upholding the right of inmates to vote in elections or the right of gays to marry one another. Instead of *respecting* the community and its decisions – something one would expect judges to be doing in a well-ordered democracy – the judges are said to have imposed their own personal moral opinions on the community, thereby denying the community its right to self-governance. In light of our earlier reflections, we are now, I hope, in a position to see the possible error in this particular objection. In ruling against a government action (for example, a statute or judicial ruling) that has the support of popular moral opinion, judges may not be acting undemocratically because they might, in fact, be *enforcing*, not *thwarting*, the community's very own constitutional morality. This will be so if the moral opinion in question is one that does not bear scrutiny under RRE. Just as a person might come to discover, when she attempts to fulfil RRE, that some of her personal moral opinions conflict with general moral norms and judgments to which she is otherwise committed, and which she is unwilling to relinquish, judges might be led to discover that the moral opinion of the community or its legislature on some issue – in our case, same- sex marriage or the right of inmates to vote in elections – conflicts with its very own moral norms, and, by implication, other true commitments of the community's morality in analogous cases – for example, those involving racial discrimination and equality between the sexes. The judges might, that is, discover that the relevant moral opinion is not a considered judgment that can remain in reflective equilibrium with these other elements of the community's own constitutional morality. Add to this the fact that the relevant principles, values, and judgments are, more often than not, ones that the law explicitly recognizes in the constitution, subordinate legislation, and legal precedent – as it has in cases involving discrimination against women and racial minorities – then a court, in upholding these elements of the community's constitutional morality, will not only be respecting the community's true moral commitments, it will, in fact, be *upholding the law*, something, of course, we want our judges to be doing whenever they decide legal cases. If this is what judicial review is really all about, then the practice seems anything but unfair and undemocratic – and so much for the popular complaint.

FURTHER OBJECTIONS

Personal Morality Still Being Imposed

Suppose judges who decide bill of rights cases try to invoke the community's constitutional morality in the manner just contemplated. They will still, a critic might insist, end up imposing their own subjective moral preferences in ways that invite the popular complaint. If, as we have been assuming all along, questions raised by the abstract clauses of a bill of rights are (partly) moral in nature, if these moral questions are ones about which there is deep disagreement and controversy within the community in question, and if it is the judges who are providing the answers, then they will be unable to do anything else but impose their own subjective moral preferences. A judge who must make a decision in such circumstances cannot avoid interpreting the bill of rights in light of her own personal morality, despite any effort and rhetoric to the contrary. And this is unfair, undemocratic, and so on.

For reasons that should now be clear, this objection is equally misguided. It is one thing to say that a bill of rights case hinges on the judge's own personal morality, and quite another to say that it hinges on her personal views *about what the community's constitutional morality requires*. The latter option describes a judgment about the true commitments of the community, not the judge. Although it is true that we must rely on the personal views of judges, and it is equally true that these views may be highly controversial, not amenable to conclusive demonstration, inconsistent with many moral opinions, and possibly biased, the fact remains that it is a personal, good faith judgment about what the community's constitutional morality actually requires. It is no more disturbing to acknowledge the need for personal judgment on such a question than it is to acknowledge that the integrity of science depends on the personal judgments of scientists about what the evidence establishes, or that the fate of defendants often turns on the personal judgments of jurors. It is also important to bear in mind that virtually every issue, moral or otherwise, that comes before an appeal court for decision is controversial and not amenable to conclusive demonstration – and yet we rely on judges' personal judgments about such matters all the time. Think of a case turning on whether a person or corporation took reasonable steps to ensure the safety of others, or on whether the defendant's actions violated community standards of decency. We have to rely on *somebody's* controversial, personal judgment about such matters, just as we must rely on *somebody's* personal judgment about the community's true moral commitments. Why shouldn't that somebody be a judge? Perhaps a judge's training renders her eminently (though not, of course, uniquely) qualified in this regard. The test of reflective equilibrium is not far removed from the more traditional task of common-law decision-making in, for example, tort and contract cases, where precedents and general principles must be reconciled with one another, and where processes such as drawing analogies, marking distinctions so as to distinguish cases, and so on, are commonplace. Considered judgments are a bit like precedents; general principles, a bit like ratios and common-law rules.[18]

[18] We will return later to this question whether judges are suitably placed to decide such questions of constitutional morality in bill of rights cases.

A Community's Constitutional Morality and Legal Precedent

Another potential objection to my proposal that judicial review be tied to the community's constitutional morality is that it seriously underplays the fact that bill of rights cases are legal cases. Bills of rights are, after all, part of constitutional *law*, not *morality*. When a court addresses a bill of rights issue, it draws support for its judgment from prior legal decisions and from legal doctrines and traditions. And when it settles an issue raised, for example, by an equality provision, a lower court is bound by the precedent set, even when that lower court thinks that the decision is incorrect in law, or is inconsistent with views generally held within the wider community – even those that satisfy RRE. In such a case, the lower court is not free to interpret the relevant provision in accordance with its own views about the true commitments of the community's constitutional morality or the corresponding views of the community. The inevitable result is this: Over time, judicial decision, not the community's own morality, sets the appropriate standards for decision in bill of rights cases. The judiciary, not individually perhaps, but as a multimember body stretching over time, is actually the force behind the creation of the norms employed in deciding bill of rights cases. The result is that the *community's* own morality fails to play the role assigned to it in the account sketched earlier. It no longer is the community's constitutional morality that is being enforced in bill of rights cases; it is the constitutional morality of the judiciary, particularly those members of the legal profession who happen to occupy the nation's supreme court. And this is undemocratic, unfair, etc.

In addressing this important objection, we should begin by stressing that precedent-setting judgments under a bill of rights' moral provisions are still, on the account herein defended, judgments about what the community's constitutional morality requires. And so it is not as if the relevant precedents are judgments stemming from the personal moralities of the judges who set them. Precedent undoubtedly plays a key role in adjudication under a bill of rights' moral provisions. But its role is to regulate judgments about what the community's constitutional morality requires, not what the judges would, themselves, prefer to see done.

A second reply is that the objection may rely on a misleading picture of the community's constitutional morality, as something wholly autonomous from the law and the decisions of judges. It is a commonplace among philosophers, as well as other legal, political, and sociological scholars, that a community's positive morality influences and shapes its law in many ways. For example, we have the criminal law we do largely because of our community's moral sense of right and wrong. Our notions of moral responsibility explain, for example, why there is more than one category of murder, and why some homicides are treated, not as murders, but as instances of manslaughter, a category reserved for cases in which responsibility is for some reason diminished. Tort law is based on moral notions of corrective justice, and so on. But the extent to which the community's morality is, in turn, shaped by law is seriously underappreciated. As Joseph Raz and Tony Honore have stressed, this is a serious mistake. The influence of law on morality is multifaceted and significant. In his "Hart Memorial Lecture," Honore reminds us that the law serves several crucial functions "in regard to gaps in morality and to moral conflicts."[19] Much as Aquinas did when he outlined the need for a human sovereign, one of whose tasks is the "determination of the common notions" set by the natural law, Honore notes that:

> ... over a wide range of cases there can be no way of determining the right course of action without a legal component. Even a society of well-disposed angels, uniformly anxious to do right, needs a system of laws in order to know the right thing to do ... law is part of the morality of any complex society ... The picture of morality as a blueprint and law as a structure put up according to or in disregard of it is ... misleading. Morality is more like an outline from which details are missing. Laws, along with conventions, fill many of these in.[20]

Honore's insightful observations provide the basis for a second, more forceful reply to the objection under consideration. If the community's constitutional morality is partly determined, in complex societies like ours, by landmark political and legal decisions, then the possibility emerges that the judges, in deciding cases under the moral provisions of a bill of rights, are, in fact, helping to shape and render more determinate the very content of constitutional morality. Legal judgments under those provisions are not to be starkly contrasted with or separated from judgments of the community's constitutional morality. On the contrary, they are an important element within that morality, just as they are in Aquinas' natural law theory. As such, precedent-setting legal judgments must be accorded significant weight in attempts to reach reflective equilibrium within a community's constitutional morality. The weight to be given these judgments presumably can vary, depending, among other things, on the fundamental secondary rules of adjudication practised within the legal system,

[19] A.M. Honore, "The Dependence of Morality on Law," (1993) 13 O.J.L.S.1 at 3. For Hart's comments on the role of law in shaping morality, see *The Concept of Law*, 2nd edn. (1994) at 200.

[20] *Ibid.* A thorough exploration of this view of morality would take us too far afield. Instead, I simply refer the reader to Raz's powerful defence in, among other places, *Engaging Reason* (1999).

and on the degree of authority we are prepared to accord our judges in deciding questions of constitutional morality on our behalf. But the fact remains that if the content of the community's constitutional morality is partly determined by important judicial decisions about its content, then in saying that judges should interpret legal rights in terms of the community's constitutional morality, one does not thereby imply that judges are free to ignore legal precedent.[21]

Judicial Discretion

The fact that judicial decisions help shape and determine a community's constitutional morality has another important consequence for debates about judicial review. As observed on numerous occasions earlier, many individuals are troubled by the idea of a system of government in which judges are either asked or permitted to decide contentious moral issues when they engage in judicial review. This seems, at the very least, to compromise our commitment to self-government. We seem to have abandoned our allegiance to democracy if we don't settle these matters among ourselves, or through the efforts of legislators who are chosen *by us* to do this *for us*.[22] Assigning the task to judges instead would be bad enough had we reason to believe that there is always a moral truth of the matter in a bill of rights case, and that judges are more likely than us or our elected representatives to discover and apply that truth when they interpret the moral norms in that bill of rights. But if Honore, Raz – and, indeed, even Aquinas – are correct in their belief that morality provides only a partial blueprint with many details missing, and that legal judgment – that is, judicial discretion – is required to fill these in, then things seem to become far, far worse for the defender of judicial review. If someone has to exercise discretion in filling in these details, should it not be the people themselves – or individuals elected by and responsible to the people for the choices they make? In representative democracies, should it not be elected legislators who fill in the blanks their society's moral blueprint leaves open?

Not necessarily. We are all familiar with the standard line that legislators, in pursuing the task of legislating on our behalf, are subject to various political pressures which often incline them (unjustly or unfairly) to side with majority

[21] Once again, I acknowledge that much more needs to be said here about the contours of "the community's constitutional morality." Fleshing out this notion and exploring how the resultant theory affects our understanding of judicial review are tasks to which I hope to turn in future studies.

[22] It is, perhaps, fair to say that this is Jeremy Waldron's principal objection to judicial review. See his *Law and Disagreement* (1999), the more recent "The Core of the Case Against Judicial Review," 115 Yale L.J. (2006) at 1346, and "Do Judges Reason Morally?" in this volume.

sentiment, or with the demands of rich, powerful minorities. There is much truth in this picture of the perils of legislating. And it should give us pause in unthinkingly assuming that elected legislators are always the best ones to fill in our moral blueprint. This will be especially so if we bear in mind our earlier reflections on RRE and on the fact that majority moral sentiment is often premised on little more than mere moral opinion, which can be at odds with the community's very own constitutional morality.

But instead of getting embroiled in this particular controversy, I wish to draw attention to some further perils of legislating, ones that arise from what might be called "the circumstances of rule making." Legislators cannot, for reasons of sheer practicality, enact legislation specific to each and every individual case that might arise in a particular social context. They must, of necessity, work with general categories covering a range of somewhat different individual cases. They must, that is, deal with types, not tokens. This, in turn, means that their rules will invariably suffer from a number of potential defects, two of which are identified by Fred Schauer as "under-inclusiveness" and "over-inclusiveness."[23] General legal rules will (arguably) fail to apply to cases to which we might later wish them to apply, and they might apply to cases to which we might later wish them not to apply. According to many theorists, this situation entails the practical necessity of having judges sort things out when problematic instances arise in particular cases. They will do so, on most theories, by exercising their discretion.[24]

Now apply all this to a context in which the problematic case involves a potential conflict with a moral norm recognized in a bill of rights. The case is one in which the enacted rule can plausibly be construed as having an unforeseen, arguably unwanted impact on a moral norm that has been included within a bill of rights, a norm like "equality" or "due process." The question in such a case is: Is the bill of rights norm infringed in a way which (we can now see) cannot be justified – that is, which renders the offending rule inconsistent with constitutional morality and hence legally invalid? Our moral blueprint may be clear on this question, in which case there seems nothing overwhelmingly problematic in allowing judges to make the appropriate call, though some will disagree. But now suppose that the blueprint is not clear enough to settle the question, perhaps because people disagree on what it requires in the particular case in question, or that the blueprint is silent on

[23] See Frederick Schauer, *Playing by the Rules: A Philosophical Examination of Rule-Based Decision-Making in Law and Life* (1991), *passim*.

[24] The most famous and influential defender of this view is, of course, H.L.A. Hart. See *The Concept of Law* (1961).

that issue. In the latter case, we might say that the blueprint is incomplete or has a gap – a gap that needs to be filled by someone exercising his/her/their discretion. If so, then who is that someone to be? Here are some reasons for thinking that a good choice just might be the judges.

Drafting workable general legislation to avoid the challenges described in the preceding two paragraphs requires abilities well beyond the best of our political actors, legislators, and constitutional drafters, thus leaving us with one of three options: (a) We can ignore the problem(s) and run the risk of allowing our legislators to compromise important norms of constitutional morality; (b) we can ask legislatures to deal with the aforementioned difficulties by clarifying or filling agreed gaps in the moral blueprint when these are brought to public attention in unforeseen cases; or (c) we can ask judges to do so, on an ongoing basis, when they decide bill of rights cases. Presumably we would like to avoid option (a). As for (b), it is not much of an option either, leaving us with option (c). The reasons why (c) is a much better option than (b) are multiple and varied, but the main one is this.[25] Cases calling for decisions about the impact of general legislation on norms of constitutional morality are best dealt with by judges if only because they are in a superior position to appreciate the particular issues raised in the cases in which these potential impacts are felt, and they are able, through use of a kind of common-law methodology with which they are very familiar, to deal with those issues in an intelligent, sensitive, case-by-case manner. The judges who do so will always have to bear in mind, of course, that their decisions and rulings will usually set precedents for others – including the community to whose constitutional morality the judge's decision contributes. But common-law methodology allows them the freedom to make their rulings with the knowledge that these can always be adjusted by later courts who will undoubtedly see further issues of relevance and further reasons, perhaps arising from strong sentiment within the community that it is well past time to change its own moral commitments, to distinguish their cases from the one(s) decided before. Through the use of what Denise Reaume aptly calls "bottom-up" modes of reasoning, judges are able to decide the unforeseeable issues of constitutional morality in ways that allow for incremental clarifications and improvements on our community's moral blueprint.[26]

[25] Once again, I direct the reader to Waluchow, *The Living Tree*, *supra* note 13, which includes a much more fully developed account of why option (b) is highly problematic and why (c) has much more going for it.

[26] See Denise Reaume, "Of Pigeonholes and Principles: A Reconsideration of Discrimination Law," (2002) 40 Osgoode Hall L.J. 113. Reaume outlines the utter mess into which Ontario antidiscrimination law has degenerated. This is largely because of misguided attempts to regulate, by way of general legislative rules, issues that are far better addressed by courts employing

Another reason for thinking it a good idea to have judges, not legislators, clarify and fill in details of the blueprint in bill of rights cases is that the resulting new details may well be more acceptable to those whose views are not reflected in them than if they were decided upon by an elected legislature. Often, those directly embroiled in conflict are not always able or willing to accept decisions that deeply affect them if those decisions are made on the basis of majority sentiment, or by way of a vote among the disputants themselves. But this is exactly what would occur were contentious issues of constitutional morality settled by referendum or through the choices of legislators responsive to majority sentiment. On the other hand, people are often more able and willing to accept and abide by a controversial decision if it is made by someone other than the parties directly in dispute – that is, by a "neutral third party." This will be so even when – perhaps *especially* when – the decision is recognized as being one that is underdetermined by the relevant factors and that therefore demands a kind of discretion or "free choice among available options." Under these conditions, the one who ends up making the decision will not be among those who profit by it. He will be an adjudicator, not an advocate. Of course, it would be foolish not to acknowledge that judges are part of the very communities in which there is disagreement about bill of rights questions, and so their views and interests will usually render them less than absolutely neutral. But despite their vested interests, it is nevertheless reasonable to hope and expect that they will be able, in filling out the blueprint, to bracket those personal interests and opinions, that is, that they will be able to display the same judicial virtues of objectivity, impartiality, and neutrality that they are generally thought to display in deciding other types of cases. In other words, we can hope that they will be able, so far as it is possible for a human being to do, to park their biases and allegiances at the door and give due weight to the considered moral views of the parties on all sides of the debate. We can also hope that, in insulating them from the forces that often plague legislators by granting them some measure of judicial independence, we will minimize the likelihood that our hopes are nothing short of naïve. If this is correct, then we should not be so quick to reject outright the suggestion that judges are in many ways better positioned than legislators to deal sensibly with some of the gaps and fuzziness to which our constitutional morality is susceptible.

common-law methodology. I suggest that much the same would occur were the issues of political morality with which bills of rights are typically concerned – equality, fundamental justice, due process – dealt with by way of statutory regulation coupled with continuous revision in light of new cases that would inevitably accompany any such move. The same kind of unprincipled, ad-hoc "pigeon-holing" that has occurred with Ontario's antidiscrimination law would likely occur in this wider context as well.

A Community's Constitutional Morality and the Protection of Minorities

Positive morality, as we have seen, is the morality properly ascribable to a community. In this way, it is distinguishable from personal morality and from the morality Kant and Plato sought to discover. In this chapter, I have argued that we can profitably view the abstract moral provisions of a bill of rights as invoking a kind (or part) of positive morality I dubbed the community's "constitutional morality." This constitutional morality is not to be identified with prevailing moral opinions any more than it is to be confused with the moral norms sitting comfortably – but inaccessibly – in Plato's world of forms. It is rooted in a community's true moral commitments, and these, as we have seen, can conflict with its more transient, possibly ill-considered moral opinions and preferences. But it is a kind of positive morality nonetheless. This raises an important question we flagged at the outset and to which I would now like to turn. Positive morality is said to be the morality of the community. But what it really amounts to (when and where it can truly be said to exist)[27] is a set of beliefs and norms of the prevailing group(s) within the community, that is *the majority*. In short, community morality is *majority morality*. By its very nature, however, a bill of rights is supposed to serve to protect vulnerable minorities and individuals against the errors, prejudices, and excesses of powerful majorities. It is, after all, a "counter-majoritarian" device. To view the rights protected by a bill of rights as a function of the moral beliefs of the very majorities against whom protection is thought essential therefore threatens to undermine the very point of having them. This is a line of argument pursued by Andrei Marmor:

> ... the idea that constitutional interpretation should be grounded on those values which happen to be widely shared in the community would undermine one of the basic rationales for having a constitution in the first place. Values that are widely shared do not require constitutional protection ... It is precisely because we fear the temptation of encroachment of certain values by popular sentiment that we remove their protection from ordinary democratic processes. After all, the democratic legislature is a kind of institution which is bound to be sensitive to popular sentiment and widely shared views in the community. We do not need the constitutional courts to do more of the same.[28]

If Marmor is correct, then my proposal threatens to undermine the very point of having a bill of rights. It would not be able to serve as the bulwark against

[27] As noted earlier, some doubt that it makes sense to speak of the positive morality of a community in pluralistic societies.

[28] Andrei Marmor, *Interpretation and Legal Theory* (rev. 2nd edn. 2005) at 161–2.

oppression that is its very reason for being. The only way to pursue minority protection effectively is presumably to interpret the moral provisions of a bill of rights, not in terms of the community's possibly biased and oppressive own morality, but in terms of Platonic morality. Judges should seek moral truth in deciding bill of rights cases, not the morality of a possibly misguided majority against whom the bill of rights is supposed to serve as protection.

We are, I hope, in a position to see why this objection fails. First, it presupposes that a community's constitutional morality is identical with "popular sentiment," that is, the moral opinions widely shared within the community. But to repeat, the role of a judge is not to bow to the moral sentiments and opinions of the majority. Her task, under the proposal herein defended, is to respect and enforce the true commitments of the community's constitutional morality in reflective equilibrium. And this morality – at least as it exists within all the contemporary constitutional democracies with which we are concerned here – thoroughly rejects any opinion that oppresses a minority group, harbours the prejudices of patriarchy, and so on. Judges within such systems, who decide on the true commitments of their community's constitutional morality in reflective equilibrium, will inevitably be led to protect minorities from the tyranny feared by Mill. They may not always succeed in making the right decisions. But to the extent that they do, minority protection will be the result. Furthermore, we must also remember that the community's constitutional morality in reflective equilibrium includes the judgments of courts in influential legal cases. In other words, we must not forget the role of legal judgments in shaping the principles of the community's constitutional morality. Both our communities' constitutional moralities and the more specific laws created to express and enforce these moralities condemn the oppression of women and minorities.

Despite the foregoing, it would be disingenuous not to acknowledge that the true commitments of a community's constitutional morality can sometimes be hostile to minority interests – in other words, there is nothing to guarantee that that morality will be anything like the kind of morality presupposed in western democracies. Once again, the morality of apartheid Africa leaps readily to mind. This fact, and the fact that, in some social contexts, judicial review can help entrench a wholly unworthy morality, might seem to undermine the position I have been defending. But against these unfortunate possibilities must be weighed all the advantages of the proposal under consideration, as well as the perils of the alternatives. It is also important to remember, as positivists have long insisted, that questions concerning legality – even those requiring appeal to a community's constitutional morality – must never be confused with, or supplant in our thinking, our ability to challenge accepted norms from the moral point of view. This includes norms of our community's constitutional morality. If radical change in a community's morality is called for, there is nothing to prevent reformers and critics from publicly pressing their case for change. There is, in other words, nothing to prevent them from saying: "The existence of law – including that part of our law which is our constitutional morality – is one thing; its merit or demerit quite another thing entirely." Judicial review, understood and practiced in the manner contemplated in this chapter, can be a powerful vehicle for moral good. But it would be both foolish, and a serious mistake, to overestimate its power, or to suppose that it is the only vehicle at our disposal.

So, a community's constitutional morality, properly understood, interpreted and enforced by judges, has the potential, within the societies with which we are concerned, to provide significant protection against Mill's tyranny of the majority. Indeed, I submit that that it is likely to provide a better guarantee than if judges were asked to decide in accordance with their own conceptions of Platonic morality. This suggestion might seem ludicrous at first glance. Surely moral truth offers far better protection to minorities than a community's constitutional morality, even when the latter has been sanitized by application of RRE. Perhaps, but there is reason to be very cautious in pursuing this line of thinking. As noted earlier, and as critics of judicial review are fond of pointing out, judges are not philosopher kings with a pipeline to Plato's heaven. They can easily get things wrong. Indeed, there is little reason to believe that a judge's personal moral convictions – that is, her beliefs about the true requirements of Platonic morality – are likely to be better than the community's constitutional morality, properly understood. A community's constitutional morality is, after all, the product of much moral and legal experience, long-standing traditions, social debate, and consensus. In other words, it is the product of sustained efforts on the part of a great many people. Given its pedigree, there is reason to believe that a community's constitutional morality will usually be closer to the ideal for that community and the circumstances in which its members lead their lives than the personal morality of any given judge whose views are significantly different.[29] It may also be true that judges will be more likely to converge in their constitutional views if their judgments are the product of attempts to discern the requirements of the community's constitutional morality. If this last conjecture is correct, then we have another reason to pursue an understanding of bills of rights in which they embody norms of a community's constitutional morality. Convergence in action and decision may not be the most important

[29] This is not to deny the possibility of judges with superior moral insight. But we lack a reliable test of who such judges might be.

values to be pursued by law, but they are certainly among the most important. Law is, after all, a social institution, which cannot do its work absent a large measure of agreement on basic conventions and shared understandings of the sort highlighted by legal theorists of all stripes.[30] These are required, not only for law's ability to offer guidance, including its guidance in filling out and clarifying Honore's moral blueprint, but because they are essential to law's very existence. If, in pursuing the community morality option – again properly conceived – judges are more likely to converge in their judgments regarding the fundamental issues raised by their bill of rights than if they pursue Platonic moral theory, we have further reason to insist that this is, in fact, what they should be doing. If there is a further convergence between the judges' beliefs and those ascribable to the community at large, then we have even more reason to pursue this option. Little is lost, but much is gained.

Judicial Determination of Rights Under a Bill of Rights is Still Undemocratic

We come now to one final objection to my proposal that we understand bills of rights in terms of the community's constitutional morality. To be sure, minority oppression is a standing threat in any democratic society. And it may be that something like a bill of rights, interpreted in light of the community's constitutional morality in reflective equilibrium, can, at least in theory, be a useful tool in working against it. It still fails to follow that citizens of constitutional democracies, faced with the many difficulties encountered in the concrete circumstances of modern politics, should pursue any such option. It most certainly fails to follow that they should entrust the interpretation and enforcement of their bill of rights protections, even when understood in this particular way, to judges. We dishonour a community's democratic representatives and the citizens they represent, if we suppose that their current judgments concerning the protections afforded by the community's constitutional morality should not be the ones that hold sway in democratic politics. Democracy demands self-government, not government by unelected elites sitting in appeal courts. It demands, in short, that the community itself do its best to determine the demands of its own constitutional morality. So we must either reject bills of rights altogether, or adopt a system in which final say on a bill of rights requirement rests with democratically chosen representatives.

[30] The exception may be some radical critical theorists who see law as a complete sham – and a very dangerous one at that – given that it is said to be a means by which the powerful within a society are able to exert their power over its weaker elements.

Unfortunately, answering this particular objection adequately requires far more space than the constraints of the current chapter permit,[31] so I will have to content myself with the following observations. Suppose that most of what I have said so far is correct: When judges decide bill of rights cases, we should take them to be attempting to clarify, supplement, and, in some instances, hold their community to its own moral commitments in particular cases. They are helping that community to abide by the demands of RRE. Now consider this: To the extent that the foregoing accurately describes their role, judges can be seen, not as thwarting the democratic enterprise, but as *contributing* to it. The reason is this: Being a morally responsible community involves taking reasonable steps to ensure that one is true to one's own moral commitments. It also involves an unwillingness to shirk these commitments whenever convenience, self-interest, or paranoia urge one to do so. Being a morally responsible community also requires a willingness to take reasonable steps to deal rationally and sensitively with difficulties that inevitably arise whenever the requirements of one's moral commitments come into play in future, unforeseen cases. All three aspects of what it is to be morally responsible are part and parcel of what it is to be a responsible community – just as they are when the morality in question is of the personal variety. But these are also, it seems to me, part of what it is to be self-governing. A self-governing community – that is, a *democratic community* – is one that does not shirk or ignore its moral commitments, does not act arbitrarily or capriciously, and does not change its moral commitments as people change their clothes. If so, then we seem led to a conclusion that many will see as profoundly paradoxical but which I hazard to suggest nevertheless: Judicial review may not only be consistent with democracy, it may well be, in the circumstances in which we find ourselves, one of its requirements.

[31] For a much fuller answer, see, once again, Waluchow, *The Living Tree*, *supra* note 13.

4 Justification and Rights Limitations

Bradley W. Miller*

INTRODUCTION

One of the most common features of contemporary bills of rights is the inclusion of one or more limitations clauses.[1] In turn, the use of limitations clauses has given rise to adjudicative structures that (at least formally) sever the definition of a right from its limitation. Bills of rights drafted in such a way are often thought of as an advance over the American model, in which reasonable limits are inherent in the conception of the constitutional rights themselves.

I intend to argue the contrary; there is no justification for the two-stage division between: (1) the definition of a legal right and determination of whether that right has been infringed in a particular instance, and (2) the determination of whether the infringement of a right is nevertheless ultimately justified. I will argue that, despite the proliferation of two-stage bills of rights, the dominant interpretation of such bills of rights creates unnecessary interpretative difficulties and threatens to distort rights adjudication.

I refer predominately to the *Canadian Charter of Rights and Freedoms* (the Charter) in this paper. As it happens, jurisprudence under the Charter is exemplary of a number of problems, and yet its structure (and its jurisprudence) is both celebrated in Canada as an advance over American jurisprudence[2] and

* I am grateful to the participants in the colloquium for their comments on this chapter, particularly T.R.S. Allan, James Allan, Grant Huscroft, and Aileen Kavanagh.

[1] There has been a proliferation of two-stage bills of rights in the post-World War era, including the *European Convention on Human Rights* (1950), the *International Covenant on Civil and Political Rights* (1976), the *Canadian Charter of Rights and Freedoms* (1982), the *South African Bill of Rights* (1996), and the *New Zealand Bill of Rights Act* (1990).

[2] E.g., P.W. Hogg argues that the implied limits placed on free speech and equal protection in American Bill of Rights jurisprudence amount to "judicial legislation" and are not authorized by the text (*Constitutional Law of Canada*, 4th edn., ch. 35.1). Jamie Cameron notes similar claims for the "textual superiority" of the *Charter* over the U.S. Bill of Rights: "(b)y guaranteeing

emulated in several jurisdictions. Notwithstanding the emphasis on the Charter, the conclusions drawn are applicable to any bill of rights that has been interpreted so as to uncouple the definition of rights from their limitation.

THE TWO-STAGE MODEL: DEFINITION AND JUSTIFICATION

We should begin by canvassing the purpose of including limitations clause(s) in bills of rights. It seems likely that limitations clauses are intended by their drafters to guide legal reasoning by drawing attention to important goods that must be borne in mind when determining the scope of rights. In some instances, such as in the *European Convention on Human Rights*, they direct the judiciary (and others guided by law) to a discrete catalogue of interests that the judiciary should take into account. In other instances, such as the Charter, there is a single, general limiting clause, which leaves the grounds of limitation to interpretation. Janet Hiebert has documented that, in the Canadian example, the purpose of the limitations clause was to bound the transfer of power to the judiciary that would result from the adoption of the Charter.[3] The purpose is both to head off concerns about the erosion of parliamentary sovereignty with the grant of unlimited, absolute rights, and to provide the judiciary with some guidance for interpreting rights.

In the Canadian example, the general limiting clause is given great prominence, being placed in the first article.[4] On the Supreme Court of Canada's method of interpreting the Charter, established in *R. v. Oakes*, the test of a statute's validity must proceed in two stages: First, the complainant has the burden of establishing that the impugned legislation has infringed some part of the Charter; thereafter, the burden shifts to the government to demonstrate that the infringement or violation of the individual section of the Charter is, nevertheless, "justified" under s. 1 of the Charter.[5] That is, once the scope of a right has been articulated, and once it has been determined that the right

individual rights and refusing to provide for their limitation, the American Constitution created an impossible contradiction.... The *Charter* addressed that flaw with unassailable logic: self-contained provisions guarantee the substantive rights and a limitations clause determines what restrictions on those rights are consistent with democratic values." ("The Original Conception of Section 1 and its Demise: A Comment on *Irwin Toy v. Attorney-General of Quebec*" (1989) 35 McGill L.J. 253 at 257–8). See also Lorraine Weinrib, "The Supreme Court of Canada and Section One of the Charter," (1988) 10 Sup. Ct. L. Rev. 469.

[3] J. Hiebert, *Limiting Rights* (1996) at 9–31.

[4] Section 1 of the *Charter* "guarantees the rights and freedoms set out in it subject only to such reasonable limits prescribed by law as can be demonstrably justified in a free and democratic society."

[5] [1986] 1 S.C.R. 103 [*Oakes*].

has been violated in the context of a particular claimant, the court turns to determine whether there are sufficient grounds to justify the limitation of the right.

The Court has thus conceived of the limiting aspect of s. 1 as not applying until *after* a court has declared that a person has a Charter right and declared that the right has been *violated*.[6] The Court thus rejects the alternative conceptualisation (fully consistent with the text of s. 1) in which Charter rights, fully specified, would be inviolable and the "reasonable limits" would be inherent in the rights themselves.

A claimant who has been successful at the first stage of the analysis is said to have suffered the infringement of a Charter right. However, it is important to note that the nature of this right infringement is substantially different than the infringement of a right under the U.S. Bill of Rights, or even (analogously) the infringement of an absolute moral right. First-stage Charter rights are much weaker entities than either constitutional rights that have been posited without limitations clauses, or fully specified, absolute moral rights.[7] To the extent that an examination of the claims and reasons that compete with the rights claimant are postponed to a second step of analysis (as with s. 1 reasoning under the Charter),[8] the first-stage analysis is not capable of generating the conclusion that there has been a violation of something with a directive strength equivalent to an absolute moral right. The product of the first stage analysis is, at most, a *prima facie* right; it is an intermediate conclusion or a placeholder. Stage one analysis can only generate a tentative, intermediate conclusion that some *claim* of constitutional right is a candidate for qualification as a genuine right on further analysis.[9] The mischief of such *prima facie* rights is explored over the balance of this paper.

[6] "... any s. 1 inquiry must be premised on an understanding that the impugned limit violates constitutional rights and freedoms – rights and freedoms which are part of the supreme law of Canada." *Oakes*, *ibid.* at para. 63 (Dickson C.J.).

[7] A fully specified, undefeated moral right, on this conception, provides a reason for action that has not been defeated by any other relevant reason for action, and is thus binding on the deliberator. Of course, among the many ways that moral rights differ from legal rights is that the former are not subject to legal enforcement.

[8] The extent to which Charter rights are internally qualified varies. Section 2(b) has minimal internal qualifications, whereas sections 7 and 8, and (arguably) 15 contain internal qualifications.

[9] This line of argument borrows from Joseph Raz's analysis of the structure of moral reasoning: "Assertions of rights are typically intermediate conclusions in arguments from ultimate values to duties. They are, so to speak, points in the argument where many considerations intersect and where the results of their conflicts are summarized to be used with additional premises when need be. Such intermediate conclusions are used and referred to as if they are themselves complete reasons." Although rights are referred to as "reasons in their own right," they are not

THE TWO-STAGE MODEL AND RIGHTS DISCOURSE

A preliminary objection to the two-stage model is its potential to significantly skew public discourse over rights. The Supreme Court of Canada often overstates the significance of its determination that a particular Charter right has been infringed. Unsurprisingly, the inconclusive nature of a finding of such a first-stage rights infringement is not well understood by non-jurists. The two-step model thus allows for the intermediate conclusion of a right infringement to trade on the higher prestige and greater strength of a moral right that provides an undefeated reason for action. To the extent that actors (particularly legislators) misunderstand the distinction between the intermediate finding of a violation of a particular section of the Charter and the finding of a violation of the Charter itself (that is, a violation that has not been found justified under s. 1), they risk exaggerating the reasons for action generated by the intermediate findings.

The alternative reading – that reasonable limits are inherent in the rights themselves – would have avoided the conceptual muddle of asserting that something that is *justified* can be judged to be, all things considered, an infringement of someone's right. To contend that state action limiting a person's claim to a benefit or liberty of action is *justified* is precisely to make the claim that there are competing demands or reasons that defeat the *claim* of constitutional right in this instance. After all, no one has a right not to be affected by fully justified state action.[10] When a government (or other party) contends that state action limiting a right is *justified*, it is arguing that notwithstanding an intermediate finding that there has been a right violation, there are nevertheless competing demands and reasons that defeat the *claim* of right in this instance. Argument at this second stage of s. 1 analysis is best understood, not as a *justification* of a right *violation*, but as the *defeat* of the claim of right, having considered the competing claims and entitlements of others.

Consider the prestige to a claimant that, under the current adjudicative structure, is generated by a judicial pronouncement that a legal restriction is *discriminatory* and thus infringes s. 15(1) of the Charter. Dicta from the Supreme

"ultimate reasons." J. Raz, *The Morality of Freedom* (1986) at 181 [Raz, *The Morality of Freedom*]. Raz, of course, is addressing the question of how *moral* rights function as reasons for action. The question in bill of rights adjudication is subtly different: It is, "Is this apparent constitutional right truly a constitutional right?" The closer analogue to Raz's question – "What reasons for action are generated by this finding of a constitutional right?" – is a question that I do not to address here.

[10] See John Finnis, *Natural Law and Natural Rights* (1980) at 220–1 [Finnis, *Natural Law and Natural Rights*].

Court of Canada often overstate the significance of a first-stage finding: In *Lavoie v. Canada*, for example, Bastarache J. states that "the government's burden under s. 1 is to *justify* a breach of human dignity, not to explain it or deny its existence."[11] The overstatement is not restricted to the courts; one commentator describes s. 1 adjudication (in the context of an equality claim) as a matter of "determining whether the government has met the burden of explaining why it should be allowed to *demean the dignity* of the vulnerable."[12]

Even where the Court's ultimate conclusion is that an infringement of a "right" is reasonable and fully justified, the Court's language (shaped by the structure of its analysis) provides inappropriate comfort to those whose claims may succeed at stage one, but are rightly refused on s. 1 analysis. Section 15(1) claims, in particular, are often claims for social recognition, and any activity that receives the protection of s. 15(1) will be popularly understood as having received the imprimatur of the Court. Now consider the case of a certain type of pedophile who brings a Charter challenge to criminal prohibitions, not simply to escape prosecution, but to advance the acceptance of pedophilia on par with other consensual sexual practices.[13] The claimant who succeeds at the s. 15(1) stage but loses under s. 1, obtains from the Court the social prestige that comes with a declaration that one has been discriminated against and had one's rights violated. Notwithstanding the caveat that the violation was held to be justified (perhaps – it may be thought by the claimant and others – on the basis of mere majoritarian preferences or animus),[14] the declaration is a powerful tool in the campaign for social recognition.[15] The finding of discrimination must impact on how the public (and the claimant) evaluates the conduct or choice in question, and shapes how future public debate will be conducted.[16]

[11] [2002] 1 S.C.R. 769 at para. 48 (Bastarache J.) [emphasis added] [*Lavoie*].

[12] S. Martin, "Balancing Individual Rights to Equality and Social Goals," (2001) 80 Can. Bar Rev. 299 at 364 [emphasis added].

[13] As was the case in *R. v. Sharpe*, [2001] 1 S.C.R. 45. "Sharpe, 67, was disappointed [with the Court's decision] but unrepentant... 'You know, kids were meant to enjoy sex and to have sex.'" Quote attributed to John Robin Sharpe, S. Bailey, "Supreme Court of Canada upholds most of child porn law as debate rages," *Vancouver Sun* (27 January 2001) A1.

[14] The argument dismissing s. 1 reasoning as a matter of applying majoritarian biases is addressed subsequently.

[15] It may be objected that *Sharpe* is a weak example. After all, whatever the Court held on the question of whether the law discriminated against Sharpe, the weight of public opinion remains decidedly against pedophilia. My point, however, is simply that the two-step model provides an unfortunate tool that has the capacity to skew discourse. I do not argue that every abuse of discourse in this way is immediately or even ultimately successful in realizing its goals.

[16] See G. Huscroft in P. Rishworth and G. Huscroft *et al.*, *The New Zealand Bill of Rights* (2003) at 373.

THE REASONABLENESS OF RIGHTS

A second, related criticism of the two-stage model is that the bifurcation of definition and limits will either result in (1) the systematic exclusion of relevant contextual factors in determining whether there has been a first-stage infringement, or (2) a collapse of the entire enquiry into either the first or second stage.

In Canada, the second scenario has played out in the context of freedom of expression adjudication under s. 2(b) of the Charter. Freedom of expression has been defined so expansively that all of the analytical work is done in the s. 1 adjudication.[17] Richard Moon argues that such a collapse was inevitable: The Supreme Court was tasked with "fitting a social or relational right . . . into an adjudicative structure that is based on an individualistic model of rights."[18] The adjudicative structure of the Charter is premised on judges being able to define individual rights without reference to a broad social context. Moon contends that whereas critics have faulted the Supreme Court for failing to keep stage-one and stage-two analyses distinct, in reality, the Supreme Court cannot satisfactorily come to a conclusion that a person's freedom of expression has been infringed without "determin[ing] the relative value/harm of a particular form or practice of expression within the social and economic context."[19] That is, in determining whether some proscribed expression is constitutionally protected, it is necessary to assess its value. Such an inquiry cannot be made in isolation from the broad-ranging social context that is to be left to s. 1. In the result, the Supreme Court has effectively abandoned the two-stage adjudicative model for freedom of expression litigation, and performs the entire analysis at the second stage. It is not, in this regard, approaching freedom of expression adjudication any differently than the U.S. Supreme Court under the Bill of Rights.

The first scenario – the exclusion of relevant contextual factors in determining whether there has been a first-stage infringement – is evident in the Supreme Court's equality jurisprudence under s. 15(1) of the Charter. Here, the Court has resisted the second scenario and struggles interminably with the proper dividing line between the definition of a right at s. 15(1) and the considerations relevant to its justification in s. 1 analysis. There has been substantial disagreement within the Court on the question of *where* in Charter adjudication competing considerations should be considered. Should it be at

[17] See R. Moon, "Justified Limits on Free Expression: The Collapse of the General Approach to Limits on Charter Rights," (2002) 40 Osgoode Hall L.J. 337.

[18] *Ibid.* at 350–1.

[19] *Ibid.* at 352.

the stage of determining whether legislation is discriminatory under s. 15(1), or is the broader context relevant *only* at the s. 1 stage, after the Court has already ruled that the impugned legislation is discriminatory? The debate over this question – essentially a question of whether governments' responsibility to act for the common good ought to be taken into account when assessing whether legislation is discriminatory – has been central throughout the development of Canadian equality jurisprudence.[20]

Justice Bastarache perhaps best articulates the current orthodoxy, writing for a plurality of the Supreme Court in *Lavoie*. There, he reiterated that discrimination is established if the claimant's feelings of indignity are judged by the Court to be reasonable.[21] It is only *after* a finding of discrimination has been made that it is appropriate to consider the public good at the s. 1 stage. The state can then attempt to "justify a breach of human dignity" by arguing that societal needs "outweigh" individual rights.[22] The Court's function under s. 15(1), he says, is to differentiate between a legislative distinction and discrimination, and to do so based on "a judicial interpretation of the normative parameters of the term 'discrimination.'"[23]

Arguing against Bastarache J. for a position close to what I advocate, Arbour J.'s concurring reasons in *Lavoie* held that s. 15(1) should be understood as having its own internal limitations.[24] This is because rights claims are "bilateral"; they are essentially "a legally binding demand for recognition of, and respect for, one's interests on the part of others."[25] As such, they ought not to be considered in isolation from their impact on the rest of society: "[f]or if others are to be duty-bound to respect one's rights, fairness requires that they be given some say, that their own interests be taken account of, in determining those rights."[26]

Justice Bastarache's reasons in *Lavoie* are a particularly instructive example of the difficultly created by the two-stage process. It seems unlikely that Bastarache J. could (or does) define the "normative parameters of the term 'discrimination'" without having any regard for the competing rights that the state is charged with safeguarding. A difficulty in Bastarache J.'s judgment is

[20] *Cf.* s. 3 of the *South Africa Bill of Rights*, which requires that the "state may not *unfairly* discriminate" (emphasis added), thus less equivocally pointing to a broad context to determine what conduct constitutes impermissible discrimination. For an account of the development of the s. 15(1) doctrine of the Supreme Court, see Justice Ian Binnie, "Equality Rights in Canada: Judicial Usurpation or Missed Opportunity?" in G. Huscroft and P. Rishworth, eds., *Litigating Rights: Perspectives from Domestic and International Law* (2002) 101.

[21] *Lavoie, supra* note 11 at para. 47.

[22] *Ibid.* at paras. 48–9.

[23] *Ibid.* at para. 50.

[24] *Ibid.* at para. 92.

[25] *Ibid.* at para. 88.

[26] *Ibid.*

the absence of an explanation of what are the "normative parameters of the term 'discrimination,'" or even an acknowledgment that one's conception of discrimination is a function of, or is related to, other conceptions of political morality that are, themselves, controversial. Justice Bastarache gives the impression that the normative parameters of discrimination are established through a supposedly uncontroversial, value-free judicial act of setting a definition. This language of "defining" obscures the value-laden and inevitably controversial nature of determining whether some legislation is discriminatory. The argument that, according to one's conception of justice and the history and culture of a given society, there are duties, obligations, and disadvantages that are unreasonable to ask others to accept, is an argument that rests on conclusions of moral and political philosophy. It demands a wide-ranging inquiry before others can be told by a court that they are guilty of having demeaned a claimant's dignity.

Justice Bastarache's division between the roles of s. 15(1) and s. 1 analysis – deferring to s. 1 any consideration of the "practical, moral, economic, or social underpinnings of the legislation in question, or . . . the need to protect other rights and values embodied in the Charter"[27] – is problematic. There is a danger that inquiries into the needs and circumstances of others that are needed in order to determine whether a claimant has, indeed, suffered discrimination will be (1) postponed to s. 1 adjudication, and then (2) devalued, because they cannot be used to argue that a claimant's treatment is not, all things now considered, truly an infringement of anyone's dignity. Indeed, Bastarache J. characterises the state's practical, moral, economic, and social arguments that some legislative distinction is not truly discriminatory, as being a matter of "counter[ing] the claimant's s. 15(1) argument with public policy arguments."[28]

The only way the proposed division between definition and limitation could work in the context of a right like s. 15(1) of the Charter would be if, as Bastarache J. suggests, s. 1 adjudication were simply a matter of weighing public policy arguments against individual rights.[29] This division is suggestive of the principle/policy dichotomy usually associated with Ronald Dworkin.[30] Such

[27] *Ibid.* at para. 48.

[28] *Lavoie, supra* note 11 at para. 48.

[29] The argument that the division is needed to shift the burden of proof from the claimant at the definition stage to the state at the limitation stage is a nonstarter. As Jeremy Gunn argues, where "issues are frequently more complicated . . . the burden of proof might properly and logically shift at different points in the proceedings." T.J. Gunn, "Deconstructing Proportionality in Limitations Analysis," 19 Emory International L.R. 465 at 481 (2005). There is no need to tie issues of burden of proof to the two-stage model of rights adjudication.

[30] E.g., Ronald Dworkin, *Taking Rights Seriously* (1977) 22, 90–4 [Dworkin, *Taking Rights Seriously*], *A Matter of Principle* (1985) at 359, 387 [Dworkin, *A Matter of Principle*].

a conception allows for bill of rights adjudication to be understood as a contest between "the individual's perspective or interest *against* the general or public good or against the claims, demands, needs, or requirements of others generally."[31]

The idea that there is a distinction between principles and policies, and that stage-one Charter adjudication is a matter of principle, whereas stage two is a function of policy concerns, would seem to be the best justification for the two-stage adjudicative structure. What can be said for this justification? It is necessary to give a brief account of this familiar argument, before attending to the equally familiar criticisms from John Finnis, Joseph Raz, Jeremy Waldron, and others.[32]

THE PRINCIPLE/POLICY DICHOTOMY

In Dworkin's theory of rights, individual rights are matters of *principle*, and are to be distinguished from the collective goals (the matters of *policy*) that would make the community as a whole better off. Appeals to "policy" are articulations of "a standard that sets out a goal to be reached, generally an improvement in some economic, political, or social feature of the community."[33] Policies are contrasted with "principles," which are standards that are to be observed "because it is a requirement of justice or fairness or some other dimension of morality."[34] In short, "[p]rinciples are propositions that describe rights; policies are propositions that describe goals."[35] Rights, Dworkin maintains, may not be abridged, even if it is in the best interests of the community to do so: Where an individual has a right, "it is . . . wrong for officials to act in violation of that right, even if they (correctly) believe that the community as a whole would be better off if they did."[36]

What follows from this conceptual division into principles and policies is a division of labour. If the determination of the scope of a right is a matter of principled argument, then it makes sense, Dworkin argues, for the judiciary to

[31] Joseph Raz, "Rights and Individual Well-being," in *Ethics in the Public Domain* (1994) at 29 [emphasis added] [Raz, "Rights and Individual Well-being"].

[32] See, *e.g.*, *ibid.*; D.N. MacCormick, *Legal Reasoning and Legal Theory* (1978) at 259–64; Finnis, *Natural Law and Natural Rights*, *supra* note 10; Finnis, "A Bill of Rights for Britain? The Moral of Contemporary Jurisprudence," (1985) 71 Proceedings of the British Academy 303 [Finnis, "A Bill of Rights for Britain?"]; and Jeremy Waldron, "Rights and Majorities: Rousseau revisited" in *Liberal Rights* (1993) at 392.

[33] Ronald Dworkin, *Taking Rights Seriously*, *supra* note 30 at 22.

[34] *Ibid.*

[35] *Ibid.* at 90.

[36] Dworkin, *A Matter of Principle*, *supra* note 30 at 359.

have the final say in such matters. Arguments before courts must be principled; courts are institutions where outcomes are determined by the quality of one's reasons.[37]

Although courts, in upholding rights, are not to be swayed by considerations of policy, the same cannot be expected of legislatures. Dworkin contends that the legislature is *also* a guardian of principle and should also be motivated by principle, but he concludes that, in practice, legislatures do not reach the heights of principle reached by courts: "[d]epressingly often . . . the process is dominated by political alliances that are formed around a single issue and use the familiar tactics of pressure groups to bribe or blackmail legislators into voting as they wish."[38] Legislative decisions are "compromised," based on "the weight of numbers or the balance of political influence,"[39] and simply reflect "what most people want."[40] Legislatures, Waldron notes, are thus dismissed by Dworkin as the venue of "deal-making, horse-trading, log-rolling, interest-pandering and pork-barreling – as anything, indeed, except principled political decision making."[41]

But is it at all reasonable to conceive of policies and collective interests in this way?[42] A better description of the practice of legislators would result

[37] *Ibid.* at 70.

[38] Dworkin, *Freedom's Law: The Moral Reading of the American Constitution* (1996) at 344 [Dworkin, *Freedom's Law*].

[39] *Ibid.* at 30, 344.

[40] *Ibid.* at 344. Dworkin also states that legislature are also guardians of principle: See *Freedom's Law, supra* note 38 at 31; Dworkin, *Law's Empire* (1986), ch 6, and can benefit from having issues framed for them by courts, *Freedom's Law, supra* note 38 at 345.

[41] Waldron, *The Dignity of Legislation* (1999) at 2. Whether or not Dworkin's cynicism about legislatures is warranted, it seems odd that it is not matched with similar cynicism about the extent to which appellate court judges can be (and at least on occasion, surely are) deflected from fully reasonable decision-making. Do judges not, from time to time, wrongly inflate the value of the good championed by favoured groups, secure the backing of other panel members on favoured decisions by trading off support in other cases, formally give reasons for judgment that do not reflect their actual reasons, and silently pass over contrary (yet binding) precedent? Do they not, in these and other ways, act in an unreasonable and unprincipled manner?

[42] Brian Leiter argues that Dworkin himself "quietly abandoned this wildly implausible claim" under pressure from Neil MacCormick, *Legal Reasoning and Legal Theory* (1978) and John Bell, *Policy Arguments in Judicial Decisions* (1983): Brian Leiter, "The End of Empire: Dworkin and Jurisprudence in the 21st Century," 35 Rutgers L.J. (2005) 165 at 173. But whatever the evidence that Dworkin has abandoned the distinction, it is still operative in Dworkin's thought in *Freedom's Law* at 344–5. Conor Gearty also appeals to a distinction between principle and policy in his work on judicial review under the *Human Rights Act*, C. Gearty, *Principles of Human Rights Adjudication* (2004): See Aileen Kavanagh's criticism of the principle/policy distinction in "Deference or Defiance? The Limits of the Judicial Role in Constitutional Adjudication" in this volume.

from the application of H.L.A. Hart's internal point of view.[43] Recall that Hart, when describing the concepts of law and rule-following behaviour, urged that explanatory priority be given to the point of view of persons who actually *use* the rules as a guide to decision and action; that is, whose actions and choices constitute the subject matter under investigation. This internal point of view of the participant better explains the practice and content of law, over the external point of view of the mere observer. Similarly, if we substitute the act of "legislating" for legal rule-following, we can say that explanatory priority ought to be given to the internal view of the legislator who is motivated to legislate out of a concern to provide to persons that which they are justly owed by government. Furthermore – and following Finnis – precedence should be given to the central case of the internal point of view; that is, legislators who *correctly* assess the matter of justice served by the adopted policy. In other words, precedence must be given to the perspective of the legislator who correctly believes in the rationality and justice of the legislation enacted. The legislator who (out of a desire to conform to the collective desires of others, or to achieve a type of social solidarity) enacts a statute *without* accepting its rationality and justice, represents a nonstandard, peripheral case of legislating from the internal point of view. Attending to the internal point of view demonstrates what Dworkin's critics have persistently argued: that much of what Dworkin would dismiss as matters of policy should be characterized as matters of right, or principle. In short, the distinction between policy and principle does not hold.

Finnis, for example, uses a nonaggregative account of the collective interests of a political community (one that has traditionally sailed under the name of the "common good"), which he defines as:

> . . . a set of conditions which enables the members of a community to attain for themselves reasonable objectives, or to realize reasonably for themselves the value(s), for the sake of which they have reason to collaborate with each other (positively and/or negatively) in a community.[44]

On such a conception, legislating for the common good is a matter of securing the background conditions necessary for each person to pursue his or her own good. The Supreme Court of Canada appeared to have in mind

[43] H.L.A. Hart, *The Concept of Law*, 2nd edn. (1994) at 95–6. This distinction has also been adopted by J. Raz, *Practical Reason and Norms*, 2nd edn. (1990) at 177, and further developed by Finnis, *Natural Law and Natural Rights*, *supra* note 10 at 11–16, and Finnis, *Aquinas: Moral, Political and Legal Theory* (1998), ch 2, esp. 38–40.

[44] Finnis, *Natural Law and Natural Rights*, *supra* note 10 at 155.

such a nonaggregative conception of collective interests when it meditated on the meaning of the common good in *Manitoba (A.G.) v. Metropolitan Stores Ltd.*:

> ... the laws which litigants seek to suspend ... have been enacted by democratically-elected legislatures and are generally passed for the common good, for instance: the providing and financing of public services such as educational services, or of public utilities such as electricity, the protection of public health, natural resources and the environment, the repression of what is considered to be criminal activity, the controlling of economic activity such as the containing of inflation, the regulation of labour relations, etc.[45]

Such a list usefully illustrates how regulation motivated by concern for the common good is a very different matter from regulation motivated by a desire to repress or injure (or even to accept such repression or injury as an acceptable side effect of legislation aimed at obtaining a benefit for some preferred group or class of favoured persons).

Respect for the common good requires that the legislator (and other law makers, such as judges) consider and give effect to each person's well being without favouritism.[46] This is not to say that the legislator is bound to accept every person's self-understanding, or to value equally every life plan. As traditionally understood, the common good is consistent with policies that are motivated by judgments that there are ranges of both valuable life plans and valueless life plans, and that a government can be justified (and sometimes required) to act so as to facilitate (or even promote) the many morally good options and discourage (or even prohibit) the morally valueless.[47]

On such a conception of the common good, there is no conflict between the common good and individual rights. Respect for each person's well being, including each person's rights, is an integral part of the common good. This is not to argue that a person's *claim* of right will never conflict with a corresponding legislature's particular determination of what the common good requires. It is only to make the argument that it is neither accurate nor helpful to talk about rights as having a conclusory status that is in conflict with the desires of some depersonalized majority or collective interest.

[45] *Manitoba (A.G.) v. Metropolitan Stores Ltd.*, [1987] 1 S.C.R. 110 at para. 55 (Beetz J.) [*Metropolitan Stores*].

[46] Finnis, *Natural Law and Natural Rights*, *supra* note 10 at 214; Robert P. George, "Individual Rights, Collective Interests, Public Law, and American Politics," (1989) 8 Law & Phil. 245 at 252–3 [George, "Individual Rights, Collective Interests"].

[47] It is therefore consistent with the perfectionist liberalism of Joseph Raz or William Galston, as well as the natural law theory of Germain Grisez, John Finnis, or Robert George.

Finnis argues that "general welfare" or "collective interests" are the welfare and interests of individuals. They cannot be aggregated in any sensible way. If legislative responsibilities include legislating in the genuine interest of all persons, and if the legislature is also a forum of principle that is to be guided by law (including principles of constitutional law), then a legislator cannot justly appeal to a conception of majoritarianism or aggregate welfare to justify disregarding a person's rights. The nonaggregative common good includes the respect for the fully specified rights of all individuals within the political community. A government that disregards these individual rights, whether in the name of advancing the goals of some collective or otherwise, damages the common good.[48]

Finnis draws a further distinction between the common good and Dworkin's concept of collective interests, one that further erodes the basis for the division between principle and policy. His argument is simply that what is called collective interests can easily be translated into claims of right.[49] One could speak equally plausibly about the criminal prohibition of anticompetitive business practices as being for the common good, as one can speak about one's own right (in common with others) that government criminalize anticompetitive business practices for one's own protection. As Robert George describes it, if we conceive of collective interests "as including a due regard for the incommensurable interests of (each individual member of) the community in, *inter alia*, fairness and a respect for individual rights – the neat contrast between matters of principle and policy and between individual rights and collective interests blur."[50]

If there is a conception of collective interests that speaks the same language as the conception of rights, what we are left with is a contest not between principles and a voluntarist imposition of majority preferences, but rather between the rights of some and the rights of others. The language on both sides of the equation can be the language of rights.

MAJORITARIAN PREFERENCES AND THE PRINCIPLES OF A "FREE AND DEMOCRATIC SOCIETY"

The principle/policy distinction seems unavailable to support the two-stage model. I think we can go further, and argue that the jurisprudence of the Supreme Court of Canada (a jurisprudence that, on this point, is supported

[48] Finnis, *Natural Law and Natural Rights*, *supra* note 10 at 168, 210–18; Robert George, *Making Men Moral* (1993) at 90–3 [George, *Making Men Moral*].

[49] Finnis, "A Bill of Rights for Britain?" *supra* note 32 at 320–1; see also Finnis, *Natural Law and Natural Rights*, *supra* note 10.

[50] George, *Making Men Moral*, *supra* note 48 at 91.

by sound philosophy) supports a conception of s. 1 that further destabilizes the distinction between the definition of rights and their limitation. I argued previously that in the context of s. 15(1), the demands of equality could not be determined without considering the needs and circumstances of persons and groups in addition to the claimant. Now I want to argue that the concept of s. 1 that the Court currently uses is not a matter of giving effect to majoritarian preferences, but is this same inquiry of establishing the common good for the whole of the community, including the claimant.

Unmistakably, while the enumerated rights are often described using florid language,[51] s. 1 is described in more prosaic fashion; it is a matter of the "realization of collective goals,"[52] a phrase open to interpretation as a matter of utilitarian cost-benefit analysis and the imposition of majority will. Similarly, the Supreme Court sometimes labels these s. 1 interests as the "collective interest,"[53] the "public interest,"[54] "social interests,"[55] the "state interest,"[56] or "policy," "public policy," or "social policy."[57]

[51] *E.g.*, s. 15(1) "reflects the fondest dreams, the highest hopes and finest aspirations of Canadian society," *Vriend v. Alberta*, [1998] 1 S.C.R. 493 at para. 67 (Cory J.) [*Vriend*].

[52] *Oakes*, *supra* note 5 at para. 65 (Dickson C.J.). Also, "[I]n a modern industrial society, it is generally accepted that many activities in which individuals can engage must nevertheless to a greater or lesser extent be regulated by the state to ensure that the individual's pursuit of his or her self-interest is compatible with the community's interest in the realization of *collective goals and aspirations*," *Thomson Newspapers Ltd. v. Canada (Director of Investigation and Research, Restrictive Trade Practice Commission)*, [1990] 1 S.C.R. 425 at 506–7 [emphasis added]; also cited in *British Columbia Securities Commission v. Branch*, [1995] 2 S.C.R. 3 at para. 56; and *RJR-MacDonald Inc. v. Canada (Attorney General)*, [1995] 3 S.C.R. 199 at para 118 (La Forest J., dissenting). Similarly, "[t]he distinction between 'objective' and 'means' is important since at this stage, the Court must ensure that the said objective is consistent with the principles integral to a free and democratic society, pressing and substantial, and directed to the realisation of collective goals of fundamental importance," *Thomson Newspapers Co. v. Canada (Attorney General)*, [1998] 1 S.C.R. 877 at paras. 23 and 38. "More than simply an instruction to courts that they defer to legislatures as a matter of policy, s. 1 of the *Charter* is a recognition that individual rights must be balanced against one another and against important collective goals," *R. v. Robinson*, [1996] 1 S.C.R. 683 at para. 86 (L'Heureux-Dubé J. dissenting).

[53] "[T]he notion that individual rights may, in some circumstances, be subordinated to substantial and compelling collective interests is itself a basic tenet of our legal system lying at or very near the core of our most deeply rooted juridical convictions." *Godbout v. Longueuil (City)*, [1997] 3 S.C.R. 844 at para. 76 (LaForest J.).

[54] *Reference Re Motor Vehicle Act (British Columbia) S 94(2)*, [1985] 2 S.C.R. 486 at paras. 80–1 (Lamer J.) [*Motor Vehicle Reference*].

[55] *New Brunswick (Minister of Health and Community Services) v. G. (J.)*, [1999] 3 S.C.R. 46 at para. 99 [*G.(J.)*].

[56] *R. v. Morgentaler*, [1988] 1 S.C.R. 30 at 74, 82, 85, 99, and 107; *Rodriguez v. British Columbia (Attorney General)*, [1993] 3 S.C.R. 519 at para. 205; *Lavoie*, *supra* note 11 at para. 47.

[57] See, *e.g.*, *Newfoundland (Treasury Board) v. N.A.P.E.*, [2004] 3 S.C.R. 381 at para. 69 [*N.A.P.E.*]; *Eldridge v. British Columbia (Attorney General)*, [1997] 3 S.C.R. 624 at para. 85; *Libman v.*

Is the Court employing a nonaggregative conception of collective interests according to which no person's interests may be justly left out of account by decision-makers, and no person's moral or legal rights may be disregarded without thereby damaging the common good?[58] Or are collective interests to be understood in the aggregate, using a utilitarian calculus? Are rights infringements to be weighed against collective goals, the significance of which is derived *not* from the reasons advanced for them by the majority (using the point of view internal to the decision maker), but rather from the external point of view that attributes significance to the desires of the majority simply because they are the desires of the majority?

To the extent that the infringement/justification model of bill of rights adjudication mirrors the principle/policy distinction – in particular, to the extent that it relies on a conception of "collective goals" drawn from the external point of view – it misdescribes what is at play in adjudication. However, I will argue that the best reading of the reasons given by the Court in its s. 1 jurisprudence – particularly its emphasis on "the underlying values and principles of a free and democratic society"[59] – supports a nonaggregative conception of collective interest and similar terminology. This conception excludes some considerations from s. 1 adjudication, while arguably admitting the whole of the morality of a free and democratic society that bears on questions of community life.

Of course, what one judges to be the underlying values principles of a free and democratic society will be largely influenced by what one judges to be sound moral and political philosophy. The Court thus set itself the contentious task of delineating a theory of political morality in which the underlying values and principles of a free and democratic society can be understood. Unsurprisingly, apart from occasional dicta from individual judges, the Supreme Court of Canada has not yet attempted to articulate a comprehensive moral and political theory thought to underlie the Canadian constitutional order.[60]

It should be noted, however, that some judges have made sweeping and highly controversial statements about the theories of political morality, which they believe underlie the Canadian constitutional order.[61] Unsurprisingly,

Quebec (Attorney General), [1997] 3 S.C.R. 569 at para. 59; and *RJR-MacDonald Inc. v. Canada (Attorney General)*, [1995] 3 S.C.R. 199 at para. 67.

[58] As articulated by George, "Individual Rights, Collective Interests," *supra* note 46 at 252–54.

[59] *Oakes, supra* note 5 at para. 64 (Dickson C.J.).

[60] Robert Bork takes the position that such a theory of the "legitimate and important objectives of government" is not "even conceivable." See, Robert H. Bork, *The Tempting of America* (1990) at 226.

[61] For example, Wilson J. in *R. v. Morgentaler*, [1988] 1 S.C.R. 30 at para. 229, refers to "... the basic theory underlying the Charter, namely that the state will respect choices made by individuals

those judges who have been inclined to this sort of exercise have substantial disagreements with each other. Whereas Wilson J., for example, cites John Stuart Mill in her interpretation that the "basic theory of the Charter" is to avoid "subordinating [individual] choices to any one conception of the good life,"[62] Gonthier J. cites Joseph Raz for the proposition that "... it is the goal of all political action to enable individuals to pursue valid conceptions of the good and to discourage evil or empty ones."[63]

Regardless of the Court's reluctance (and perhaps, inability) to engage in political philosophy in the abstract, it must inevitably articulate some aspects of what constitutes the good of a free and democratic society in order to establish why particular Charter rights infringements are or are not justified in particular instances.[64] In many (perhaps most) cases, there is agreement about the justification, and thus no impetus to explore disagreement over the grounds for the justification. Nevertheless, we do have some insight into what the Court considers to be the underlying values and principles of a free and democratic society.

Uncontroversially, free and democratic principles include "the protection of competing rights."[65] We also know that s. 1 principles are not restricted to considerations emanating from the enumerated rights. As Dickson C. J. stated in *Slaight Communications Inc. v. Davidson*, "[t]here are many diverse values

and, to the greatest extent possible, will avoid subordinating these choices to any one conception of the good life," and quotes J.S. Mill in support [*Morgentaler*]. Such general statements can, of course, command wide assent while masking deep disagreement over what constitutes "the greatest extent possible." For two very different readings of Mill, which would generate two different answers to the question of what is the greatest extent to which the state can respect choices made by individuals, see Dworkin, *Taking Rights Seriously*, *supra* note 30 at 259–65, and C. Taylor, *Philosophical Arguments* (1995) at 257–58.

Similarly, we can contrast Lamer C.J.'s dicta in *Rodriguez v. British Columbia (Attorney General)*, [1993] 3 S.C.R.519 at para. 59, that "the *Charter* has established the essentially secular nature of Canadian society," with La Forest J.'s willingness to consider "long-standing philosophical and religious traditions" in his s. 15(1) analysis in *Egan v. Canada*, [1995] 2 S.C.R. 513 at para. 21. See also the Court's holding that the *B.C. School Act's* requirement that schools be run on "strictly secular" principles "does not mean that religious concerns have no place in the deliberations and decisions" of a school board: *Chamberlain v. Surrey School District No. 36*, [2002] 4 S.C.R. 710 at para. 19.

[62] *Morgentaler*, *ibid.*

[63] *Sauvé v. Canada (Chief Electoral Officer)*, [2002] 3 S.C.R. 519 at para. 112 (Gonthier J. dissenting), citing J. Raz, *The Morality of Freedom*, *supra* note 9 at 133.

[64] "[W]hen a court interprets legislation alleged to be a reasonable limitation in a free and democratic society as stated in s. 1 of the Charter, the court must inevitably delineate some of the attributes of a democratic society." *Vriend*, *supra* note 51 at para. 141.

[65] *Sauvé v. Canada (Chief Electoral Officer)*, [2002] 3 S.C.R. 519 at para. 20 [*Sauvé*].

that deserve protection in a free and democratic society such as that of Canada, only some of which are expressly provided for in the *Charter*."[66] In *R. v. Big M Drug Mart Ltd.*,[67] the Court tracked the language of the *European Convention on Human Rights* in defining s. 1 principles as those "limitations as are necessary to protect *public safety*, *order*, *health* or *morals* or the fundamental rights and freedoms of others . . . "[68] Additionally, from *Oakes*, Dickson C. J. provided a further specification:

> The Court must be guided by the values and principles essential to a free and democratic society which I believe embody, to name but a few, respect for the inherent dignity of the human person, commitment to social justice and equality, accommodation of a wide variety of beliefs, respect for cultural and group identity, and faith in social and political institutions which enhance the participation of individuals and groups in society.[69]

It has been argued that by not repeating *Big M*'s litany of public safety, order, health, or morals in *Oakes*, the Court abandoned this list of limiting factors.[70] However, the Court has characterized *Oakes* and *Big M* as consistent with each other: "the factors set forth in *Big M* . . . are really an earlier and simpler formulation of values later incorporated in the more complex s. 1 formulation devised in *Oakes*."[71] Of course, the strongest evidence that the Court accepts public order, health, and morality as s. 1 principles is its actual use of such principles in determining whether specific Charter rights limitations are justified in cases dealing with, for example, obscene or racist expression.[72] In *Lavoie*, a plurality of the Court reaffirmed the broad nature of s. 1 principles:

> This justification [of rights infringements] may be established by the practical, moral, economic, or social underpinnings of the legislation in question, or by the need to protect other rights and values embodied in the *Charter*. It may be further established based on the requirements of proportionality, that

[66] [1989] 1 S.C.R. 1038 at 1056.

[67] *R. v. Big M Drug Mart Ltd.*, [1985] 1 S.C.R. 295 [*Big M*]. At issue was the constitutionality of a prohibition against Sunday trading. The Court found that the prohibition violated freedom of religion, and was not justified under s. 1.

[68] *Ibid.* at para. 95 [emphasis added].

[69] *Oakes*, *supra* note 5 at para. 64 (Dickson C.J.).

[70] As held, for example, by the trial judge in *R. v. Butler*, [1989] 72 C.R. (3d) 18 at 43 (Man. Q.B.).

[71] *Ross v. New Brunswick School District No. 15*, [1996] 1 S.C.R. 825 at para. 74.

[72] *R. v. Keegstra*, [1990] 3 S.C.R. 697; *R. v. Butler*, [1992] 1 S.C.R. 452; *Little Sisters Book and Art Emporium v. Canada (Minister of Justice)*, [2000] 2 S.C.R. 1120; and *R. v. Sharpe*, [2001] 1 S.C.R. 45.

> is, whether the interest pursued by the legislation outweighs its impact on human dignity and freedom.[73]

The litany of practical, moral, economic, or social reasons seems to represent a very wide scope, arguably encompassing the whole of the political morality of a free and democratic society.

One's answer to the question whether particular practical, moral, economic, or social reasons are sufficiently important to justify particular rights infringements must be a function of one's understanding of what constitutes the well-being of persons and groups (including, but not limited to, political society as a whole), as well as one's understanding of the proper function and jurisdiction of government. In other words, it is determined, or strongly influenced, by one's answers to the questions: (1) Is the impugned activity truly worthwhile (or at least, not harmful and worthless to the actor and others)? (2) Does the impugned activity hinder other persons in the pursuit of some aspect of their genuine well being? (3) What are the contours of the government's obligation to act so as to assist persons in their pursuit of genuine well being?

We should then ask, what has the Supreme Court of Canada held to be the good of the community – the collective interests – that the state has a duty to promote? In contemporary adjudication, the Court has said that government has the obligation "to stimulate and preserve the community's economic and social welfare."[74] What then are the components of this welfare?[75] The Court has identified some of the goods that the state, in this capacity, is to provide, including national security,[76] the administration of justice,[77] health care,[78] civil infrastructure,[79] public safety,[80] the regulation and co-ordination of the economy,[81] the preservation of the physical environment,[82] and the

[73] *Lavoie, supra* note 11 at para. 48 (Bastarache J., for the plurality).

[74] *Lavigne v. Ontario Public Service Employees Union*, [1991] 2 S.C.R. 211 at 314 (La Forest J.).

[75] One might also ask for *which communities* the government has a responsibility to promote well-being. It is evident from the jurisprudence of the Charter era that the common good of the Canadian political community includes the preservation and enhancement of French and English linguistic communities, aboriginal communities, religious and cultural groups, and families.

[76] *Suresh v. Canada (Minister of Citizenship and Immigration)*, [2002] 1 S.C.R. 3 at para. 85.

[77] *Reference re: Manitoba Language Rights*, [1985] 1 S.C.R. 721; *Reference re Remuneration of Judges of the Provincial Court of Prince Edward Island*, [1997] 3 S.C.R. 3.

[78] *Eldridge v. Canada*, [1997] 3 S.C.R. 624 at para. 94; *RJR–Macdonald Inc. v. Canada (Attorney General)*, [1995] 3 S.C.R. 199 at para. 170.

[79] *Just v. British Columbia*, [1989] 2 S.C.R. 1228.

[80] *Reference re: Firearms Act (Can.)*, [2000] 1 S.C.R. 783 at para. 4.

[81] *Reference Re Anti–Inflation Act*, [1976] 2 S.C.R. 373 at 425.

[82] *114957 Canada Ltée (Spraytech, Société d'arrosage) v. Hudson (Town)*, [2001] 2 S.C.R. 241.

prevention of moral corruption.[83] Although diligent and skilful attention to these and other government responsibilities is essential to the good of a free and democratic society which s. 1 of the Charter makes paramount, they are nevertheless sometimes oddly mischaracterized (as by Arbour J. in *Lavoie*) as "less valued state objectives," which are contrasted with "society's most cherished values" embodied in the rest of the Charter.[84]

Can we rule out some values and principles as being *inconsistent* with the principles of a free and democratic society? From the jurisprudence of the Court, we can start the list with the "values" of hate-mongers,[85] child pornographers,[86] and totalitarian regimes.[87] We can add "a simple majoritarian political preference for abolishing a right altogether,"[88] which would exclude accepting as a sufficient justification the brute fact that a decision was favoured by a majority. But are appeals to economic criteria also ruled out in a free and democratic society?

There has been some controversy over whether fiscal considerations or economic criteria can come within the values and principles of a free and democratic society. The Supreme Court of Canada, in a series of cases that address what has become known as the "dollars versus rights" controversy,[89] repeatedly refused to accede to government arguments to justify rights infringements on the basis of unacceptable financial cost. Justice Wilson, in *Singh v. Canada (Minister of Employment and Immigration)*, expressed her "considerable doubt that the type of utilitarian consideration brought forward ... can constitute a justification for a limitation on the rights set out in the *Charter*."[90] Similarly, Lamer C. J. declared that "a measure whose sole purpose is financial, and which infringes Charter rights, can never be justified under s. 1."[91]

[83] *R. v. Butler*, [1992] 1 S.C.R. 452; *R. v. Keegstra*, [1990] 3 S.C.R. 697.
[84] *Lavoie, supra* note 11 at para. 91.
[85] *R. v. Keegstra*, [1990] 3 S.C.R. 697. (In the context of s. 319 of the *Criminal Code*, RSC 1985, c. C-46, anyone who "incites hatred against an identifiable group where such incitement is likely to lead to a breach of the peace" is guilty of an offence. An identifiable group is defined in s. 318 as "any section of the public distinguished by colour, race, religion, ethnic origin or sexual orientation.")
[86] *R. v. Sharpe*, [2001] 1 S.C.R. 45.
[87] A totalitarian regime being the opposite of a "free and democratic society."
[88] *Sauvé, supra* note 65 at para. 20.
[89] *Singh v. Canada (Minister of Employment and Immigration)*, [1985] 1 S.C.R. 177 [*Singh*]; *R. v. Lee*, [1989] 2 S.C.R. 1384; *Schachter v. Canada*, [1992] 2 S.C.R. 679; *Reference re Remuneration of Judges of the Provincial Court of Prince Edward Island*, [1997] 3 S.C.R. 3; and *Nova Scotia (Workers' Compensation Board) v. Martin*, [2003] 2 S.C.R. 504.
[90] *Singh, ibid.* at para. 70.
[91] *Reference re Remuneration of Judges of the Provincial Court of Prince Edward Island*, [1997] 3 S.C.R. 3 at para. 284 (Lamer C.J.).

Nevertheless, in *Newfoundland (Treasury Board) v. Newfoundland Association of Public Employees*, the Court, for the first time, accepted a fiscal justification for a rights violation. In the result, the Court held that the Newfoundland government violated the s. 15(1) equality rights of female public sector workers by enacting legislation delaying the implementation of a pay equity settlement. It further held that the violation was justified under s. 1, on the grounds that there was a fiscal crisis facing Newfoundland.

The claimant, the Newfoundland Association of Public Employees, supported by the intervener Women's Legal Education and Action Fund (LEAF), argued that economic criteria should not be sufficient to justify limitations on the enumerated Charter rights. LEAF argued that "monetary considerations should not be available as a justification in the context of equality violations," claiming that fiscal considerations and the goal of remedying discrimination are incomparable.[92] LEAF further argued that allowing fiscal considerations a place in s. 1 adjudication "allows majoritarian democracy to trump substantive democracy."[93]

LEAF's objection is precisely that the government's s. 1 argument, in this case, conceives of s. 1 as a forum of policy, in which majoritarian interests threaten to trump rights. Were this, in fact, the government's argument, it would, indeed, be objectionable, and inconsistent with what I have argued is the Court's interpretation of the underlying values and principles of a free and democratic society. However, LEAF misconceives the government's argument because it overlooks the transparency of budgetary decisions.[94] A decision to spend or not to spend government funds is not typically an end in itself. It is instrumental to achieving some purpose. It is this underlying purpose that must be evaluated, and not the bare decision to spend or not to spend. At the end of the day, a decision not to spend funds can be judged to have been made for either a sufficient reason or an insufficient reason. In order to determine whether what has been described as a fiscal decision is justified, one must attend to the moral evaluations motivating the fiscal decision. This point was well understood by the Supreme Court of Canada, which rejected the characterization of the government's purpose as majoritarian self-interest, and instead characterized it as having been undertaken in service of the common good. Furthermore, the Court resisted the characterization of the contest as

[92] N.A.P.E., *supra* note 57 (Factum of the Intervenor: LEAF at para. 60), reprinted in Fay Faraday *et al.* eds., *Making Equality Rights Real* (2006) at 471–92.

[93] *Ibid.* at para. 66.

[94] On the transparency of reasoning, see J. M. Finnis, *Fundamentals of Ethics* (1983) 70–4.

being between individual rights and the financial benefit to some collective, and instead identified the individual rights all around:

> The government in 1991 was not just debating rights versus dollars but rights versus hospital beds, rights versus layoffs, rights versus jobs, rights versus education and rights versus social welfare. The requirement to reduce expenditures, and the allocation of the necessary cuts, *was* undertaken to promote other values of a free and democratic society . . . [95]

The Court appropriately conceives of the common good in nonaggregative terms, and identifies the reasons underlying what, at first glance, might appear to be purely economic decision-making. Without this further step in the analysis, it is not possible to get beyond the simplistic and highly misleading rhetoric of "dollars versus rights."[96]

Not every aspect of the Court's reasoning in *N.A.P.E.* is sound. The Court was unduly concerned with the objection that a government, acting unreasonably, could counter rights claims with the defence that the claims would cost too much, and that the limited funds available have already been allocated to more important and pressing matters. The Court's answer was to characterize the situation facing the Newfoundland government as extreme and exceptional because it was an emergency; Newfoundland was faced with the prospect of a loss in credit rating and a loss of ability to borrow funds. No more money was available, or at least was available only on unacceptable terms. The Court suggested that although fiscal choices can justify the infringement of a right, this justification is limited to situations of emergency.

The Court's concession was premature. Once a fiscal choice is translated in terms of the government's obligations towards all persons in a free and democratic society, the presence of an emergency will be sufficient but not necessary to establish the grounds for the limit. It is hard to tell what the presence of an emergency adds to the mix. Furthermore, what constitutes an emergency is contestable. One can argue that there was no emergency in Newfoundland, only a situation in which a proportion of public revenue would be consumed by servicing debt. This is not an emergency, just a worsening economy with losses to be shared by all.

To the extent that it made the existence of an emergency a necessary condition for "justifying" a rights infringement, the Court erred. The source of the

[95] *N.A.P.E.*, *supra* note 57 at para. 75.

[96] For a version of the argument criticized here, see M. Randall, "Equality Rights in the Charter: reconceptualizing state accountability for ending domestic violence" in Fay Faraday *et al.* eds., *Making Equality Rights Real* (2006) 275 at 281–91.

error was, again, the inflation of the status of the "right" that was held to have been infringed at the first stage of the analysis. As I have argued throughout, in determining whether there has been an infringement of a fully specified right (rather than an intermediate, first-stage conclusion that a right has been violated), one must take into account competing interests. There is no reason to grant automatic priority to the rights enumerated in the Charter over the justificatory values identified (however vaguely), by s. 1 of the Charter. Where fiscal concerns can be translated into moral arguments about the entitlements of persons, and the government has not engaged in impermissible bias or neglect of any person or group in coming to its allocation, then the fiscal justification ought to stand, regardless of whether it can be characterized as an emergency. In *N.A.P.E.*, it ought to have been sufficient for the Court to accept the government's argument that it would be unfair to the people of Newfoundland – contrary to the underlying values and principles of a free and democratic society – to accede to the demands of the claimants.

If the presence of an emergency cannot act as the limiting factor, and the principle/policy distinction does not hold, what are the bounds to fiscally based rights limitations? There is no simple formula; certainly there is nothing as simple and elegant as the proposed principle/policy distinction. Section 1 of the Charter requires courts to review the legislature's exercise of its responsibility for the claimant's rights and the needs and well being of others. A fiscal justification should be inadequate when it is proffered in the place of an argument as to why some limitation on a right is fitting in a free and democratic society. So, for example, a fiscal justification should fail if a government cannot demonstrate how, as a consequence of its action, the legitimate claims of others would go unmet, or the common good would otherwise be impaired; a government is unable to establish that it would be unfair to require society to bear additional costs to meet the claim of right; or a government had not taken the needs of the right claimant into account in its decision-making (*e.g.*, has not considered them even to reject them, or has rejected them because of some animus or inaccurate stereotyping). There is no shortcut through this sort of reasoning.[97]

In *N.A.P.E.*, two disparate conceptions of s. 1 reasoning collide. The one strand, beloved of claimants' counsel, characterizes collective interests in an aggregated way, and holds them in opposition to individual rights. When collective interests are conceived of in this way, it is a simple matter to hold that

[97] On the perennial question of whether legislatures or courts are better placed to answer these sorts of questions see Jeremy Waldron, "Do Judges Reason Morally?" and Aileen Kavanagh, "Deference or Defiance? The Limits of the Judicial Role in Constitutional Adjudication," both in this volume.

they can be defeated by rights in "the forum of principle." The second strand, which won out in *N.A.P.E.*, is a product of sound philosophy, acknowledging the legislature's responsibility to legislate for the common good, understood as providing the background conditions necessary for individuals to pursue their own good.

CONCLUSION

I have argued that the inclusion of limitations clauses in bills of rights provides an unnecessary invitation to the judiciary to inflate individual rights at the expense of the political community. Reasoning under bills of rights, I have argued, should not be unreasonably fettered or deflected by an unwarranted ascription of conclusory force to preliminary findings of rights infringement. However, such an unwarranted ascription often (but not always) results from the Supreme Court's interpretation of the structure of the Charter as requiring a two-step process of definition and limitation. It can be, and intermittently is, overcome by attention to the nature of the reasons that are offered in support of legislation. Legislation that is for the common good is a matter of the legislature providing persons with that which they are justly owed or (equivalently) respecting the rights of persons. When rights are conceived of along these lines, the principle/policy distinction falls away and a less restricted, more defensible s. 1 reasoning can take root.

The Supreme Court of Canada, among other courts, is heavily invested in a two-step adjudicative structure. Much as I find *Oakes* and its progeny regrettable, there is clearly no prospect that the two-stage approach will be reconsidered. It does not follow, however, that there can be no practical consequences from the foregoing analysis. Bills of rights are in the service of the entire political community. To the extent that a constitutional interpretation works injustice on that community, it should not be followed. Those courts that are not willing to abandon the two-stage structure can, and should, relax the demand that the analysis conducted at each stage be kept distinct. A court that draws watertight distinctions between definition and limitation can only do so artificially – there are only so many reasons to go around.

PART TWO

JUDICIAL REVIEW, LEGITIMACY, AND JUSTIFICATION

5 Constitutions, Judicial Review, Moral Rights, and Democracy: Disentangling the Issues

Larry Alexander*

Should countries have constitutions? Should there be American or Canadian-style judicial review of constitutional questions? Should constitutions have provisions establishing rights? Or is there a fundamental right to decide democratically the most important issues confronting us and, particularly, the content of the rights we possess?

These questions are frequently not distinguished, with the predictable result that an answer to one is taken to be an answer to another. I intend, however, to make it clear that and why they are separate questions.

I. SHOULD COUNTRIES HAVE CONSTITUTIONS?

First, what does it mean to have a constitution? Answering this question is not easy.

For one thing, a constitution need not be written. It is oft said that the British have an "unwritten constitution," which is not just an ironic way of saying they do not have one. And there are numerous treatises and other scholarly works devoted to British "constitutional law." There are, of course, quite compelling reasons why modern constitutions tend to be written, especially if they are lengthy and complex. But nothing in the nature of constitutions requires that they be written.

A more promising way of thinking about constitutions is in terms of their being "higher law." Put differently, constitutions are what validate ordinary law – the law produced by legislative and administrative bodies and by

* I wish to thank the organizers of the conference on Interpreting the Constitution, Grant Huscroft, Brad Miller, and Randal Graham, for their hospitality, and all of the conference participants for their comments and criticisms.

common-law courts. Ordinary law is valid law, when it is so, just because it is authorized by the higher law of the constitution.

Still another way we might distinguish constitutions from ordinary law is in terms of degrees of entrenchment. In most democracies, ordinary laws are relatively unentrenched and can be amended or repealed by democratic majorities. Constitutional provisions, on the other hand, cannot be amended or repealed by democratic majorities.

The higher law and relative entrenchment accounts of constitutions typically go hand in hand. Constitutions are generally higher up the validity chain than ordinary laws and also more entrenched than ordinary laws. Still, neither account seems sufficient by itself (although the validity account seems necessary).

The validity account seems insufficient because parts of what everyone would concede is a constitution occupy different locations in the validity chain. Consider, for example, Article VII of the U.S. Constitution.[1] Article VII declares how the entire U.S. Constitution became the U.S. Constitution (that is, through ratification by a sufficient number of States). Thus, Article VII is higher up the validity chain than, say, Article V,[2] which specifies how the U.S. Constitution can be validly amended. And Article V is thus higher up the validity chain than the twenty-seven Amendments added in pursuance of its terms. And these are higher up the validity chain than laws passed by Congress. So although it is true that the Constitution is higher on the validity chain than acts of Congress – which are higher than rules enacted by administrative agencies or state legislatures (in areas of concurrent power) – some parts of the Constitution are higher up the validity chain than others.

The degree of entrenchment is also insufficient for demarcating constitutions and distinguishing them from ordinary laws. For one thing, constitutions need not be entrenched against majority repeal. For another, ordinary laws *may* be entrenched. (Some scholars believe, for example, that the U.S. Congress has the power to entrench its legislation against majoritarian repeal.[3] Although I believe they are mistaken,[4] there is nothing illogical about that position, even if it is normatively unattractive. Nor would such an entrenched piece of ordinary

[1] U.S. Const. Art. VII: "The Ratification of the Conventions of nine States shall be sufficient for the Establishment of this Constitution between the States so ratifying the Same."

[2] U.S. Const. amend. V.

[3] See, *e.g.*, Eric A. Posner and Adrian Vermeule, "Legislative Entrenchment: A Reappraisal," 111 Yale L.J. 1665 (2002).

[4] See Larry Alexander and Saikrishna Prakash, "Mother May I? Imposing Mandatory Prospective Rules of Statutory Interpretation," 20 Const. Comm. 97 at 107 note 22 (2003); John O. McGinnis

legislation be a constitution, though insofar as it is entrenched it would share a characteristic common to most constitutions.)

A constitution may be repealable by majority vote, and ordinary laws may be entrenched against majority repeal. These two points are often overlooked because they produce a very unstable state of affairs and are thus relatively uncommon. In any country in which the constitution is, itself, subject to amendment or repeal by majoritarian processes, and in which the entrenchment of ordinary (nonconstitutional) laws is authorized, majoritarian overturning of entrenchments would merely have to proceed by first overturning the constitution's authorizing provision (and then reinstating it once the entrenched law was eliminated). If there are going to be laws entrenched against majoritarian repeals, it makes more sense for them to be higher in the validity chain rather than lower. Relatedly, if there is going to be a validity chain – so that the validity of a law is tested by reference to some higher, validating law – it makes sense for the validating law to be more difficult to change than the laws it validates.

We can therefore see why constitutions: (1) tend to be written; (2) are invariably higher in the chain of legal validity than ordinary laws (though not all parts of a constitution need be on the same level in that chain); and (3) are almost always more entrenched than ordinary laws (though some laws at the level of ordinary laws in the validity chain may also be entrenched against majoritarian repeal). Because there are many positions in the legal validity chain, and because neither writtenness nor entrenchment is a necessary or sufficient characteristic of constitutions, the line between constitutions and ordinary laws will be a contentious one, and that, in turn, affects the question of whether a country should have a constitution. For it may be the case that every country already has one.

Take the British example again. The anti-constitutionalist might argue that Britain has gotten along without a constitution rather nicely, thank you, and so has no need to enact one. But has it? If so, what are all those scholarly treatments of British constitutionalism about?

The anti-constitutionalist might point out that in Britain, Parliament is supreme, and Parliament acts by majority vote. But there are all sorts of background rules at work here, most of which have never been enacted by a majority vote in Parliament. There are rules defining Parliament itself, rules about what counts as a vote, *etc., etc.* When a British court is asked to apply British law,

and Michael R. Rappaport, "Symmetric Entrenchment: A Constitutional and Normative Theory," 89 Va. L. Rev. 385 (2003) [McGinnis & Rappaport, "Symmetric Entrenchment"].

it must determine whether what is asserted to be an act of Parliament really is such. And that inquiry will take it into territory not occupied by acts of Parliament – constitutional territory, if you will.[5]

Moreover, these background, constitutional rules are entrenched against parliamentary majoritarian repeal – not by formal rules, but by the informal practices and understandings of the British legal community. Because of their informality – which explains their unwrittenness – they can be easily overlooked. But because passing a law by a majority vote in Parliament is not a brute fact but an institutional one, it is subordinate logically to those practices and understandings that make it possible and that count as the British constitution.

Now because I have said that the British constitution is constituted by the practices and understandings of the British legal community, it may appear that I have described the British system as aristocratic rather than democratic. After all, the democratic body – Parliament – must act in pursuance of constitutive rules, the source of which is the practices and understandings of elites. But the picture is, I believe, more complicated than this. First, the constitutional rules of Britain are relatively unconstraining of parliamentary action – unlike, say, those of the U.S. Constitution *vis-à-vis* Congress. Although Parliament, to enact laws, must act in accordance with constitutional norms, whatever a parliamentary majority wants, it can usually get.

Second, the constitutional norms themselves, though they rest on elite practices and understandings, ultimately rest on acceptance by the people of Britain, for the elites whose norms they are have only the authority recognized by the citizens. All law, and thus all constitutional law, written or unwritten, deeply entrenched or unentrenched, rests on acceptance.[6] That is true in Britain. That is true in the United States and Canada. If Article VII of the U.S. Constitution is the highest law in the validity hierarchy of the United

[5] Now, someone may object at this point and say that I have not described judicial review of parliamentary acts on constitutional grounds. Rather, what I have described is nothing more than judicial recourse to those informal understandings that constitute the rule of recognition. And, of course, not only judges, but all officials – indeed, private citizens as well when they need to identify who the officials are and what their official acts are – must necessarily have recourse to the legal system's rule of recognition. But the rule of recognition is not the constitution, and deciding that Parliament has not officially acted is different from deciding that it has acted unconstitutionally.

I disagree. There is no bright line between a rule of recognition and a constitution. There are just rules that stand in a hierarchical relationship to one another in terms of legal validity, with the rules at the apex resting on nothing more than acceptance. (I owe this footnote to my colleague Steve Smith, who *did* raise this objection.)

[6] See Matthew D. Adler, "Popular Constitutionalism and the Rule of Recognition: Whose Practices Ground U.S. Law?" 100 Nw. U. L. Rev. 719 (2006).

States, Article VII itself owes its validity to its moment-to-moment acceptance by the people of the United States. If I were to draft my ideal constitution and then put in it my equivalent of Article VII – "this Constitution shall be deemed the law of the U.S. when Larry Alexander sings 'Begin the Beguine'" – then sing Begin the Beguine, my constitution just would be the U.S. Constitution if, but only if, the rest of the people began regarding it as such.[7] In such an unlikely case, the old U.S. Constitution and its Article VII would be just worthless scraps of paper, as my constitution is overwhelmingly likely to turn out to be.

So all constitutions ultimately rest on acceptance – which makes them not democratic, but anarchic. And all democracies have constitutions – relatively entrenched norms, written or unwritten, which validate the ordinary enactments of democratic majorities.

Once we recognize this, the question of whether to enact a constitution looks ill-posed. The better questions to ask are: Should we formalize the constitution, and if so, how much law should be constitutionalized as opposed to left to democratic majorities?

A simple, unicameral parliamentary system can operate with rather few constitutional rules. These would be rules defining the parliament, rules defining and regulating voting, rules about agenda control and like matters (rules of parliamentary procedure), and perhaps a few others. Once one introduces bicameralism, or a separate executive branch, or federalism, the need for a formal, written constitution appears compelling.

II. SHOULD THERE BE AMERICAN OR CANADIAN-STYLE JUDICIAL REVIEW?

If one accepts that it is desirable to entrench some rules against parliamentary majoritarian repeal – for example, rules defining parliament or establishing a bicameral system, rules separating the powers of the executive, the legislature, and the courts, or rules establishing a federal system – the case for judicial review seems to follow inexorably. If the constitution is higher law than legislation, and if the courts must apply the law to disputes before them, then unless judicial interpretations of these rules are less authoritative than legislative or executive interpretations, the courts must refuse to apply legislative and executive acts that contravene the constitutional rules. Moreover, if the rules are unclear – and if their interpretation turns on discerning the intended

[7] See Larry Alexander, "Originalism, or Who Is Fred?" 19 Harv. J. L. & Pub. Pol'y 321 (1996); Frederick Schauer, "Amending the Presuppositions of a Constitution" in Sanford Levinson ed., *Responding To Imperfection* (1995) 145–61.

meaning of the constitution's authors – then judges are better equipped than other officials or ordinary citizens to get that meaning right. If one objects to judges doing this (instead of, say, legislatures), it must be because one objects to constitutionalizing the issue in the first place. Thus, if one accepts the wisdom of settling and entrenching, say, a specific division of power between the executive and the legislative, or between the federal government and provincial governments, and if the terms of that settlement require ordinary interpretive techniques of the kind courts employ routinely, then one should have no objection to judicial review of disputes over the terms of the settlement.

Of course, if one objects to entrenching a settlement of the issue, one can object, as well, to judicial enforcement of the settlement. More significantly, if it appears the constitution's authors did *not*, in fact, *settle* the matter – that is, they authored, not a determinate *rule* that refers to matters of fact, but an indeterminate *standard* calling for evaluative judgments rather than interpretation, the case for judicial review rather than legislative constitutional determinations is weakened. Many, for example, think of the scope of the commerce power under the U.S. Constitution as involving an evaluative standard rather than a determinate rule, and one that Congress is better able to apply than are the courts.[8] Of course, even if the scope of that power is a standard, it does not follow that Congress's evaluative judgments in applying that standard are superior to the courts'. The courts may be better situated than Congress epistemically or motivationally. I shall return to this point subsequently.

III. SHOULD CONSTITUTIONS HAVE PROVISIONS ESTABLISHING RIGHTS?

The U.S. and Canadian constitutions have rights-establishing provisions. Is that a good idea? Here I want to make several distinctions.

First, one should distinguish between provisions that, themselves, establish a constitutional (legal) right and those that purport to incorporate into the constitution a pre-existing moral right. Is freedom of speech a particular set of privileges and immunities established by the First Amendment to the U.S. Constitution,[9] or is it a pre-legal human right that the First Amendment incorporates into the Constitution by reference?

Second, if the right is one established by the Constitution rather than one that exists independently of it, is it embodied in a rule or in a standard? Some

[8] See, *e.g.*, *United States v. Lopez*, 514 U.S. 549 at 604–14 (1995) (Souter J., dissenting).

[9] U.S. Const. amend. I: "Congress shall make no law . . . abridging the freedom of speech . . ."

believe that the U.S. Constitution itself establishes certain rights, but it does so through evaluative standards rather than rules. If true, then the constitutional interpreter must employ evaluative judgments without there being an independent moral referent for those judgments to track. Is that possible?

I'm inclined to doubt it. Suppose, for example, that there is no moral right of freedom of expression.[10] And suppose a constitution declares freedom of expression to be a constitutional right. Now, it might be the case that this right is embodied in a determinate rule or set of rules. Many believe the First Amendment in the U.S. Constitution was intended by its authors to be no more than a rule against prior restraints such as requirements to seek a government license before publishing. In that case, the absence of a moral right of freedom of expression makes no difference to constitutional jurisprudence. But if the constitutional right of freedom of expression is meant to be a standard requiring evaluative judgments, it is hard to see what those judgments could be based upon in the absence of a moral right.

Should constitutions establish and entrench rights-defining rules? Surely some rules of that type are desirable because they are simply corollaries of the basic governmental structures that it is desirable to establish constitutionally, or instrumentally necessary to the proper function of those structures. A right to petition the government, or a right to criticize candidates, seems to go hand in glove with representative democracy. So constitutional rights of these types are desirable if constitutions are desirable. These instrumental rights may be embodied in rules, in which case, judicial review of their application should be uncontroversial. Alternatively, they may be embodied in standards requiring evaluations in the form of instrumental, not moral,[11] judgments. If so, judicial review will be more controversial, just as it is when the U.S. Supreme Court treats the commerce power as a standard but then rejects Congress's judgment regarding its scope.

Finally, should constitutions establish and entrench rights-defining rules that are viewed as capturing at least part of some real moral rights rather than as implementing constitutional structures? There are, for example, provisions of the U.S. Constitution that are in the form of rules, establish rights, and appear to be unconnected to structures. The prohibition on religious tests for

[10] See Larry Alexander, *Is There a Right of Freedom of Expression?* (2005).

[11] It is a fair question whether instrumental judgments can ultimately be pried apart from moral ones. Deciding upon which means to adopt in pursuit of some end involves weighing the costs of various means, which costs are measured in terms of competing ends that will be set back. And weighing setbacks to some ends against promotion of others will require an evaluative scale that may ultimately be a moral one.

office, or the bill of attainder clauses, may be such rights, though structural accounts of them may be available.

Is it appropriate for constitutional authors to establish and entrench rules implementing moral rights? One argument in favor of this is that moments of constitutional founding or amendment are propitious for accurately capturing the requirements of morality. At such moments, there is substantial deliberation. People are serious and attentive. And a super-majority is typically required for passage.[12] On the other hand, future majorities (short of the super-majorities required to amend the constitution) do have the advantage of historical experience.

IV. SHOULD CONSTITUTIONS ENTRENCH MORAL RIGHTS – AND IF SO, WHAT ARE THE IMPLICATIONS FOR JUDICIAL REVIEW?

Finally, should constitutions entrench moral rights, as many such as Ronald Dworkin believe the U.S. Constitution's framers intended to do?[13] And if so, should those moral rights be judicially enforced against the legislature (and the executive)? Those are the questions I shall devote the bulk of this chapter to answering.

The first step toward answering these questions is to point out that if real moral rights are to be constitutionalized, they must be truncated. Suppose we, the constitutional authors, carefully delineate in specific rules how the branches of government shall be selected and operate, how powers shall be divided among them, and so on. And then we add on provisions that purport to constitutionalize real moral rights. It may turn out that our successors will conclude that, as they see them, real moral rights are inconsistent with the various specific provisions in the constitution setting up the governmental institutions and their powers. If, for example, the due process clause of the Fifth Amendment to the U.S. Constitution refers, *inter alia*, to the real moral

[12] See McGinnis and Rappaport, "Symmetric Entrenchment," *supra* note 4 at 417–26 (arguing the virtues of supermajoritarian rules); John O. McGinnis and Michael B. Rappaport, "Our Supermajoritarian Constitution," 80 Tex. L. Rev. 703 (2002). But see Ethan J, Leib, "Why Supermajoritarianism Does Not Illuminate the Interpretive Debate Between Originalists and Non-Originalists," 2007 Nw. U.L. Rev. Colloquy 7 (disputing the claim that the supermajoritarian origins of the U.S. Constitution support the wisdom of its original meaning); Andrei Marmor, "Are Constitutions Legitimate?" (2007) 20 Can. J. Law & Juris. 69 at 80 (disputing the expertise of the founders regarding morality, though without adverting to the possible moral wisdom of the supermajoritarian and highly deliberative process of constitutional ratification).

[13] See Ronald Dworkin, *Freedom's Law: The Moral Reading of the American Constitution* (1996) at 7–8 [Dworkin, *Freedom's Law*].

right to equal treatment,[14] and if real equality among voters is inconsistent with giving small states equal representation in the Senate,[15] then the Fifth Amendment made the Senate unconstitutional two years after the Senate was established! Of course, no one believes that the Fifth Amendment did this, including those such as Dworkin who argue that the constitutional framers meant to constitutionalize real moral principles. The reason they believe that the Senate was not rendered unconstitutional by the constitutionalized right of equality, however, has to be that the constitutionalized real moral rights operate only within the boundaries laid down by the institutional provisions. In other words, they have to hold that if real moral principles are constitutionalized, they are constitutionalized only in truncated form because that truncation was what was intended.

Now, I am very skeptical that this position is credible as an account of what the framers intended. It is true that if they did intend to constitutionalize real moral rights, they did not see those rights as inconsistent with the constitutional structures they had just labored to define.[16] But Dworkin and his ilk are willing to set aside framers' (mis)interpretations of moral principles in other contexts. (Dworkin, for example, is adamant that the framers of the Eighth Amendment meant to forbid punishments that were really, as a moral matter, cruel and unusual, even if that prohibition covered punishments, such as executions, that the framers believed were not cruel and unusual.[17])

Not only must real moral rights, if constitutionalized, be truncated so as to avoid making the basic constitutional structures themselves subject to constitutional challenge, but, more importantly, *the real moral rights constitutionalized must be subordinated to institutional decisions defining and implementing them.* What do I mean by this? Only the banal but often overlooked point that whatever institution has the final legally authoritative say regarding what the constitution means – whether it is the Supreme Court or the legislature – all actors in the system must treat that institution's decisions defining the constitution's moral rights as correct even if the decisions are incorrect from the other

[14] See *Bolling v. Sharpe*, 347 U.S. 497 (1954) (holding that the due process clause of the fifth amendment, which binds the federal government, contains an equality principle similar to the one binding the states in the fourteenth amendment's equal protection clause).

[15] See *Reynolds v. Sims*, 377 U.S. 533 (1964) (holding that election districts for state senates must be drawn according to the equipopulous "one person, one vote" principle despite the fact that the U.S. Senate itself is not based on population).

[16] And is there any reason to believe that the framers' views of what constitutional structures were consistent with real moral rights will turn out to be inferior to some later court's view, given the deliberations that took place at the "constitutional moment" and the supermajoritarian standard for ratification?

[17] See Dworkin, *Freedom's* Law, *supra* note 13 at 291–302.

actors' point of view. That means that for legal purposes, except for the final authoritative decision maker, it is not real moral rights but rather that decision maker's view of real moral rights that is constitutionally controlling. If that were not the case, then anyone who had a view of real moral rights that was at odds with the final decision maker's would regard himself as *legally* entitled to ignore the final decision maker. The legal system could not perform one of its paramount functions – namely, settlement of moral disagreements.

So the first step in answering the questions of whether real moral rights should be constitutionalized and what are the implications of doing so for judicial review is to point out that constitutionalzing real moral rights requires domesticating them and rendering them subordinate to constitutional structures and institutional decisions – something in tension with their nature as real moral rights and, as such, overriding in practical reason.[18] The second step is to note the oddity of the first question. After all, whether or not we constitutionalize real moral rights, we are nonetheless subject to them.[19] We need not entrench them in our constitutions to be subordinated to their demands. We are always so subordinated. And so, irrespective of whether we put them in our constitutions, they are entrenched norms superordinate to all constitutional and subconstitutional norms – and entrenched, not just against majority repeal, but against any human repeal whatsoever. (Whether God can alter morality is, of course, a much mooted philosophical/theological matter that is fortunately immaterial to my point.)

So whether or not we formally constitutionalize them, real moral rights are already entrenched and superordinate to all legal decisions. What is really at stake, then, in the debate over whether to constitutionalize real moral rights is not whether our legal decisions are to be subordinated to real moral requirements, but instead whether our ordinary legal decisions – legislative, executive, and judicial – are to be legally subordinated to *some institution's view of those moral requirements*.

More precisely, Jeremy Waldron's jeremiads against rights-based constitutional judicial review can read as follows: Legislatures, when enacting and repealing legislation, are always bound by the requirements of morality. (Aren't we all, and all the time?) Thus, when legislatures act, we can assume it is their judgment that their actions pass moral muster. The legislature's view of what morality really requires is therefore implicit in the laws it passes, fails to pass,

[18] See Larry Alexander and Frederick Schauer, "Law's Limited Domain Confronts Morality's Universal Empire," 48 William & Mary L. Rev. 1579 (2007). The subordination of moral conclusions to legal ones is the basic subject of Emily Sherwin's and my recent books. *See* Larry Alexander and Emily Sherwin, *The Rule of Rules* (2001), esp. Ch. 4; *Demystifying Legal Reasoning* (forthcoming).

[19] See, *e.g.*, Joseph Raz, "Incorporation by Law," 10 Legal Theory 1 at 8–10 (2004).

and repeals. What is objectionable then is not making legislation subordinate to real moral rights, whether or not those are found in a constitution, but *making legislation legally subordinate to the judiciary's view of what those rights entail.*[20]

v. IS THE DEMOCRATIC CRITIQUE OF MORAL-RIGHTS-BASED JUDICIAL REVIEW COMPELLING?

This, then, is where the analysis stands. Moral rights and the principles that support them are always "entrenched" and superordinate to legislation and, indeed, to super-majority-enacted constitutional rules. In that sense, entrenching them in constitutions makes them no more trumps of legislation than they already are. Rather, on this level, the question is how to keep them from running roughshod over the other parts of the constitution, the parts that constitute the government and the powers and procedures of its branches.

The real question is not whether to constitutionalize moral principles and rights but is instead which institution's view of morality will be superior within the legal system. Whose say will be final and entrenched (unless it is altered by processes of constitutional amendment)? And it is to this question, I believe, that Waldron's democratic critique is, or should be, directed.

Waldron argues that the legislature's view of the moral constraints on law should be controlling because the legislature is the most democratic institution of government. For the moment, let us accept the contention that the legislature *is* the most democratic institution. Why does that count against judicial review based on morality? As I see it, there are three types of arguments that one can rely upon to reject such judicial review and support legislative supremacy: (1) an argument based on a moral right to democratic decision-making; (2) an argument based on the relative trustworthiness of legislative and judicial determinations of moral matters; and (3) an argument based on the relative ease with which legislative and judicial decisions can be reversed.

Let me begin with the last. It is really but a corollary of the others. Legislative decisions that are made democratically can be reversed democratically. Judicial decisions of the highest court based on constitutional grounds can be reversed by the highest court itself "democratically" – by a majority vote of the justices[21] – but can be reversed by the citizenry only through the super-majoritarian

[20] See generally Jeremy Waldron, "The Core of the Case Against Judicial Review," 115 Yale L.J. 1346 (2006) [Waldron, "The Core of the Case"].

[21] Of course, majoritarian decisions among oligarchs are "democratic" only within the oligarchy. Waldron claims that there is no obvious argument for why judicial decisions on multi-member courts are taken by majority vote, and he vehemently denies that courts' deciding by majority vote makes those decisions "democratic." I assume that the majority vote decision

processes of constitutional amendment.[22] (In some countries, such as Canada, the highest court's ruling can be circumvented legislatively even if it cannot be overturned.)

Now, if one thought that the courts were otherwise better suited to settle moral matters than were legislatures, the fact that only they, by majority vote of the justices, could easily overturn their decisions on moral matters would count in *favor* of letting them have the final say within the legal system. That is why the relative entrenchment argument against judicial review is not independent of the other arguments.

Let me then, working backwards, address the argument regarding (relative) competence. Are legislatures better than courts at determining what morality requires of government actors? Which institution is situated more favorably epistemically? Which institution is better motivated to discover the right answer?

The questions assume that there are correct and incorrect answers to moral questions (or at least better and worse ones). They also assume that we have some epistemic access to those answers, and that some methods, procedures, and motivations are epistemically superior to others.

So then the question becomes: Given how legislatures and courts operate when, respectively, they make law or decide cases, and the characteristic motivations to which legislators and judges are subject, are legislative decisions about the moral constraints on law more likely, as likely, or less likely to be correct than judicial ones? Waldron, at times, appears to argue that they are more likely to be correct. If the conditions the Condorcet Jury Theorem demands are met, and if the theorem otherwise applies to most legislation, then a decision endorsed by several hundred legislators is more likely to be correct than one endorsed by five Supreme Court justices, at least if the issue is a binary one

procedure, although it may owe something to the Condorcet Jury Theorem, is most likely based on practicality: Any other decision procedure might result in stalemate and the absence of a decision, giving an advantage to the judicial status quo ante (the lower court's decision). Obviously, if decisions of multimember courts were to be determined by some substantive standard, such as which judge's opinion is the best reasoned, there would need to be a procedure for determining *that*, and no improvement over the majority-of-judges-rule principle would be accomplished. It would be possible, on the other hand, to give the votes of the judges different weights based on some nonsubstantive principle, such as the most senior judges' votes count for more than the votes of the less senior judges.

[22] Note that if the highest court's decision rests on its interpretation of real moral rights that it finds in the constitution, the overruling amendment would have either to gainsay the court on whether the provision in question did refer to real moral rights, or to gainsay it on the meaning the court gave those real moral rights. And because the citizenry cannot change real moral rights, no matter how supermajoritarian the change, it can repudiate the court's meaning only in the sense of enacting a formal rule excluding it.

("Is this law forbidden by morality?").[23] But there is, or must be, a *ceteris paribus* clause here; and the *ceteris* covers a huge domain.

The question whether the epistemic arguments against judicial review based on morality outweigh those in favor is one I am going to leave unresolved here. It is not that I believe that question is beside the point. Indeed, I believe it is crucial and should be determinative. It is just that answering the question is above my pay grade.[24]

So let me turn to the first argument against such judicial review – namely, that it is undemocratic, and that its undemocratic character is sufficient to condemn it. What is the basis of this argument?

In some places, the democratic arguments against judicial review predicated on morality sound in, or at least give off a whiff of, moral skepticism. Moral skepticism is weaponry much too powerful for this more targeted attack. If moral rights do not exist, then it follows that no moral right to democratic decision-making exists. As elsewhere, thoroughgoing skepticism undermines the skeptic's own position.

At other times, the democratic argument sounds not in moral skepticism per se, but rather in skepticism about moral knowledge – epistemic moral skepticism. Again, however, skepticism is unhelpful to the democratic argument. Leaving aside the oddity of postulating the existence of morality – the overriding reasons by which we should be guided – to which we have no epistemic access, if we cannot claim knowledge of morality, then we cannot then claim knowledge of a moral right to democratic decision-making.

Much more plausible is a softer skepticism, one that accepts both that morality exists and that we can know it, but one that also notes the inherent controversiality regarding both morality's content and the appropriate methodology for obtaining knowledge of that content. The controversiality argument is not one of skepticism but of humility. And humility, this argument goes, argues in favor of democratic resolution of those moral issues that law must, perforce, resolve. Resolution by a (majority of a) court manifests judicial arrogance when humility is due.

[23] See Jeremy Waldron, *Law and Disagreement*(1999); Waldron, "The Core of the Case," *supra* note 20 at 1393.

[24] David Estlund has written extensively on the epistemic qualities of democratic legislation. See, *e.g.*, David Estlund, "Democracy and the Jury Theorem: New Skeptical Reflections" (unpublished MS, 2006); "What's So Rickety? Richardson's Non-Epistemic Democracy," 71 Phil. & Phen. Res. 204 (2005); Book Review, 115 Ethics 609 (2005). See also Frederick Schauer, "Legislatures as Rule-Followers," in R. W. Bauman and T. Kahana eds., *The Least Examined Branch* (2006) at 468–79 (discussing motivational problems that legislatures face with respect to rights that ought to constrain them).

But how does this argument stack up if we resolve the epistemic/motivational superiority issue in favor of courts? Moral issues and methodologies may be inherently controversial, but if courts are better suited than legislatures epistemically and motivationally, humility seems beside the point. I do not want my doctor to humbly defer to my self-diagnoses if her diagnoses are superior to mine. If humility applies here at all, it is I who am arrogant in insisting that my own diagnoses be followed, not she in insisting on following hers.

This brings us then to the final pro-legislature trump card: the moral right of the majority to have its way even when its way is morally wrong. My view is that as an argument in favor of legislatures over courts on matters of moral rights, it is incomplete; and even if the argument is completed, it is, I believe, unpersuasive.

The argument is incomplete because if there *is* a moral right of the majority to prevail even when it is morally wrong, it is presumably a moral right of the majority of *citizens* or *all people affected*, *not* a moral right of the majority of *legislative representatives*.[25] The latter may not accurately mirror the judgments of the former. Indeed, as a general argument against judicial review, and not a parochial one aimed at the U.S. or Canadian courts, the argument overlooks the possibility that the judges themselves might be democratically elected and/or might have to stand for democratic re-election. If judges were elected at large, but legislators were elected by geographic districts, it would be plausible to claim that the courts' decisions had more democratic warrant than the legislature's.[26] So suppose we complete the argument by excluding democratically elected courts from its purview. The legislature now has superior democratic credentials to those of courts. Do its democratic credentials trump courts' hypothesized superior epistemic credentials on moral matters? Do democratic assemblies have a moral right to be morally wrong on all matters within their purview?

I cannot fathom the claim that they do. I have a number of stock examples that I trot out to illustrate my objection, but this one, oft-used, will suffice.

[25] On this point – Who comprises the demos? – see the very important recent article by Robert E. Goodin, "Enfranchising All Affected Interests, and Its Alternatives," 35 Phil & Pub. Aff. 40 (2007) [Goodin, "Enfranchising All Affected Interests"].

[26] The democratic argument for preferring that moral decisions be made legislatively rather than judicially often does presuppose a nonelected judiciary. After all, appellate courts, like legislatures, decide matters by majority vote and are thus "democratic" in that sense. And if judges were elected, they would be as "democratic" as legislatures in that sense as well. The only remaining difference would be that legislatures are typically larger bodies than appellate courts. But if that's dispositive, it suggests that plebiscites should be regarded as superior to legislation for making morally freighted decisions.

In the novella *The Ox-Bow Incident*,[27] a posse has captured two men that most believe, given the evidence before them, are guilty of cattle rustling and murder. The choice the posse faces is between taking the captives back to the nearest town with a court for the two to stand trial, with full due process, or to hold its own trial without legal due process, and if it finds the two guilty, itself administer the requisite punishment (hanging). The majority of the posse opts for the latter course of action.

There are two dissenters. In the story, they argue strenuously for taking the captives to a court for a legal trial, but in the end they lose, and the captives are adjudged guilty and lynched by the posse. And, of course, it turns out that the captives were actually innocent.

Suppose, however, that the two dissenters, employing the element of surprise, could have pulled their guns on the majority, forced it to turn over the captives to them, and then brought the captives to a court. *Would the dissenters have been wrong to do so? Did the majority have a moral right to have its morally wrong way?* Is the latter position even coherent if we assume that majorities, no matter how overwhelming, cannot alter moral rights?[28]

Remember that we are assuming that the epistemic argument has been resolved in favor of courts, not legislatures. So we are faced with this question: If it is likely that the court is morally correct and the legislature is morally wrong, is it nonetheless morally wrong to impose the likely morally correct result and thereby refuse to enforce the likely morally incorrect result? Or, to telescope, does a democratic majority have the moral right to trample others' moral rights? If we block the retreat to the epistemic question, then this is the question. And for me, "no" is the obvious answer.[29]

[27] Walter van Tilburg, *The Ox-Bow Incident* (1940).

[28] Waldron has objected that the scenario portrayed in the story does not resemble a typical legislative procedure. The posse was adjudicating guilt (like a jury) and not legislating. There were no committees, second and third readings of bills, and so on.

These points are correct but not decisive. Suppose the posse were deciding whether to adopt the rule "lynch on the spot" or the rule "transport suspects to the legal authorities." And suppose it set up a committee, which duly reported its recommendation to the entire posse, which then debated the issue and took a succession of votes, with "lynch on the spot" prevailing overwhelmingly. The points in the text would still apply.

[29] See, for further argument on this point, Larry Alexander, "What Is the Problem of Judicial Review?" 31 Austral. J. Legal Phil. 1 at 11–12 note 16 (2006).

I should point out that others have argued, not only that Waldron fails to establish a moral right of democratic legislatures to have their way even when morally wrong, but also that there is a moral right to judicial review of democratic legislation. See Yuval Eylon and Alon Harel, "The Right to Judicial Review," 92 Va. L. Rev. 991 (2006). Eylon and Harel's argument rests on the insensitivity of legislative bodies to the effects of their general laws on particular individuals – that is, on the ever present possibility that legislation that is morally benign may

Now, I want to remind the reader that I am agnostic on the epistemological (and motivational) competence question. Waldron levels some very persuasive criticisms at the way the U.S. Supreme Court approaches moral questions, such as that of abortion. Its tendency to convert moral questions into more legalistic sounding ones is surely to be regretted if what we want is real moral deliberation.

On the other hand, those who argue for legislative supremacy in the resolution of moral issues need to be interrogated about several matters:

1. How are legislatures to be constructed? Through geographic, winner-take-all districting? Through proportional representation of political parties? *Etc.* The inputs of legislative construction will affect the output of moral decisions.
2. If democratic resolution of moral issues is desirable – and if, as is true, the Chinese, say, have a stake in moral decisions made by the U.S. government – then should we not have worldwide democratic decision-making?[30] At what level should moral decisions be made – international, national, state or provincial, municipal, or individual? Do future (and perhaps past) people have a right to have a say – after all, their interests are affected by what our government does – and if so, how can that right be implemented?[31] How do bicameralism, federalism, and separation of powers affect matters?
3. Why favor legislatures over, say, the President, who, in the United States, is elected by the entire citizenry? Or why not advocate plebiscites on moral questions? Or why not prefer democratically elected courts to legislatures? Democratic credentials are not the sole possession of legislatures.
4. To whom do we extend the franchise? Currently, the vote is denied based on age, residence, felony-conviction, and – for some types of

violate moral rights in some fraction of its applications that escape the notice of the legislature. Put differently, their argument might be construed thusly: (1) Even rights-sensitive legislatures are likely to enact laws that, although not intrinsically rights-violative, will violate the rights of particular individuals in certain unforeseen circumstances. (2) Individuals have a moral right not to have their moral rights put at undue risk. (3) Even rights-sensitive legislatures will put individuals' moral rights at undue risk per (1). (4) Judicial review reduces that risk to a morally tolerable level. Therefore, (5) there is a moral right to judicial review. Eylon and Harel's argument could be viewed as a variant on the epistemic/motivational superiority of courts to legislatures, a superiority that forms the basis of a derivative moral right to judicial review.

[30] See, *e.g.*, Goodin, "Enfranchising All Affected Interests," *supra* note 25.

[31] *Ibid.* at 51–5.

legislation – the lack of property-owning taxpayer status. How do these exclusions affect the argument for legislative supremacy?[32]

5. If moral decisions in legislatures are not binary – as most will not be – then how are the intransitivity problems predicted by Arrow to be avoided?[33] Which one of his conditions should be sacrificed, and how does this affect the legislature's democratic credentials?
6. Are electors – and then the legislators they elect – to vote their interests or their judgments? And if the latter, do they vote their conclusions or their principles? And with respect to the electors, how do they trade off their various policy and moral preferences when deciding which legislator to support, and how should those trade-offs be "combined"? Such trade-offs are inevitable and make the legislature's determinations extremely unlikely to reflect the electorate's.
7. Finally, what are we to say about the rights that commentators such as John Ely argued were preconditions for truly democratic decision-making?[34]

VI. IMPLICATIONS

It is time to draw all these threads together. If my analysis on each point has been correct, then what are its overall implications? Here is what I believe follows from the previous discussion:

1. There is a good argument for super-majoritarian establishment of the basic constitutive rules of the government – the rules that define governmental constitutions, their processes, and their procedures – and their entrenchment against repeal by less than super-majorities. Perhaps in a country with a relatively homogeneous and stable elite legal culture, these rules need not be formalized or formally enacted. Perhaps they can remain unwritten and customary. But that possibility does not refute the general point. Nor is there any reason for courts not to enforce the constitutional ground rules or defer to the legislature's interpretations of those ground rules – unless the ground rules are not rules but standards requiring evaluations that the legislature is better equipped to make.
2. There may be a good case for formal super-majoritarian enactment and entrenchment of constitutional rights that reflect the super-majority's

[32] *Ibid.*

[33] See Kenneth J. Arrow, *Social Choice and Individual Values* (1963) at 2–8.

[34] John Hart Ely, *Democracy and Distrust: A Theory of Judicial Review* (1980).

perception of real moral rights. If the super-majority percentage requirement is sufficiently high, and if the epistemic conditions are favorable – conditions of serious and sober deliberation – then there is reason to trust the super-majority's perception more than that of present bare legislative majorities. But for the super-majority's entrenchment of its perception of rights to succeed, it must convert moral rights into formal determinate rules that courts can enforce through ordinary processes of legal interpretation and without recourse to the *courts'* moral views. If the enacting super-majority merely refers to real moral rights without "rulifying" those rights, it will have failed to entrench *its* view of what those rights entail.

3. With respect to real moral rights, as opposed to the founding super-majority's perception and translation of those rights into rules, there is, in one sense, no need to entrench them in a constitution, as the government is always subordinate to moral reasons, whether or not the constitution so says. If the constitution does refer to real moral rights, however, the implication of its so doing is either: (i) to give everyone *legal* warrant for disregarding laws, judicial decisions, and all other governmental commands on moral grounds; or (ii) to give *courts*, and only courts, legal warrant for overriding laws and other governmental actions on moral grounds. Alternative (i) results in anarchy; even judicial opinions are undermined. Alternative (ii) is what critics such as Waldron oppose and others, such as Dworkin, commend.
4. With respect to constitutional judicial review – judicial review, the products of which are only reversible by super-majorities or by the courts themselves – the real issue then is whether to allow the courts to impose *their* view of moral requirements on other governmental actors, including legislative majorities. If legislatures have an epistemic/motivational advantage with respect to morality, then we surely should not hamstring it with morality-based judicial review. On the other hand, if the epistemic/motivational advantage lies with the courts, then there is no reason not to constitutionalize real moral rights and thereby convert them into judicially enforceable legal rights. *At least, that is the case so long as the real moral rights do not undermine the other parts of the constitution or even judicial review itself.*

What do I mean by this last sentence? If the constitution were understood to have made real moral rights into *fundamental law*, there would, in theory, be nothing to prevent citizens from ignoring judicial decisions regarding those rights if the citizens understood moral rights differently from the courts. After all, they would then be *legally* disagreeing as well. The same point holds for lower courts and all other government actors. Thus, to prevent anarchy, the constitution should be understood to have incorporated real moral rights for purposes of the highest court's jurisprudence; but for all other purposes, it should be understood to have incorporated either real moral rights or the highest court's view of real moral rights, with the former legally subordinate to the latter.

This much may be clear enough. But why do I also say that the real moral rights enforced by the courts should not be interpreted to undermine governmental structures? If the founding super-majority set up structures at odds with the real moral rights they also constitutionalized, why should the courts not overturn those structures? Perhaps there is no convincing reason against so doing. One would have to argue that although the courts' view of morality is more trustworthy than the legislature's, it is less trustworthy than the founding super-majority's. If the courts view morality as inconsistent with the basic constitutional structure, they are more likely to be mistaken than correct. But unless one accepts this argument, constitutional structures will always be at risk of judicial invalidation in the name of real moral rights. (Indeed, the courts might even find *themselves* to be unconstitutional on this ground.) And that provides a reason to be leery of constitutionalizing real moral rights.

* * *

I have not attempted to settle the debates over judicial review in general or over judicial review on moral grounds in particular. What I have attempted to do is set forth a clear analytical map of the terrain on which those debates occur. My modest hope is that analytical clarity will keep the debaters from arguing past each other, which is what I suspect is occurring a good deal of the time.

6 The Incoherence of Constitutional Positivism

David Dyzenhaus*

"[Positivism's ideal] is, I suspect . . . rather futile . . . the only effective technique for reducing the common law to a set of rules is codification, coupled of course with a deliberate reduction in the status of the judiciary and some sort of ban on law reporting. But to portray the common law as actually conforming to this ideal is to confuse the aspirations of those who are attempting to arrest the collapse of a degenerate system of customary law with the reality."[1]

A. W. B. Simpson

INTRODUCTION

The term constitutional positivism refers to a family of positions in legal and political theory, many of which are influential in contemporary debates. Members of this family include critics of judicial activism and academics who advocate an enhanced role for legislatures in constitutional interpretation and a diminished role for judges. They tend to see originalism, the idea that there is some original, factually determinable meaning of the constitution that it is the judicial duty to transmit to legal subjects, as a way of disciplining judges in order to confine their activism and diminish their role in legal order.

It is important at the outset to appreciate that constitutional positivism, although a member of the positivist tradition, has a rather complex relationship

* I thank all the participants in the colloquium on constitutional theory at which this chapter was first presented for a most stimulating two days of discussion and, in particular, Grant Huscroft, the colloquium organizer, who prohibited formal presentation of papers, thus ensuring that the two days were entirely devoted to discussion. I also thank Rayner Thwaites for an excellent set of written comments on the first draft of the chapter.

[1] A. W. B. Simpson, "The Common Law and Legal Theory" in A. W. B. Simpson, ed., *Oxford Essays in Jurisprudence* (2nd series, 1973) 77 at 99.

with it.[2] Traditionally, positivism is hostile to judicial review for political reasons to do with ensuring that the law is made by the legislature, because it is in the legislature that collective judgments about the common good are most appropriately made. Positivists from this tradition wish to avoid installing any resource in legal order that will allow judges to claim that they are interpreting the law when, in fact, positivists argue, judges are substituting their own judgment about the good for the legislative one.

I will call this tradition political positivism, to distinguish it from its conceptual descendant in the work of H. L. A. Hart and Joseph Raz, who purport to be engaged simply in describing law, and so claim to be agnostic about such issues as the wisdom of entrenching rights. And I call it political rather than democratic positivism because, as its founder Jeremy Bentham showed, its opposition to bills of rights can be consistently maintained only if one supposes that the decision to entrench a bill of rights is a mistake even when it is taken by the democratically elected representatives of the people who have the overwhelming support of their electorate. When Bentham said that rights talk is "nonsense upon stilts" he did not mean only that such talk is politically dangerous because it gives to judges the opportunity to grab or usurp legislative power. He also meant that to adopt a bill of rights that judges have final authority to interpret is a grave political mistake, no matter how much popular support that measure had and continues to enjoy.

But even if we understand the tradition to which constitutional positivists belong as political, thus avoiding confusion with the late twentieth century offshoot in conceptual positivism, we have to appreciate the feature that distances it from political positivism. Constitutional positivism is political in nature, and shares enough, at least rhetorically, with the tradition of political positivism to make it plausible to think of its proponents as neo-Benthamites. But it is very watered down.

Political positivists do not traditionally argue for an enhanced role for legislatures in constitutional interpretation as an independent good. That is because they are altogether opposed to constitutional interpretation, by which I mean interpretation of allegedly fundamental principles of legal order. Indeed, the very idea that there are such principles, whoever is to interpret them, is

[2] My account here relies on my "The Unwritten Constitution and the Rule of Law" in Grant Huscroft and Ian Brodie, eds., *Constitutionalism in the Charter Era* (2004) 383 at 385–91 [Huscroft and Brodie, *Constitutionalism in the Charter Era*] as developed in chapter 2 of Dyzenhaus, *The Constitution of Law: Legality in a Time of Emergency* (2006) [Dyzenhaus, *Constitution of Law*].

anathema to political positivism. As we will see, constitutional positivists, in contrast, not only concede that such interpretation is desirable, but are also prepared to include rights among these principles. They appear to accept that a society should ensure that its law is consistent with the kind of constitutional commitments commonly found in entrenched bills of rights, as well as with the general array of human rights found in international human rights documents. Thus, the two prominent constitutional positivists on whom this chapter focuses – Jeremy Waldron and Jeffrey Goldsworthy – claim only that we are better off when our formal institutional mechanisms give the legislature, rather than judges, the final say over the interpretation of our society's constitutional and human rights commitments.

I will suggest both that to regard such an enhanced role for the legislature as an independent good becomes possible largely as a result of the kind of judicial role political positivists traditionally dislike and that such activity might be necessary for legislatures to play an enhanced role effectively. But, as we will see, constitutional positivists think that an enhanced role for legislatures is a zero sum affair – what the legislature gains, the judges must give up. I will argue that in making these claims, constitutional positivism reveals itself as deeply incoherent. I will conclude by suggesting that this incoherence affects the positivist tradition in general, including conceptual positivism.

WALDRON ON JUDICIAL REVIEW

Jeremy Waldron has argued in the past that the democratic adoption of a bill of rights is analogous to a situation in which the people of a properly functioning democracy have decided to change to rule by dictator. It amounts to "voting democracy out of existence, at least so far as a wide range of issues of political principle is concerned."[3] More recently, his argument appears to have changed somewhat. The issue for him is not so much whether a bill of rights is adopted, but the formal institutional mechanisms for realizing such rights.[4] Indeed, he assumes that the society in which he will provide his argument – the "core case"– against judicial review has a strong commitment to the idea of individual and minority rights, even a constitutional document that contains a bill of rights.[5]

[3] For such a claim, see Jeremy Waldron, "A Right-Based Critique of Constitutional Rights," (1993) 13 O.J.L.S. 18 at 46.

[4] Jeremy Waldron, "The Core of the Case Against Judicial Review," 115 Yale L.J. 1346 (2006) [Waldron, "The Core of the Case"].

[5] *Ibid.* at 1360.

Waldron seeks to limit his target to what he calls "strong form judicial review," where courts have the "authority to decline to apply a statute in a particular case (even though the statute on its own terms plainly applies in that case) or to modify the effect of a statute to make its application conform with individual rights (in ways that the statute itself does not envisage)."[6] He contrasts "weak form judicial review," where courts "may scrutinize legislation for its conformity to individual rights but they may not decline to apply it (or moderate its application) simply because rights would otherwise be violated."[7] And he cites as examples of weak form review the United Kingdom, where courts may issue a formal declaration of incompatibility of a statute with the rights set out in the *Human Rights Act* but may not invalidate the statute or decline to apply it, and New Zealand, where the *New Zealand Bill of Rights Act* gives courts only the authority to prefer interpretations of legislation that are consistent with the rights and freedoms set out in the Bill. He notes the existence of some "intermediate cases" – for example, Canada, where section 33 of the *Canadian Charter of Rights and Freedoms* gives the national and provincial legislatures the authority to override, for a limited period of time, judicial determinations that a statute is of "no force or effect" because it is "inconsistent with the provisions of the Constitution."[8] But because the override is rarely invoked, Waldron says that the "Canadian arrangement" is a form of strong judicial review.[9]

Waldron quotes the objection made by Jeffrey Goldsworthy that the fact that section 33 is rarely used should not affect one's evaluation of it:

> [S]urely that is the electorate's democratic prerogative, which Waldron would be bound to respect. It would not be open to him to object that an ingenuous electorate is likely to be deceived by the specious objectivity of constitutionalized rights, or dazzled by the mystique of the judiciary—by a naïve faith in judges' expert legal skills, superior wisdom, and impartiality. That objection would reflect precisely the same lack of faith in the electorate's capacity for enlightened self-government that motivates proponents of constitutionally entrenched rights.[10]

[6] *Ibid.* at 1354. [7] *Ibid.* at 1355.

[8] Section 52(1) of the *Constitution Act*, 1982.

[9] Waldron, "The Core of the Case," *supra* note 4 at 1356–7.

[10] *Ibid.* at 1357, quoting from Jeffrey Goldsworthy, "Judicial Review, Legislative Override, and Democracy" in Tom Campbell, Jeffrey Goldsworthy, and Adrienne Stone eds., *Protecting Human Rights: Instruments and Institutions* (2003) 263 at 267. [Goldsworthy, "Judicial Review"]. Waldron's references are to the same essay as it appeared in 33 Wake Forest L. Rev. 451 at 454–9 (2003).

Waldron's response is that the problem with section 33 is that it "requires the legislature to misrepresent its position on rights. To legislate 'notwithstanding the Charter' is a way of saying that you do not think Charter rights have the importance that the Charter says they have," whereas the real issue is different interpretations of the Charter by groups who all think Charter rights are important. In Waldron's view, the problem is not, as Goldsworthy suggests,[11] the wording of section 33 but that as a "matter of practical politics, the legislature is always somewhat at the mercy of the courts' public declarations about the meaning of the society's Bill or Charter of Rights."[12]

But Goldsworthy is surely right. If the distinction between weak and strong form judicial review depends not on constitutional form, by which I mean the formal structure prescribed by some written text, but on how seriously the public takes what judges say, then Waldron's focus on strong form judicial review is misconceived. If, in the United Kingdom, Parliament always amends legislation that has been declared incompatible with human rights, such a declaration is no less powerful a form of review than a formal authorization to judges to invalidate statutes. As Goldsworthy points out, if this proves to be the case, it "will not follow that the judiciary has been given power to trump the democratic process. The democratic process will determine what is or is not politically feasible."[13]

Moreover, when New Zealand courts strain to find an interpretation of a statute that will make it consistent with the rights commitments in the *New Zealand Bill of Rights Act*, or British courts do the same as they seek to comply with the interpretative obligation in section 3 of the *Human Rights Act*, they are engaging in what Waldron seems to think amounts to strong form judicial review – modifying the "effect of a statute to make its application conform with individual rights (in ways that the statute itself does not envisage)."[14] At least they are so engaging if one assumes, as Waldron appears to assume in his description, that there is a fact of the matter about what the statute envisaged such that a rights-conforming interpretation changes the statute's meaning.

At most, in my view, one can say that judges who do not accept that they are under an interpretative obligation to give a rights-conforming interpretation are likely to come to different conclusions from those who do. But to say that the latter judges are changing the meaning begs the question about how meaning is most appropriately determined, whether or not the obligation is one imposed

[11] Goldworthy, "Judicial Review," *ibid.* at 276.

[12] Waldron, "The Core of the Case," *supra* note 4 at n. 34.

[13] Goldsworthy, "Judicial Review," *supra* note 10 at 268.

[14] Waldron, "The Core of the Case," *supra* note 4 at 1354.

by statute, as in New Zealand or the United Kingdom after the enactment of their human rights statutes, or, as some judges thought in those countries prior to the enactment of these statutes, the obligation is one inherent in the common law tradition. Perhaps there is an ambivalence in Waldron's argument at this point between a political positivist position that says that judges should avoid interpretative techniques that strain to preserve rights, even in a legal order that is publicly and legally committed to the protection of rights, and a position that says that those techniques are legitimate when, but only when, they are legislatively prescribed.

This second position would involve a reluctant move away from political positivism, forced by the legislative command imposing on judges the interpretative obligation that the common law tradition always claimed existed to interpret the law in accordance with their understanding of the legal order's constitutional principles. However, as I have suggested and will elaborate subsequently, political positivists should continue to oppose this mode of interpretation even when it is imposed by statute, indeed, even when it is comes about through a popular decision to entrench a judicially enforced bill of rights. Conversely, opposition to strong form judicial review on the basis of such bills of rights should extend through human rights statutes, such as we find in the United Kingdom and New Zealand, to old-fashioned judicial review of executive action on the basis of common law principles of legality.

Waldron's inconsistency in this regard is further revealed by the fact that his choice to make strong form judicial review his sole target means that he excludes from his discussion judicial review of executive action, of which he has this to say:

> [I]t is almost universally accepted that the executive's elective credentials are subject to the principle of the rule of law, and, as a result, that officials may properly be required by courts to act in accordance with legal authorization. The equivalent proposition for legislators has been propounded too: Judicial review is just the subjection of the legislature to the rule of law. But in the case of the legislature, it is not uncontested; indeed that is precisely the contestation we are concerned with here.[15]

In a footnote to the quotation, he says that more could be said about whether his argument "might also extend to judicial review of executive action in the light of statutes enacted long ago or statutes whose provisions require extensive interpretation by the courts," and he adds that "[p]ursuing the matter in this

[15] *Ibid.*

direction might be considered either a *reductio ad absurdum* of my argument or an attractive application of it."[16]

I suspect, for the reason just outlined, that the terminus is a *reductio*, not an attractive application. Indeed, one can make the same argument I sketched about what we can think of as informal declarations of incompatibility. Consider the situation of a common law judge in a legal order with no written constitution, who finds that he has no choice but to conclude that a statute is intended to violate the rule of law. For example, the statute gives to public officials the authority to detain individuals considered to be security risks and states that those individuals are not entitled to a hearing to determine whether or not they have been lawfully detained. Although the judge might decide that he has no choice but to let the individual rot in his legal black hole – a space created by law but in which the writ of the rule of law does not run – he may still, in his judgment, make the informal equivalent of a formal declaration of incompatibility under the *Human Rights Act* by declaring emphatically that the legislature has violated the rule of law. Of course, his declaration might fall on deaf ears. But let us assume, with Waldron, that the society has a strong commitment to the idea of individual and minority rights, sufficient for such an informal declaration of incompatibility to chime with a general public respect for legality.

In such a societal context, the government might feel no less pressure than it does in other constitutional orders to respond positively to a strong judicial statement that a statute contravenes the requirements of the rule of law. That society would, on Waldron's terms, have in respect of judicial judgments of constitutionality – judgments about the requirements of the common law constitution – strong form judicial review, despite the fact that judges not only lacked formal authority to avoid applying an unconstitutional statute, but did not even claim an informal one.[17]

Waldron is in particular trouble on this point because, in making his core case against judicial review, he assumes a societal commitment to human rights. It is the third of four assumptions, the others being that there are: (1) democratic institutions in good working order, including a representative legislature elected on the basis of universal suffrage; (2) a set of judicial institutions, again in reasonably good order; and (3) persisting, substantial, and good faith

[16] *Ibid.* at note 21.

[17] See further on this point, Mark Tushnet, "Weak Form Judicial Review: Is Implications for Legislatures" in Huscroft and Brodie eds., *Constitutionalism in the Charter Era, supra* note 2 at 215 and Paul Rishworth, "The Inevitability of Judicial Review under 'Interpretive' Bills of Rights: Canada's Legacy to New Zealand and Commonwealth Constitutionalism," *ibid.* at 233.

disagreement about rights among the members of the society who are committed to the idea of rights.[18] These assumptions might seem to lead naturally to a conclusion that strong form judicial review is appropriate, especially since Waldron is prepared to pack into his third assumption that it is appropriate in a society that "cherishes rights" to adopt a written declaration of such a rights – a bill of rights.[19]

The apparent naturalness of the path to such a conclusion seems part of the reason that Waldron not only adopts the assumptions, but also makes them explicit, given that his argumentative strategy is to show why the core of the case against strong form judicial review succeeds, even when all the ingredients for such review are in place. However, it is possible that, in contrast to the tradition of political positivism, he is no less an enthusiast of human rights than any proponent of judicial review; all he contests is the most appropriate mechanism for ensuring that such rights are respected.

There is yet another reason for Waldron to adopt these assumptions. They allow him to speak to an audience of scholars either in societies in the "modern Western world,"[20] or in developed societies that have adopted the institutions and moral commitments of the West. In such societies, any democratic case against judicial review has to be made despite these assumptions, because many of the scholars as well as large swaths of "the people" will not take seriously an argument that requires that the society be reformed in such a way that assumption (1), (2), or (3) is dropped. Each is considered crucial to the health of the society.

Assumption (4) can be viewed in this light, but also as simply an inevitable feature of any society in which there is a reasonable plurality of political views. Waldron's argument depends heavily on it, because his core case boils down to the claim that, given the fact of pluralism, one should prefer legislative interpretations of rights to judicial interpretations. He accepts that it is important for a legislature to be alerted to issues of rights that might arise through the application of legislation, but takes this factor to argue for either weak form judicial review or some kind of *ex ante* check – for example, the Attorney General in New Zealand or, a very interesting example to which he does not allude, the Joint Committee on Human Rights in the United Kingdom.[21] I have already noted that the concession to weak form judicial review, together

[18] Waldron, "The Core of the Case," *supra* note 4 at 1360.

[19] *Ibid.* at 1365.

[20] *Ibid.* at 1361.

[21] *Ibid.* at 1370. For the role of such a committee in a theory of constitutional democracy, see David Dyzenhaus, "Deference, Security and Human Rights," in Benjamin J. Goold and Liora Lazarus eds., *Security and Human Rights* (2007) 125 [Dyzenhaus, "Deference"].

with the concession to judicial review of executive action, should not be so lightly made, but for the moment I will focus on the issue of why the legislature should be preferred as the body that finally decides issues of rights. The point, Waldron says, is "as old as Hobbes: We must set up a decision-procedure whose operation will settle, not reignite, the controversies whose existence called for a decision procedure in the first place."[22]

The main reasons to support strong form judicial review when it comes to issues of rights are, in Waldron's view, that rights are presented to courts in the context of specific cases; that the courts will orient their decisions to the bill of rights; and that reasoning and reason-giving play a prominent role in judicial deliberation.[23] Against the first reason, Waldron points out that by the time the issues get to the highest appellate courts, they are often framed in the most abstract fashion, whereas legislatures can consider legislation on the basis of individual cases.[24] Against the second, he seems to argue that when deciding issues of rights, an orientation to a bill of rights is an unhelpful distraction because such bills are platitudinous, tend to encourage "rigid textual formalism," and prevent judges from going directly to the moral reasons at stake in the case.[25] In regard to the third, Waldron finds judicial reason-giving cramped and unhelpfully focused on relevant law, in contrast to the full range of moral reasons legislators can take into account when they are minded to do so.[26] His point seems to be that if we want decisions about the content of our laws to be morally justified, we should give a monopoly on making law

[22] Waldron, "The Core of the Case," *supra* note 4 at 1371, referring to Thomas Hobbes, Richard Tuck ed., *Leviathan* (1996) 123 [*Leviathan*]. Hobbes, however, was far from supporting Waldron's position. Although Hobbes was opposed to the common law, he regarded judges as under a duty to interpret enacted law in the light of their understanding of the principles of legality that inhere in every legal order, his laws of nature. In addition, when Hobbes stated his regress argument – that the sovereign has to have the final authority to interpret the law, otherwise he would not be the sovereign – he was careful explicitly to confine the argument to enacted law and to exempt the principles of legality; see *Leviathan* at 224. Finally, it is important for Hobbes that, in any legal order, the final authority is an interpretative authority, which is to say, not a power to override. (See my essay, "Hobbes' Constitutional Theory," in Ian Shapiro ed., Hobbes, *Leviathan* (forthcoming). Only if the legislature offers an interpretation do judges owe the legislature deference properly so called. For a careful discussion of deference in the constitutional context, see Aileen Kavanagh's contribution to this volume, "Deference or Defiance? The Limits of the Judicial Role in Constitutional Adjudication." For an excellent discussion of Hobbes in the context of the overarching themes of this volume, see Mark Walters, "Written Constitutions and Unwritten Constitutionalism," in this volume.

[23] Waldron, "The Core of the Case," *supra* note 4 at 1379.

[24] *Ibid.* at 1380.

[25] *Ibid.* at 1382.

[26] *Ibid.* at 1382–6. He provides an example of legislative debate in the United Kingdom, where the legislators engaged in a full and mutually respectful moral deliberation on the deeply contentious issue of abortion.

to the forum in which uninhibited and full moral reasoning can take place. In addition, he points out that even in judgments that are regarded as moral landmarks, the space given to this kind of reasoning is usually small and the quality of the reasoning, evaluated from the perspective of moral philosophy, is not first rate.

In the final result, Waldron's core case seems to amount to the claim that as long the legislature in a democratic, rights-respecting culture is functioning normally, given that contentious issues about rights will be ultimately resolved by majority vote – whether in the appellate courts or in the legislature – it is better that the legislature, with its democratic credentials and its capacity to engage in full deliberation, take the final decision about rights. Only if his assumptions do not hold – especially, it seems, the assumption that the legislature in a democratic, rights-respecting culture is functioning normally – is there, he thinks, a possible case for strong form judicial review.

There are at least six things wrong with this argument. The first is its selectivity. That parliaments on occasion engage admirably in moral debate is to be welcomed. But constitutional positivists are just as prone as common law enthusiasts, if not more so, to romanticize their favoured institution – one whose reputation among the people often seems rather low these days because of the popular perception that legislatures act as rubber stamps for powerful governments. Far from being reason-debating forums, they often fail even to be reason-demanding forums.[27] Consider, for example, that when the United Kingdom renewed the *Anti-Terrorism, Crime and Security Act*, an Act driven through Parliament in 2001 by a government uninterested in debate, this was done by ministerial order, discussed before an almost empty chamber.

Second, very important in compelling the kind of moral debate Waldron regards as paradigmatic are judicial decisions that call into question whether a statute is compatible with constitutional commitments. I am by no means suggesting that judges are the only agents of promoting such debate. Parliamentary committees that are given the role of requiring that Parliament engage in such debate might be even more effective, if they are given the right kind of institutional teeth and, even more important, if they operate in a political culture in which politicians are willing to take the committees seriously. But even if it is right that such committees might be more effective than judges, the issue is not an either/or one. If judges are an essential element in sustaining the culture, the point is to work out how best these institutions should interact. Thus, as I suggested, the enhanced role for legislatures in ensuring that

[27] See Dyzenhaus, "Deference," *supra* note 21.

their legislation complies with and furthers constitutional commitments often comes about because they are prompted – even forced – by other institutions of legal order to debate their commitments.

Third, there is a problem about regarding the kind of debate in which legislators at their best engage as paradigmatic, so that judicial reasoning, even at its best, falls short.[28] If one task of judges is to ensure that the decisions and actions of other officials are faithful to law, including constitutional commitments, one would expect their reasoning to be driven by legal reasons, not by the all-things-considered kind of moral reasoning in which legislators might engage. It would be instructive in this regard to compare the reasoning that appears in Hansard when legislators do take the time to engage in moral debate, with the reasoning in the reports of a conscientious legislative committee such as the Joint Committee on Human Rights and the reasoning of the judges of the House of Lords in a human rights decision. Although each forum will consider the same range of issues, the way those issues are formulated and discussed is quite different.

The Joint Committee lists concerns about the human rights implications of government actions and proposed legislation, relying on a wide range of material: judicial decisions, international legal documents, comparative material, its discussions with government ministers, and reports of other legislative committees. These concerns provide a resource for legislative and public debate as well as for judicial deliberation, should legislation be challenged. Legislative debates are, for the most part, concerned with the justifications in policy and morality of proposed legislation. Legislators do not engage in legal argument, even though there are often many lawyers among them, and even when they are reacting to a judicial decision that a statute is incompatible with constitutional commitments. Rather, they make claims and assertions about the compliance of their proposed measures with constitutional commitments.

In all three of these forums, then, there will figure elements of moral, legal, and policy-based reasoning, but which elements dominate will depend on the attributes of the forum and all, I suspect, are necessary if the legal order is to satisfy a requirement that I take to be the ultimate commitment of legal order.

[28] In my view, the problem is compounded by Waldron's contribution to this volume, "Do Judges Reason Morally?" There, Waldron seems to argue that the kind of moral reasoning judges are ill-equipped to undertake is the kind of reasoning in which all that matters is moral considerations – uncluttered, that is, by constitutional and other legal commitments. No one would disagree with that proposition. The issue is surely whether judicial review, whether strong or weak form, is illegitimate, in part because it involves judges making moral judgments about the consequences of their society's legal commitments. Waldron does not, in his contribution to this volume, appear to argue that it is illegitimate.

I mean here the commitment that all public decisions be fully justified, where part of that requirement is that the decisions are shown to be at least consistent with constitutional commitments and, preferably, as advancing the project of a progressive realization of such commitments. In addition, that commitment depends far more on legal culture than it does on the formal institutions of legal order. That the equivalent of the Joint Committee on Human Rights in Australia is far less effective in promoting compliance with rights has, I would suggest, much to do with the astonishingly positivistic ethos that prevails among Australian judges and lawyers in general.[29]

The fourth problem is that Waldron does not appear to take into account the function of judicial decision-making that involves applying general rules to particulars.[30] The issue is not so much whether, as he thinks, legislation can be generated because of a single case, but whether the legislature might appropriately decide single cases; and here one would have to take into account the possibility that such decisions could amount to bills of attainder. Conversely, when judges decide single cases in which the content of the law is in issue, although their reasoning is framed by the case, the question for them is how to understand the law given the problems thrown up by the case. And of course "law" here does not mean, say, just the statute that is most directly relevant, but all the relevant law, including constitutional principles. Legislatures could try to engage in this kind of reasoning, but then their reasoning would mimic the reasoning that Waldron disparages.

The fifth problem that affects Waldron's position stems from his thought that, whereas strong form judicial review is inappropriate in a well-functioning democracy, it might be appropriate in other political orders. It is worth recalling here that John Austin made a significant break with Bentham when he argued that judges were not only in the business of making law, but that they did not do enough of this. And he made that break because he thought that Bentham had not foreseen the dangers of concentrating a monopoly of law-making power in a legislature that would be captured by the ignorant masses. In other words, Austin wished to carve out a space in positivist legal theory for a judicial elite who could counter a legislature controlled by the enfranchised masses.[31]

Curiously, Jeffrey Goldsworthy suggests the same idea as lying behind the post-Second World War turn to judicial enforcement of constitutional rights.

[29] For a comparison of the two committees, see Carolyn Evans and Simon Evans, "Legislative Scrutiny Committees and Parliamentary Conceptions of Human Rights," [2006] 4 P.L. 784.

[30] See T. R. S. Allan's contribution to this volume, "Constitutional Justice and the Concept of Law."

[31] John Austin, *Lectures on Jurisprudence* Vol. II (1885) at 532–3.

It "shifts power to people (judges) who are representative members of the highly educated, professional, upper-middle class, and whose superior education, intelligence, habits of thought, and professional ethos are deemed more likely to produce enlightened decisions."[32] This, he says, is a return to "mixed government"; an "aristocratic" element is reinserted "into the political process to check the ignorance, prejudice and passion of the "mob."[33] Although he, like Waldron, is opposed to this idea in well-functioning democracies, both he and Waldron seem to suggest that such an aristocratic element might well be appropriate in legal orders that have not yet made the transition to liberal democracy.

But Goldsworthy leaves out the main political impetus for the rights and constitutional revolutions of the period since the Second World War. The impetus was a reaction against a particular kind of elite rule, the rule of highly authoritarian elites, including fascists, Nazis, communists, and the political relicts of colonialism, notably the Afrikaner Nationalist governments of apartheid South Africa. In some of these, it is true that the regime managed to secure the enthusiastic support of a "mob," which formed some significant part of the population. But the reaction was not to mob rule in itself; rather, it was to the power of governments to oppress.

Moreover, it took some serious self-examination for some societies, notably the United Kingdom, to realize that their governments were also capable of at least small-scale oppression of human rights, so that human rights protections were needed there as well, not just for those in their nonage. A hard-won insight for most parents, or at least for me, is that one of the benefits of bringing up children is an insight into one's own "self incurred" immaturity, so that one can make a belated, but hopefully not unsuccessful, attempt to finally grow up. And the reaction by governments such as the United States of America, the United Kingdom, Canada, and Australia to the phenomenon of international terrorism might well serve as examples of the ever-present danger of immaturation. In the light of such developments, I think we should question the resurgence of the kind of utilitarianism that informed Britain's colonial policy – the view, aptly termed "Government House utilitarianism,"[34] that peoples in their "nonage" (as Mill famously put it in *On Liberty*)[35] cannot be trusted

[32] Goldsworthy, "Questioning the Migration of Constitutional Ideas: Rights, Constitutionalism and the Limits of Convergence," in Sujit Choudhry ed., *The Migration of Constitutional Ideas* (2006) 115 at 122 [Goldsworthy, "Questioning the Migration"].

[33] *Ibid.*

[34] Amartya Sen and Bernard Williams, "Introduction: Utilitarianism and Beyond" in Sen and Williams eds., *Utilitarianism and Beyond* (1982) 1 at 16.

[35] John Stuart Mill, *On Liberty*, in Richard Wollheim ed., *John Stuart Mill: Three Essays* (1975) 1 at 15–16.

to govern themselves. Indeed, it was just this view that led to Britain being the principal force in drafting the *European Convention on Human Rights* to govern the untrustworthy Europeans, but not, of course, the always trustworthy government and legislature of the United Kingdom.[36]

The sixth and final problem has to do with my claim that Waldron's acceptance of judicial review of executive action might prove a *reductio* of his case against strong form judicial review. Consider again a society in which there is no entrenched bill of rights, but there is a human rights culture such that the public expects legislators to amend a statute to bring it into line with judicial decisions that pronounce the statute valid but express concern about the fact, as the judges understand it, that the statute violates the human rights commitments of their society. Moreover, the legislators always live up to that expectation. As I have already suggested, such a society is, in substance, no different from one in which there is a fully functional entrenched bill of rights.

In sum, for a political positivist, the deep mistake should be a change in political culture from one in which it is a sufficient condition for the legitimacy of a political decision that it has been voted into law by a majority in Parliament to a human rights culture, where a decision must also comply with human rights and other constitutional commitments. But what matters is that the mistake is made, not the form in which it manifests itself. Moreover, it is important to see that the issue need not be characterized as grandly as one about a human rights culture. It could just as well be characterized as one about a culture of legality, in which principles such as those that figured on Lon L. Fuller's list[37] are associated with the society's commitment to the rule of law. If, for example, the public expects that the legislature will amend a statute that is pronounced by judges to be valid but also close to a bill of attainder, and thus in violation of the principle of generality, and the legislature always reacts positively to such pronouncements, then the same mistake is made.

In other words, the objection of the tradition of political positivism to entrenched bills of rights is that their entrenchment is designed to promote, even to create, a human rights culture. For example, the entrenchment of the *Canadian Charter of Rights and Freedoms* was certainly intended to bring about a qualitative change in Canada's human rights culture – that is, a culture that already existed but the further development of which required the Charter, whereas, and more dramatically, the Interim and Final Constitutions of

[36] See A. W. B. Simpson, *Human Rights and the End of Empire: Britain and the Genesis of the European Convention* (2001).

[37] Lon L. Fuller, *The Morality of Law*, rev. edn., (1969) ch. 2.

post-apartheid South Africa were meant to be important elements in creating such a culture.[38]

The first attempt has been very successful and it remains to be seen what will happen with the second. But it is important to know that in the debates both before and after entrenchment in Canada, critics of that project complained precisely because they foresaw that entrenchment would bring about a change in political culture. Moreover, these critics saw the Charter as the consolidation and deepening of a project that had existed for as long as common law judges had used presumptions of statutory intent to mould the content of legislation into a shape more consistent with the judges' understanding of the rights and interests protected by the common law.

As John Willis, Canada's leading public lawyer of the twentieth century and one of the common law world's foremost critics of judicial review, said, such judges are engaged in an attempt to create a "common-law Bill of Rights."[39] They invoke their preferred maxims of statutory interpretation "not as a means of discovering an unexpressed intent but as means of controlling an expressed intent of which they happen to disapprove,"[40] and they seek thereby to install what Willis called a "Pseudo Bill of Rights."[41] But, it is important to emphasize, Willis was not advocating the installation of genuine, entrenched bill of rights through the democratic process. He was objecting to the thin edge of the wedge that he detected in traditional, common law review of executive action.

Willis and his heirs, most prominently located in the United Kingdom at the London School of Economics and in Canada at Osgoode Hall Law School, represent, in my view, a more authentic manifestation of twentieth century political positivism than do either Waldron or Goldsworthy.[42] They espouse a kind of leftwing neo-Benthamism, a political positivism that regards law as the necessary instrument for conveying judgments about collective welfare to the officials who will have to implement those judgments. Law is the commands of an elite, who make judgments about utility that are then put into practice by expert officials. Official expertise is required because the commands are that

[38] Though the creation was not entirely ground-up. As I have argued elsewhere, the practice of some lawyers and judges during the apartheid era, a practice that depended on a commitment to common law principles of legality, was an important ingredient in the respect for legality on the part of important individuals in the liberation struggle – see David Dyzenhaus, *Judging the Judges, Judging Ourselves: Truth, Reconciliation and the Apartheid Legal Order* (1998).

[39] John Willis, "Administrative Law and the British North America Act," 53 Harvard L. Rev 251 at 274 (1939) [Willis, "Administrative Law and the BNA Act"].

[40] *Ibid.* at 276.

[41] *Ibid.* at 281.

[42] Perhaps the best known work of this group is J. A. G. Griffith, *The Politics of the Judiciary*, 5th edn., (1997).

legislative mandates be carried out, and that means that expertise is necessary to develop as well as to apply the mandates.

It is important to see that it is not only law that has an instrumental role in the neo-Benthamism of these leftwing lawyers. The institutions of democracy, including parliament, also have an instrumental role. Parliament is useful in so far as it provides the forum in which judgments about utility or welfare can be given proper legal form, so that the executive can get on with the job. It follows that legitimacy in their theory comes from success – from successful delivery of social programs. They might not, then, be best understood as seeking to provide what we might think of as a normative account of law, an account of law's authority, nor even of politics or democracy. Rather, their theory is completely parasitic on the existence of a social democratic program. If such a program is in place, they have a theory about how best to deliver it.

The role of judges is thus vexed within their theory. Because law is simply an instrument of the social policy of the powerful, the only analytical apparatus one needs to understand law is something like H. L. A. Hart's rule of recognition,[43] which provides technical or factual criteria for what counts as authoritative. The only institutional apparatuses one should have in place are, first, the legislative body that frames the policy of the government as law. Second, there are the administrative officials who see to it that law is implemented effectively and who will also, under conditions of complexity, have a limited law-making function. Finally, one needs a staff of judges, but only in the sense of a supervisory staff of officials who are capable of checking that the administrative officials stay within the limits of the law, where the determination of such limits is conceived as a technical or factual task – that is, one that does not require the supervisory officials to do more than check on jurisdictional limits; for example, to ensure that tax officials do not decide immigration matters.

In sum, these left neo-Benthamites are opposed not only to bills of rights, to formalized "nonsense upon stilts." They are also opposed to any account of the rule of law that includes principles capable of being elevated by supervisory officials or judges into unwritten constitutional principles, which can then be abused to control "an expressed intent of which they happen to disapprove."[44]

To the extent that such neo-Benthamites concede that there are principles of legality that go beyond those that serve to determine factually conceived legislative intent, they compromise their theory. However, it is worth remarking that almost without exception they have not been able to avoid such compromises. The idea that the rule of law is a set of unwritten constitutional

43 H. L. A. Hart, *The Concept of Law* (1961) ch. 6 [Hart, *The Concept of Law*].

44 Willis, "Administrative Law and the BNA Act," *supra* note 39 at 276.

principles that should inform the determination of the limits of the law has a siren-like effect on almost all twentieth-century neo-Benthamites. Although, at times, they might advocate creating a world in which there is law but no judges, they find great difficulty in maintaining that stance. Often, their fervent opposition to the judiciary turns into the whimper of counsels of judicial restraint, with no principled basis offered for when judges should intervene or when they should not. Instead, they find themselves drawn into discussions of when judges overstepped the line, and so, almost despite themselves, they presuppose the legitimacy of the judicial review, as long as judges stay within the (unelaborated) limits of their role, which brings me to my critique of Goldsworthy.

GOLDSWORTHY ON CONSTITUTIONAL INTERPRETATION

Goldsworthy's writings on constitutional interpretation are especially susceptible to the problem just sketched. He has recently argued that non-originalism – the theory that judges may, by interpretation, give new meanings to constitutional provisions – is refuted by consideration of the provision in the Australian Constitution that the national Parliament is to make laws "for the peace, order, and good government" of Australia.[45] Read literally, Goldsworthy says, this phrase appears to give judges the authority to invalidate legislation that, in their view, is contrary to peace, order, and good government – for example, laws that are not in compliance with contemporary understandings of human rights. But it is obvious, he claims, that judges may not do this, because the phrase is clearly understood to be a stock one, used by the Imperial Parliament to confer "unlimited, plenary power with respect to the subject-matters listed,"[46] a power that does not contain judicially enforceable limits. Indeed, Goldsworthy says this example is a *reductio ad absurdum* of non-originalism, one not confined to this sweeping, general phrase, given that it "applies to all legislative powers," including "more specific words, defining particular powers or rights, when they too have a clear, original meaning."[47]

However, the Imperial Parliament did not say that the Australian Parliament had an "unlimited, plenary power." It spoke, for instance, of "good government." If the Australian Parliament sought to change the system of government by installing a dictatorship, a power that was once thought to be both non-justiciable and without limit, could, for good reason, be found by judges to be both limited and justiciable. Goldsworthy's claim about this provision is no

[45] Goldsworthy, "Questioning the Migration," *supra* note 32 at 130.
[46] *Ibid.* at 131.
[47] *Ibid.* at 131–2.

less vulnerable than claims that used to be made about the non-justiciability of the prerogative.

It fails, therefore, to follow from this example, as Goldsworthy thinks it must, that judges are only entitled to give a new meaning to a constitution because an original meaning cannot be discovered, so that it may be said both that there is an indeterminacy and that judges are entitled to rectify it.[48] First, for judges to accept this as an account of what they either do or should be doing, they would have to reject a feature of adjudication that Goldsworthy himself relies on in criticizing Raz's argument that "courts have a moral authority to change constitutional meaning, even when it is determinate, in the interests of justice or good government."[49] As Goldsworthy notes, and as Ronald Dworkin has emphasized, judges "take great pains to demonstrate that their interpretation is faithful to the constitution as it is."[50] However, as Dworkin has pointed out, if we are to take those pains seriously, the idea that judicial interpretation works in two stages "suggests a plainly inadequate phenomenological account of the judicial decision."[51] Indeed, originalist and non-originalist judges disagree about how to interpret, but agree that it is not legitimate for judges to change the law. Goldsworthy's claim that judges have discretion when law – on some originalist or plain fact understanding – runs out, is as at odds with this feature of adjudication as is Raz's claim that judges should decide their constitutional cases on the basis of morality, rather than law. From the judicial perspective, the moment of indeterminacy, in the sense that Goldsworthy uses that term, never arrives.

Of course, judges might well be lying, a possibility Goldsworthy does contemplate.[52] But, still, it is worth keeping in mind that although judges will often use various expressions to indicate that the problem of interpretation facing them is a difficult one, they regard themselves as under a duty to find an answer to the problem that they can present as fully determined by all the

[48] *Ibid.* at 132.

[49] *Ibid.* at 128, referring to Joseph Raz, "On the Authority and Interpretation of Constitutions: Some Preliminaries," in Larry Alexander ed., *Constitutionalism: Philosophical Foundations* (1999) 152 at 177, 180–1, 182–3, 186, and 189.

[50] Goldsworthy, "Questioning the Migration," *supra* note 32 at 128.

[51] Ronald Dworkin, "Hard Cases," in *Taking Rights Seriously* (1977) 81 at 86.

[52] See his contribution to this volume, "Unwritten Constitutional Principles." In that chapter, Goldsworthy seeks to drive a wedge between myself and T. R. S. Allan by arguing that there is a tension in our common law position manifested in the fact that Allan believes that a statute inconsistent with the common law constitution is invalid, whereas I hold that it might be valid though in some significant sense illegal. In my view, this difference is about judicial remedies, not about substance, and Goldsworthy's attempt to make more of it than that exhibits a positivist obsession with validity.

relevant legal reasons. The idea that law is indeterminate in Goldsworthy's sense figures, to my knowledge, only in the rhetoric of originalist judges as the moment when they might resort to norms of a different legal regime from the one they take themselves to be ordinarily confined.

For example, if originalist judges are interpreting a statute, these might be the norms of the common law or of noncustomary or unincorporated international law, and if they are interpreting a constitutional text, these might be the norms of a foreign constitution or the norms of the common law or of noncustomary or unincorporated international law. But, as I have indicated, the moment of indeterminacy – the occasion on which they are entitled to resort to these alien norms – never arrives. Rather, the claim that the judges would, on the right occasion, rely on the norms is used to pay some kind of lip service to this different legal regime just because its existence cannot be denied. But its norms are not permitted entry into the interpretative field of what originalist judges consider to be relevant law. Originalists are committed, in other words, not only to a variety of kinds of dualism, but also to keeping the different legal regimes apart, unless the one in which they feel most at home – the regime established by statute law – compels them to do otherwise.[53]

Indeed, the judicial version of constitutional positivism is a stance of judges who try to follow a positivist ideal of fidelity to law despite the fact that they work within legal orders in which the Benthamite dream of a completely codified legal order, one in which all law is enacted positive law with a determinate content, was not realized.[54] They are thus forced to try to make the legal order in which they find themselves conform as far as possible to their understanding of law and the rule of law.[55]

These judges are committed by their understanding of the doctrine of legislative supremacy to applying the law enacted by their legislatures in a manner true to the idea that the legislature has a monopoly on law-making, so that judges should seek to understand statutes as providing rules with a factually determined content. But as judges in a common law legal order, they have to

[53] For an exploration of dualism in this context, see chapter 4 of Dyzenhaus, *Constitution of Law*, *supra* note 2. For a defence of dualism from a perspective much influenced by both Waldron and Scalia, see James Allan and Grant Huscroft, "Constitutional Rights Coming Home to Roost? Rights Internationalism in American Courts," (2006) 43 San Diego L. Rev. 1. I suggested at the colloquium that there might be another member or version of the positivist family whom we have to take into account in understanding the phenomenon of constitutional positivism – nationalistic positivism, a stance that seeks to insulate a legal order from "polluting" outside sources, especially international law, but including foreign law from whatever source.

[54] I take James Allan's argument in this volume, "The Travails of Justice Waldron," to support this claim.

[55] See David Dyzenhaus, "The Genealogy of Legal Positivism," (2004) 24 O.J.L.S. 39–67.

contend with the fact that they have an interpretative role that goes far beyond what political positivism considers ideal, a role premised on the idea that their judgments are authoritative expositions of the law. They do their best to make sense of that role through a rigid doctrine of the separation of powers. Whereas the legislature has a monopoly on law-making, judges have a monopoly on law interpretation. But they exercise their monopoly by seeking to be true to their ideal of law and so seek to tether themselves to what they claim to be the factually determined content of the legislature's commands. If their legal order includes an entrenched bill of rights that either gives them or is taken to give them an authority to invalidate statutes that conflict with the bill, they will, in turn, interpret the provisions of the bill as a set of commands, each with a factually determinable content, and thus will limit the scope of judicial review to clashes between facts about a statute and facts about the bill of rights.

It is important to note two features of this stance, both of which are problematic for constitutional positivism, and even more problematic for the tradition of political positivism. First, constitutional positivists advocate originalism as a means of curbing judicial activism – the propensity of judges to affirm their interpretation of a bill of rights over the legislature's. However, originalism does no better on this score than any other theory of interpretation. Because originalism is a set of interpretative techniques judges use to resolve hard cases – cases in which there is reasonable disagreement about what the law requires – whether originalist judges will affirm their interpretation depends on whether they "discover" inconsistencies between alleged facts about their bill of rights and alleged facts about statutes. If the judges discover these often, they will be, by definition, activist, which goes a long way to show the unhelpfulness of that label.

Second, originalist judges are, in their own way, true to Dworkin's description of the phenomenology of adjudication. If we advert to Hart's well-known distinction between the core of determinate law and the penumbra where law is indeterminate,[56] one could say that they accept that distinction but never happen to find themselves in the penumbra, the area in which they would have to exercise a discretion based on moral considerations and arguments.

So whereas Waldron's neo-Benthamism is an unsuccessful attempt to dislodge judges from their constitutional place, Goldsworthy attempts to stabilize their place along neo-Benthamite lines, by resorting to a moderate originalism. But Goldsworthy's argument also fails because his theory of interpretation relies on an understanding of judicial discretion that the judges most sympathetic to

[56] H. L. A. Hart, "Positivism and the Separation of Law and Morals," in Hart, *Essays in Jurisprudence and Philosophy* (1983) 49 at 64.

his arguments would reject. Indeed, while I have dealt with these two leading constitutional positivists for the most part in separate sections, the problems identified for each also affect the other, with some slight variations. That is because their problems are symptomatic of positivism's struggle to survive in a legal world that has changed in ways that make its relation to legal practice ever more tangential.

POSITIVISM AND CONSTITUTIONALISM

At issue in the debates about constitutional interpretation is not whether judges have to exercise judgment about how to interpret the law. Rather, the issue is how to understand that judgment; whether, with political positivists, as a political judgment ultimately unconstrained by law that settles by quasilegislative fiat law's content, or, with Dworkin, as a matter of principles already implicit in the law that determine the answer to the case in the sense that the judge's interpretation strives to represent the law in its best moral light. As Dworkin has consistently argued against conceptual positivists, that debate does not turn on an inevitable fact of the matter, whether judicial judgment is more as a matter of fact like legislation or like interpretation, but on political commitments to do with the point of legal order. Is the point of law to be an effective instrument of the powerful, or is it to ensure that political power is exercised in accordance with principles of legality?

Judges, as we know, are required to adopt the second position. The constitutional positivists among them will attempt to limit their understanding of principles of legality to those that help determine a content that can be represented as the content the legislature, in fact, intended to transmit to legal subjects. But whether such judges are in a common law legal order, or in a legal order in which there is weak or strong form judicial review, they find that their understanding of their obligation of fidelity to law is inconsistent with many of the pieces of constitutional furniture in place.

Legal theorists who belong to the same family – for example, Waldron and Goldsworthy – do not seem, at least at the present time, to know what to do about that furniture. Neither seems to want to do what A. W. B. Simpson, in the epigraph, taken from what is in my view a classic contribution to legal philosophy, describes as necessary to make legal order conform to a positivist ideal. They will not, that is, strip the legal order bare, perhaps because they sense that such a stripped-down legal order would not count as such. It would, at the least, be bereft of much of what they, themselves, associate with legality. But the tensions in their position mount with every extra piece of furniture they are willing to leave in place.

Conceptual positivism does not have the same problem. Conceptual positivists turn the debunking account of judicial discretion given by political positivists into an allegedly descriptive account. They are thus doomed to concluding that the core of law recedes as legal orders use entrenched bills of rights and other written instruments both to make constitutional commitments explicit and to add to them, and as international human rights law plays a more pervasive role in domestic law. But – the lesson we can learn from Simpson – this process merely accentuates problems that conceptual positivism always encountered in explaining the common law or, as Fuller argued, any standard list of principles of legality. Whereas some, like Raz, seem cheerful enough at the prospect of a theory that has no serious connection with contemporary legal practice, or perhaps with practice at any time, others have felt compelled to take account of what we can think of as the real world of constitutionalism. Hence the development of inclusive legal positivism, the version of conceptual positivism that asks us to be aware of the logical possibility of a legal order not based on constitutional or fundamental moral principles of legality, but, when it comes to the real world of law, abandons that possibility and adopts a more or less Dworkinian mode of understanding law.[57]

Note that Kelsen's legal theory is quite different from all the variants of legal positivism described so far. Constitutionalism, by which he understands an entrenched bill of rights that judges have the final authority to interpret, is not just a contingent fact about some legal orders. Rather, it is an essential step along the path to a destination that has been described in the most illuminating discussion I know of his legal theory as a "utopia of legality."[58] That is, constitutionalism is essential to the full realization of the principle of legality, a principle that Kelsen took to be the fundamental principle both of legal order and of liberal democracy. Moreover, Kelsen argued that full realization of that principle also requires particular legal orders to subordinate their law to international law.[59]

Kelsen's legal theory should thus be seen as a reconstructive inquiry into the developmental history of legal orders, of the sort later taken up by Jürgen Habermas,[60] but, in my view, most powerfully articulated by Wolfgang Schluchter, in a book that unfortunately seems to have made little impact on legal scholarship in English: *The Rise of Western Rationalism: Max Weber's Developmental*

[57] See the very intelligent account by Wil Waluchow, "Constitutions as Living Trees: An Idiot Defends," (2005) 18 Can J. L. & Jur. 207.

[58] Lars Vinx, *Hans Kelsen's Pure Theory of Law: Legality and Legitimacy* (2007).

[59] It seems to me that Waldron's position is developing in a Kelsenian direction.

[60] Jürgen Habermas, *Between Facts and Norms: Contributions to a Discourse Theory of Law and Democracy* (1996) [translated by William Rehg].

History.[61] As I understand such a history, it is, in a sense, an account of legal order from the external perspective conceptual legal positivists sometimes seem to advocate. It wishes, that is, to provide a theory of law that can account for legal orders at all times and in all places. But it differs from conceptual legal positivists in that it argues that what counts as a legal order will depend on what one takes the principle of legality to be, a normative question. Whatever one's answer to that question, some orders that count as such will be regarded, to use Hart's term from *The Concept of Law*, as more "primitive" exemplars,[62] while others, to use Simpson's term from the epigraph, will be regarded as "degenerate," verging on having little claim to be a legal order.

The principle of legality cannot, however, be confined to this somewhat external perspective, the individuation and understanding of particular legal orders. In addition, it is the principle that should guide legal officials, including judges, in their deliberations about what the law requires, since part of their task is to make decisions that conform both to the principle and to the positive law of the legal order. Such officials owe an obligation of fidelity to law, to determine that all acts of state, including statutes, conform to the overarching commitment of the legal order to legality. It is true that Kelsen regards any such determination as ultimately discretionary, an act of will. But if, from the fully internal perspective that a legal official must adopt in making such a determination, she may rely only on reasons that can be authentically presented as legal reasons, and if, in addition, the official must present an argument as to why her conclusion is the best given available reasons, then all the essential components of a Dworkinian theory of adjudication will be in place in every legal order that deserves that title.

On my argument, then, problems encountered by the positions within the family I have called constitutional positivism arise because they all seek a reconciliation with legal orders that are on a developmental path quite different from the one advocated by the patriarch of their more extended family of political positivists, Jeremy Bentham. On the basis of Simpson's essay, one might say that these positions need to put forward grander proposals for legal reform than they presently do if they are to avoid incoherence. To quote again from the epigraph, at the least they need to advocate "codification, coupled of course with a deliberate reduction in the status of the judiciary and some sort of ban on law reporting."

[61] (1981) [translated by Guenther Roth].

[62] Hart, *The Concept of Law*, *supra* note 43 at 89.

7 The Travails of Justice Waldron

James Allan*

Imagine for a moment that there exists a smart, well-read, articulate legal academic, well-versed in constitutional law and more so in legal philosophy (indeed in moral and political philosophy as well). Imagine, too, that this person has taken a particular interest in bills of rights. He has written extensively about how such instruments fail to take seriously the right to participate in social decision-making, including decisions about rights and how rights ought to play out and rank against each other. In other words, he has turned the strong-rights-based arguments grounded in autonomy and equality – arguments relied on by so many bill of rights supporters – back onto those same people who defend the privileged position such instruments afford to unelected judges. Imagine, indeed, that this person has attempted to run through all the arguments made in favour of strong judicial review under a bill of rights and to rebut each and every one of them and that, to some readers, perhaps more than some, he has been immensely successful in those attempts.

Let me stop. There is no need to *imagine* any of the above. Jeremy Waldron is, without doubt, the leading bill of rights critic writing today and what I just set out was nothing more than an abbreviated, and thinly veiled, description of his stature and position. There is no need to imagine critics of bills of rights and no need to imagine a particular one who is all of the above.

Still, there is a role for your imagination in this chapter because I do want you (this time seriously) to imagine something that has not already happened. I want you to imagine what would happen if Waldron, *mirabile dictu*, were invited to serve on the U.S. Supreme Court (or, for that matter, the Supreme Court of Canada, the House of Lords, or the New Zealand Supreme Court).

* The author wishes to thank Andrew Geddis, Jeff Goldsworthy, Grant Huscroft, Richard Kay, Richard Posner, Peter Skegg, and John Smillie for their comments, criticisms, and suggestions on earlier versions of this chapter.

Could he accept? And if he were to accept, what would it be like for him as Justice Waldron? How would he decide the bill of rights cases that came before him?

That is the topic of this chapter. Put in less playful and more universally applicable terms, my objective is to raise the general issue of how an actual judge who was convinced by Waldron might behave (and relatedly, how that behaviour would measure up against Waldronian values). In other words, how does Waldron's jurisprudence play out in a world full of bills of rights and judges to apply them?

Notice that this is far more a live issue in practice than is whether or not to adopt (or jettison) a bill of rights. I share Waldron's opposition to these instruments in the context of functioning democracies.[1] Yet, outside Australia, where I work, every democracy has by now adopted either a constitutionalized[2] or statutory[3] bill of rights. Nor, sadly, is there much prospect of any of these countries jettisoning the charter or bill they have, at least any time soon. So in one very tangible, practical sense – the sense in which theoretical, philosophical arguments are brought to bear on important issues of the day with the chance such analyses and argumentation will influence what occurs – Waldron's critique, albeit powerful, wide-ranging, and (to more than a few of us) persuasive, is most directly relevant to Australia and attempts to forestall the adoption of a bill of rights there.[4]

Everywhere else in the democratic world the live issue, at least for those of us who think the role given to unelected judges under these instruments is a puffed-up, illegitimate one, is how to limit the judiciary. How can we keep to a minimum the moral input and rights-based social decision-making of these

[1] See, for instance, my. "Bills of Rights and Judicial Power – A Liberal's Quandary?" (1996) 16 O.J.L.S. 337; *Sympathy and Antipathy: Essays Legal and Philosophical* (2002); "Rights, Paternalism, Constitutions and Judges" in G. Huscroft and P. Rishworth eds., *Litigating Rights: Perspectives from Domestic and International Law* (2002); "Oh That I Were Made Judge in the Land," (2002) 30 Federal L. Rev 561; "Paying for the Comfort of Dogma," (2003) 25 Sydney L. Rev. 63; "A Modest Proposal," (2003) 23 O.J.L.S. 197; "An Unashamed Majoritarian," (2004) 27 Dalhousie L.J. 537 [Allan, "An Unashamed Majoritarian]; "Portia, Bassanio or Dick the Butcher? Constraining Judges in the Twenty-First Century," (2006) 17 King's College Law Journal 1 [Allan, "Portia, Bassanio or Dick the Butcher?"]; and "Thin Beats Fat Yet Again – Conceptions of Democracy," (2006) 25 Law & Philosophy 533 [Allan, "Thin Beats Fat"].

[2] E.g., the U.S. and Canada.

[3] E.g., New Zealand and the U.K.

[4] Indeed, since Waldron started his attack on bills of rights [see "A Right-Based Critique of Constitutional Rights," (1993) 13 O.J.L.S. 18], the U.K. enacted one in 1998 (*U.K. Human Rights Act*). Australia has one for the capital city territory of Canberra (the *Human Rights Act* 2004) and for one of the states, Victoria (*Charter of Human Rights and Responsibilities Act* 2006), but there is not one in any other state or federally at the Commonwealth level.

committees of ex-lawyers and so maximize the role of the elected parliament in a free and democratic society? Imagining the travails of Justice Waldron is a vehicle to explore that very live and relevant question.

I will proceed as follows. In Part I, I will distinguish between "inside the core" and "outside the core" instances of countries with "democratic institutions in reasonably good working order, including a representative legislature elected on the basis of universal adult suffrage."[5] The distinction is Waldron's, not mine.[6] *Inside the core*, absent evidence that this or that society's citizens reject rights,[7] bill of rights-style judicial review is illegitimate. In here, says Waldron, "the society in question ought to settle the disagreements about rights that its members have using its legislative institutions."[8] By contrast, *outside the core*, where the electoral and legislative arrangements are deemed *not* to be in reasonably good shape, this sort of judicial review *may* (but only may) be justified. Or so says Waldron. Accordingly, our imagined Justice Waldron needs first to decide whether the United States or Canada (or indeed New Zealand or the United Kingdom) is or is not an "inside the core" society.

In Part II, I consider how Justice Waldron might decide the bill of rights cases that come before him. In Part III, I shift focus northwards to Canada to consider the effect, if any, of a power in the legislature to overcome judicial decisions on an imagined Mr. Justice Waldron there. I end, in Part IV, with a question deliberately left for last: Could Professor Waldron accept the job on a top court?

I. IN OR OUT?

Let us assume for the moment that Professor Waldron, for whatever reason, agrees to join the top court and become Justice Waldron. He needs first to decide whether, in this jurisdiction, it is politically legitimate "for decisions about rights made by legislatures to be second-guessed by the courts."[9] Is this

[5] Jeremy Waldron, "The Core of the Case Against Judicial Review,"(2006) 115 Yale L.J. 1346 at 1360 [Waldron, "Core of the Case"].

[6] See, in particular, Waldron, "Core of the Case," *ibid.*, section VII, from 1401.

[7] And as Waldron himself points out, assuming "a general commitment to rights in [a] society . . . is fairly easily satisfied, given that the case for judicial review almost always assumes that somehow the society for which judicial review is envisaged has a Bill of Rights which stands in some real relation to the views of citizens" (*ibid.* at 1402). In other words, given that the societies we are imagining or supposing will offer Waldron a top judging job are societies that have already adopted some sort of bill of rights, making the case that rights are rejected in those societies will be an uphill struggle, to say the least.

[8] *Ibid.* at 1360.

[9] *Ibid.*

an "inside the core" jurisdiction with electoral and legislative arrangements in reasonably good shape, or is it an "outside the core" one where they are not in reasonably good shape?

This matters. It matters not least because our Justice Waldron thinks bill of rights-style judicial review is illegitimate for jurisdictions "inside the core." So how he would decide bill of rights cases that came before him would presumably be affected (at times decisively affected) by this first inside-or-outside determination.

One's initial reaction would be to say that the United States and Canada, and, for that matter, the United Kingdom, Australia, and New Zealand, are obviously "inside the core" countries – countries with democratic institutions in reasonably good working order.[10] If not them, then who?

This instinct is buttressed by Waldron's explicit proviso that the requirement for electoral and legislative arrangements to be in reasonably good shape is "not unrealistic."[11] "[W]e are not entitled to demand perfection,"[12] he cautions, going so far as to remind us it is *not* the case "that judicial review of legislation is defensible"[13] just because perfection is absent.

So the fact that all of us can point to what we see as imperfections in the electoral and legislative arrangements of Justice Waldron's jurisdiction is far from enough to qualify it as a jurisdiction that is "outside the core." True, Canada has an unelected upper house filled with appointed placemen and party hacks. And the United Kingdom, too, also lacks a genuine, elected house of review, to say nothing of the democratic deficiencies some would claim flow from membership in the European Union. The United States has notorious problems with gerrymandering and campaign finance deficiencies that overplay the role of money in elections.[14] Tiny New Zealand, meanwhile, has no upper house, genuine or otherwise, and also lacks federalism.[15] Only Australia

[10] I say this despite the Chief Justice of Canada's rather self-satisfied (and patently wrong) implications to the contrary. She implied that Australia, the U.S., New Zealand and the UK were "self-proclaimed democracies" only in the course of her 5-4 majority judgment in *Sauvé v. Canada (Chief Electoral Officer)*, [2002] 3 S.C.R. 519 at para. 41 – refering to the countries discussed in the dissent at paras. 125, 130, and 131 [*Sauvé*].

[11] Waldron, "Core of the Case," *supra* note 5 at 1402.

[12] *Ibid.* at 1402.

[13] *Ibid.*

[14] For more on all of this, see James Allan and Andrew Geddis, "Waldron and Opposing Judicial Review – Except, sort of, in New Zealand," (2006) N.Z.L.J. 94 [Allan and Geddis, "Opposing Judicial Review"].

[15] In a short (and to my eyes surprising, almost strange) article, Waldron condemns the electoral and legislative arrangements of his native New Zealand as much inferior to those of the U.S. See Waldron, "Compared to What? Judicial Activism and New Zealand's Parliament," (2005) N.Z.L.J. 441. ("For my money . . . the legislatures in the US have much more dignity in their own right than the craven submission of the New Zealand Parliament . . ." *ibid.* at 445) [Waldron,

(with federalism, a genuine elected house of review Senate, no American-style gerrymandering, a preferential voting system – indeed compulsory voting, and good campaign finance rules) appears immune from easy faultfinding.

Again, though, much more is needed to move a jurisdiction "outside the core" than an ability to spot imperfections. "The arguments . . . [are] in large part comparative,"[16] advises Waldron – namely a comparison between the extent to which people's right to participate is upheld when unelected judges make social policy decisions under a bill of rights versus when the elected legislature (with its warts and all) does.

On that comparative basis, none of the Anglo-U.S. countries discussed earlier looks anywhere near being "outside the core." From a Waldronian starting point where one values rights in a strong way – meaning individual autonomy and treating each person as a moral equivalent, so that the right of each person to participate in social decision-making stands as a sort of "right of rights" – no one could say that in any of our countries the unelected judges outscore the elected branches in giving people a say, in counting their actual views, or in having actual decisions determined by their participation.

This is no surprise, of course. It would be odd, indeed, if all Waldron's many articles and books, with their powerful, persuasive arguments against strong judicial review and judicial activism, were not meant to apply to the sort of countries mentioned. Indeed, as regards the United States, Waldron has been explicit, noting without demurring that "I am known as a fanatical opponent of strong judicial review in the United States."[17]

In other words, there will be no easy way out for our Justice Waldron. He has accepted a job on the top court in a country where he believes "decisions about rights made by legislatures [ought not] to be second-guessed by courts,"[18] where society's "disagreements about rights [ought to be settled] using its legislative institutions."[19]

How then, given the political illegitimacy he thinks attaches to the task, might Justice Waldron decide the bill of rights cases that come before him? Speculating on that is the subject of the next part of this chapter.

"Compared to What?"]. For my and Andrew Geddis's response and attempted rebuttal of that claim, see Allan and Geddis, "Opposing Judicial Review, *supra* note 14.

[16] Waldron, "Core of the Case," *supra* note 5 at 1402. See, too, "Compared to What?" *supra* note 15 at 441.

[17] Waldron, "Compared to What?" *supra* note 15 at 442. See, too, Waldron's "A Right-Based Critique of Constitutional Rights," (1993) 13 O.J.L.S. 18, which indicates the same point, implicitly, as regards the U.K.

[18] Waldron, "Core of the Case," *supra* note 5 at 1360.

[19] *Ibid.*

II. WHAT TO DO?

Our Justice Waldron might surprise even himself. Once in the job, he might find he adopts something like the Holmes or Frankfurter or Posner approaches – or stated approaches – to dealing with bill of rights cases. Let's call this the "can't help it" or "puke test" approach.[20] Justice Waldron's basic stance, on this approach, will be one of deference to the elected legislature. He will accept that disagreements about rights ought to be settled by the legislature. Or rather, he will accept that that is the appropriate stance to take in the vast preponderance of cases.

Justice Waldron recognises that the rights in a bill of rights are expressed in indeterminate, amorphous terms; they are expressed as moral abstractions. When cases come before him, he will be asked *not* to approve the fine sentiments that lie behind these abstractions (who wouldn't?) but, rather, to apply them to specific situations down in the quagmire of social policy line-drawing. He will be asked to rule on the desirable scope and ambit of these indeterminate rights, on how they might rank against one another, and on what limits on them are thought to be reasonable and justifiable. On all these questions, people just disagree. More importantly, that disagreement takes place between reasonable, well-meaning, smart, even nice people and does so on questions over which the judiciary has no obviously greater moral perspicacity than anyone else. That is what makes the elevated, puffed-up role and powers of unelected judges operating a bill of rights so illegitimate. That is why Justice Waldron will think his task, at core, is illegitimate.

And yet the odd case – more likely, only the exceptionally odd, rare, and unusual case – may come before him in which deference to the elected legislature would make Justice Waldron want to puke (metaphorically, at any rate). How optimistic can we be – how optimistic can our Justice Waldron, himself, be – that in such situations he will swallow hard or hold his nose and defer? Do not forget, he has accepted a job in which *his view* (assuming he happens to vote with the majority of others on the top court) *is determinative*. He can strike down legislation he wants struck down (under the constitutionalized bills of rights of the United States and Canada). He can use the "reading down"

[20] Richard Posner describes (approvingly) Holmes' approach in just these terms. See "The Problematics of Moral and Legal Theory," 111 Harvard L. Rev. 1638 at 1709 (and note 148) (1998) and "2004 Term Foreword: A Political Court," 119 Harvard L. Rev. 31 at 84 (2005). On the Posner account, "Holmes ascribed no special virtue to legislatures, but then he ascribed no special virtue to judges either. With their relative capabilities a wash, Holmes was content to let the more representative body have its head." (E-mail to the author from Richard Posner, April 11, 2006.)

provision to rewrite any legislation he wants to rewrite (under statutory bills of rights).[21]

A clear and present danger, or at least likelihood, is that Justice Waldron may not be able to help himself in such situations. He has been given the power to second-guess. He believes the contested statute to be morally deficient, and considerably so. Most human beings, rather than resign,[22] would, at some point, exercise those powers. Odds are, I think, that Justice Waldron would, too.

Of course, few judges who, like Waldron, accept the basic illegitimacy of committees of ex-lawyers and of ex-law professors having this second-guessing power will also follow Posner and Holmes in so explicitly setting out or articulating a "can't help it" or "puke" test. Some may even come to rationalise what they are doing in other, less troubling terms.

Notice, too, that I am *not* mooting some moralizing judge who is wholly convinced of his or her own ability to achieve justice, to be on the side of the angels, to do the right thing, to keep pace with civilization, to know what highly indeterminate rights guarantees require down in the quagmire of social policy-making detail, to keep flowing the pipeline to God.[23] That is partly the problem. I am mooting just the opposite of that sort of judge. Yet under the dynamics of bill of rights adjudication, even our Justice Waldron-type judge will find himself, I suspect, second-guessing the elected legislature, though of course much, much less frequently than those who have no doubts or qualms about the legitimacy of what they are doing.

Still, if our goal is to limit and keep to a minimum the moral input (largely exercised via rights-based decision-making) of unelected judges, this sort of Holmesian or Frankfurterite or Posnerite approach will likely appear attractive – not perfect, but as good as it gets in practice.[24] It may even lessen the tendency of judges to fall victim to moral self-righteousness or sanctimoniousness.[25] Of course there will still be the "thin skin" problem. The threshold of

[21] Section 3 in the *U.K. Human Rights Act* and section 6 of the *New Zealand Bill of Rights Act*. See Allan, "Portia, Bassanio or Dick the Butcher?" *supra* note 1 at 10 for a discussion of how this, in fact, is happening in the UK and New Zealand.

[22] The obverse but related side of this issue, whether Waldron could accept a job on the top court, I leave until the end of this chapter.

[23] Though, of course, we could all quite easily begin to compile a list of this sort of judge (from all of the jurisdictions under consideration).

[24] One could argue, I think, that a strong attachment to originalism as a mode of interpretation also lessens the judge's personal moral input. In a sense I agree. See Allan, "Portia, Bassanio or Dick the Butcher?" *supra* note 1. Note also Mark Tushnet's speculations as regards deferential approaches to judging in Mark Tushnet, "Scepticism about Judicial Review: A Perspective from the United States," in Tom Campbell, K.D. Ewing, and Adam Tomkins eds., *Sceptical Essays on Human Rights* (2001) 359 at 371.

[25] See, *e.g.*, note 10, *supra*.

what makes a judge want to puke will be markedly lower for some than for others. And this is true even if all judges were open and honest about what they were doing when applying this puke test (which seems to me to be a highly implausible assumption).

Nevertheless, our Justice Waldron might, himself, come to see the attractions of the relative moral minimalism (as regards judges) of this "can't help it" or "puke" test. As I said at the outset of this Part, he might surprise himself.

Whether he did or not would depend on how constraining Waldron's preferred interpretive approach, a form of textualism, proved to be when it comes to bill of rights adjudication. Does the text of a bill of rights secure predictability? Or is it "general, ... ambiguous, ... vague, and ... [full] of terms that would leave the citizen at the mercy of the interpreter's judgment or discretion"?[26]

Let us consider the case law for a moment. The texts of all our Anglo-American bills of rights make mention of a right to "freedom of speech" or to "freedom of expression." Canada's *Charter of Rights and Freedoms* and New Zealand's *Bill of Rights Act* also make explicit that rights and freedoms can be limited by laws where the limit is deemed (by the judges) to be reasonable and justifiable.[27] In the United States, this is implicit.[28]

So how constraining on the point-of-application interpreters is the injunction to guarantee freedom of speech and expression, subject to reasonable limits? How does it affect, say, campaign finance rules, hate speech provisions, or defamation regimes? To my mind, it seems abundantly clear that "the citizen [is largely] at the mercy of the interpreter's judgment or discretion."[29] Just compare *RAV* v. *City of St Paul*[30] with *R* v. *Keegstra*[31] (criminalization of hate speech in the United States and Canada) or *New York Times* v. *Sullivan*[32] with *Hill* v. *Church of Scientology*,[33] *Lange* v. *Atkinson*,[34] and *Reynolds* v. *Times Newspapers*[35] (defamation liability in the United States, Canada, New Zealand, and the United Kingdom). Or look at how the right is interpreted to affect campaign spending[36] or the openness of trials.[37]

[26] Jeremy Waldron, *Law and Disagreement* (1999) at 83–4 [Waldron, *Law and Disagreement*].

[27] See s. 1 of the *Canadian Charter of Rights and Freedoms* and s. 5 of *The New Zealand Bill of Rights Act*.

[28] See my "An Unashamed Majoritarian," *supra* note 1.

[29] Waldron, *Law and Disagreement*, supra note 26 at 83–4.

[30] 505 U.S. 377 (1992).

[31] [1990] 3 S.C.R. 697.

[32] 376 U.S. 254 (1964).

[33] [1995] 2 S.C.R. 1130.

[34] [2000] 3 N.Z.L.R. 385 (C.A.).

[35] [2001] 2 A.C. 127.

[36] Compare *Buckley v. Valeo*, 424 U.S. 1 (1976) and *Harper v. Canada (Attorney General)*, [2004] 1 S.C.R. 827.

[37] Compare *Nebraska Press Association v. Stuart*, 427 U.S. 539 (1976) with *Gisborne Herald Co. Ltd. v. Solicitor-General*, [1995] 3 N.Z.L.R. 563 (C.A.).

Or take just about any of the other rights enumerated in these instruments. Does a textualist interpretive approach tell us where to draw the line when it comes to voting,[38] or who can marry,[39] or limits on advertising?[40] Does it help us decide what does or does not constitute "cruel and unusual punishments," "due process of law," "unreasonable search and seizure," "reasonable and demonstrably justified limits," or any of the other openly moral mandates? Does it foreclose finding or discovering some further broad right, say one to privacy, in the "penumbras, formed by emanations" of existing rights to due process, freedom from unreasonable searches, and against self-incrimination (then finding a more specific further unwritten right in the penumbra of this discovered privacy right's emanation)?[41] Are any of the rights in a bill of rights "specific rather than general, univocal rather than ambiguous"?[42] Is a bill of rights like a tax statute or campaign finance statute or criminal statute (or code) or corporations statute in terms of its determinacy, specificity, and "core of settled meaning"?[43]

I do not think anyone can answer "yes" to these questions honestly or while keeping a straight face. Justice Waldron may believe that, in normal circumstances, democratic considerations dictate that "legislators are entitled to insist on the authoritativeness of the text and nothing but the text,"[44] supplemented only by "the meanings embodied conventionally in the text."[45] This may even be a powerful position to take as regards interpreting the vast preponderance of statutes.[46] With bills of rights, however, it is akin to handing the judiciary (and himself) a blank cheque. Textualism or a plain meaning approach constrains

[38] See *Sauvé, supra* note 10.

[39] See *Halpern v. Canada (Attorney General)* (2003), 65 O.R. (3d) 161 (C.A.); *Quilter v. Attorney-General*, [1998] 1 N.Z.L.R. 523 (C.A.) and *Joslin et al v. New Zealand*, Communication No. 902/1999, UN Doc. A/57/40 at 214 (2002); and *Goodridge v. Mass. Department of Public Health*, 440 Mass. 309, 798 NE2d 941 (2003).

[40] Consider *RJR-MacDonald v. Canada*, [1995] 3 S.C.R. 199.

[41] See *Griswold v. Connecticut*, 381 U.S. 479 (1965) and *Roe v. Wade*, 410 U.S. 113 (1973).

[42] Waldron, *Law and Disagreement, supra* note 26 at 83.

[43] This term was coined by H.L.A. Hart in his masterpiece, *The Concept of Law* (1961) at 140 *inter alia* [Hart, *The Concept of Law*]. Notice, too, that statutory bills of rights with their reading down provisions (see, for example, section 3 in the *U.K. Human Rights Act* and section 6 in the *New Zealand Bill of Rights Act*) positively invite indeterminacy. Consider *Ghaidan v. Mendoza*, [2004] 3 All E.R. 411 (H.L.) and my comments on that decision in Allan, "Portia, Bassanio or Dick the Butcher," *supra* note 1.

[44] Waldron, *Law and Disagreement, supra* note 26 at 145.

[45] *Ibid.*, at 142.

[46] For my argument that this case can be made (though, also, that it involves a sort of reliance on originalism) see "Constitutional Interpretation v. Statutory Interpretation: Understanding the Attractions of 'Original Intent'," (2000) 6 Legal Theory 109. See, too, Jeffrey Goldsworthy, "Interpreting the Constitution in its Second Century," (2000) 24 Melbourne U.L.R. 677.

the bill of rights interpreting judge hardly at all. Waldron seems to me to imply as much himself.[47]

Hence, our Justice Waldron, a judge well aware of the political illegitimacy that attaches to second-guessing the elected legislature and one intent on minimizing the judiciary's moral input, would have to shun textualism as regards bill of rights adjudication. Even more obviously, he would have to eschew progressivist or "living tree" or "living constitutionalism" type modes of interpretation – approaches grounded on the notion that the meaning of rights in bills of rights evolves and changes in accordance with the needs of contemporary society[48] (or more honestly put, in accord with the judges' views of those needs).

That is why I mooted that our Justice Waldron might surprise even himself and come to see the attractions of a Holmesian or Frankfurterite or Posnerite approach.

Another possibility is this: Perhaps our Justice Waldron, a former student of Ronald Dworkin's, might decide that, broadly speaking, he likes the Herculean best fit approach to interpretation, but that in his jurisdiction the best understanding of the first nine chapters – of all the settled law, cases, constitutional provisions, and conventions – is an overarching commitment by society to a right to participate in social decision-making, even about rights. In other words, all the provisions in a bill of rights would need to be interpreted against this synthesizing, all-embracing, fundamental, best fit commitment to letting the numbers count when it comes to resolving where to draw the myriad lines rights-based adjudication requires. Justice Waldron would direct himself, in other words, to interpret bill of rights disputes in the light of society's strong *prima facie* commitment to majority rules.

On this sort of approach, our Justice Waldron might end up with a very strong presumption in favour of the challenged piece of legislation that was the product of the democratically elected legislature. Only where some enumerated right appeared to give him abundantly clear warrant to strike down (under a constitutionalized model) or to re-write under the guise of interpreting (under a statutory model) some statute would our Justice Waldron use the bill of rights to do so.

In a sense, this would be a sort of redirected Dworkinianism, one in which the mythical Hercules is taken to pay a good deal more attention to his homeland being the birthplace of democracy.[49]

47 See Waldron, *Law and Disagreement*, *supra* note 26 at 83–4, not least note 41 therein.

48 For more detail on why this is obvious, see James Allan and Grant Huscroft, "Constitutional Rights Coming Home to Roost? Rights Internationalism in American Courts," 43 San Diego L.R. 1 at 31 (2006).

49 For a powerful argument to the effect that Dworkin's best-fit interpretive prescription is open to being used at the second-order level in order to sanction just about any desired first-order

More to the point, this redirected Dworkinianism appears likely to produce just about the same outcomes as the more spartan, less varnished (and possibly more plain dealing) Holmesian or Frankfurterite or Posnerite approaches. There would be an awful lot of deference coupled with a scintilla or dash of juristocracy or kritarchy. The architectural designs and justifications would be much more elaborate; the finished product pretty much the same.

There is yet another alternative. This one involves a John Hart Ely-type[50] distinction between those rights that further or make possible voting and canvassing and campaigning and participating in social decision-making and so majority rules and letting the numbers count, on the one hand, and all other rights on the other. As Amartya Sen notes, "[e]ven elections can be deeply defective if they occur without the different sides getting an adequate opportunity to present their respective cases, or without the electorate enjoying the freedom to obtain news and to consider the views of the competing protagonists."[51]

In other words, "majority rules" or "letting the numbers count" is a deceptively simple-seeming notion, one that, in fact, requires some sort of moral overlay to give life to the notion of having a right to participate. Value judgments and choices need to be made about voting systems, campaign finance rules, access to media, district- or boundary-drawing mechanisms, defamation regimes, and more. At some point, a jurisdiction's choices may mean that the numbers do not really count. People having to vote by raising their hands in the presence of men with machine guns is a blatant example. More debatable examples might include countries with only government-controlled broadcasting and newspapers or those with swingeing defamation laws or those with locked-in gerrymandering. At some point – and no doubt different people would draw the line at different places – the numbers really stop counting, and who governs and becomes legislators is really not determined by the preferences and choices of the majority.

So maybe our Justice Waldron might adopt two different approaches as regards the rights in his jurisdiction's bill of rights. Those rights, those moral abstractions, raising issues related to how governments are chosen (so as to ensure the numbers really do count) might be treated one way. All other rights and value judgments – those linked to the scope of and reasonable limits on

outcome, see J.L. Mackie's "The Third Theory of Law," in Joan Mackie and Penelope Mackie eds., *Persons and Values*, (1985) at 132–44.

50 See John Hart Ely, *Democracy and Distrust: A Theory of Judicial Review* (1980), especially chapter four.

51 Amartya Sen, "Democracy as a Universal Value," (1999) 10 Journal of Democracy 3 at 9. For my response to Sen's advocacy of a fat conception of democracy, see Allan, "Thin Beats Fat," *supra* note 1.

freedom of religion, say, or of privacy, or of search and seizure, or of immigration policy, or of how to spend society's limited resources on health or education, and so much more – might be treated in another.

In instances of the latter, our Justice Waldron would be almost wholly deferential; in instances of the former, however, perhaps he would be much less so. To ensure the numbers really do count, our Justice Waldron might be more prepared to second-guess, to inject his own moral input, to draw some of the social policy lines rights-based instruments allow him (if he so desires) to draw.

And yet not so. Some may find attractive this Ely-type distinction with its two-speed approach to the level of judges' moral input and intrusiveness. But Waldron does not.[52] Even here, he thinks, it is not for the judges to intervene (and for what it is worth, I agree).

Is there anything more, then, on which we can speculate as regards how our Justice Waldron might decide the bill of rights cases that come before him? In fact, there may be. In one of his recent articles,[53] Waldron throws us hints of something more. Although I am unsure what to make of this article as a whole,[54] there does appear to be the suggestion that judges *can* use the bill of rights when statutes (and maybe case law) are silent and the issue is an open question – when it falls into what H. L. A. Hart called "the penumbra of uncertainty."[55] Consider this passage:

> Another way of putting the matter is this: We may have simply decided, as a matter of national will, not to rule out the death penalty altogether. But a case can still be made that *we* should not just *decide* whether it is cruel or unjust to execute adults for crimes committed when they were children. Since it is an open question in our system whether this practice is constitutional, *we* should look not just for a decision but for a way of figuring out the complex rights and wrongs of the matter, as well as the vexing issues of culpability and responsibility. In addressing this problem, *we* need all the help *we* can get. If these issues have been wrestled with in a number of other jurisdictions, then *our* commitment to the pursuit of justice should lead *us* to examine the end product of their labors for guidance. So even if the modern death

[52] See Waldron, *Law and Disagreement*, *supra* note 26 at 295–6 *inter alia* and "A Right-Based Critique of Constitutional Rights," (1993) 13 O.J.L.S. 18 at 39.

[53] See Jeremy Waldron, "Foreign Law and the Modern *Ius Gentium*," 119 Harv. L. Rev. 129 (2006) [Waldron, "Foreign Law"].

[54] I consider this article at length in "Jeremy Waldron and the Philosopher's Stone," San Diego L.R. (2008, forthcoming).

[55] See Hart, *The Concept of Law*, *supra* note 43 at 131 *inter alia*. Hart also calls this the "penumbra of doubt" (at 119, *inter alia*).

> penalty is quintessentially and peculiarly American, the accumulated legal wisdom of mankind, embodied in *ius gentium*, may still have something to offer *us*.[56]

Waldron is writing here in the course of arguing that it may sometimes be "appropriate for American courts to cite or defer to foreign law."[57] That is why I have put all the first person plural pronouns (save for the first one) in italics. In the context of his paper, it is clear that all these italicised pronouns refer to the unelected judiciary, *not* to all the voters who have a right to participate in social decision-making, even about whether to execute adults for murders committed when children. Each "we" and "us" who will be struggling with "whether the Eighth Amendment forbids the juvenile death penalty"[58] refers to a judicial "we" or to a judicial "us." And by not making that as clear as he might have, by hiding behind a deceptively embracing pronoun, Waldron seems open to the charge he has in the past levelled at others – of using weasel words.

Elected U.S. legislatures looking to foreign legislatures and open to being guided by them (or even by foreign courts), but always remaining accountable to voters for doing so, is one thing. Unelected U.S. judges looking to foreign courts to reach decisions about what the U.S. Constitution requires – decisions that, for all practical purposes, can never be overturned by legislators or by all the many citizens with a Waldronian right to participate in social decision-making – are a wholly different thing. Use of the first-person plural pronoun very effectively blurs the distinction.

Still, that is a digression. I raise the matter here solely because of the suggestion in Waldron's passage that judges may have more room – more legitimate room – to decide difficult social policy issues when they are "open question[s] in our system."[59]

Could our Justice Waldron, the same Justice Waldron who thinks "disagreements about rights [ought to be settled] using . . . legislative institutions,"[60] endorse rights-based decision-making by unelected judges provided only that the decision is in an area at present left open or not yet dealt with by the legislature?

[56] Waldron, "Foreign Law," *supra* note 53 at 140. The second and penultimate italics in the original; the rest are mine.

[57] *Ibid.*, at 129.

[58] *Ibid.*, at 140.

[59] Waldron, "Foreign Law," *supra* note 53 at 140. Elsewhere in "Foreign Law," Waldron says "the fact that an appeal to the law of nations is precluded in some contexts does not necessarily make it unavailable in others" (p. 133) and "[i]n subject areas where municipal legal systems already have their own applicable law, the function of *ius gentium* is not to pre-empt that law but to guide its elaboration and development" (at 139).

[60] Waldron, "Core of the Case," *supra* note 5 at 1360.

I think not. Admittedly, decisions by judges in these unsettled areas of law would not, strictly speaking, amount to second-guessing the elected legislature. *Ex hypothesi* we are now speculating about issues and questions that, at the time of the judicial decision, remain "open question[s]."[61] Yet this is a casuist's or, worse, a sophist's response. If it be politically illegitimate for judges to gainsay what the elected legislature has already decided about rights – for all the strong-rights[62] reasons grounded in autonomy and equality that Waldron himself gives – then how, precisely, does it become somehow legitimate simply by virtue of the judges happening to get to the issue first?[63] Remember, when the judges do happen to get to an issue first, and they then make a decision under the aegis of the constitutionalized bill of rights, the legislature is shut out, foreclosed from overruling the judges.

I cannot see how our Justice Waldron could justify that sort of temporal distinction, between the illegitimacy of (later in time) second-guessing by judges and the legitimacy and acceptability of (earlier in time) foreclosing by judges. Surely our Justice Waldron would think both illegitimate.[64]

Of course some non-Americans will immediately protest. Canadians will point to the "notwithstanding clause" – s. 33 of the *Canadian Charter of Rights and Freedoms* – that gives legislatures the ability to respond to the judges. New Zealanders and those from the United Kingdom, meanwhile, will insist that their statutory bills of rights do not actually empower judges to strike down or invalidate legislation.

However, both sorts of protest are specious, in my view, as I have argued elsewhere already.[65] Moreover, I will have more to say about the Canadian notwithstanding clause in Part III.

Before leaving this second Part of the paper, though, let me recap. I have speculated that our Justice Waldron will not be able to resort to textualism

[61] Waldron, "Foreign Law," *supra* note 53 at 140.

[62] For my distinction between strong-rights theories and weak rights theories, see "Bills of Rights and Judicial Power – A Liberal's Quandary," (1996) 16 O.J.L.S. 337.

[63] Furthermore, as Richard Kay suggested to me, legislatures either regulate or they do not regulate. Yet there are no obvious grounds for treating the latter course as not having dealt with the situation, as opposed to having made a decision to leave it alone.

[64] I say this solely on the basis of the weakness of the distinction. Of course one could also point out how easy it would be, in practice, to frame most issues that come before the courts as 'open questions,' meaning that any halfway competent ex-lawyer could say he or she was almost never second-guessing the legislature.

[65] As regards statutory bills of rights, see Allan, "Portia, Bassanio or Dick the Butcher?" *supra* note 1 and "The Effect of a Statutory Bill of Rights Where Parliament is Sovereign: The Lesson from New Zealand" in Tom Campbell, K.D. Ewing and Adam Tomkins eds. *Sceptical Essays on the Human Rights Act 1998* (2001) at 375, and as regards Canada, see my "An Unashamed Majoritarian," *supra* note 1, and "The Author Doth Protest Too Much, Methinks," (2003) 20 N.Z.U.L.R. 519.

when interpreting the rights in a bill of rights; such an interpretive approach will hardly constrain the point-of-application interpreter at all; it will not minimize, or much reduce, the judge's moral input. Instead, I have conjectured that our Justice Waldron might surprise even himself by coming to see the attractions of a Holmesian or Frankfurterite or Posnerite approach to interpreting bills of rights. He might do this directly, or perhaps he might reach much the same endpoint by means of some sort of more superd-up Dworkinian vehicle.

I have also suggested our Justice Waldron would reject the Ely-type approach, and that he would – or should – also reject anything turning on whether an issue first arose before the elected legislature or the unelected courts.

We need now to head north.

III. NOTWITHSTANDING'S MANIFEST DESTINY

In this Part I speculate on whether our Justice Waldron might find his task easier in Canada. What if, in adopting a bill of rights, the elected legislators give themselves a way ultimately to gainsay the unelected judges by inserting a notwithstanding or override clause? What if the majority vote to entrench a justiciable bill of rights, but only do so if it contains one of these notwithstanding clauses? Unelected judges may strike down the statutes passed by the democratically elected branch of government, but that same democratically elected branch of government can then reassemble and in a simple majority vote, override the judges.

Does such a clause lessen or eliminate the illegitimacy that our Justice Waldron believes attaches to bill of rights adjudication? Does this free him up to be less deferential to the legislature?

This is more or less the question Jeffrey Goldsworthy has posed.[66] I have considered it before in the context of whether the consequentialist is better placed to answer it than is the nonconsequentialist or strong-rights adherent.[67] Here, though, let us just consider how such a notwithstanding clause might affect our Justice Waldron's task.

At first glance, it appears as though at least some of the political illegitimacy attaching to unelected judges second-guessing the elected branches on rights issues has been dissipated. The elected branches can override or gainsay the second-guess; Parliament can do so on a 50 per cent plus one basis; it does

[66] See Jeffrey Goldsworthy's "Judicial Review, Legislative Override, and Democracy," in Tom Campbell, Jeffrey Goldsworthy, and Adrienne Stone eds., *Protecting Human Rights: Instruments and Institutions* (2003) at 263–79. See also David Dyzenhaus, "The Incoherence of Constitutional Positivism," this volume, at 141–2.

[67] See my *Sympathy and Antipathy – Essays Legal and Philosophical* (2002) at 283–6 [Allan, *Sympathy and Antipathy*]. I think the consequentialist is better placed to respond.

not appear that an earlier generation (the one opting for judicial oversight) is locking in a later one.

Concomitantly, someone like our Justice Waldron – unlike the consequentialist or utilitarian defender of rights and, in particular, of a right to participate in social decision-making – can hardly point to and castigate the fact that these autonomous voters and their elected representatives choose never (or virtually never) to use the override, that they are overawed by the language of rights, or that they need protecting from their own follies and have to be made less cavalier about excluding themselves from the decision-making process.

As Jeffrey Goldsworthy argues,[68] a strong-rights, nonconsequentialist defender of the right to participate, someone like our Justice Waldron, might, in theory, think that a good deal of the illegitimacy of his job has been abated by such an override clause.

Of course the question is wholly theoretical, as Goldsworthy himself concedes,[69] because the actual Canadian notwithstanding clause, s. 33 of the Charter,[70] is, itself, highly flawed. It applies only to some, not all, of the enumerated rights; it allows legislation to be passed only for five-year periods (though it can be renewed); it has been held, by the judges,[71] not to apply retroactively; and so it clearly leaves judicial supremacy as the default position.

In addition, it has never been invoked, not one single time, by the Canadian Parliament.[72] This may be, in part, because of its wording. Section 33 authorizes

[68] See note 66, *supra*.

[69] See *ibid.*, and "Legislation, Interpretation and Judicial Review," (2001) 51 U.T.L.J. 75. Grant Huscroft makes the same point in "Rights, Bills of Rights, and the Role of Courts and Legislatures" in Huscroft and Rishworth eds., *Litigating Rights* (2002) 12 and "'Thank God We're Here': Judicial Exclusivity and its Consequences," (2004) 25 Sup. Ct. L. Rev. 241.

[70] Section 33 of the Charter provides as follows:

1. Parliament or the legislature of a province may expressly declare in an Act of Parliament or of the legislature, as the case may be, that the Act or a provision thereof shall operate notwithstanding a provision included in section 2 or sections 7 to 14 of this Charter.
2. An act or a provision of an Act in respect of which a declaration made under this section is in effect shall have such operation as it would have but for the provision of this Charter referred to in the declaration.
3. A declaration made under subsection (1) shall cease to have effect five years after it comes into force or on such earlier date as may be specified in the declaration.
4. Parliament or the legislature of a province may re-enact a declaration made under subsection (1).
5. Subsection (3) applies in respect of a re-enactment made under subsection (4).

[71] See *Ford v. Quebec (Attorney General)*, [1988] 2 S.C.R. 712.

[72] At the provincial level, outside of Quebec, which did not sign on to the 1982 repatriation of the Constitution with its Charter, section 33 has been used not more than a handful of times, and *never* to overturn a court decision.

Canadian legislatures to declare that their enactments "shall operate notwithstanding a provision included in [specified sections] of this Charter." In other words, it implies, incorrectly and inaccurately, that the purpose of the notwithstanding clause is to override the Charter itself. It does *not* say that the elected legislature has a power to override disputed and debatable judicial interpretations of the Charter – and this is what is needed to avoid begging the question *by assuming* that judges' views are a better indication of what the Charter does or does not require than are the views of the elected legislators.[73]

Put differently, Canada's section 33 notwithstanding clause makes a legislative response extremely unlikely by making it seem as though legislators, when invoking this section, are against the *Charter* and against rights.

Of course, Goldsworthy concedes as much,[74] so the simple answer to the question I posed earlier is "No." Our Justice Waldron will not find his task any easier in Canada because the notwithstanding clause, as worded, does not lessen or eliminate the illegitimacy attaching to bill of rights adjudication. (And one could add that, in fact, there never was any referendum in Canada on whether to adopt the *Charter*, nor any election – federal or provincial – on the issue either. A majority of Canadians never voted to entrench the *Charter*, however popular it may now be.)

However, Goldsworthy can be read as asking us to imagine a properly worded notwithstanding clause (one, I would add, that is part of a *Charter* – *mirabile dictu* – that *has* been put to a referendum or election and *has* received the support of the majority). This is clearly *not* the Canadian reality. Goldsworthy accepts that. He simply asks, "what if?" What if there were a jurisdiction with an override or notwithstanding clause that did not beg the question, that did not imply legislators had to be against rights in order for it to be invoked, that applied to all the enumerated rights, that was permanent and not having to be renewed, that had received majority support in advance of coming into effect, *etc.*? In such an admittedly nonexistent jurisdiction, would our Justice Waldron – a self-declared strong-rights adherent who seemingly forswears consequentialism[75] – still think rights-based second-guessing by the judges politically illegitimate?

[73] Waldron, too, makes this same point about section 33's flawed wording in "Core of the Case," *supra* note 5 at 1357 and in "Some Models of Dialogue Between Judges and Legislators," in Huscroft and Brodie eds., *Constitutionalism in the Charter Era* (2004) 7 at 30–7 [Waldron, "Some Models of Dialogue"]. See, too, *supra* note 69 for the same point.

[74] *Supra* note 66.

[75] Waldron says that "[i]f there is a democratic objection to judicial review, it *must* also be a rights-based objection" (*Law and Disagreement, supra* note 26 at 282, [emphasis added]). I agree with Goldsworthy (see "Judicial Review, Legislative Override, and Democracy," *supra* note 66 at 270) that this assertion by Waldron is wrong.

The question seems a good one to me. Waldron, in his pre-judicial incarnation, attempts to answer it in this way:

> Goldsworthy says there is no need for a "notwithstanding" clause to create this impression [of the legislators being against rights and against the Charter rather than having simply differed with the judges about how some right is to play out in situations characterized by reasonable, smart, nice people regularly disagreeing amongst themselves about that best or most moral playing out of the right]. It *could* provide explicitly for the legislature to insist on its (disputable) conception of Charter rights over the courts' (disputable) conception of those rights. But in fact it does not. And I believe it is no accident that it was drafted in that way. I do not think one could never [sic] get a Canadian enthusiast for the Charter to accept a "notwithstanding" clause that involved an honest acknowledgment that rights might be disputable, or an honest acknowledgment that a federal or provincial legislature might have a view of rights that was, though controversial, no less reasonable than the view arrived at by the judiciary.[76]

Notice that Waldron's answer is a purely empirical one – that a fair, non-question-begging override will never come into existence. The proponents of bills of rights will never allow the legislative/judicial disagreements about rights to be characterized in this way, he replies.

What do we make of this answer? As an empirical claim or prediction, I think Waldron is correct. It is overwhelmingly unlikely, I agree, that we will ever, in fact, see anything approaching a notwithstanding provision that is acceptably drafted and that does not beg the question at issue by making it seem as though legislators have to be against rights before it can be invoked.

Yet somehow that answer strikes me as not good enough. We want to know whether an acceptably worded notwithstanding provision would change things, would make our Justice Waldron's rights-based adjudicating less illegitimate, from his point of view. Professor Waldron shunts us aside by saying this situation simply will not arise, or at least that it is extremely unlikely ever to transpire. If that were the test, though, it is not clear to me why Waldron bothers to write about what things would be like without strong judicial review. In the U.S. context, we all know the Bill of Rights is here to stay.

Lots and lots and lots of theoretical writing – at which Waldron himself excels – involves thinking about and speculating on states of affairs the likelihood of which coming into existence hovers only marginally above zero.

[76] Waldron, "Some Models of Dialogue," *supra* note 73 at 38–9, italics in the original and internal footnote omitted.

As I said earlier, I think Goldsworthy's question is a good one. As it happens, I agree with Goldsworthy that consequentialists *can* answer it;[77] they *can* say why even an acceptably worded override – one that is never invoked because most citizens happen to be happy with an unelected judiciary drawing all the difficult lines that rights disputes give rise to and that bills of rights hand to the judges – will not do anything to diminish the bad consequences of an uninvolved, deferential, apathetic citizenry.[78]

I am not sure, though, what a strong-rights adherent like Waldron could say.

So, in practice, in Canada today, our Justice Waldron would face the same "what to do" dilemma as he does in the United States. The task of rights-based adjudication is politically illegitimate in both jurisdictions.[79] A "notwithstanding clause" does not lessen the illegitimacy. And Professor Waldron is probably correct that the people who push bills of rights would never allow a non-question-begging notwithstanding clause to come into existence.

That said, it strikes me that if, against all odds, such a clause were to materialise, our Justice Waldron should find his task of rights-based adjudicating much less illegitimate, perhaps not illegitimate at all. Of course an imagined Justice Bentham would *not* think an acceptably worded notwithstanding clause did anything to improve the bad consequences of committees of ex-lawyers

[77] See *supra* notes 66 and 67.

[78] There is also the political science point related to burden shifting. Even with an acceptably worded override, it is still the case that for a disagreeing legislature to trump a judicial decision, it requires the legislature to pass the same Act twice. This requires expenditure of legislative time and attention and of political capital. Hence there will be times when the majority wants it but it will not happen.

[79] I would go further and say the same applies to statutory bills of rights as well. The two main tools of judicial power under a statutory model are, firstly, reading down provisions (provisions that ask judges to do all that they can to interpret other statutes in a way the judges consider to be a human rights friendly manner – see section 3 of the *U.K. Human Rights Act* and section 6 of the *New Zealand Bill of Rights Act*) and, secondly, Declarations of Incompatibility or Inconsistency (see section 4 of the *U.K. Human Rights Act* and the case of *Moonen v. Film and Literature Board of Review*, [2000] 2 N.Z.L.R. 9 (CA), in New Zealand, where the judges gave themselves this power). The reading down power is more insidious. In my view, the legislature cannot respond to it. Declarations of Incompatibility are, in theory, more honest, but thus far the legislature has shown no willingness to second guess the judges here either. According to Klug and Starmer ("Standing Back from the Human Rights Act: How Effective Is It Five Years On?" [2005] P.L. 716 at 721), "[i]n *every case* where remedial action had not been taken before the [judicial] declaration was made, the government responded by repealing, amending or committing to repeal or amend, the relevant provision" ([emphasis added]. Note that the authors see this as a good thing). For my full argument on this point, see Allan, "Portia, Bassanio or Dick the Butcher?" *supra* note 1 and "The Victorian Charter of Human Rights and Responsibilities: Exegesis and Criticisms," [2006] M.U.L.R. 28. To be perfectly honest, it is not at all clear to me what Waldron's considered view is of the legitimacy or otherwise of statutory bills of rights.

imposing their own moral views on the rest of us – whether we want them to or not – and so did nothing to ameliorate the political illegitimacy of his job. But our Justice Waldron, who appears to forswear appeals to consequences, has different bases and justifications for upholding the right to participate than an imagined Justice Bentham.

Accordingly, I say again that Goldsworthy's question strikes me as a good one, one that is tough for the nonconsequentialist to answer.

IV. OH THAT I WERE MADE JUDGE IN THE LAND

This chapter has thus far begged the most interesting question. Could Professor Waldron accept the job on a top court? I want to be deliberately provocative and suggest that the situation Waldron faces is the obverse of that faced by some of the judges in apartheid South Africa. They could either stay, and make a bad system more palatable and less harsh than any likely replacement, or resign. Waldron can either take the job, and lessen the illegitimacy of the system more than any likely alternative appointee (by keeping to a bare minimum any second-guessing of the elected legislature), or decline the offer.

Yes, the degree or amount of political illegitimacy between the two systems differs substantially. An apartheid regime is far worse, far more politically illegitimate, than is a system in which society's rights-based decision-making and line drawing is handed over to committees of unelected ex-lawyers.

Nevertheless, for a person like Waldron, someone fundamentally committed to letting the numbers count and giving real effect to the right to participate as *the* right of rights, the difference is one of degree or amount (of illegitimacy) only. He faces the same calculation as the apartheid South African judge – either take part, because the likely replacement or alternative will be worse, or have nothing to do with the illegitimate system.

Observe that the choice to follow the first fork in the road – to undertake politically illegitimate judging – appears defensible only on a utilitarian (or other consequentialist) basis. The thinking would be: "I can do more to diminish second-guessing and the inputting of judges' moral views and sentiments[80] than the sort of person who is otherwise likely to be offered (and take) the job." The likely good consequences of me being in this position, in other words, outweigh the likely bad ones – including the perceived legitimacy the system garners by virtue of having someone like me in the job.

[80] Or in the apartheid context, I can do more to ameliorate the harshness of a wicked system.

In contrast, the decision to follow the second fork – to refuse to accept the judging job or to resign from it – can be justified on either a consequentialist/utilitarian basis or on a deontological/nonutilitarian basis. It is the former when one decides that the bad consequences of being a part of the system – say, in terms of perpetuating it by reducing its rigours – are likely to outweigh any good one can do as a judge in the system. It is the latter when one forswears or disavows all appeal to consequences and just says "this is wrong" or "I will not be tainted."

Here, I do no more than suggest that people of a nonutilitarian or deontological inclination will lean towards not taking (or not keeping) the judgeship. Consequentialists have the harder task. Some will weigh up things and think it right to accept; others will reach the opposite conclusion.[81] And the degree of perceived illegitimacy of the system will affect their calculations. The worse the system, the more offsetting good one needs to think he or she can do by being a judge. Thus, it is a possibility – because one scenario is more illegitimate than the other – that the same person might calculate that he should resign from his job in the apartheid scenario but that he should take the judging job in the scenario we are considering in this chapter.

I suspect, as well, that any consequentialist or utilitarian weighing up of likely consequences – or, at any rate, any honest weighing up – needs to factor in the probability that once in the job anyone, even our Justice Waldron, will, to some extent, succumb to the temptations of moral second-guessing of having a largely unchecked power to impose his own moral sentiments on the rest of us. Differently phrased, there is the possibility that what Waldron would advocate be done in his role *as a professor* might not align perfectly with what he, as Justice Waldron, would, in fact, do *once a judge*. The job, as it were, might go to his head; he might start putting more stock than before on his own moral antennae; he might fail to spot all the sycophancy and flattery that goes with the job; the ability to achieve justice, do the right thing, and know what is needed to keep pace with civilization might appear to be more judgelike attributes once in the job.[82] In short, there is no necessary 1:1 correlation between the opinions of Waldron *qua* professor and Waldron *qua* judge.

A thorough consequentialist weighing-up of whether to take the job would need to factor in that possibility as well.

[81] This is because utilitarianism provides an approach – look to the future and weigh up likely consequences. It does *not* provide answers. See Allan, *Sympathy and Antipathy*, *supra* note 67.

[82] Mark Tushnet thinks this is a likely outcome, too. See *supra* note 24 at 371.

I say no more than that. Certainly, I do not presume to say whether Waldron should, or should not, take up the offer to become a top judge, or even whether there is a right answer (or indeed a right approach to finding an answer) to such a question.

Actually, I will say more than that because I have, thus far, overlooked the relevance of the judicial oath, "to do justice according to law."[83] Were Waldron to take the top judging job, the very fact he swore or affirmed the judicial oath might give rise to an interesting complication. Would our newly appointed Justice Waldron (because of the judicial oath) now have a legal obligation to enforce the bill of rights regardless of his political and moral objections to it? More to the point, would he have a moral obligation to comply with his legal obligation?

Obviously that would depend, in part, on how constraining the enumerated legal rights were taken to be. The more amorphous, vague, and indeterminate these bill of rights-enumerated rights are taken to be, the more this becomes a nonquestion.

That, in turn, though, raises issues about *stare decisis*. The rights themselves may be phrased in woolly, ambiguous, vague terms, leaving much to the interpreting judge's discretion. But maybe the case law generated by the hyperconstitutionalized legal environment has significantly expanded the core of settled meaning pertaining to some of these rights?[84]

Or perhaps not. Ironically, it is just those judges who are most attracted to progressivist "living tree" modes of interpretation who are least bothered by the "according to law" suffix of the judicial oath. They blithely go about keeping pace with what they see as the demands of civilisation and the needs of contemporary society. Justice Waldron, I suspect, will be far more concerned about pre-existing constraints.

Once we head down this road, other issues spring up, too. We would need to distinguish between a theory of interpretation and a theory of judicial disobedience – of when it is justifiable and defensible to disobey the law or to lie about what it requires. (And here one might want to claim that the degree of illegitimacy of the system *does* matter vis-à-vis a theory of judicial disobedience more tellingly than it does vis-à-vis a theory of interpretation.) We might also want to allow for the Waldronian judge who reckons it best (in a long-term

[83] I thank Richard Kay and Jeffrey Goldsworthy for bringing this point to my attention.

[84] If so, as Andrew Geddis noted to me, the puke test then becomes ambiguous. A legislative enactment could induce the puking reaction, but then so could some past precedent of the court. If it be the latter, can Justice Waldron circumvent that? Or does that constrain him, meaning his legal obligations are less than vague sometimes?

sense) to overturn legislation as liberally as possible, to give the community just the juristocracy they seem to crave (in the hope such activism might awaken them from their foolishness).

Any greater consideration of these ancillary issues, however, is beyond the scope of this chapter. No doubt, there is much that is uncertain. All we can be sure of is that there exists an asymmetry here. The Waldrons of the world will hesitate and ponder and be unsure of whether to take the job as top judge. They will see political illegitimacy in the task of bill of rights adjudication and this will have a bearing on their decision. Meanwhile, bill of rights proponents – at least those who see nothing illegitimate in unelected judges settling disagreements about rights for the rest of us – will have no concerns about the propriety of their required task, no qualms about accepting the job.

Over time, assuming all other things to be equal,[85] how many bill of rights sceptics – how many Waldrons – should we expect to find on our highest court?

[85] And of course all other things are unlikely to be equal over time. We should expect law schools to produce a preponderance of bill of rights proponents, lawyers' groups to be strong supporters (for self-interested and non-self-interested reasons) and any bill of rights sceptic nominated for judicial appointment to be characterised or vilified (by bill of rights proponents) as beyond the pale.

8 Deference or Defiance? The Limits of the Judicial Role in Constitutional Adjudication

Aileen Kavanagh*

INTRODUCTION

We are all familiar with infamous cases from various jurisdictions, in which judges have refrained from striking down grossly unjust legislative provisions or refused to overturn unjust decisions made by the executive branch. Rather than use the legal tools at their disposal to oppose such measures, judges have, instead, chosen to defer to the elected branches of government. Some of the most notoriously acquiescent decisions are handed down in time of war or when there is a perceived threat to national security, but deferential judicial decision-making is, by no means, confined to these circumstances. Although judicial deference has attracted the criticism that it represents an abdication of the judicial duty to enforce human rights, it has also attracted some notable support. Thus, Alexander Bickel argued that rather than being a judicial vice, a degree of deference to the elected branches of government was one of the "passive virtues" that good judges should display.[1]

In this chapter I will address two main questions: (1) Why do judges sometimes refrain from using the full amplitude of their powers to adjudicate constitutional issues and prefer, instead, to defer to the elected branches of government, and (2) should they defer? Are there reasons why judges ought to be

* I would like to thank members of the colloquium and the Public Law Discussion Group at the University of Cambridge for extremely helpful feedback on this paper. I would also like to thank the British Academy for funding a visit to the Faculty of Law at the University of Toronto, where I began my research into the doctrine of deference.

[1] See generally Alexander Bickel, "The Supreme Court 1960 Term – Foreword: The Passive Virtues," (1961) 75 Harv. L. Rev. 40 [Bickel, "The Passive Virtues"]; Bickel, *The Least Dangerous Branch: The Supreme Court at the Bar of Politics* (1963) ch. 4. For a classic statement of the duty of judicial deference, see also James Thayer, "The Origin and Scope of the American Doctrine of Constitutional Law," (1893) 7 Harvard Law Rev. 129.

deferential rather than defiant? In other words, is there some virtue in judicial deference as Bickel suggests, or is deference a vice to be avoided by self-respecting judges? Of course, we cannot hope to provide satisfactory answers to these questions without having a clearer idea of what deference actually requires of judges. Therefore, the first part of the chapter is devoted to an analysis of the various ways in which deference operates in practical (and judicial) reasoning, before going on to examine its rationale and justification.

Two clarifications are in order before I begin. First, the focus of this chapter is on judicial deference to the elected branches of government in the course of constitutional adjudication. It is not directly concerned with the role of deference in other legal contexts – that is, where judges defer to precedent or the factual findings of lower courts or the decisions of specialist tribunals, *etc.* Secondly, the question of whether judges should defer to the elected branches is not about the legal powers judges possess. Rather, it concerns the appropriateness of judges *not* exercising those powers, or at least being restrained in exercising them. As Lord Steyn of the House of Lords put it: "The existence of jurisdiction does not mean that it ought always to be exercised."[2] So, whilst much of constitutional law theory is concerned with finding justifications for the immense powers judges often possess in constitutional adjudication, this paper will focus on the nature of, and justification for, judicial self-restraint – that is, the self-imposed limits judges place on their power to review and scrutinise Acts of Parliament and executive decisions.[3]

THE STRUCTURE OF DEFERENCE

Deference is a familiar feature of legal adjudication, but it is familiar in nonlegal contexts as well. We often defer to doctors on appropriate medical treatment or to financial advisers on financial matters or, indeed, to friends or family on a whole range of questions about how to conduct our lives. But what do we do when we defer? The answer suggested here is that *deference is a matter of assigning weight to the judgment of another, either where it as at variance with one's own assessment, or where one is uncertain of what the correct assessment should be.* It introduces what might be called a "systematic bias"[4] into one's

[2] Lord Steyn, "Deference: A Tangled Story," [2005] P.L. 346 at 349 [Steyn, "Deference"].

[3] For an overview of the various doctrines of judicial self-restraint, see John Daley, "Defining Judicial Restraint," in Tom Campbell and Jeffrey Goldsworthy eds., *Judicial Power, Democracy and Legal Positivism* (2000).

[4] Stephen Perry, "Second-Order Reasons, Uncertainty and Legal Theory," 62 S. Cal. L.R. 913–94 (1989) [Perry, "Second-Order Reasons"].

practical reasoning. So, if A defers to B's judgment, he assigns more weight to it than he would otherwise judge it to possess on his own determination of what the balance of reasons requires. He treats the case for the conclusion favoured by B as being stronger to some degree than it actually appears on A's assessment.[5] Clearly, if A's assessment of the issue leads to the same conclusion as B, A does not defer to the latter's judgment by agreeing with it. A is simply acting on his own understanding of what the balance of reasons requires. It is only if the judgment differs from A's own assessment, but he nonetheless assigns additional weight to it, that it becomes an instance of deference to B's judgment. But deference is also a rational strategy for dealing with uncertainty about what the balance of reasons requires.[6] Thus, A can defer to the judgment of B in a situation where A does not know, or is uncertain about, what the correct solution to the problem is. Deference is a rational response to uncertainty.

The second general point is that deference is a matter of degree depending on *how much* weight A assigns to B's judgment. It could range from treating B's judgment as a persuasive reason (of various strengths) to treating it as a conclusive reason for supporting the outcome favoured by B. Treating B's judgment as a persuasive reason amounts to what can be called *partial deference* because it does not preclude or pre-empt A's own judgment of the issue. It is a factor of variable strength that weighs into A's deliberation. However, treating B's judgment as a conclusive reason amounts to *absolute or complete deference*. Here, A surrenders his judgment to B. He declines to make his own assessment on the merits of the issue, deferring completely to B's judgment. Thus, one could say that the House of Lords' deference to its own precedents is partial rather than absolute because although its precedents are authoritative for it, their Lordships are not barred from overruling previous authority. It simply means that it would take a strong reason to outweigh the force attached to the precedent.[7]

These preliminary points are borne out by many of the judicial dicta about the need for judicial deference in the case law arising under the U.K. *Human Rights Act* (HRA). Many judges speak in terms of according a "degree of deference" to the legislature or executive[8] when the context justifies it, and many use the metaphor of attributing (a variable degree of) weight to the decisions of

[5] Thus, Perry refers to the reason to defer to an authority as a "re-weighting reason," *ibid.* at 932.

[6] *Ibid.* at 933.

[7] As Perry puts it, the courts tend to apply a "high weighting threshold to overruling" (*ibid.* at 977).

[8] See, *e.g.*, *Poplar Housing & Regeneration Community Association Ltd. v. Donoghue*, [2002] Q.B. 48 at para. 69 [*Poplar Housing*]; *A v. Secretary of State for the Home Department*, [2005] 2 W.L.R. 87 *per* Lord Rodger at para. 175 [*A. v. Secretary of State*].

Parliament or the executive.[9] Moreover, the case law reveals that judicial deference under the HRA tends to be partial rather than absolute. As Lord Hope put it in *Wilson v. First County Trust*, the need for judicial deference does not mean that "the court is absolutely disabled from forming its own view" on constitutional issues.[10] So, legislative or executive decisions may provide persuasive reasons (of varying strengths) in favour of deferring to the solution chosen by Parliament, but they are not conclusive reasons.[11] This means that it is wrong to assume that judicial deference means an unquestioning acceptance of the determination made by Parliament or the executive. Rather, it is a matter of degree that does not necessarily result in a judicial decision favorable to the elected branches, even if the degree of deference is substantial.[12] Deference to the elected branches does not preclude disagreement with them.[13]

THE RATIONALE OF DEFERENCE

We now have a very rough sketch of the structure of deference, but we need to know about its rationale. When is it appropriate to defer to the judgment of another? I want to suggest that the primary reason for deferring to the judgment of another is when that person's judgment is worthy of respect. A's judgment will be worthy of respect from B if A possesses some qualities superior to those possessed by B, that is, if A has some skill, expertise, or knowledge that B does not possess, or at least not to the same degree.[14] So the reason for deferring to doctors' advice is that they possess medical training and expertise we lack. Even in examples in which the relationship between A and B is not one between an expert and a layperson with no specialist knowledge, the primary rationale for deference is respect for the acknowledged superior claims or qualities of the other. When we defer to the judgments of our friends, partners, or family about what to do, it is generally because we believe that their judgment is likely to be sound.

9 See, *e.g.*, *Brown v. Stott*, [2001] 2 W.L.R. 817 *per* Lord Bingham at para. 39; *International Transport Roth GmbH and others v. Secretary of State for the Home Department*, [2003] Q.B. 728, [*Roth*] *per* Simon Brown L.J. at para. 26, *per* Laws LJ at para. 8; *Secretary of State for the Home Department v. Rehman*, [2002] 1 All E.R. 123 [*Rehman*] *per* Lord Steyn at para. 31; and *A v. Secretary of State*, *supra* note 8 *per* Lord Bingham at para. 29 [*A v. Secretary of State*].

10 [2003] 3 W.L.R. 568 at para. 116.

11 *R v. Lichniak*, [2003] 1 A.C. 903 at para. 14 [*Lichniak*].

12 See, *e.g.*, *Roth*, *supra* note 9.

13 See Timothy Endicott, "International Meaning: Comity in Fundamental Rights Adjudication," (2001) 13 Int'l. J Refugee Law 280 at 286 [Endicott, "International Meaning"].

14 Philip Soper also argues that the primary value underlying deference is respect for others. See *The Ethics of Deference: Learning from Law's Morals* (2002) at 181.

I have been careful to say that deference out of respect for the superior judgment of another is the *primary* rationale of deference. But it is not the only rationale. Sometimes, we defer to others even if we do not respect their judgment. For example, if I want to choose a film to see with a friend, I may defer to her judgment even if I know that her taste in films is poor and is in no way superior to my own. My reason for deferring here is one of courtesy: I want to *show* or *manifest* respect for her, despite the fact that I do not rate her judgment highly. It is a way of *signalling* my respect for her and how I value our friendship.[15] This example shows that there are two reasons for deference, both of which are intimately related to respect: One is respect for the superior judgment of another; the other is that it can be a way of showing respect to another whose relationship one values. This elaboration reveals one important aspect of the nature of deference – namely, that it can perform an expressive function: It creates the *appearance* of regard or respect for another. This expressive function means that I can be deferential towards another person for entirely self-interested or prudential reasons. For example, many people defer to their boss even if they have no regard for their superior qualities, simply because they want to keep their job or get promoted or avoid having acrimony in the workplace. However, even if the real reasons for deferring are self-interested rather than based on respect, one can only achieve those (self-interested) aims if deference communicates an attitude of respect.[16]

This analysis can be applied to judicial deference. Judges owe a degree of deference to the elected branches of government because of "that respect which one great organ of the State owes to another."[17] In other words, it is a requirement of *interinstitutional comity* – the requirement of mutual respect between the branches of government.[18] Although comity does not require the courts to agree with everything Parliament or the executive does, it does

[15] For the idea of deference as a way of *signalling* respect, see Soper, *ibid.* at 25; see also Cheshire Calhoun, "The Virtue of Civility," (2000) 29 Philosophy & Public Affairs 251, at 255, and Sarah Buss, "Appearing Respectful: the Moral Significance of Manners," (1999) 109 Ethics 795 at 801.

[16] I will not rely on the distinction proposed by David Dyzenhaus between "deference as respect" and "deference as submission." See "The Politics of Deference: judicial review and democracy," in Michael Taggart ed., *The Province of Administrative Law* (1997) 279 at 303. On my analysis, deference is *always* due to respect, but varies *in degree* such that it sometimes amounts to what I have called complete deference (what Dyzenhaus calls "deference as submission").

[17] *Buckley v. Attorney General*, [1950] I.R. 67, at 80 *per* O'Byrne J. (referring to the reason for the presumption of constitutionality in Irish constitutional law). For the link between the presumption of constitutionality and the duty of deference to the legislature, see Thayer, *supra* note 1 at 142, 149.

[18] See, *e.g.*, *R. (on the application of Jackson) v. A.G.*, [2005] 3 W.L.R. 733 (the fox-hunting case) at para. 125 (per Lord Hope): "the delicate balance between the various institutions is . . . maintained to a large degree by the mutual respect which each institution has for the

require them to pay respect to their decisions.[19] They do so by attaching weight to them, but also by treating them with courtesy. Even when judges disagree with a decision made by the elected branches, they must, nonetheless, do so respectfully – that is, in a way that does not belittle or ridicule those decisions or delegitimise them. Finally, judges sometimes defer to the elected branches for what I call prudential reasons – that is, to placate a hostile legislature or to avoid making an unpopular decision or one that might bring the judicial role into disrepute. I will consider deference on these grounds later in the chapter.

A QUESTION OF TERMINOLOGY

In a recent case before the House of Lords, Lord Hoffmann suggested that the term deference is an inappropriate way of describing the relationship between the judicial and the other branches of government because of its "overtones of servility, or perhaps gracious concession."[20] It is certainly the case that when we describe someone as "deferential," it can carry negative connotations of behaving in an obsequious, fawning, or servile way. There is a suggestion of humiliation or abasement, of kowtowing to a superior. However, the term deference does not necessarily carry these pejorative overtones. Nor are they central to the meaning of deference. Rather, they refer to being (or appearing) *inappropriately deferential*, either by being too deferential (giving too much weight to the judgments of another) or by being misplaced (paying deference to someone to whom it is not due). So, the overtones of servility refer to a misuse of an approach to practical reasoning that is often perfectly appropriate and sensible. I can pay absolute deference to my doctor's advice, without in any way behaving in an obsequious or fawning way. Nor does it make me a deferential sort of person. It may simply be that this is the most sensible and responsible way for me to make decisions about medical treatment, given my lack of medical knowledge or expertise.

Lord Hoffmann's comments serve to warn us of the mistake of assuming that judicial deference is the same as judicial abasement or submission to the elected branches. But they do not warrant abandoning the terminology of deference altogether. Once we remember that deference is a matter of according various degrees of weight to the judgments of the elected branches out of respect for

other"; see also Chief Justice Beverley McLachlin, "Charter Myths," (1999–2000) U.B.C. L. Rev. 23 at 36 [McLachlin, "Charter Myths"].

[19] Endicott, "International Meaning," *supra* note 13 at 286; see also Timothy Endicott, "The Reason of the Law," 48 Am. J. Juris 83 at 101 (2003).

[20] R. *(on the application of Pro-Life Alliance)*, [2004] 1 A.C. 185 *per* Lord Hoffman at para. 75.

their superior expertise, knowledge, or legitimacy, the overtones of servility Lord Hoffman finds objectionable are subdued, if not removed altogether.

DEFERENCE AND INTERPRETATION

One final explanatory issue concerns the relationship between deference and interpretation. Clearly, the doctrine of deference features in constitutional law decisions about how to interpret legal provisions, but is it a doctrine *of* constitutional interpretation? In order to answer this question, we need some clarification about what interpretation is. I have argued elsewhere that legal interpretation is always driven by evaluative judgments of two kinds.[21] The first is the *substantive evaluation*; the second is what we might call the *institutional evaluation*. The substantive evaluation refers to an evaluation of the merits of interpreting a particular constitutional (or legislative) provision in one way or another. Following Joseph Raz, we can call the reasons for the interpretive outcome that derive from this evaluation "merit reasons."[22] The *institutional evaluation*, on the other hand, engages judges' views about the extent and limits of their own role (including the limits of interpretation) and the implications they have for the correct judicial decision in the circumstances of the particular case.[23] The doctrine of deference is part of the *institutional evaluation* since it concerns the desirability of the judiciary interfering with a legislative or executive decision based on concerns about the limits of their institutional role in the constitutional framework. This part of the evaluation is constituted by "nonmerit reasons." Nonmerit reasons are independent of the substantive evaluation because they are not related to the merits of one substantive outcome over another.[24] So, the doctrine of deference is, indeed, a doctrine of constitutional interpretation, but it is not part of the (central) substantive evaluation. Rather, it features in the institutional evaluation that typically accompanies it.[25]

[21] Aileen Kavanagh, "The Idea of a Living Constitution," (2003) Can. J. L. & Jur. 55 at 65–6.

[22] For the distinction between merit reasons and nonmerit reasons, see Joseph Raz, "On the Authority and Interpretation of Constitutions: Some Preliminaries," in Larry Alexander ed., *Constitutionalism: Philosophical Foundations* (1999) 152 at 173–4, 187–9 [Raz, "Authority and Interpretation"].

[23] For a similar distinction, see Thayer, *supra* note 1 at 144; see also Bickel, "The Passive Virtues," *supra* note 1 at 74.

[24] It should be noted that whilst these two evaluations are conceptually distinct, they are often mixed and difficult to distinguish in practice.

[25] For the view that the substantive evaluation (and the merit reasons that support it) are central or primary because they define the task of the courts in constitutional interpretation, see Raz, "Authority and Interpretation," *supra* note 22 at 187.

MINIMAL AND SUBSTANTIAL DEFERENCE

I have noted that there are varying degrees of deference that judges owe the elected branches. We can now distinguish between *minimal* and *substantial deference*. I shall argue that judges always owe a duty of *minimal deference* to legislative and executive decision-making, but *substantial deference* is only owed exceptionally. *Minimal deference* is the judicial attribution of some presumptive weight to the decision taken by the elected body, but it is not a very strong presumption. It simply requires that the legislature's or executive's decisions are treated with respect in the sense that they should be taken seriously as a bona fide attempt to solve whatever social problem they set out to tackle. Whilst ordinary citizens can view legislative or executive actions in a sceptical way (presuming them to be erroneous or misguided unless proven otherwise) this is an inappropriate attitude for the judiciary to adopt. Judges must always give (minimal) weight to the fact that this is the solution chosen by the legislature or the executive and cannot therefore dismiss it without good reason. Deference in this minimal sense means that judges acting in their judicial capacity cannot make light of, or be sceptical about, attempts by the legislature to solve a social problem in legislation. Moreover, even if judges ultimately disagree with a legislative provision or find it incompatible with bill of rights guarantees, their duty of *minimal deference* means that they should, nonetheless, *display* respect for it.[26]

The duty of *minimal deference* accounts for the fact that judges ought not invalidate an executive decision, or declare legislation to be incompatible with a bill of rights, *merely* on the basis that they disagree with it or because they might have come up with a different solution if they had had the power to make the primary decision. Rather, the error of the legislation must be sufficiently grave to override the presumptive weight in its favour. As Kennedy C. J. put it in the English Court of Appeal: "if the law falls within a reasonable range of alternatives the court will not find it over broad *merely because they can conceive of a better alternative*."[27] This highlights an important aspect of the judicial role – namely, that judges reviewing legislation or executive decisions are secondary rather than primary decision-makers. Even if they might have come to a different decision had they been the primary decision-maker, this, in

[26] As Ruth Gavison puts it, even if courts criticise or even invalidate decisions by the elected branches, they should not "delegitimise" them: "The Role of Courts in Rifted Democracies," (1999) 33 Isr. L.R. 216 at 241.

[27] *R (Pearson) v. Secretary of State for the Home Department*, [2001] H.R.L.R. 39 (emphasis added). Chief Justice Beverley McLachlin has described the approach of the Supreme Court of Canada in similar terms. See McLachlin, "Charter Myths," *supra* note 18 at 29.

itself, does not entitle them to declare that the legislation is unconstitutional. Judges do not have primary responsibility, but rather a secondary responsibility, to ensure that the primary decision-maker has acted in accordance with the requirements of legality. If it violates those requirements, then this must be substantial in order to outweigh the systematic bias in favour of the legislation.

Out of deference to the *competence*, *expertise*, and *constitutional legitimacy* of Parliament as the lawmaking body, the courts in many jurisdictions typically adopt a "reasonableness" rather than a "correctness" standard of review.[28] Under a reasonableness test, the court assesses whether the legislative or executive decision falls within a range of reasonable options. An option is reasonable if it is supported by reasons and is open to justification.[29] Under a correctness test, the court assesses whether the legislative or executive decision is the best one. Under such a test, the court would simply substitute its view for that of the primary decision-maker. Judges are reluctant to substitute one primary decision for another using their own standards of correctness.[30] Rather, having regard for the choice made by the elected branches of government in the particular context, they will assess whether the legislative or executive response was a reasonable one, with compliance with human rights being one of the factors determining its reasonableness. As we will see, a court will only use a correctness standard when it concludes that it is in a better position to deal with the issue and it is convinced it has got the right answer. In that situation, both *reasons of authority* and *epistemic reasons* point in favour of a nondeferential decision. In other words, the court believes it ought to decide this issue as a matter of political responsibility, and it is certain it will do so correctly as a matter of expertise and competence.

So minimal deference applies across the board in all cases. Not so with *substantial deference*. *Substantial deference* has to be earned by the elected branches and is only warranted when the courts judge themselves suffer from particular institutional shortcomings with regard to the issue at hand. These are cases in which they judge the legislature or the executive to have:

a. more institutional competence,
b. more expertise, and/or
c. more legitimacy to assess the particular issue.

[28] For further comment on this distinction, see Perry, "Second-Order Reasons," *supra* note 4 at 938.

[29] In the U.S., the reasonableness test is also referred to as the rational basis test when the question is whether the policy has a rational basis.

[30] See, *e.g.*, Lord Phillips in *R (Mahmood)* v. *Secretary of State for the Home Department*, [2001] 1 W.L.R. 840 at para. 38 (CA): "The court does not substitute its own decision for that of the executive. It reviews the decision of the executive to see whether it is permitted by law – in this instance the Human Rights Act 1998."

These are the three main grounds for substantial deference, and I will consider each in turn.

THE ARGUMENT FROM INSTITUTIONAL COMPETENCE

One institutional limitation that prompts courts to defer to the legislature or the executive is the fact that judicial powers of law-reform are generally piecemeal. Judges' training and expertise equip them to deal with detailed problems arising from the application of existing legal doctrine. They are able to extend or contract the operation of these doctrines to resolve disputes in light of changing conditions. However, they are generally not equipped to engage in radical reform of an entire area of the law.[31] When a case concerns an issue that demands widespread or radical reform of various interlinked areas of the law, a responsible judge will, sometimes, pay substantial deference to the superior *law-making competence* of the legislature. This arose in the House of Lords case of *Bellinger v. Bellinger.*[32]

The issue in that case was whether a postoperative transsexual female could be treated as "female" for the purposes of subsection 11 (c) of the *Matrimonial Causes Act* 1973, which required that the parties to a marriage be "respectively male and female." The House of Lords decided that it was inappropriate to interpret that subsection to include transsexuals such as Mrs. Bellinger because "this would present a major change in the law, having far-reaching ramifications. It raises issues whose solution calls for extensive inquiry and the widest public consultation and discussion."[33] The uncertainty surrounding the circumstances in which gender reassignment could be recognised for the purposes of marriage meant that it was necessary to come up with "objective, publicly available criteria by which gender reassignment is to be assessed,"[34] criteria the Court was not in a position to devise. Because the Court was focused on the facts and evidence pertaining only to Mrs. Bellinger, it did not consider that it would be responsible to change the law on the basis of one individual case.[35] This issue was "part of a wider problem which should be considered as a whole and not dealt with in a piecemeal fashion."[36] Moreover, the recognition of gender reassignment for the purposes of marriage had implications for many other areas of the law, such as education, childcare, criminal law, birth certification, *etc.* Parliament had the lawmaking ability to deal with the varied subject matter and was able to regulate the area in a way that would provide

[31] See generally Joseph Raz, *The Authority of Law: Essays on Law and Morality* (1979) at 196.

[32] [2003] 2 A.C. 467 [*Bellinger*].

[33] *Ibid. per* Lord Nicholls at para. 37.

[34] *Ibid.* at para. 42.

[35] *Ibid.* at paras. 39–44.

[36] *Ibid.* at para. 45.

certainty for those affected. For all of these reasons, the Court decided that the necessary comprehensive reform should be left to Parliament.

The *Bellinger* case highlights another limitation of judicial decision-making that may account for the degree of deference judges pay to the legislature or the executive. This is that judges typically deal with a bivalent form of dispute.[37] Judges are equipped to deal with the question: "Does this legislative provision violate Convention rights?" but not the more general question of how transsexuality should be regulated in disparate areas of the law. In the *Bellinger* case, the Court had no difficulty in establishing that nonrecognition of gender reassignment for the purposes of marriage was incompatible with articles 8 and 12 of the *European Convention on Human Rights* (ECHR)[38] and made a declaration of incompatibility to this effect. No deference was needed here. It was with reference to the broader questions of how the law should be reformed in order to achieve such recognition in a fair way that the Court paid deference to the superior law-making ability of Parliament.

This is not to say that substantial deference is *always* justified even in such situations. The duty of deference is not absolute even in cases in which judges have less institutional competence than the legislature or the executive. If the existing legal doctrine has severe negative consequences for the litigant, and the court believes that the legislature is unwilling or unable to engage in the required radical reform, they may consider it necessary to engage in partial reform in order to achieve justice in the individual case, despite the possible shortcomings of this sort of reform. So, the desirability of deference in cases in which radical law-reform is needed is not a blanket rule. It is a matter of balancing the judicial obligation to do justice in the individual case against the possible disadvantages of partial or incremental reform.[39]

THE ARGUMENT FROM SUPERIOR EXPERTISE

One of the most common arguments advanced in favour of substantial judicial deference is that the courts should defer to the legislature and/or the executive

[37] See Timothy Endicott, "The Impossibility of the Rule of Law," (1999) 19 O.J.L.S. 1 at 15.

[38] *Bellinger*, *supra* note 32 at para. 53.

[39] The Chief Justice of the Supreme Court of Canada, Beverley McLachlin, argues along similar lines that although, as a general rule, the public interest is best served if judges engage in "cautious, incremental, case-by-case adaptation of the law to current circumstances," if the matter is of central importance to society and the rule of law, and there is a legislative inability or unwillingness to address the pressing problem at stake, the courts are justified – albeit rarely – in changing the law dramatically. See "The Supreme Court and the Public Interest," (2001) 64 Sask. L. Rev. 309 at 319.

on questions of "public policy" or matters that are in the public interest. The argument is that the expertise of the courts is in matters of law, not policy, so they should show deference when policy questions arise. The alleged dichotomy between questions of law (which are appropriate for the courts) and questions of policy (which are not) recalls Ronald Dworkin's well-known argument that judges should base their decisions on matters of principle rather than policy, where a "principle" is defined as a "requirement of justice or fairness or some other dimension of morality"[40] and "policy" is defined as "a kind of standard that sets out a goal to be reached, generally an improvement in some economic, political or social feature of the community."[41] So, arguments of principle identify rights, whereas arguments of policy assert that some decision or law will promote the general welfare, the public interest or the collective good. Of course, the plausibility of this suggestion depends on being able to make a meaningful distinction between principles and policies, a possibility doubted by many.[42] But even if it is granted that this distinction can be made, its normative import (the claim that judges *should not* rely on policy arguments) is open to objection.

It should be noted at the outset that it is a recommendation for judges to refrain from doing something they do all the time. Any first-year law student will know that the courts consider alleged social harms when developing the common law or interpreting statutes. They do not consider rights in isolation from those harms, but rather attempt to balance one value against another. Judicial evaluation of policies and legislative goals (including their consequences for society) is part of the "traditional judicial toolkit."[43] But this fact alone does not undermine the normative claim, because it may be (though unlikely, given its pervasiveness) that these decisions are illegitimate on this basis. Luckily, the normative claim can be rejected on its own terms. Judicial decisions take effect in the world in which we live, and to be just, they must take into account the consequences or implications they may have for the various goals the law serves. So, for example, when judges are deciding medical negligence cases, it

[40] Ronald Dworkin, *Taking Rights Seriously* (1977) 22.

[41] *Ibid.*

[42] See Kent Greenawalt, "Policy, Rights, and Judicial Decision," in Marshall Cohen ed., *Ronald Dworkin and Contemporary Jurisprudence* (1983); John Bell, *Policy Arguments in Judicial Decisions* (1983) [Bell, "Policy Arguments"]; Joseph Raz, "Prof Dworkin's Theory of Rights." (1978) 26 Political Studies 123 at 128; John Finnis, "A Bill of Rights for Britain? The Moral of Contemporary Jurisprudence," (1985) 71 *Proceedings of the British Academy* 303 at 315; see also Bradley Miller's contribution to this volume, "Justification of Rights Limitations."

[43] Justice Antonin Scalia, "Judicial Deference to Administrative Interpretations of Law," (1989) Duke L.J. 511 at 515.

is entirely legitimate for them to consider (as they often do) the impact their decision will have on medical practice.[44] Similarly, if judges have to decide whether a member of the police force owes a duty of care to members of the public, they must consider the impact this would have on the conduct of police business and their ability to suppress crime, as well as consequences for legal development and the role of the courts.[45]

This is the familiar floodgates argument, familiar because it is such a common and accepted feature of judicial decision-making. If judges made these decisions without any consideration of collective goals and practical consequences, their decisions would be profoundly unjust. Lord Steyn has pointed out that not only is it "an everyday occurrence" for courts to consider matters of policy, "it would be a matter of public disquiet if the court did not do so."[46] The reason for this is that the just resolution of any case requires that the facts of that case should be viewed in light of the social realities that attend them. Judges have a responsibility to ensure, to the extent that they can, that their decisions are correct and one factor determining the correctness of their decisions will be whether they correctly evaluate the policy issues that inevitably arise in the course of their decisions.[47]

Aside from the moral responsibility to consider the policy implications of the decisions they make, they, in fact, have no alternative but to do so when making many decisions under the HRA. After all, many of the freedoms protected by the Convention are expressly subject to limits necessary in a democratic society in the interests of various public goals, such as "national security," "public safety," "the economic well-being of the country," and "the prevention of disorder or crime." All these matters involve policy issues and it would be an abdication of the judicial function to say that they are nonjusticiable when judges are given a mandate by Parliament to adjudicate them under the HRA.[48] This reflects a more general point, namely, that to the extent that a statute explicitly promotes collective goals, judges cannot interpret those laws faithfully without some consideration and evaluation of how best to promote them.[49]

The principle/policy distinction has been resurrected by Conor Gearty to show that when a case arising under the HRA is a matter of legal principle,

[44] Lord Woolf, "Are the Courts Excessively Deferential to the Medical Profession?" (2001) 9 Med. L. Rev. 2.

[45] See, *e.g.*, *Hill v. Chief Constable of West Yorkshire*, [1989] A.C. 53 *per* Lord Templeman at 65.

[46] Steyn, "Deference," *supra* note 2 at 357.

[47] See Andrew Ashworth, "Interpreting Criminal Statutes: a Crisis of Legality," (1991) 107 L.Q.R. 419 at 443.

[48] Steyn, "Deference," *supra* note 2.

[49] See Bell, "Policy Arguments," *supra* note 42 at 222.

the courts should be activist, but deference is required when policy issues are involved. He relies on the metaphor of a swimming pool "with the shallow end marked 'legal principle' and the deep end marked 'public policy'."[50] Judges can be assured and assertive when adjudicating at the former end, but should recognise that they are "entirely out of their depth"[51] in the latter. This claim is open to the objections already levelled at Dworkin's distinction. But there is another problem that besets this analysis, namely, that the cases under the HRA (or indeed any other constitutional document guaranteeing rights) do not arise in separate categories marked "legal principle" or "public policy." Rather, they are often, if not typically, entwined. In fact, all of the interesting and difficult cases involving the desirability of deference do not lie at either end of Gearty's metaphorical pool. Rather, they are cases that simultaneously involve both legal principle of the highest constitutional order *and* public policy. One might say that they are simultaneously in the shallow and the deep end of the pool and, because this is a conceptual impossibility, the metaphor seems unhelpful as a way of illuminating the question of the desirability of judicial deference.[52]

The real distinction here is that between *the type of policy decision appropriate to the institutional features, competence, and legitimacy of the courts and the type of policy decision that is beyond that competence*. Though certainly not as succinct or as pleasingly alliterative as the "principle/policy" distinction, it brings us to the heart of the real concerns and difficulties surrounding judicial deference. First, it emphasises that if a case contains an element of public policy, this does not mean that the issue is necessarily beyond review by the courts, or that substantial deference is *automatically* required. Rather, it means that the courts must fulfil their duty of upholding constitutional principle, whilst bearing in mind any limits on their expertise, competence, or legitimacy that may warrant a degree of deference. Secondly, it emphasises that the determination of how much deference is due to the elected branches of government is deeply contextual and cannot be answered by simply demarcating subject-areas where deference is appropriate. Rather, it is the (complex) task of assessing whether the court's competence, expertise, and legitimacy equip them to judge this particular issue with confidence. So, instead of seeking to solve the issue of

[50] Conor Gearty, *Principles of Human Rights Adjudication* (2004) at 121.

[51] *Ibid.* at 122.

[52] Admittedly, Gearty seems to allow for the possibility of some cases being located on a sort of borderline between principle and policy (*i.e.* the middle of the pool) where judges "assert[] an issue to be one of legal principle while all the time they are sliding into ever-deeper water," *ibid.* at 122. However, it is not clear how to apply this metaphorical description to the caselaw other than to say that such cases simultaneously involve a strong principle *and* policy dimension.

deference by asking "Is this a case involving immigration policy or housing policy or national security etc.?" judges have to embark on the much more difficult and multifaceted inquiry into relative institutional competence, bearing in mind all the factors relevant in the context of the individual case. These will include not only the policy context of the case and the relative expertise and competence of the courts (and the judicial process) in dealing with that context, but also the degree of intrusion into Convention rights, the nature of the right at issue, and the extent (and type) of law-reform necessary to rectify the alleged rights violation. So although the subject matter of the case is relevant to the appropriate degree of deference, it is not determinative.

It should be conceded straight away that the distinction proposed here fails to provide us with a clear-cut method of identifying in advance which subject-matter is appropriate for judicial decision-making and which is not. The allure of the principle/policy distinction was that it purported to do this. However, it could not deliver on this promise, partly because it exaggerated the differences between the subject matter and decision-making processes appropriate to the judicial bodies on the one hand, and the elected branches on the other. In so doing, it distorted the extent to which *both* principle *and* policy have a role to play in both spheres. The distinction proposed here attempts to be faithful to the reality (and complexity) of the tasks facing the courts when they have to decide whether, and to what extent, to defer to the elected branches.

The more contextual approach entailed by this distinction can be illustrated by the House of Lords case of *Ghaidan v. Mendoza*.[53] The issue there was whether the word "spouse" in the *Rent Act 1977* could be read to include homosexual partners so as to enable a gay man to succeed to a secure tenancy on the death of his partner. Although there were precedents for substantial deference in the area of housing policy,[54] the House of Lords found in favour of the claimant. Whilst the Court acknowledged that Parliament is charged with "the primary responsibility for deciding the best way of dealing with social problems,"[55] this did not mean that the court ought not to intervene. Even if a case arises in an area in which "Parliament has to hold a fair balance between the competing interests of tenant and landlords taking into account broad issues of social and economic policy," the existence of possible discrimination meant that the courts would scrutinise with intensity any reasons in favour of the discriminatory regime.

[53] [2004] 3 W.L.R. 113 [*Ghaidan*].

[54] Counsel for the defendant relied on *Poplar Housing*, supra note 8, when arguing for a deferential judicial approach.

[55] *Ghaidan*, *supra* note 53 at para. 19.

Three points are worth noting about this decision. First, although the Court was cognisant of, and sensitive to, the policy context in which Parliament enacted the legislation under scrutiny, this context did not preclude intense scrutiny by the courts of the justification for the policy. Secondly, we should note Lord Nicholl's use of the word "primary" in his judgment in *Ghaidan*. Although Parliament is the primary decision-maker on matters of policy and therefore an assessment of its merits is *primarily* for Parliament, it is not *exclusively* so. We must remember that the courts have a legitimate reviewing role that involves them in making their own assessment of the legislative provision with reference to standards of legality. Of course, they do not have general jurisdiction to assess the pros and cons of legislation all things considered, but they are charged with the task of assessing legislation's compliance with Convention rights. After all, if Parliament were the sole judge of all the advantages and disadvantages of legislative policy, this would emasculate the courts' reviewing role.

Nor should it be assumed that simply because the courts may not have the competence to make the primary decision, they will *therefore* lack the competence to engage in (forthright) secondary review of that decision. In other words, even though we would not allocate to the courts the job of devising a comprehensive housing policy for the whole country, it does not necessarily follow that they are ill suited to the task of reviewing part of an existing policy for compliance with human rights standards. Finally, the Court was certain that the legislation was discriminatory.[56] Their confidence that there was a clear violation of rights led to less deference being paid to the primary decision-maker.[57] Therefore, whilst being aware of the policy context of the legislation, the crucial factors determining the degree of deference will be (a) whether there is a *clear* violation of rights, (b) whether the legal change required to rectify that violation lies within the court's law-making competence, and (c) whether the reform is likely to upset the whole legislative framework set up by Parliament to tackle the social problem at issue. All three factors were present in the *Ghaidan* case.

So substantial deference must be earned rather than assumed. The courts need to be vigilant in scrutinising whether there are any particular claims of

[56] The fact that the legislation was discriminatory was accepted without much discussion by all five members of the House of Lords, including Lord Millett, who dissented on the issue of whether the discrimination could be removed by way of interpretation, *ibid.* at para. 55.

[57] Perry, "Second-Order Reasons," *supra* note 4 at 938, argues that there is often an inverse relationship between deference and the strength of the judge's conviction that the primary decision maker has erred. Interference with the primary decision will only occur if the conviction rises above a certain epistemic threshold.

superior expertise and competence in the context of the individual case, rather than adopting a crude subject-based approach that predetermines the issue.[58]

THE ARGUMENT FROM DEMOCRATIC LEGITIMACY

The final reason for substantial deference is that of superior institutional legitimacy. Do the courts owe the elected branches of government substantial deference out of respect for the latter's superior institutional legitimacy? Of course, this begs the question whether the elected branches of government actually have more institutional legitimacy than the courts. A comprehensive answer to this question would require us to identify the different sources of legitimacy for all three branches of government and compare them – a task beyond the scope of this chapter. Instead, I will concentrate on the narrower question of whether the superior *democratic* legitimacy of the elected branches of government warrants deference from the courts.

On my analysis, the democratic legitimacy of the elected branches of government is one of the reasons why the courts owe the decisions of the elected branches *minimal deference*. Judges ought to respect the decisions made by the elected branches, in part because they have been made by a body that has been democratically elected. As Lord Bingham put it in *R. v. Lichniak*: "The fact that a statutory provision represents the settled will of a democratic assembly is not a conclusive reason for upholding it, but a degree of deference is due to the judgments of the democratic assembly on how a social problem is best tackled."[59] Our political system, being a democratic one, necessarily values democratic legitimacy and allocates the primary lawmaking power to those who possess it. Therefore, the decisions made by that body are worthy of respect.

But does superior democratic legitimacy also warrant *substantial deference*? We noted earlier that substantial deference needs to be earned rather than assumed. If superior democratic legitimacy warranted substantial deference across the board, it would emasculate the judges' reviewing role in the constitutional framework. So, if deference is owed to the elected branches on this ground, then it must be justified in the circumstances of the individual case. Can such a justification be found? Although it is hard to generalise here,

[58] For a rejection of the subject-based approach to deference along similar lines, see Murray Hunt, "Sovereignty's Blight: Why Contemporary Public Law Needs the Concept of 'Due Deference'," in Nicholas Bamforth and Peter Leyland eds., *Public Law in a Multi-Layered Constitution* (2003) 337 at 351; see also T.R.S. Allan, "Common Law Reason and the Limits of Judicial Deference," in David Dyzenhaus ed., *The Unity of Public Law* (2004) 289 at 294–5.

[59] *Lichniak*, *supra* note 11 at para. 14.

one can imagine cases in which judges (rightly) believe that it is inappropriate for them to change the law on a particularly sensitive issue about which there is widespread social controversy, because such a decision would have a greater chance of being accepted in society if it were introduced by the elected branches of government.[60] This may be attributable, in part, to the resources available to the elected branches – they will be able to consult with relevant interest groups, promote and get in involved in public discussion, set up advertising campaigns and educational programmes in order to ensure that the legal change has greater chances of being accepted and supported. But beyond these mechanisms, there is also the very fact of democratic legitimacy that, depending on the legal and political culture, may make societal acceptance of the legal change more likely.

It should be noted that deference on grounds of superior democratic legitimacy has attracted some criticism in the United Kingdom. For example, Jeffrey Jowell has argued that whilst one can accept the need for judicial deference on grounds of superior institutional competence, one cannot accept it on grounds of superior democratic legitimacy.[61] He advances three arguments in favour of this proposition. First, if we accept the argument for deference based on superior democratic legitimacy, the courts would be required to defer automatically, on constitutional grounds, on any occasion in which a qualified right was claimed to be limited by the public interest.[62] Secondly, the HRA has fundamentally altered the constitutional landscape in the United Kingdom so that "the primacy of representative status and political accountability has been erased."[63] The courts should not presume that elected branches are constitutionally best suited to decide a matter "simply because of their representative character and the fact that they are politically accountable to the electorate."[64] Finally, it would be an abdication of the court's constitutional responsibility to yield its decisions about the balance between rights and the public interest to the legislature or any other body.[65]

A number of responses need to be made to these claims. First, it does not necessarily follow that if we accept superior democratic legitimacy as a factor justifying judicial deference, the courts should therefore "delegate"[66] all their decisions to the elected branches. As noted earlier, deference is not an all or

[60] This was Lord Hoffmann's concern in *Rehman*, *supra* note 9 at para. 62.

[61] See Jeffrey Jowell, "Judicial Deference: Civility, Servility or Institutional Capacity?" (2003) P.L. 592 at 596; see also Steyn, "Deference," *supra* note 2 at 358.

[62] Jowell, "Judicial Deference and Human Rights: A Question of Competence," in P. Craig and R. Rawlings eds., *Law and Administration in Europe* (2003) at 73.

[63] *Ibid.* at 75.

[64] *Ibid.*

[65] *Ibid.* at 80.

[66] *Ibid.*

nothing matter; it is a matter of degree and will vary in accordance with the context of a case, the nature of the decision, the extent of the rights violation, *et cetera*. There is no reason to believe that superior democratic legitimacy, even if accepted as a legitimate reason for judicial deference, would be a conclusive (rather than persuasive) reason in its favour.

The argument for deference on grounds of democratic legitimacy does not mean that judges should deny their own authority on any issue that touches on "public policy." On the contrary, the judiciary should not doubt their own legitimacy to carry out the tasks allocated to them – namely, to apply, interpret, and develop the law in a responsible way, in light of existing legal doctrine and the demands of justice in individual cases. Judges are under an oath to uphold the administration of justice and would abdicate their duty if they were to pay substantial deference to the elected branches in a *routine* manner, simply because they do not possess democratic legitimacy. There may be *exceptional cases* in which a particular law reform would cause widespread upheaval in society and, in these cases, the democratic legitimacy of the elected branches of government might be an advantage in securing support and consensus behind the change. As such, it would be a factor leading to a degree of judicial deference.

Secondly, whilst it is certainly the case that the HRA has brought about significant changes in U.K. constitutional law, it seems hyperbolic to claim that it has "erased" the primacy of representative government and democratic accountability. That the U.K. courts now possess greater powers to protect rights than before does not undermine the fact that the primary law-making powers still rest with the elected branches of government. These branches draw their legitimacy (in part) from the fact that they have been chosen by a majority of people to represent them. As Jowell points out, we should not equate democracy with majority rule – we also expect our elected representatives to make good decisions.[67] But just as majority rule is not all there is to democracy, nor can it be dismissed as irrelevant to the legitimacy of the elected branches. Simply put: The fact that Parliament is popularly elected and subject to removal by the electorate is one of its institutional features that warrants respect from the judiciary.

A final question is whether Parliament is entitled to more judicial deference than the executive, given that the latter does not have the same degree of democratic legitimacy as the former. This was suggested by Lord Justice Laws

[67] For an argument that the condition of good government is of central importance for the justification of democratic authority, see Aileen Kavanagh, "Participation and Judicial Review: A Reply to Jeremy Waldron," (2003) 22 Law & Phil. 451 at 460.

in *International Transport Roth GmbH and others v. Secretary of State for the Home Department*, in which he claimed that "greater deference is to be paid to an Act of Parliament than to a decision of the executive or subordinate measure."[68] Although he did not explain the rationale of this principle, a likely candidate is that Parliament has more democratic legitimacy. I do not think that this is a principle of general import. The reason is that the degree of deference in any particular case will be dependent on the overall context as determined by a number of different factors, such as the expertise of the primary decision-maker, the policy context in which the decision was reached, whether the court would be more or less likely to reach the right decision, which Convention right is involved and the extent of the alleged breach, and so on. Democratic legitimacy is one (often subordinate) factor in this overall assessment. If it were the only relevant factor, then it might be true to say that greater deference is to be paid to an Act of Parliament than to a decision of the executive. But it is not the only relevant factor, often not even the most significant factor. Therefore, it is dubious as a general principle.

DEFERENCE FOR PRUDENTIAL REASONS

Doctrines of deference are sometimes invoked by judges for what might be called prudential reasons.[69] One has a prudential reason to perform an act if performing it will, in some way, advance one's interests or prevent them being adversely affected. So, for example, a court may be deferential in order to placate a hostile legislature, which might otherwise limit the powers of the court. Or it may wish to preserve the court's reputation as an impartial enforcer of the law, so as to ensure that confidence in its judgments is not undermined[70] or to allay fears of those keen to criticise it.[71] It has sometimes

[68] *Supra* note 9 at para. 71.

[69] Bickel believed that prudence (rather than principle) underpins judicial decisions to withhold judgment on the merits of a constitutional dispute. See Bickel, "The Passive Virtues," *supra* note 1 at 49, 68, and 79.

[70] Lord Steyn suggests that when developing the common law, judges must "proceed with caution lest they undermine confidence in their judgments." See Steyn, "Deference," *supra* note 2 at 348. See also Thayer, *supra* note 1, at 142, who argues that if judges interfere too readily in decisions of the elected branches, "it must diminish the reverence for the laws which is essential to the public safety and happiness."

[71] See, *e.g.*, Lord Bingham, who observed extra-judicially that the courts would pay deference to the elected branches under the HRA because "to do so would certainly help to allay the fears of those who see incorporation as an objectionable judicial usurpation of democratic authority"; see "Incorporation of the ECHR: The Opportunity and the Challenge," [1998] 2 Jersey L. Rev. 257 at 269–70.

been claimed that the European Court of Human Rights is deferential to national governments because of "the strategic argument about the risk of loss of state support"[72] – that is, the fear that an adverse decision from the court would lead to the withdrawal of a State party from the Convention.[73] Reliance on prudential or strategic arguments such as these has tended to give judicial deference a bad name: It has led to claims that it is a self-denying ordinance that provides a cloak for excessive judicial timidity in the face of serious rights violations.[74] This, critics argue, is nothing short of "an abdication by the court of its enforcement responsibilities."[75]

Furthermore, deferential decisions seem all the more objectionable because the courts sometimes conceal their prudential reasons for deferring, emphasising instead an aspect of the *substantive evaluation* that leads them to a judgment in favour of the elected branches. Let us deal with this objection about concealment first. It is certainly the case that judges sometimes underplay the political considerations affecting their decisions. The politics of judicial decision-making is such that judges are often under considerable political pressure to make it seem as if the outcome of the case follows only from an assessment of the substantive legal issues involved. However, it can be self-defeating to make one's actual reasons for deference explicit. As noted at the beginning of this chapter, deference can be a way of *showing* or *manifesting* respect, and it would be counterproductive to make explicit the fact that it is only a matter of show. It would be pointless for judges to adopt a deferential decision and advance as the only reason in support of it that they wish to placate a hostile legislature. Only a decision that *seems* genuinely respectful to the legislature's decision is likely to placate the legislature. So concealing judicial reservations about or, indeed, outright disapproval of, a decision of the elected branches may be the only way of preserving the rationale of deference.

Aside from this issue of strategic advantage, many will find the prospect of judicial reliance on prudential reasons deeply objectionable on more substantive grounds. They will say that judges ought to confine themselves to

[72] See Susan Marks, "Civil Liberties at the Margin: the UK Derogation and the European Court of Human Rights," (1995) 15 O.J.L.S. 69 at 93 [Marks, "Civil Liberties at the Margin"].

[73] Though this strategic reason seemed to have more force in early decisions of the Court. See Tim Jones, "The Devaluation of Human Rights Under the European Convention," [1995] P.L. 430 at 437 [Jones, "The Devaluation of Human Rights"].

[74] See, *e.g.*, Marks, "Civil Liberties at the Margin," *supra* note 72 at 76.

[75] See Jones, "The Devaluation of Human Rights," *supra* note 73 at 432. For other examples of deference for prudential reasons under the ECHR, see Yutaka Arai-Takahashi, *The Margin of Appreciation Doctrine and the Principle of Proportionality in the Jurisprudence of the ECHR* (2002), at 99 and 232.

the substantive evaluation involved in the case, and if this leads to an outcome unfavourable to the elected branches of government, so be it. The courts should decide on the law and not get involved in prudential calculations about possible (political) consequences for them or anyone else. Their job is to enforce existing rights – the likely reaction of others is entirely irrelevant.[76] I do not agree with this argument because it relies on an unduly narrow conception of the judicial role. As noted earlier, judges have not one but two general tasks when making their decisions: The first is to decide on the substantive merits of the individual case; the second (related) task is to make a decision on the extent and limits of their own institutional role. It would be irresponsible for judges to decide cases whilst remaining oblivious to their possible consequences,[77] and these include prudential concerns such as whether a particular judicial decision would produce a backlash in society; whether society is ready for the legal change; whether it might be counterproductive to introduce it at this particular time; and whether the elected branches of government would then move to curtail the powers of the courts as a result.

Although judges have an obligation to do justice in the individual case, that is not their only obligation. They also need to ensure that the courts, themselves, are respected not only in society as a whole, but also amongst the other branches of government and that none of their decisions bring them into disrepute. Moreover, they need to understand the political context in which they operate. They are the weakest branch of government and are dependent on the other branches of government to respect and implement their decisions. Given this dependence, the continued power of the courts to make law and do justice in individual cases depends, in part, on not alienating the legislature and executive. This is a reason in favour of restraint in judicial decision-making. It means that nonmerit reasons can sometimes defeat merit reasons in constitutional adjudication.

However, that is not to say that judges should kowtow to the elected branches whenever they issue a threat to curtail the powers of the courts or attempt to undermine their decisions. Judges must assess the seriousness of the threat, whether it is a matter of empty political posturing or, alternatively, whether it is underpinned by a serious drive to change the law; whether it is made by the

[76] I take T.R.S. Allan to make a sophisticated version of this basic claim. See T.R.S. Allan, "Human Rights and Judicial Review: A Critique of 'Due Deference'," (2006) 65 Cambridge L.J. 671 at 683 and 688–9.

[77] As Lord Bingham pointed out (extra-judicially), the courts make their decisions "in the light of legal principle and such authority as there is, *and having regard to the apprehended practical consequences of one decision as opposed to another*, what the law should be." See Lord Bingham, "The Courts and the Constitution," (1996/7) 7 King's College L.J. 12 at 16 [emphasis added].

head of government, or the leader of the opposition whose popularity is waning; *etc.* Even if it is serious, this does not necessarily mean automatic or complete deference. It may simply mean that judges have to *present* their decisions in a deferential manner, even if they ultimately oppose the elected branches in the substance of their decision.[78] Or it may mean that judges should be strategic in their decision-making. They may consider it prudent to be deferential in one case in order to win themselves more freedom to do justice in future cases. Moreover, the judges may be aware that their decisions will be supported by the public at large, even if they are irksome to the government of the day. This can embolden them to resist the political pressure to hand down deferential decisions. But it would be foolhardy for judges to be oblivious to any serious proposals to change the law in a significant way, in particular, if it would reduce their powers. Just as they are concerned to do justice in the individual case, they must also be concerned with their more long-term ability to fulfil this role. This is not to say that prudential reasons are always of overriding importance. There are cases in which the courts decide (rightly) to move more quickly than the pace of society and do justice in the instant case, despite (legitimate) worries about the feasibility of implementation.[79] It may be that the injustice is so heinous that the courts feel they have no other option, especially if there is no sign of reform coming from any other branch of government.

Finally, it should not be assumed that the "prudential" reasons for deference outlined in this section are completely detached from moral reasons. In fact, when judges assess the desirability of deference, the prudential and moral reasons in favour of it are deeply intertwined. For example, the argument that judges ought not to interfere with a legislative or executive decision because of fear of a future legislative attack on their independence is partly based on institutional self-interest and self-preservation. But underlying this is a (moral) concern to preserve the reputation of the courts and the laws they uphold, thus enhancing their ability to decide cases justly. A decision not to introduce a legal change because the courts believe that society is not ready for the change, or at least not ready for the change to be introduced *by them*, again presents a mixture of different types of reasons. The courts may not want to aggravate the legislature or go against the prevailing tide. But there may also be

[78] What I have in mind here are *obiter* judicial comments that emphasise a judicial acceptance that Parliament is the primary law-making body and that judges have a duty to respect Parliament's will, *etc.*

[79] In the U.S. context, *Brown v. Board of Education*, 347 U.S. 483 (1954), is the classic example. However, the difficulty in implementing *Brown*, which lasted for decades, shows that the prudential and moral reasons in favour of postponing such a legal change can have tremendous force. See Andrei Marmor, *Interpretation and Legal Theory*, 2nd edn. (2005) at 162.

good moral reason not to introduce untimely change, for which the majority of people in society are not ready. It might be better (both for prudential and moral reasons) to postpone legal change until it would be better received and easier to implement. So prudential reasons and moral reasons are often deeply intertwined and mutually supportive.[80] This is not surprising. Judicial deference is part of the *institutional evaluation* judges must always undertake when they interpret legal texts. It engages concerns about the separation of powers and the relative role of institutions in the constitutional order, which is, at bottom, a moral issue. Because these division-of-labour questions underlie the prudential reasons we examined, it follows that judges must act on the moral considerations that apply to these questions when considering whether they ought to defer. One final point: It might be thought that when judges defer completely to the elected branches, they thereby avoid relying on their own view of the moral issues involved. This is a mistake. Even when deferring completely to the elected branches, judges are still acting on their own (moral) judgment. By deciding that it is appropriate to defer, they have come to a moral view about what constitutional propriety demands of them and which institution should prevail.

DEFERENCE AND NATIONAL SECURITY

I have argued that subject matter is not a conclusive factor leading to substantial deference. However, where issues of national security have been involved, there has been a judicial tendency towards substantial, if not complete, deference. So it is worth taking a look at the particular issues arising from cases involving national security. Historically in the United Kingdom, "the mere incantation of the phrase [national security] of itself instantly discourage[d] the court from satisfactorily fulfilling its normal role of deciding where the balance of public interest lies."[81] However, in recent years the United Kingdom courts have been less awestruck by "the mantra of national security"[82] and more ready to scrutinise the weight of claims made by the executive under this

[80] The fact that it is sometimes hard to divide judicial reasoning into moral and prudential reasons may support Raz's view that when we deliberate, we just consider which reasons are most pressing in a way that defies the common division of practical thought into moral and self-interested reasons. See Joseph Raz, *Engaging Reason: On the Theory of Value and Action* (1999) at 303. For discussion of the implications of this insight in understanding the type of moral reasoning found in judicial decision-making, see Jeremy Waldron, "Do Judges Reason Morally?" in this volume.

[81] Simon Brown L.J., "Public Interest Immunity," (1994) P.L. 579 at 589.

[82] *Ibid.* at 590.

heading. At the very least, there is now widespread judicial support for the view that national security is not nonjusticiable.[83] However, there is still no doubt that substantial deference remains the order of the day, with judges according the views of the executive and Parliament "great weight" on such issues.[84]

There are three main reasons why decisions made in the national security area tend to attract substantial deference from the courts. First, when issues of national security are involved, the executive or legislature often claim that some of the information on which their decision was based must be kept secret.[85] National security issues present the courts with a dilemma. On the one hand, they have a constitutional mandate to ensure that decisions made by the elected branch comply with the rule of law and with human rights. On the other hand, they acknowledge the peculiar expertise of the elected branches in making decisions in this area and therefore owe them substantial deference. This dilemma is heightened by the secrecy that attends many questions of national security.[86] Clearly, if a court, in carrying out its reviewing role, does not have access to all the information on which the primary decision was based, this fact alone will (rightly) lead it to pay more deference to the primary decision-maker because it will be less confident that it could arrive at a better decision than the primary decision-maker. As noted earlier, deference is a rational response to uncertainty, and uncertainty will be heightened in a case in which secrecy surrounds some of the relevant facts. The courts have no other choice but to be deferential in such a situation and to give the elected branches of government the benefit of any doubts they may have, either about the executive decision itself or the intelligence on which it is based. Without access to independent sources of information, or their own intelligence service, it is very difficult for the courts to challenge executive decisions on a sure footing when they are not in possession of the information leading to the decision.[87]

[83] Lord Steyn in *Rehman*, *supra* note 9 at para. 31.

[84] See, *e.g.*, *A v. Secretary of State*, *supra* note 8 *per* Lord Hope at para. 112, *per* Lord Walker at para. 192.

[85] Thus, in *A. v. Secretary of State*, *ibid.*, the higher courts were not invited by the Attorney General to look at the closed material relevant to the case, as noted by Lord Hope para. 117; Lord Bingham para. 27; and Lord Hoffman, para. 94.

[86] *A. v. Secretary of State*, *ibid. per* Lord Walker at para. 193.

[87] Of course, this is not a knockdown argument in favour of substantial judicial deference. Rather, it could ground an argument in favour of imaginative institutional design so that specialist courts could be set up with expertise in national security matters, equipped to deal with confidential and sensitive security information. My point is simply that *if* courts are not in possession of the information on which the primary decision was based (which, as things stand, they often are not), substantial deference may be the appropriate judicial response.

Secondly, judges' awareness of the life and death consequences of some decisions made in the national security area will cause them to err on the side of caution and safety. They are aware that they could get the decision wrong as well as the possibly catastrophic consequences of such an error. This worry about the consequences of error in this area was made explicit in the judgment of a specialist court set up to adjudicate immigration issues in the United Kingdom: It stated that when there is a "risk of destruction and mayhem on a very substantial scale, those responsible for deciding whether the risk exists and what measures are necessary to try and ensure that it is not translated into a reality must be allowed a reasonably wide margin of discretion."[88] Judicial awareness of their limitations is, therefore, especially acute in the area of national security. The chances that a court would "second-guess" some national security decisions, under these conditions of inadequate information and fear of error, are slim. Thirdly, many decisions made in the national security area are anticipatory. They are based on factual predictions of what people might or might not do – in other words, they involve risk assessments about possible future events. Especially when courts are prevented from seeing the intelligence on which such predictions are based, they are not well placed to challenge them.

It might be thought that these factors contradict the point made earlier that there should be no predetermined subject-areas automatically beyond the competence of the court. Surely cases involving national security are beyond judges' competence, expertise, and legitimacy, and should attract substantial deference across the board? This conclusion is too rash. The three grounds of deference outlined earlier help to explain why substantial deference is *sometimes* warranted in the national security area. But this is a far cry from saying that judges should *always* defer, and *never* have a useful role to play in adjudicating national security issues. Cases involving national security cover a large variety of decisions, some of which are beyond the expertise or competence of the court to challenge, some of which are not. The nature of the decision (its gravity, urgency, and sensitivity, as well as its impact on human rights) determines the degree of deference that is appropriate.[89] This can be illustrated

[88] The Special Immigration Appeals Commission (SIAC), established by the *Special Immigration Appeals Commission Act* 1997, in *A. v. Secretary of State, supra* note 8 at para. 21. For comment on SIAC's decision, see Mark Elliott, "Constitutional Developments: United Kingdom," (2003) 1 Int. J. Con. L. 334 at 339.

[89] For discussion of the "differential character of issues for which the shield of national security may be claimed," see David Feldman, "Proportionality and the Human Rights Act," in Evelyn Ellis ed., *The Principle of Proportionality in the Laws of Europe* (1999) 117 at 133.

by the recent House of Lords decision in *A v. Secretary of State for the Home Department*, known as the "Belmarsh prison" case.[90]

There, the nine people detained in Belmarsh prison under section 23 of the *Anti-Terrorism, Crime and Security Act 2001* claimed that this section violated articles 5 and 14 of the ECHR. Section 23 contained the power to detain indefinitely non-nationals in circumstances in which they had been determined by the Secretary of State to be a security risk but could not be deported. When enacting this provision, the U.K. government derogated from Article 5 of the Convention, which precludes indefinite detention. The detainees had two main arguments. The first was that there was no emergency "threatening the life of the nation" as required by Article 15 of the Convention to justify a derogation. Secondly, even if there were such an emergency, the decision to detain indefinitely non-nationals without trial was not "strictly required by the exigencies of the situation" as required by Article 15. The central issue in the case concerned the appropriate standard or intensity of review with which the court should assess these two questions. Acting on behalf of the Secretary of State, the Attorney General argued that it was for Parliament and the executive to assess the threat facing the nation, as well as for those bodies (and not the courts) to judge the response necessary to protect the security of the public. The elected branches of government were entitled to a wide margin of appreciation on both questions, especially as they were matters of national security and the courts must accept that such matters fell within the discretionary area of judgment belonging to the democratic organs of the state. In short, the Attorney General's argument was that both issues were essentially nonjusticiable.

The House of Lords rejected this submission. Its reasoning is interesting and, for the most part, supports the account of deference provided here. First, their Lordships made clear that although substantial deference may be appropriate in matters of national security, complete deference was not. Even on the question of whether the derogation was justified, the Court warned that deference "cannot be taken too far. Deference does not mean abasement to [the views of government or Parliament], even in matters of national security."[91] Although the decisions and views of the elected branches should be given great weight in this area, deference did not mean that the Court was disabled from assessing the merits of the decisions. Secondly, the Court emphasised

[90] [2005] 2 A.C. 68 [*Belmarsh Prison*]. For a more detailed analysis of this case, see David Dyzenhaus, "Deference, Security and Human Rights," in Benjamin J. Goold and Liora Lazarus, *Security and Rights* (2007) [Dyzenhaus, "Deference, Security and Human Rights"].

[91] *Belmarsh Prison, ibid. per* Lord Rodgers at para. 176; see also Lord Bingham at para. 41.

that since "national security" can sometimes be used as a pretext for bringing in measures that are not objectively justified, the judiciary must be vigilant to scrutinise those measures to check whether they are strictly required in the exigencies of the situation.[92] In other words, the doctrine of judicial deference in appropriate circumstances did not preclude the court from subjecting decisions about national security to scrutiny.[93] Deference was not to be equated with an uncritical review.

Thirdly, Lord Bingham clarified that although "any decision made by a representative democratic body must of course command respect, the degree of respect will be conditioned by the nature of the decision."[94] The Court paid more deference to the executive and Parliament on the question of the justifiability of the derogation than on the question of the particular means chosen by them to meet the state of emergency. The Court accepted that the question of whether there is an emergency and whether it threatens the life of the nation are "pre-eminently a matter for the executive and for Parliament. The judgment that has to be formed on these issues is outside the expertise of the courts."[95] It is worth noting that the Court did not see some "closed material" related to the decision to derogate and decided to defer to the judgment of the Special Immigration Appeals Commission, which had seen this material and had concluded that there was a public emergency threatening the life of the nation. Although Lord Scott expressed "very grave doubt" about whether the public emergency was one that justified the description of threatening the life of the nation, he was, nonetheless, prepared to allow the Secretary of State "the benefit of the doubt on this point."[96] The judges' comments on this issue remind us of the point made earlier: Deference is a rational response to uncertainty. Lord Scott could not challenge the decision of the Secretary of State on a sure footing because he was not in possession of all the information on which the decision was made. Mere "doubt," no matter how grave, cannot ground a judicial finding against the Secretary of State, because in order to be justified as an interference with an executive decision, the doubt must be substantiated. So, if judges are in doubt, the benefit goes to the Secretary of State.[97]

[92] *Ibid. per* Lord Rodgers at para. 177; Baroness Hale at para. 226; Lord Hope at para. 108; and Lord Bingham at para. 41.

[93] *Ibid. per* Lord Bingham at para. 42.

[94] *Ibid.* at para. 39.

[95] *Ibid. per* Lord Hope at para. 116.

[96] *Ibid.* at para. 154

[97] Dyzenhaus, "Deference, Security and Human Rights", *supra* note 90 at 7, 8 suggests that the House of Lords should have applied a more probing standard of scrutiny to the question of whether the derogation was justified. However, he concedes that in order to do this, the court would have needed to see the closed material on which the decision was based. In fact, he argues that more rigorous Parliamentary scrutiny of the executive decision to derogate would

On the question of whether the means chosen by Parliament to respond to the threat were "strictly necessary," the Court adopted a more stringent standard of review. Relevant here was the fact that section 23 constituted a derogation from article 5 of the ECHR "at the extreme end of the severity spectrum,"[98] because the person who is detained under the section would not be accused of any crime but merely be reasonably suspected by the Secretary of State to be a terrorist. The individual could then be detained indefinitely. Many of their Lordships adverted to the fact that there was a clear and substantial violation of article 5 in this case,[99] and that the government had provided "no persuasive explanation"[100] why the security threat called for a power of indefinite intention in the case of non-nationals but not in the case of nationals. So this issue warranted less deference because human rights were engaged and the courts have a mandate under the HRA to guard against their violation, either in legislative or executive decision-making.[101] Therefore, they have a particular role of vigilance with regard to them. Moreover, the Court had no doubt that the detainee's right to liberty was violated by section 23 and that no cogent justification for the violation had been provided.

HOW SHOULD A JUDGE SHOW DEFERENCE?

Beyond respecting the decisions of the elected branches by giving weight to them and treating them with courtesy in judicial decisions, does deference require judges to adopt any particular course of action in their decisions? For example, in the United States, it is sometimes assumed that when the Supreme Court strikes down legislation, it is being activist; when it refrains from striking down, it is being deferential. Does deference require courts to refrain from striking down legislation whenever possible? On the analysis provided here, judges are always under a duty to pay minimal deference to the legislature and, exceptionally, substantial judicial deference may be warranted on grounds of superior competence, expertise, or legitimacy. The degree of deference

enhance the judicial ability to review this question, because it would place more information about it in the public domain, see 37; see also David Feldman, "Human Rights, Terrorism and Risk: The Role of Politicians and Judges," [2006] P.L. 364 at 380.

[98] *Belmarsh Prison*, *supra* note 90 *per* Lord Scott at para. 155.

[99] *Ibid. per* Lord Scott; *per* Lord Rodger at para. 178 (describing the inroad into the appellant's liberty in Belmarsh as "far reaching"); and *per* Baroness Hale at para. 222 (describing executive detention without trial as the antithesis of the right to liberty and security of person).

[100] *Ibid. per* Lord Nicholls at para. 78; Lord Bingham at para. 43.

[101] *Ibid. per* Lord Nicholls at para. 80.

deemed appropriate in any particular case clearly will impact on the decision about whether or not to strike down legislation, but it does not determine that issue. A court could pay substantial deference to the legislature, but still decide to strike down the legislation, or it could pay minimal deference to the legislature and refrain from striking down. The doctrine of deference does not require one option or the other.

The point is that it is too simplistic to equate striking down with activism and failure to strike down with deference. For one thing, such an equation ignores the various ways in which courts can defer to the elected branches, stopping short of striking down. For example, many constitutional courts have the option of postponing the striking down, in order to allow the elected branches time to adjust to the change and produce a constitutionally satisfactory solution to the problem.[102] Such a postponement can be attributable to a perceived need for judicial deference. In addition, the equation severely underestimates the creative potential of statutory interpretation as a way of rectifying a potential constitutional problem, thus forestalling the need to strike down. The interpretive techniques of "reading in" and "reading down" mean that judges can modify the express words and consequently the effect of a statute in order to make it conform to constitutional rights. By going down this "interpretive" route to achieving compliance with constitutional rights, it is the judges who carry out the necessary legislative modification.[103] But when judges *invalidate* or strike down legislation on constitutional grounds, it is up to the elected branches to decide how they will respond to the judicial decision, whether by enacting an appropriate replacement provision or changing the legislation root-and-branch. The upshot is that when a potential constitutional problem is "solved" through interpretation, this may involve a greater judicial intrusion on the legislative sphere than if the provision were simply struck down.[104] The judicial choice in such situations is not between striking down and doing

[102] The prevalence of the deferential strategy when courts have faced the issue of same-sex marriage is noted by Nicholas Bamforth, "Same-sex Partnerships: Some Comparative Constitutional Lessons," [2007] E.H.R.L.R. 47 at 57.

[103] This goes to support the view that even when judges adjudicate under statutory bills of rights, such as those in the U.K. and New Zealand, they are still engaging in "strong form judicial review." For further discussion, see David Dyzenhaus's contribution to this volume, "The Incoherence of Constitutional Positivism."

[104] See, *e.g.*, Frederick Schauer, "*Ashwander* Revisited," 1995 Sup. Ct. Rev. 71 at 93 (1995). Grant Huscroft voices similar worries about the power of interpretation under the Canadian Charter. See "A Constitutional 'Work in Progress'? The Charter and the Limits of Progress of Interpretation," in Grant Huscroft and Ian Brodie eds., *Constitutionalism in the Charter Era* (2004) 413 at 422.

nothing. Rather, it is between striking down the legislation and utilizing the methods of interpretation. It is by no means clear that the latter option is more deferential than the former.

This point applies (perhaps even with more force) to the situation in the United Kingdom. Under section 3 of the HRA, U.K. courts are under a duty to read and give effect to legislation in a way that is compatible with Convention rights if it is possible to do so.[105] If it is not possible, they have the power under section 4 to declare that legislation is incompatible with the Convention. But this declaration has no legal impact on the legislation and does not amount to the power to invalidate primary legislation. Does it follow that judges who issue a declaration of incompatibility are being more deferential to Parliament than those who engage in a section 3 interpretation? As we have seen, there will sometimes be good reason for judges to opt for a declaration of incompatibility rather than a rights-compatible interpretation, because of the judiciary's need to pay deference to Parliament's superior lawmaking competence (as in the *Bellinger* case). So considerations of deference can certainly ground a decision in favour of a declaration of incompatibility. But it does not follow from this that the declaration of incompatibility is *generally* more deferential than a section 3 interpretation. It all depends on the context. Sometimes, it becomes clear during the oral argument of a case that the government would prefer the court to adopt a section 3 interpretation. This may be because a declaration of incompatibility, though carrying no legal effect, can be more embarrassing for the government than a Convention-compatible interpretation. Moreover, a practice seems to be emerging whereby the elected branches do not reject the declarations. In fact, all the declarations of incompatibility to date have been followed. As time goes on, this may give declarations of incompatibility the same status *de facto* as a judicial striking down. Either way, the point remains that what deference requires depends on the legal and political context of the individual case. It is therefore difficult to generalise.

CONCLUSION

It has been argued that judges owe a degree of deference to the elected branches of government as a matter of constitutional principle, but also for prudential reasons. The primary constitutional principle involved is that of interinstitutional comity. Even when judges defer for "prudential" reasons, I argued

[105] Section 3(1) reads: "So far as it is possible to do so, primary legislation and subordinate legislation *must* be read and given effect in a way which is compatible with the Convention rights" [emphasis added].

that deference was ultimately rooted in a judgment of political morality about appropriate institutional roles. Deference requires judges to be aware of their institutional limits and to ensure that they make the decisions to which they are best suited, but leave others to the legislature or the executive. Sometimes judges are criticised for being too timid and asserting themselves too little against a powerful legislature or executive. Cases in which judges are too deferential to the elected branches of government give deference a bad name. They create the impression that judicial deference is to be equated with excessive or ill-placed deference. On the analysis provided here, even when deference is due, it does not mean that judges blindly or routinely endorse the view of the elected branches and adopt a completely uncritical approach to adjudication. Rather, it is a matter of assessing the factors that justify giving more or less weight to the view of the elected branches in the circumstances of the individual case.

So, judicial deference is not, in itself, either a vice or a virtue – it all depends on how it is used and whether the judge has made the correct assessment of whether it has been earned and to what degree. It is a vice if it is excessive or is paid to elected bodies in a routine fashion or for no good reason. But it can be a virtue (what Alexander Bickel referred to as one of the "passive virtues"[106]) if its use is warranted in the context of a particular case. To be sure, standing up against the pressure exerted by popular opinion or a hostile legislature sometimes requires judicial courage, and in a case in which the court has the expertise to make the decision and the justice of the case so demands, it is a weak and timid court that capitulates to those pressures. However, there are also cases in which the best and most responsible judicial decision is one that is more deferential. Therefore, deference, when it is a matter of being *appropriately respectful*, is part and parcel of a court's responsibility, rather than an evasion of it.

[106] Bickel, "The Passive Virtues," *supra* note 1.

PART THREE

WRITTEN AND UNWRITTEN CONSTITUTIONAL PRINCIPLES

9 Constitutional Justice and the Concept of Law

T. R. S. Allan

> There are certain vital principles in our free Republican governments, which will determine and overrule an apparent and flagrant abuse of legislative power. . . . An act of the Legislature (for I cannot call it a law) contrary to the great first principles of the social compact, cannot be considered a rightful exercise of legislative authority.
>
> *Calder v. Bull* 3 US (3 Dall) 386 at 388 per Chase J. (1798).

INTRODUCTION

If we begin our reflections on constitutional jurisprudence from the legal positivist's notion of law – law as whatever is commanded by those who wield established authority – we face great difficulties in accounting for much of our legal experience. Can the familiar associations between law and liberty, or between law and justice, as daily exhibited in the practice of liberal democracy, really be only contingent connections, wholly dependent on the specific wording of a particular constitutional text? And is it true that, in the absence of such a text, all the liberties of the citizen are necessarily at the mercy of the current legislative majority? Are the unwritten principles of liberal constitutionalism, frequently acknowledged by courts as well as jurists, only optimistic presumptions – entirely subservient to the clear instructions of the text, which may or may not sustain them? Why should we try so hard to marry such a notion of "law," having echoes of a brigade commander's instructions to his troops, with the complex content of a jurisprudence apparently devoted to securing the legitimacy of official coercion?

Instead of treating law largely as an instrument of government policy, we do better in constitutional theory to embrace a subtler, more sophisticated concept of law. The connections between law, liberty, and justice are better understood when we grant the importance of the idea of the *rule of law* – or the special constitutional value of legality – to our concept of law.[1] I shall argue that law is an institution that presupposes the importance of respecting human dignity and individual autonomy in the conduct of public affairs. Legal obligations are those duties that a conscientious citizen, who acknowledges the legitimate demands of the public good, *ought* to recognize. Such a citizen is supported by an independent and impartial judiciary when he challenges dubious infringements of his liberty, just as his true interests are defended, in principle, by his elected representatives in parliament when they pursue a genuine common good. The integrity of the judicial process, accordingly, is an ineradicable feature of law: No judge can properly connive at its corruption or unwarranted interference, any more than a citizen can honourably collaborate with (what he takes to be) grave injustice (to himself or others). But there is more to judicial process than impartiality and procedural rectitude; its integrity is intimately bound up with the nature of the rules it is invoked to enforce.

An appropriate account of the rule of law, forging the requisite links with freedom and justice, would "render many of our written constitutional rights redundant"[2] only if the "law" is conceived as whatever is imposed by clear legislation, subject only to express constitutional constraints. Contrary to recent assertions of the Supreme Court of Canada, there are no "compelling reasons to insist upon the primacy of our written constitution"[3] if to do so is to misunderstand the true foundations of constitutional freedom. Nor should special honour be accorded to the values of "legal certainty and predictability" at the expense of those of constitutional justice. A written constitution is, first and foremost, an attempt to articulate the main components of the rule of law: Its true meaning and moral force must be sought in an understanding of the nature and implications of that ideal.

If, moreover, the supremacy of law and the exclusion of arbitrary power mean only a formal equality of all before the law, including officials, it is the ideal of the rule of law that is "trivialized" rather than the written constitution.[4]

THE CONCEPT OF LAW

Fuller's precepts of procedural legality (his "internal morality of law") can readily be seen to protect the citizen's freedom by curtailing the scope for

[1] The importance of explaining the value of legality in the context of other political values is emphasized by Ronald Dworkin: See Dworkin, *Justice in Robes* (2006) ch. 6.

[2] *British Columbia v. Imperial Tobacco Canada Ltd*, [2005] 2 S.C.R. 473 at para. 65.

[3] *Ibid.*, citing *Reference re Secession of Quebec*, [1998] 2 S.C.R. 217 at para. 53.

[4] *Ibid.* at paras. 58–9, 66–7.

arbitrary coercion.[5] Their primary focus is the formulation and application of statutory criminal prohibitions: They constitute the essential conditions of the constitutional principle, *nulla poena sine lege*. It is only if the rules of criminal law are clear, consistent, and prospective; are duly published; and do not command the impossible or change too frequently, that the citizen can escape punishment by avoiding the commission of offences. As Fuller notes, strict liability offences and *ex post facto* laws wreak grave injustice.[6] If, moreover, the administration of the laws were to diverge from their published content, the citizen would become subject to arbitrary punishment – punishment for any reason that appealed to officials. Adherence to the rule of law therefore renders the "law" fit to be a bulwark between governors and governed: The citizen can be punished only for conduct that is clearly proscribed in advance.

A critical element of the law's protection – one that Fuller neglected in his initial account – is its *generality*.[7] The law is a barrier to the exercise of arbitrary power because it is general in form, applicable to everyone whose conduct may fall within its scope rather than to a limited number of specified persons. And because the law's application is ultimately in the hands of independent courts, the lawmakers cannot choose specific individuals to be the beneficiaries or victims of the rules on grounds that are irrelevant to their supposed rationale. The separation of powers is, then, an integral feature of the rule of law. Changes in the law may only be made in general and, normally, prospective terms; and those officials who exercise coercive power in particular cases, whether judges or government ministers or their agents, must act in accordance with existing rules. As Hayek explained, in an influential exposition of the rule of law, our freedom is secured in the sense that "when we obey laws, in the sense of general abstract rules laid down irrespective of their application to us, we are not subject to another man's will."[8]

As a body of general rules that meets the formal conditions of procedural legality, the law does not necessarily confer specific domains of freedom: Its prescriptions may make oppressive demands on the citizen. Even in this basic form, however, the rule of law safeguards liberty as independence – no one is at the mercy of an arbitrary will because people's obligations are defined

[5] Lon L. Fuller, *The Morality of Law* (rev. edn. 1969) [Fuller, *Morality of Law*].

[6] *Ibid.* at 59, 77–8.

[7] Fuller emphasised the importance of generality in his response to criticisms of the initial account of the inner morality of law. The shift of emphasis marked a transition from an instrumentalist to a constitutionalist understanding of law, moving the focus from a lawmaker's to a citizen's perspective on law: See Allan, *Constitutional Justice: A Liberal Theory of the Rule of Law* (2001), chs. 2 and 3 [Allan, *Constitutional Justice*].

[8] F.A. Hayek, *The Constitution of Liberty* (1960) at 153.

and limited by published rules. In this sense, liberty is the opposite of the condition of slavery: A slave enjoys such freedom as he possesses solely at his master's pleasure. The law secures liberty as independence in two ways. First, it precludes the exercise of an arbitrary governmental will, as regards the fortunes of particular persons; secondly, it protects the citizen from lawless violence at the hands of other citizens, who may interfere in his affairs only in the manner and to the extent that the law permits. The law can serve its primary function of securing independence from the will of others only when the various precepts of the rule of law are duly observed.[9]

The connection between law and liberty lies at the heart of the republican tradition of political thought, in which liberty is viewed as the product of law. Interference in people's affairs, moreover, is not regarded as infringing liberty when it is not arbitrary and does not represent a form of domination. An interference is arbitrary when it is performed at the intervener's pleasure, without reference to the interests or opinions of those affected. Properly constituted law is constitutive of liberty by conforming to people's common interests: A true polity is one in which the laws constrain those who would otherwise wield arbitrary power over others, and do not confer arbitrary powers on officials.[10]

The centrality of the idea of the rule of law to our concept of law confirms the existence of important conceptual connections between law and liberty. Law is the foundation of freedom in the sense that it provides for independence or nondomination: Its essential purpose is to curtail the exercise of arbitrary power. If, however, what is nonarbitrary is ultimately a matter of what is acceptable to the citizen – what he or she can reasonably be expected to acknowledge as legitimate interference, leaving liberty intact – there is also a necessary link between law and justice. Law is legitimate only when it serves the interests of those it purports to rule, according to their own collective understanding of what these interests truly are. Fuller suggested that compliance with the rule of law marked respect for human dignity: It entailed a view of man as a "responsible agent, capable of understanding and following rules, and answerable for his defaults."[11] But the mere form of law is not sufficient alone to explain the connection. The law is addressed not merely to an individual, who must choose between compliance and punishment for disobedience. It is addressed to the *citizen*, seeking his co-operation in the legitimate pursuit of the common good.

If, then, we grant the central importance of the antithesis between law and arbitrary power, we cannot rest content with a conception of law that guarantees only a *formal* equality between citizens. The law is no safeguard against the

9 See N.E. Simmonds, *Law as a Moral Idea* (2007) at 99–111.

10 See Philip Pettit, *Republicanism: A Theory of Freedom and Government* (1997) at 35–7 and 55.

11 Fuller, *Morality of Law*, *supra* note 5 at 162.

abuse of governmental power if its generality is only a veneer, permitting the lawmakers to target an unpopular group by a suitably nuanced description. If it is a fundamental requirement of law that the rules should be framed in such a manner as to protect the citizen from the whims of those responsible for their enforcement, it is equally important that the rules should, themselves, embody a coherent rationale, consistent with a plausible account of the public good. Laws may discriminate between persons for good reasons; but if law is meant to be a safeguard against arbitrary power, those reasons must, in principle, be capable of public explanation and defence. The distinctions drawn between persons must be shown to relate to public objectives that everyone could acknowledge without abandoning their self-respect as equal citizens. We cannot anticipate that everyone will, in practice, endorse the public policy the rules are meant to further; but we can insist, nonetheless, that the policy should be justified by appeal to features of the public good that all can reasonably be expected to acknowledge as worthy of pursuit and protection. Governance according to law ultimately is distinguished from arbitrary rule by its commitment to *justification*: The law imposes its demands on the citizen in the interests of the common good – a good that he can affirm in virtue of his allegiance to the political community.[12]

Because the rule of law, as a general principle of legality, does not command the adoption of any specific conception of substantive justice, we cannot make any simple equation of law with justice. We should acknowledge, nonetheless, that our concept of law is intimately connected with our *pursuit* of justice: Its utility for government lies in the standards of rectitude it imposes both on lawmakers and on judges and officials. Law, whatever its specific content, aims to be general and impartial, allowing discrimination between persons only for defensible reasons – reasons that can be inspected, debated, and affirmed or rejected on the basis of rival accounts of a genuine public good. Moreover, these ambitions are internal to the form of law as an expression of "obligation": Legal rules and requirements carry an implicit claim to legitimacy, which the citizen is invited to endorse by his obedience (but which he may sometimes repudiate by disobedience). Claims of authority or obligation appeal to the rational assent of those addressed; it is assumed that such claims are capable of recognition and acceptance by anyone acting as a rational agent, willing to co-operate in the pursuit of the common good.[13]

These conclusions about the nature of law have important implications for courts and adjudication. Because adherence to legality, or fidelity to law, defines a court's quintessential constitutional duty, judges cannot properly act

[12] For an elaboration of these large claims, see Allan, *Constitutional Justice*, *supra* note 7.

[13] See R.A. Duff, "Legal Obligation and the Moral Nature of Law," (1980) Juridical Review 61.

in defiance of the rule of law. Dicey's account of the rule of law, as the "absolute supremacy . . . of regular law as opposed to the influence of arbitrary power," was rightly presented as a "fundamental principle" of the British constitution.[14] Although Dicey's doctrine is often treated as a merely formal one, having no implications for the content of law, it is clear that it was intended to reflect and inform judicial practice. Parliamentary sovereignty was consistent with the rule of law because Acts of Parliament were subject to judicial interpretation; and the judges could be trusted to interpret statutes in accordance with the general principles of the common law.[15] Insofar as the common law protected a range of specific rights and liberties, statutory rules would be construed accordingly – preserving the integrity of such rights and liberties unless there was good cause to justify their curtailment.

The concept of law – law as a bulwark against arbitrary power – ascribes a central role to courts as authoritative interpreters of law. Although the law may consist of general rules or principles, capable of relatively abstract formulation, its meaning and application in specific instances depend on impartial judicial deliberation in which, so far as possible, the state's general purposes are reconciled with the litigant's particular circumstances. The court's impartiality and independence are intrinsic to law, when law is understood by reference to the principles of the rule of law; and judges whose impartiality and independence are compromised, or who allow their own ideas of public policy to displace those reflected in the law, fail to act as judges. The rule of law is not merely a set of injunctions to legislators, but a governing ideal for judges in their interpretation and articulation of legal rules and principles. If a statute lacks the clarity it needs to give firm guidance, it is the courts' responsibility to protect the citizen from adverse consequences: He must be given the benefit of the doubt as a matter of reasonable interpretation. The common law presumptions in favour of requiring *mens rea* for criminal offences, and against retrospective laws, are necessary features of interpretation attuned to the requirements of the rule of law.

Fuller's distinction between the internal and external moralities of law marked the boundary between judicial adherence to the rule of law, on one hand, and loyalty to the democratic process, on the other. Although remaining neutral among the moral positions open to statutory regulation on such matters as sexual morality or gambling, a judge must be actively committed to the requirements of internal morality: It would be "an abdication of the

[14] A.V. Dicey, *An Introduction to the Study of the Law of the Constitution* (1885; 10th edn., 1959) at 202.

[15] *Ibid*. at ch. 13.

responsibilities of his office if the judge were to take a neutral stand between an interpretation of a statute that would bring obedience to it within the capacity of the ordinary citizen and an interpretation that would make it impossible for him to comply with its terms."[16] Although the two moralities often overlapped and interacted in complex ways, a court could not properly substitute its own conception of the public good for the opinions of elected officials. There is, therefore, a tension between two responsibilities that must be resolved according to the circumstances arising: There is a duty to protect the integrity of the judicial process as well as a duty to administer the law as it is given by established sources, including legislation. The former duty may qualify the latter because the obligation to observe legality is paramount.

A statute that imposes imprisonment for an offence of absolute liability, authorizing the punishment of a person who may be innocent of any intentional wrongdoing and who has acted with due diligence, contravenes the rule of law – unless perhaps there is some special emergency that could provide an extraordinary justification. It defeats the point of the rule of law, as a protection against arbitrary interference, to punish those who, without fault, are unaware of the circumstances giving rise to liability. Because, moreover, the punishment is excessive, in the sense that it is, by definition, disproportionate to the offence, it denies the basic equality of citizens. In holding such a statute to be a violation of section 7 of the *Canadian Charter of Rights and Freedoms*, as a deprivation of the right to life, liberty, and security of the person contrary to the principles of fundamental justice, the Supreme Court of Canada affirmed its allegiance to the rule of law.[17]

If the principles of fundamental justice lie not in "the realm of general public policy but in the inherent domain of the judiciary as guardian of the justice system,"[18] it is because they embody the requirements of the rule of law, adapted as necessary to the concrete arrangements of Canadian constitutionalism. The various requirements of fundamental justice, as illustrated in the specific provisions of the Charter, represented principles that had been recognized by common law and in international conventions "as essential elements of a system for the administration of justice which is founded upon a belief in the dignity and worth of the human person and the rule of law."[19] Although the Court could not question the legislative wisdom of creating an absolute offence – it could not intrude into the merits of government policy – it must refuse to act unjustly by collaborating in (what would amount to) the

[16] Fuller, *Morality of Law*, *supra* note 5 at 132.

[17] *Reference re (British Columbia) Motor Vehicle Act*, [1985] 2 S.C.R. 486.

[18] *Ibid.* at para. 30.

[19] *Ibid.* at para. 61.

infliction of a grave injustice. If the "conscience of the court would be shocked and the administration of justice brought into disrepute by . . . an unreasonable and extravagant penalty,"[20] the judges must resist the legislative instructions in order to protect their own integrity as a court of justice.

THE RULE OF LAW AND THE INTEGRITY OF JUDICIAL PROCESS

In deciding any question of law, a judge must be faithful to the requirements of the rule of law. Liberal democracy amounts to an ideal of constitutionalism in which the impartial application of law by an independent judiciary is an essential element. The separation of powers ensures that the judicial function cannot be usurped by other branches of government, but that separation is predicated on certain assumptions about the special *nature* of the judicial function. It is implicit in the separation of judicial power that the law will consist of general rules or principles, rather than directions for the disposal of the particular case. It is also implicit that, in the application of such general rules, a court must act fairly and impartially in ascertaining the pertinent facts, so that the general law is correctly applied. A court must therefore act in accordance with natural justice, allowing the litigants a reasonable opportunity to present their evidence and arguments and to challenge the cases of their opponents. A court should also give reasons for its decision to show that it has adhered, to the best of its ability, to the relevant legal criteria, ignoring personal or political considerations properly viewed as extraneous to the legal questions arising.

The High Court of Australia has acknowledged the implications for judicial process that follow from the separation of judicial power, inferred from the vesting of the judicial power of the Commonwealth in the High Court and other federal courts by section 71 of the Australian Constitution. Legislation cannot require or permit such courts to exercise judicial power in a manner "inconsistent with the essential character of a court or with the nature of judicial power."[21] As Deane J. explained in *Polyukhovich v. The Commonwealth*, the requirements of due process followed from the purpose of the separation of powers, which was the exclusion of arbitrary power. The "life, liberty, and property of the subject" could be shielded from arbitrary interference, unregulated by law, only if the exercise of judicial power could be guaranteed to conform to "traditional judicial procedures, remedies and methodology."[22] Otherwise,

20 *Ibid.* at para. 127 (per Wilson J.).

21 *Chu Kheng Lim v. Minister for Immigration* (1992), 176 C.L.R. 1 at 26–7.

22 (1991) 172 C.L.R. 501 at 606–7 [*Polyukhovich*].

the law is, in practice, no barrier to wrongful invasions of liberty, committed in violation of established legal safeguards.

An important application of the implicit requirement of due process, of course, is the right to a fair criminal trial. A court's power to stay proceedings as an abuse of process, when, for example, pretrial delay or publicity has caused the defendant serious prejudice, must be considered an intrinsic feature of the separation of judicial power.[23] Similar considerations apply when the proceedings threaten to place the defendant in double jeopardy, or when, in the absence (through no fault of his own) of legal representation, there cannot be a fair trial of serious or complex charges.[24] A court could proceed to conduct what it regarded, by comparison with ordinary circumstances, an unfair trial only at the price of repudiating the rule of law. Legislative instructions to conduct such a trial, even if such instructions were really intelligible, would necessarily lack validity (whether the constitution be written or unwritten); a court that obeyed them would have ceased to act, on a proper understanding, as a court of *law*.

The paradigm legislative usurpation of the judicial power is the act (or bill) of attainder, or bill of pains and penalties, which inflicts punishment on specific individuals or identifiable members of a group. The two cardinal features of judicial process are absent: The defendant is deprived of both the protection of a general rule and the safeguards of fair procedure. As a "special rule for a particular person or a particular case,"[25] such a measure violates the principle of the rule of law and is therefore necessarily invalid. No formally entrenched prohibition (such as that in Article 1, section 9, of the United States Constitution) is needed because it is already inherent in the separation of powers as a "general safeguard against legislative exercise of the judicial function, or more simply – trial by legislature."[26]

The distinction between a general rule, on one hand, and a specific measure, on the other, must not be understood in a purely formal sense: An enactment would not cease to be an act of attainder if, though avoiding proper names or descriptions of specific individuals, it sought to penalize an identifiable group who had incurred the displeasure of the legislature. Moreover, an *ad hominem* statute does not meet the requirements of the rule of law merely by leaving a residual function to the courts. The statute that provided for the trial, conviction, and punishment of government opponents, according to special rules

[23] See *Jago v. District Court (of New South Wales and others)* (1989), 168 C.L.R. 23.

[24] See *Connelly v. DPP*, [1964] A.C. 1254; *Dietrich v. R* (1992), 177 C.L.R. 292.

[25] *Hurtado v. California*, 110 U.S. 516 at 535–6 (1884).

[26] *United States v. Brown*, 381 U.S. 437 at 442 (1965) [*U.S. v. Brown*].

passed for the purpose, was rightly struck down in *Liyanage v. R.*[27] The necessity for a trial did not obscure the removal of the ordinary protections of general rule and standard judicial procedure. Nor was the *Community Protection Act 1994*, enacted by the New South Wales Parliament, saved by reserving to the Supreme Court the duty of imposing a special form of preventative detention on a specific individual.[28] In the absence of any requirement for the trial of an offence against the general law, according to normal judicial procedures, the legislation was rightly condemned as an attempt at the arbitrary infliction of punishment.

These examples are sufficient to show that we should not identify the rule of law with the preservation merely of *formal* equality. It is not sufficient that a statute abstains from interference with the judicial application of law to particular cases, if it makes arbitrary distinctions between persons unrelated to any plausible account of the common good. *Ad hominem* legislation is only the starkest example of violation of the requirement of generality: The rule of law requires, not merely the "equal protection of the laws," in the sense of the consistent enforcement of the law according to its strict terms, but the protection of equal laws, at least in the sense that the distinctions drawn between persons must be capable, in principle, of a rational justification. The standards of rational justification cannot, of course, be given by conceptual analysis: They depend on general considerations of justice and liberty drawn from the broader constitutional culture. But that point does not devalue the importance of the test: It shows that our legal judgments are necessarily dependent on our underlying moral commitments to the values of a liberal democracy based on respect for the equal dignity of citizens.

The connection between equality and the integrity of judicial process was clearly made by Gaudron J. in *Leeth v. Commonwealth*, a case in which the High Court of Australia examined the claims of equality to be an implicit feature of constitutional law: The "concept of equal justice – a concept that requires the like treatment of like persons in like circumstances, but also requires that genuine differences be treated as such – is fundamental to the judicial process."[29] It followed that a statutory provision requiring a court to determine an offender's eligibility for parole, having "regard to the matters to which it would have regard if the law of the State . . . in which the offender was convicted were applicable," was invalid: An exercise of power that involved

[27] [1967] 1 A.C. 259 [*Liyanage*]. See Allan, *Constitutional Justice, supra* note 7 at 233.

[28] *Kable v. Director of Public Prosecutions* (NSW) (1996), 189 C.L.R. 51. See Allan, *Constitutional Justice, supra* note 7 at 234–8.

[29] (1992) 174 C.L.R. 455 at 502 [*Leeth*].

impermissible discrimination between federal offenders was inconsistent with judicial process. It was "manifestly absurd" that the penalties attaching to breach of Commonwealth law should vary according to the location of the court in which proceedings were brought.

Gaudron J. drew a doubtful distinction, however, between due process in the exercise of a judicial power and equality as regards the content of substantive law. Yet the difference between exercise of a judicial discretion, according to specified statutory criteria, and application of rules determining rights and duties is surely a difference of degree rather than kind. The application of rules is not merely a matter of logical deduction on the basis of uncontroversial classification of facts: It entails, like judicial discretion, an exercise of *judgment* in which the stipulated criteria are adapted to the context of the circumstances.[30] The application of law and the exercise of discretion are, alike, dependent on *evaluation*; it follows that a "constitutional guarantee of equality before the courts," if it is genuine, entails a basic "immunity from discriminatory laws."[31] So a court that objects to the application of arbitrary criteria, in exercise of judicial discretion, must equally object to their application in deciding a question of substantive law. Deane and Toohey J. J. based their decision squarely on the "doctrine of legal equality" that was implicit in the Constitution's separation of judicial power, requiring "a court to extend to the parties before it equal justice," treating them "fairly and impartially as equals before the law" and refraining from "discrimination on irrelevant or irrational grounds."[32] Brennan J. held that the relevant provisions were necessary and the discrimination justified, but he affirmed that the *maximum penalty* prescribed for an offence must be the same throughout the Commonwealth.[33]

If the law exists to protect the citizen from arbitrary power, wielded by potentially hostile authorities or influential private interests, its generality is an inherent feature, which must be respected in its administration by courts. The integrity of the judicial process is undermined, in criminal proceedings, as much by the imposition of unequal penalties as by failures of natural justice. If it would be contrary to proper judicial process to admit hearsay testimony against the defendant, in breach of the ordinary rules of evidence, or to convict

[30] *Cf.* H.L.A. Hart, *The Concept of Law*, 2nd edn. (1994) at 124–36.

[31] *Kruger v. The Commonwealth(Stolen Generations Case)* (1997), 190 C.L.R. 1 at 112. *Cf.* Dawson J., *ibid.* at 63–8.

[32] *Leeth, supra* note 29 at 487. See further, Mark Walters' contribution to this volume, "Written Constitutions and Unwritten Constitutionalism" [Walters, "Written Constitutions and Unwritten Constitutionalism"].

[33] The majority held, like Brennan J., that the provisions did not, in context, entail a departure from the judicial function.

solely on the basis of his disposition to commit similar offences, it must be equally improper to inflict a harsher than normal punishment on an offender who has incurred governmental displeasure, or whose offence has attracted special media attention and consequent public outrage. The latter corrupts the fair and impartial administration of justice as much as the former. Yet the rule of law could not coherently distinguish between such an abuse of judicial *discretion*, in respect of sentencing, on one hand, and the infliction of special punishment on a specific category of despised offenders, in performance of a statutory duty, on the other. Such a statutory duty would turn the process of criminal justice into a political weapon against hated opponents, making the courts an instrument of oppression. It follows that, like the ban on acts of attainder, the prohibition of cruel and unusual punishments is implicit in the rule of law: No formally entrenched constitutional provision is needed.[34]

When we perceive that the rule of law demands more than merely formal equality, which is compatible with arbitrary invasions of liberty under a mere cloak of legality, we can see that the integrity of judicial process is inseparably linked with the nature and purpose of the laws that the courts are required to enforce. The protection of liberty from arbitrary interference entails the prohibition of *ex post facto* criminal laws: The infliction of punishment for conduct that was lawful at the time contradicts the rationale of the rule of law. Such a measure is, in its very nature, "cruel and unjust," as Blackstone observed,[35] and the connection with judicial process is readily established. Because those whose conduct is officially condemned, in retrospect, are, in principle, identifiable at the time of the measure's enactment, an *ex post facto* law is a species of illegitimate *ad hominem* legislation. Its application amounts to a "travesty of the judicial process" because it is a "law invented to fit the facts after they have become known," so that the proceedings are not truly directed to ascertaining guilt or innocence but, rather, "to ascertaining whether the Parliament had perfected its intention of declaring the act in question an act against the criminal law."[36]

If the rule of law were satisfied merely by formal equality, it would be possible simply to distinguish (as Mason C. J. sought to distinguish) between retrospective legislation that leaves to the courts the task of deciding whether the

[34] George Winterton is skeptical, but accepts, nonetheless, that legislation imposing "barbarous sentences" would be unconstitutional as requiring the courts to "exercise a power which was incompatible with the role of the judiciary in a civilised society": See Winterton, "The Separation of Judicial Power as an Implied Bill of Rights," in Geoffrey Lindell ed., *Future Directions in Australian Constitutional Law* (1994) at 207.

[35] Sir William Blackstone, *Commentaries on the Laws of England*, 9th edn. (1783), vol 1 at 46.

[36] *Polyukhovich*, *supra* note 22 at 705 (*per* Gaudron J.).

accused had performed the prohibited act, and an *ex post facto* law that, itself, adjudged guilt and imposed punishment.[37] Because, however, the *ex post facto* law is a species of *ad hominem* legislation, it constitutes a "trial by legislature," in breach of the separation of powers, by blurring the fundamental distinction between specifying prohibited conduct, on one hand, and identifying those persons thought to deserve punishment, on the other. The line between the specification of general criteria for legal coercion and the designation of the persons considered to fall within their compass may be a fine one, in many instances, but when the law operates retrospectively the line disappears altogether. It was breached by the statute condemned in *United States v. Brown*, which made it an offence for anyone who had, in the previous five years, been a member of the Communist party to serve as an officer of a labour union.[38] Rather than being a general rule providing that persons who had committed certain acts or possessed certain characteristics, indicating that they were likely to initiate political strikes, should not hold union office, the statute designated a group of persons who (in the opinion of Congress) exhibited the requisite traits.

What then does the rule of law require? It requires a judicial examination of the nature of a purported law in order to ensure that it serves a legitimate public purpose – a purpose compatible with a plausible conception of the common good, consistent with whatever constitutional rights are generally recognized and officially affirmed. Moreover, the rigour of the court's scrutiny – or the "intensity" of its review – must reflect the scale of the threat of departures from equality or generality to the integrity of the judicial process. In the administration of ordinary civil and criminal law, unequal provisions call for a skeptical inquiry: It is part of our concept of law that departures from the even application of equal laws are in need of persuasive justification. In the broader field of public law, there is usually greater scope for special regimes to govern disparate areas of public policy, according to the reasonable choices of elected officials and expert administrators. The scope for departures from equality is reduced, however, when regulation affects the enjoyment of constitutional rights, which preserve a sphere of personal autonomy from governmental interference. The rule of law makes the justification of differential treatment, at appropriate levels of reasoned consistency, an internal feature of law and hence of legal validity.

At its core, the rule of law requires the impartial administration of a body of general rules by an independent judiciary; but it can accommodate departures from generality and the high standards of judicial process when they can be

[37] *Ibid. per* Mason C.J. at 536.

[38] *Supra* note 26.

justified as a reasonable adaptation of the rule of law to the exigencies of practical administration. When it is necessary for a legitimate public purpose to permit the exercise of executive discretion, the rule of law requires only that the discretion be exercised fairly – for the proper purpose and in a manner that causes no unnecessary injury to the interests of persons particularly affected. The constraints of equality and due process are the more demanding, however, the closer a discretionary power impinges on the rights or interests that, by virtue of their significance for freedom and dignity, define the substance of equal citizenship. When, for instance, a government minister or agency wields powers concerning the prosecution of suspects or the punishment of offenders, the requisite standards of procedural fairness and equality of treatment will be appropriately severe. A quasi-judicial power must be exercised in a manner that approaches the judicial; and if essentially judicial functions are imposed on executive officials, they are required to act – if they are permitted to act at all – as judges would be obliged to act in similar circumstances. When English Home Secretaries were permitted to set minimum "tariff" sentences for murderers, whose formal statutory sentence was life imprisonment, the House of Lords rightly held that they must act judicially, ignoring public clamour.[39]

A recent case, *Lewis v. Attorney General of Jamaica*, in which the Judicial Committee of the Privy Council heard appeals from the Court of Appeal of Jamaica regarding the standards of natural justice applicable to the exercise of the prerogative of mercy, provides an apt illustration of the requirements of the rule of law.[40] The applicants had each been convicted of murder and sentenced to death. The Governor-General was advised on his exercise of the prerogative of mercy by a committee (the "Jamaican Privy Council"), which was required by the Constitution of Jamaica to consider the trial judge's written report and such other information as the Governor-General might require to be provided. The applicants had appealed, *inter alia*, on the ground that their constitutional right to "protection of the law" had been contravened by a denial of natural justice: They had not been shown the material placed before the advisory committee or been permitted to make representations in regard to it. Rejecting the earlier view, affirmed by precedent, that exercise of the prerogative of mercy was a wholly unregulated personal discretion – the "exemplar of a purely administrative act," impervious to judicial review[41] – the Court upheld

[39] *R v. Secretary of State for the Home Department, ex parte Venables and Thompson*, [1998] A.C. 407. See further, Allan, *Constitutional Justice*, *supra* note 7 at 133–48.

[40] [2000] 2 A.C. 50.

[41] *de Freitas v. Benny*, [1976] A.C. 239 at 247 (Trinidad and Tobago); see also *Reckley v. Minister of Public Safety and Immigration (No. 2)*, [1996] A.C. 527 (The Bahamas).

the claims to procedural propriety, as a matter of legal right. The formal constitutional provisions should be supplemented by the appropriate requirements of natural justice, and the courts could require the relevant officials to proceed accordingly.

The Court was justified in overturning the precedents because the official exercise of a wholly unregulated discretion, in a matter that concerned not only the administration of criminal justice but the prisoners' rights to life and liberty, was incompatible with the rule of law. Judicial recognition of nonjusticiable, arbitrary powers contravenes the rule of law; the precedents were not, accordingly, a valid source of law. For similar reasons, the Court was rightly unwilling to distinguish the case from the earlier cases on the ground that the formal arrangements for exercise of the power varied between the different jurisdictions, affecting the status of the advisory committee. The right to make representations in relation to a petition for mercy was held to be the same in all cases: A shared "common law," correctly interpreted, affirmed the true requirements of the rule of law.

LAW, JUSTICE, AND PRACTICAL REASON

I have argued that there are moral constraints on the scope of law-making power that derive from our concept of law, which is elucidated by reflection on the idea of the rule of law. The general requirements of equality and procedural fairness make questions of moral justification pertinent to the content of law. All distinctions between persons, whether made by legislation or administrative order, must serve a defensible view of the public good; and, though they will normally leave ample scope for the exercise of democratic judgment and official expertise, the basic demands of justice are an essential part of the public good. If the law makes a moral claim to obedience, on the ground of its service to the common good, the reasonableness of that claim, in the circumstances arising, is a condition of its validity. Legality and legitimacy are thereby brought into harmony: The law is a product of the exercise of legitimate authority, consistent with the requirements of the rule of law.

Although the general form of the rule of law is universal, dictating similar requirements of legality in every just constitutional order, its detailed implementation will vary from jurisdiction to jurisdiction. The prohibition of acts of attainder and *ex post facto* criminal laws is an entailment of the rule of law; but the principle of equality it reflects is vindicated by consistent application of the general rules adopted for legitimate public ends. The principles of natural justice or procedural fairness are implicit in governance according to law, but their precise requirements will depend on context, reflecting local practice.

Every just legal order will honour the freedoms of speech, conscience, and association because they lie at the heart of a liberal-democratic polity based on equal citizenship, but the specific contours of these liberties will be framed by experience and settled legal tradition. We cannot draw a clear line between the conceptual implications of the rule of law and the content of the legal tradition it nourishes in any particular jurisdiction. The conceptual implications are continuous with the practical wisdom their implementation requires: A court is necessarily both a defender of law (or the rule of law) and an interpreter of law at one and the same time.[42]

Every judicial decision, accordingly, has two dimensions. It appeals to shared standards and settled tradition, but at the same time reflects the judge's view of the moral basis of those standards and the grounds of the legitimacy of that tradition. Because the settled law is underpinned by a conception of the rule of law that safeguards individual liberty, it represents (at least approximately) an interpretation of justice that deserves respect. It is the judge's responsibility to renew and develop the tradition by adapting its standards to novel circumstances, or to familiar circumstances in the light of changing social mores. Every case tests the judge's commitment to the legal order: It obliges him to renew his faith in the constitution by squaring his legal and moral judgments. He cannot acknowledge that the law is gravely morally deficient, obliging him to repudiate the fundamental requirements of justice, without undermining his own allegiance to the constitution as a just order of governance. But because his role is a partly creative one – an active participation in the development of the tradition – he has no reason to deny his own deepest commitments. He will preserve his loyalty to the just constitution by refusing to do injustice in the particular case; he will interpret the relevant sources of law appropriately.

If the law's content were simply determined by authoritative directives, irrespective of the moral considerations arising in particular cases, it would make sense to distinguish between validity and justice. When, however, the law is understood to embody a scheme of justice, reflecting the moral traditions of the community, the resolution of particular cases must be sensitive to the demands of those traditions. Legal rules are only convenient guides for just determination of cases within the relevant classes or categories; they cannot bind the decision-maker in any case in which their application would plainly cause injustice. The unforeseen or exceptional or borderline case serves to illustrate the proper limits of the rule. The rule's "authority" is a *prima facie*, contextual

[42] Hence the implausibility of legal positivism in the context of a legal order acknowledging human dignity as a fundamental value: See also David Dyzenhaus, "The Incoherence of Constitutional Positivism," in this volume.

one: It surrenders to contrary argument whenever there are good grounds for thinking that its application would threaten the integrity of the constitutional order. The written law is always underpinned and informed by the unwritten, reflecting the discourse of reason.[43]

A complaint that a legal rule is unjust, either generally or in the circumstances of a particular case, is, therefore, fundamentally an objection to the law's *administration* – that its manner of application is unfair and irrational, failing to match, in practice, the standards of justice that are defended in theory. It makes no difference, moreover, whether the rule is merely a generalization drawn from previous judicial decisions or a carefully articulated provision formally enacted by the legislature: Its validity and legitimacy alike depend on its capacity to serve the legal and constitutional order, interpreted as a collaborative scheme of just governance. No official institution can lawfully violate the constitution it is designed to serve, and if it acts unjustly, according to established moral standards, it thereby exceeds its constitutional authority. Because this is as true for the constitutional court as for a parliament, it is the citizen who is the ultimate arbiter of the law: He or she must finally decide, as a matter of moral conviction, whether or not a (purported) rule *deserves* obedience.

When the rule of law is embraced as a constitutional ideal, the authority of courts and legislatures is subservient to the associated requirements of justice. Statutes and precedents obtain their force from the strength of their claims to embody the demands of justice, or at least to offer guidance consistent with justice. Because legislation awaits interpretation at the hands of those who must seek to apply its strictures to specific instances, its true meaning is always a matter of *argument*; as a contribution to the existing order of justice, it invites moral scrutiny and deliberation. And because every judicial ruling, whether interpreting legislation or expounding common law, purports to be an accurate reflection of existing law, it must be received in that spirit. Its authority is a function of the plausibility of that claim: Its power to settle a general question of law, rather than merely to decide the specific case, depends on the cogency of the reasons supplied. Moreover, whatever authority is granted to statutes or precedents – or the rules they are taken to establish – is a strictly temporary and tentative authority. As circumstances change or new information becomes available, or better arguments are offered, previous rulings will need to be revised. Statutes must be reinterpreted and precedents reconsidered as deliberation over questions of law and justice proceeds in the new conditions.[44]

[43] See Walters, "Written Constitutions and Unwritten Constitutionalism," *supra* note 32.

[44] *Cf.* Jeremy Waldron, "The Rule of Law as a Theatre of Debate," in Justine Burley ed., *Dworkin and his Critics* (2004) at 319.

In practice, the law-abiding citizen will accept the authority of many official actions or decisions he thinks mistaken. It is implicit in a collaborative venture that there must be a degree of give and take: No one could reasonably expect the law's administration to be fully in accordance with his own opinions about its true content. A citizen's right to interpret the law according to his own best judgment – implicit in the constitutional freedom of conscience – comes at the cost of the similar right enjoyed by other citizens. The accommodation of these rights depends on mutual respect and the practice of civility: The right to have one's argument fairly heard implies an equivalent readiness to consider alternative points of view. It is easier, moreover, to live with official decisions one dislikes or deplores if one is assured of their corrigibility. A merely provisional determination of rights and duties can often be embraced as a current approximation to legal correctness, in anticipation of future progress. But granting the temporary authority of statutory rules or judicial decisions is not the same as acknowledging their correctness: The citizen's true allegiance is to the law, which he must honour insofar as the requirements of civility allow.[45]

A person who rejects a statutory provision or judicial decision on grounds of justice therefore denies its legal status: *lex injusta non est lex*. Such a provision or ruling exceeds the legitimate scope of reasonable interpretation that the fair-minded citizen accords the pertinent official bodies. Naturally, the legislature must be granted a larger sphere of discretion than other branches of government given that it is empowered to change the (ordinary) law rather than apply it. The legislature must, nonetheless, comply with fundamental constitutional principles, as settled by legal tradition, informed by an understanding of the nature and purpose of law. It is empowered to bring current rules into harmony with justice, adapting the body of law to the demands of justice made by novel circumstances or by changes in social and moral attitudes; it is not empowered to violate the fundamentals of justice or legislate in contravention of the rule of law.

It does not follow that a judge has jurisdiction to "strike down" a measure as null and void for all purposes: That will depend on the jurisdictional rules of the legal system in question. He may have no power to remove an offending measure from the statute book; the measure may retain its *formal* status as "law." If, however, a court declines to give a provision any effect in the circumstances of a particular case on the ground that it would be unjust to do so, it loses much of its authority. If a subsequent case can be appropriately distinguished, the provision may retain a limited legal effect; but if, in practice, circumstances

[45] *Cf.* Stephen Macedo, *Liberal Virtues: Citizenship, Virtue, and Community in Liberal Constitutionalism* (1991) ch. 3.

are unlikely to arise in which it would be permitted to alter the previous law, the measure is, to all intents and purposes, a dead letter. In substance, then, validity is a matter of degree: A statutory provision is truly law only to the extent that it is *accepted as authoritative* by those it purports to bind. Its meaning and effect are, alike, in the hands of its interpreters, whether judges, officials, or private citizens.

In practice, the limits of legislative discretion may well be controversial – whether or not such limits are enshrined in a written fundamental text or a bill of rights. It is, nonetheless, the prerogative of every citizen of independent mind and conscience to determine their true content, challenging a measure that breaches their requirements. He cannot be expected to acquiesce in what he thinks is grave injustice, done to others, any more than we could expect him to submit to violations of his own fundamental rights – rights, most especially, to participate in the democratic process, to freedoms of speech and conscience, to due process in his personal dealings with public authority, particularly in matters concerning his liberty. The citizen does not repudiate such violations as the wrongful imposition of unjust laws. As a participant-member of the legal community, he must be understood to deny their validity: They are not, from the perspective of the legal and constitutional order he affirms, truly laws at all.

Although generally treated by legal theorists as a repudiation of governmental authority or flouting of legal obligations, "civil disobedience" is better understood as an insistence on the prevailing limits of authority – a denial that the official demands in question constitute genuine legal obligations. The dissentient's disobedience is a plea for the return of legality – for the organs of state to acknowledge their breach of constitutional principle. Even if the roots of dissent lie in religious or ethical scruples that are not widely shared, the dissentient seeks only the protection accorded by the just constitution – the constitution he affirms alongside the religious or ethical commitments he cannot conscientiously renounce. The Jehovah's Witness who declines to salute the flag invokes a right to freedom of conscience that he believes his constitution, properly understood, affirms.[46] The pacifist who refuses to enlist invokes the same freedom, expecting the courts to confirm the legality of his recalcitrance even if the executive proves obdurate.

Furthermore, because the member of a true rule-of-law community accepts a responsibility to interpret the constitution, ultimately, for himself, resisting injustice so far as possible even when powerful officials prove unrelenting, his

[46] Respecting the flag "as a symbol of fairness and justice," he nevertheless refuses to join a ceremony condemned by his religion: See *West Virginia Board of Education v. Barnette*, 319 U.S. 624 (1943) [*Barnette*].

deliberations cannot be curtailed by a judgment of the highest or constitutional court. It is one thing carefully to consider the arguments of judges or officials, assessing their strength in the light of fundamental principle; it is quite another to surrender one's own judgment in the face of coercive authority. If the conclusions of the supreme court are not persuasive, the dissentient is entitled to sustain his contrary opinion: He denies that the court has correctly interpreted the law.

A person who challenges a judicial decision should be understood as offering a competing account of the shared constitutional order. If the challenge were made by appeal to conceptions of justice that were *not* widely shared, at least at a comparatively abstract level, it would plainly have no serious prospect of success. The dissentient appeals to the principles that underlie the legal order, as a settled framework for the pursuit of a genuine common good: There is an interaction and interdependence between legal doctrine and moral judgment. By appealing to settled principles and arguing from accepted paradigms, the dissentient pursues his ambition to convert others to his own interpretation of the constitution. So long as he retains his faith in the scheme of justice, acknowledging his duty to obey legal obligations properly imposed, his conscientious dissent in the matter in dispute must be seen for what it really is – an appeal to others to adhere more closely to their own professed ideals of liberty, justice, and law.

Ronald Dworkin rightly rejected the view that Jehovah's Witnesses were obliged to accept the decision of the U.S. Supreme Court in 1940 that a West Virginia law requiring students to salute the flag was valid – a decision soon afterwards reversed in *West Virginia State Board of Education v. Barnette*.[47] He argued correctly that a "citizen's allegiance is to the law, not to any particular person's view of what the law is."[48] The dissentient acts fairly "so long as he proceeds on his own considered and reasonable view of what the law requires." In Dworkin's view, however, a citizen must grant the courts the general power to alter the law by their decisions; and his right to follow his own judgment applies only where "the law is uncertain, in the sense that a plausible case can be made on both sides."[49] But unless very carefully handled, these qualifications will engulf the general principle Dworkin purported to defend.

Although judicial decisions, if well reasoned, will exert an important influence on the law's development, it is the primary function of courts to apply (and clarify) existing law. A judicial decision may, if it secures wide acceptance,

[47] 319 U.S. 624, reversing *Minersville School District v. Gobitis*, 310 U.S. 586 (1940).
[48] Ronald Dworkin, *Taking Rights Seriously* (1977) at 214.
[49] *Ibid.* at 215.

settle an uncertain question that arises within the constraints of established principle; it may even overturn familiar doctrine when earlier decisions are no longer thought to reflect the requirements of principle, correctly conceived. But because judicial decision-making must keep faith with the past – with the legal tradition in which it operates and which it has a responsibility to sustain – judges' decisions, even in the highest courts, are subject to appraisal in the light of principles they cannot change at will. No one should grant the courts the right to contravene constitutional fundamentals; and no one, acting conscientiously, need accept another's opinion about whether the courts have stayed within the proper limits of their powers. The law is more fundamental and enduring than the judgments that exemplify it – or purport to exemplify it – because such judgments are only partial insights, drawn from reflection on the details of particular cases. Future cases, raising new and unforeseen complexities, will serve to broaden our moral vision, deepening the law. And if the law is more fundamental even than the presently established paradigms, it is certainly superior to an erroneous judgment of the constitutional court – even if the error, or supposed error, is not (yet) generally acknowledged.

The law is uncertain, moreover, whenever any citizen struggles to square his loyalty to the constitution with other moral obligations he cannot conscientiously deny. A "plausible case can be made on both sides" whenever a person, who otherwise acknowledges the legitimate claims of the legal order, is compelled to resist the demand of a public authority as a matter of personal integrity. If the rule of law is a moral ideal, claiming the allegiance of every citizen on the basis of his duty to respect the needs of justice and the common good, his consent to law cannot be taken for granted. The constitutional court can offer him good reasons for its conclusions about the law; but because it cannot oblige him to accept them, we cannot condemn his dissent as an assault on the rule of law. He honours the rule of law by seeking to integrate his legal with his other responsibilities; and we dismiss his objections as "implausible" at the risk of impugning his honesty and good faith as a loyal member of a just community.

The citizen who rejects the opinion of the constitutional court is in much the same position as a judge who reaches a different conclusion from that of the majority. And a judge who accepts the dissentient's case is bound by the rule of law to give judgment accordingly, even when the majority is adamantly opposed. A well-reasoned dissenting judgment makes a valuable contribution to the legal process, obliging others to attend to the reasons given and, in due course, to reconsider their weight. In *Liversidge v. Anderson*,[50] the House of

[50] [1942] A.C. 206.

Lords majority held that the Secretary of State could detain a person without trial, under wartime regulations, without any requirement to satisfy a court that he had reasonable cause to do so. Lord Atkin's scornful dissent, comparing the minister's attitude to the prerogative claimed by Charles I, enshrined a contrary view in the record of the highest court, enabling subsequent generations to connect their more jealous approach to executive power with earlier legal tradition, correctly conceived.[51] Justice Harlan's dissent in *Plessy v. Ferguson*[52] foreshadowed its eventual overruling in *Brown v Board of Education*.[53]

A powerful dissent cannot be stifled by the mere existence of the court's decision: Its ability to shape the law and legal understanding depends on its reception by the legal profession and, ultimately, by society at large. Nor is a judge obliged to change his opinion if there is little likelihood that the court will accept it in the foreseeable future. The deeper his convictions about the demand of justice, in the circumstances under review, the more persuasive the contrary opinions must be to alter his view of what the legal tradition truly requires. At the limits of conscience, the judge must strike out along his own path, harnessing whatever the resources of statute, precedent, and practice can provide in favour of his own viewpoint. The force of his argument will determine his success; but its novelty is not an insuperable barrier. There is no judicial decision, however firmly established, that cannot ultimately be challenged by appeal to a new interpretation of the general principles that inform the legal and political deliberations that the rule of law requires.

A judge who questions the justice of a statute or precedent seeks to preserve the integrity of the legal order, repudiating a rule or decision at odds with fundamental principle. Whether or not he could ever accept its validity, in spite of his misgivings, will depend on the scale of the threat he perceives to the law's integrity. If the offence to basic rights or freedoms is grave, the judge will accord the rule or decision no force in his account of the present law, correctly understood: To grant its validity would undermine the coherence of the constitutional scheme of justice. If an erroneous decision is formally binding on him, as the ruling of a higher court, he must try to distinguish it in subsequent cases – matching the ingenuity of his reasoning to the level of his repugnance. A judge cannot properly acknowledge an *absolute* obligation to follow an erroneous ruling of a higher court, for his ultimate commitment is

[51] For an important discussion of the dissents in *Liversidge* and in *R v. Halliday, ex parte Zadig*, [1917] A.C. 260 (Lord Shaw), see David Dyzenhaus, *The Constitution of Law: Legality in a Time of Emergency* (2006) at 149–60.

[52] 163 U.S. 537 (1896).

[53] 347 U.S. 483 (1954) [*Brown*].

one of fidelity to law – a commitment vindicated whenever his senior judges concede, in retrospect, that their own previous decision was wrong.

The judge will typically draw no sharp distinction between just governance, as a matter of abstract political theory, and the essentials of constitutional law. The latter is legitimate only insofar as it embodies or approximates the former, as mediated by a shared history and experience. Justice Jackson's references, in *Barnette*, to Roman efforts to stamp out Christianity and the efforts of the Inquisition to impose religious unity show that his understanding of the nature of American constitutionalism, while based on legal tradition, reflected his broader conception of legitimate government. Philosophy and history combined to illuminate the basic character of the State: "We set up government by consent of the governed, and the Bill of Rights denies those in power any legal opportunity to coerce that consent."[54] Constitutional law embodies the demands of justice; constitutional justice is defined, in large part, by an accurate understanding of the legal tradition.

Justice Blackmun's dissent in *Bowers v. Hardwick*[55] invoked an indissoluble mixture of legal precedent and political theory, identifying a conception of American constitutionalism as the basis of legitimate government. He cited *Barnette's* proclamation of the "freedom to be intellectually and spiritually diverse or even contrary" in support of his view that restrictions on liberty could not be justified on the mere basis of majority opinion about sexual morality. His denial that the proscription of private homosexual relations could be justified by appeal to "traditional Judeo-Christian values" expressed the basic character of the legal order, as Justice Blackmun understood it: "The legitimacy of secular legislation depends . . . on whether the State can advance some justification for its law beyond its conformity to religious doctrine." Although Justice Blackmun's hope that the Court would soon reverse its decision was not fulfilled, he was entitled to reject its authority in anticipation of the eventual vindication of his view.

CONCLUSION

I have argued that our concept of law is internally related to the preservation of liberty in the primary sense of independence: Law is the antithesis of arbitrary power. Because the law is addressed to every citizen, invoking his presumed commitment to justice and the common good, its requirements must be *acknowledged* as legitimate; unjust or arbitrary demands, violating

[54] *Barnette, supra* note 46 at 641.

[55] 478 U.S. 186 (1986) [*Bowers*].

the constitutional authority that the reasonable citizen affirms, fail to generate genuine legal obligations. The public *justification* of law is a necessary part of its claim to legitimacy, as well as its correct interpretation. The principles of equality and procedural fairness impose conditions on both the form and content of law, which reproduce most of the fundamental constraints characteristic of a bill of rights. They also preserve an ideal of judicial process that insulates adjudication, as a matter of conceptual coherence, from threatened departures from the rule of law.

When law is regarded as the measure of justice, the legal tradition is continuously tested and refined by internal challenge to its moral legitimacy. When the tradition is understood to be a guarantor of basic liberties, its extension and adaptation to current needs entail rigorous examination of the underlying public philosophy of freedom. Although paradigmatic judicial decisions and accepted understandings will help to focus the debate and promote a fair degree of unanimity, at least about many aspects of constitutional propriety, the legal interpreter must use his own moral compass when confronted by any doubtful question of law. He must think and reason as a member of the community, having regard to the character of the polity as other citizens understand and defend it; his arguments must be addressed to that general understanding, conceding the necessity to offer the more powerful reasons in proportion to the unpopularity or novelty of his opinions. But because he defends a vision of legitimate governance that he believes is true – the correct understanding of liberty or human dignity for his fellow citizens at this point in their collective political history – he must attune the theoretical sophistication of his case to the strength of his convictions.[56]

Justice Blackmun's dissent in *Bowers* drew on both First Amendment and Fourth Amendment jurisprudence in support of his reading of the requirements of due process under the Fourteenth Amendment. His view of the requirements of constitutional privacy was built on his understanding of the contribution of sexual intimacy to identity and personality. Distinguishing between matters of public decency and those of "private morality," Justice Blackmun denied that popular disapproval of a homosexual lifestyle could "justify invading the houses, hearts, and minds of citizens who choose to live their lives differently."[57] His constitutional judgment was ultimately, and necessarily,

[56] *Cf.* Ronald Dworkin, *A Matter of Principle* (1986), ch. 1, and *Law's Empire* (1986), ch. 6. Dworkin, however, defends a distinction between the "grounds" and "force" of law (see *Law's Empire* at 108–13) that I am contesting here.

[57] *Bowers*, *supra note* 55 at 213.

grounded in a theory of legitimate governance, applicable to the society and polity of which he was proud to be a member.[58]

In the case that finally vindicated Justice Blackmun's view, *Lawrence v. Texas* (overruling *Bowers*), the Supreme Court observed that the due process clause granted protection to personal decisions relating to a range of matters central to personal dignity and autonomy – marriage, procreation, contraception, family relationships, child rearing, and education.[59] *Bowers* had been wrong when it was decided, but had been further undermined by subsequent decisions affirming the scope of the liberty secured by the Fourteenth Amendment. The decision is as much an affirmation of the requirements of legitimate government, wherever the constitutional values of liberty, autonomy, and personal dignity are duly guaranteed, as an interpretation of the U.S. Constitution; the reference to the decision of the European Court of Human Rights in *Dudgeon v. United Kingdom*,[60] in refutation of the "sweeping references" in the *Bowers* judgment to the "history of Western civilization," helps make this clear. What would amount to an overblown rhetoric, as a narrowly technical reading of a specific constitutional text, is more naturally understood as the expression of a deeper philosophy of lawful governance, befitting the liberal democratic polity that the country had become. The petitioners were entitled to respect for the liberty of their private lives: "The State cannot demean their existence or control their destiny by making their private sexual conduct a crime." The implications of the Fifth and Fourteenth Amendments would become apparent only with the passage of time: "As the Constitution endures, persons in every generation can invoke its principles in their own search for greater freedom."[61]

There is plainly no inconsistency between believing, as a matter of personal morality, that certain sorts of private sexual relationship are wrong or demeaning, and holding as a question of political morality that individuals should be free to choose the nature of their own relationships. The *Lawrence* case was fairly straightforward: There was simply no "legitimate state interest" that could justify the intrusion into the sphere of personal freedom. There is no good reason, however, for thinking that more difficult, or finely balanced, cases do not require a similar approach: The legal or constitutional question is always a matter of ascertaining the morally appropriate boundary between personal liberty, on one hand, and legitimate state interest, on the other. Cases involving abortion or pornography or assisted suicide may be harder to resolve

[58] Compare Stevens J., *ibid.* at 217.

[59] 539 U.S. 558 at 574 (2003) [*Lawrence*].

[60] 45 Eur. Ct. H.R., Series A, No 45 (Judgment of 22 October 1981), 4 E.H.R.R. 149 [*Dudgeon*].

[61] *Lawrence, supra* note 59 at 578–9.

because there are genuine public interests to be reconciled with individual autonomy; but where all those involved acknowledge both dimensions of the moral question at hand, even if they differ over matters of precise definition and weight, they are engaged in the same deliberative endeavor. The debate is a moral debate about the true requirements of law – what is appropriate and legitimate in a political community committed to the fundamental ideas of liberty, equality, and human dignity that underpin a liberal democracy, having the specific character and history of the polity in question.[62]

Justice Scalia's dissent in *Lawrence* did not so much defend an alternative view of constitutional justice as deny the Court's jurisdiction to do justice at all. He thought it enough to establish a legitimate state interest that the statute reflected majority opinion about the morality of certain forms of sexual relationship; there was no requirement that legislation should be proportionate, based on specific considerations of public welfare sufficient to outweigh the deleterious effects on personal privacy and freedom. Justice Scalia observed that "criminal laws against fornication, bigamy, adultery, adult incest, bestiality, and obscenity" equally reflected conventional morality, suggesting that no such laws could now survive rational-basis review.[63] But judicial review should surely be more discriminating. The question of justice in each case must be whether or not a specific prohibition can be defended by recourse to reasons that the autonomous citizen, duly respectful of other people's interests and concerns, could fairly be expected to acknowledge. For Justice Scalia, it was a merit of democratic regulation, as opposed to judicial reason, that "the people . . . need not carry things to their logical conclusion"; they can draw lines that reflect degrees of moral disapprobation rather than any general principle. But this amounts to the withdrawal of law in favour of arbitrary will: Reason simply surrenders to passion or prejudice. Government retains its legitimacy only when it preserves the connections with liberty and justice that the rule of law makes an inherent feature of law.

[62] For valuable contributions in this spirit, see especially Ronald Dworkin, *Life's Dominion: An Argument about Abortion and Euthanasia* (1993), and Alan Brudner, *Constitutional Goods* (2004) ch. 9.

[63] *Lawrence, supra* note 59 at 599.

10 Written Constitutions and Unwritten Constitutionalism

Mark D. Walters

INTRODUCTION

Defending the idea of "unwritten law" has never been easy. Jeremy Bentham thought the very expression to be a "paradoxical and unmeaning epithet."[1] In his view, social reform required "fixed and accurate" laws – laws that "[w]e see, we hear, we touch; in short we handle . . . "[2] This empirical concept of law follows from the ideal of law as something produced by conscious acts of sovereign will. Central to this concept are, to use H.L.A. Hart's expression, "rules of change" that permit societies to escape the confines of "primitive" custom.[3] The progressive march of legal theory, it may be said, has been away from medieval notions of law as customs practiced time out of mind or as the immutable dictates of natural law, away from the fiction that judges discover rather than make law, and towards modern notions of law as creative political acts recorded in writing.

In terms of constitutional law, this march leads to the idea of written constitutionalism, a destination that the rebelling American colonists are often said to have reached first.[4] It was a task especially "reserved" to the American people, wrote Alexander Hamilton, to demonstrate to the world that constitutions might be established through "reflection and choice" rather than "accident and force."[5] In contrast to the unwritten British constitution, about

[1] Jeremy Bentham, A Comment on the Commentaries: A Criticism of W. Blackstone's "Commentaries on the laws of England," in C.W. Everett ed. (1928) at 156.

[2] *Ibid.* at 126.

[3] H.L.A. Hart, *The Concept of Law* (1961) at 89–94.

[4] Richard S. Kay, "American Constitutionalism," in Larry Alexander ed., *Constitutionalism: Philosophical Foundations* (1998) at 16.

[5] "Federalist No. 1," in Terence Ball ed., *The Federalist with Letters of 'Brutus'* (2003) at 1 ["Federalist No. 1"].

which there was "nothing visible, nothing real," the U.S. Constitution was a "certain and fixed" law "delineated by the mighty hand of the people," the "work or will" of a populace acting in its "original, sovereign, and unlimited capacity."[6] Its virtue lay not just in the hope of certainty that the prospect of a written instrument nourished, but also in the idea that this instrument was the product of a conscious and collective political act – "a compact," as John Jay observed, "deliberately formed, maturely considered, and solemnly adopted" by "the will of the people."[7] Like written law in general, written constitutional law manifests the creative potential of humanity and the aspirations of liberal modernity: We are to celebrate the fact that "[t]he Enlightenment hope in written constitutions is sweeping the world."[8]

But is this all that laws and constitutions really are? Is there no aspect of legality or constitutionality that transcends the politics of law-making and constitution writing? If, as Lon Fuller said, it is impossible to convert all of the "implicit demands of legal decency" – all aspects of the ideal of legality or the rule of law – "into explicit constitutional limitations,"[9] must the ideal of legality always give way to the sovereignty of texts and their writers?

From time to time, judges in places that have written constitutions talk about an unwritten constitutional law that somehow seems to *be* without ever having been *made*, a body of legal values with a persistence that defies its ethereal nature and the contingencies inherent in constitution writing. True, judges do not often resort openly to this unwritten law, but they appear sincere when they do. The acknowledgement in Australia in 1926 that an "unwritten constitution" forms "part of the fabric on which the written words of the Constitution are superimposed," has influenced the modern doctrine of constitutional implications in that country.[10] The Supreme Court of Canada has stated that the Canadian constitution is "primarily a written one," but "[b]ehind the written word" are "vital un-stated assumptions upon which the text is based," a series of "unwritten constitutional principles" to which judges may give "powerful

[6] *Vanhorne's Lessee v. Dorrance*, 2 U.S. (2 Dall.) 304 (C.C.D. Pa. 1795) at 307–9 (Patterson J.).

[7] *Henfield's Case*, Whart. St. Tr. 49 (C.C.D. Pa. 1793) at 58 [*Henfield's Case*]. *Cf. Re Representation in the House of Commons* (1903), 33 S.C.R. 475 *per* Mills J. at 586: Canada's constitution "is the result of compact" made by "representative men in self-governing provinces"; *Cunliffe v. Commonwealth of Australia* (1994), 182 C.L.R. 272 (HC) at 340 (Deane J.: Australia's "Constitution [was] adopted by the people as the compact of our nation").

[8] Bruce Ackerman, "The Rise of World Constitutionalism," 83 Va. L. Rev. 771 (1997) at 772.

[9] Lon L. Fuller, *Anatomy of the Law* (1971) at 92 [Fuller, *Anatomy of the Law*].

[10] *The Commonwealth v. Kreglinger & Fernau Ltd.* (1926), 37 C.L.R. 393 (HC) at 413–14 (Isaacs J.), cited in *Nationwide News Pty. Ltd. v. Wills* (1992), 177 C.L.R. 1 (HC) at 69 [*Nationwide News*]; *Australian Capital Television Pty. Limited v. The Commonwealth of Australia* (1992), 177 C.L.R. 106 (HC) at 135 and 230 [*Australian Capital Television*].

normative force."[11] Even in the United States, where the written constitution occupies an almost sacred place within the national imagination, the idea expressed by a mid-nineteenth century judge – that there is "back of the written Constitution, an unwritten Constitution" that protects rights "not preserved by express constitutional provisions" – continues to find its supporters.[12]

If statements such as these are taken seriously, then the stories told about the writing of constitutions by the "mighty hand of the people" must be taken a little less seriously. We would have to say that the sovereign capacity of constitution makers is not unlimited but exercised within (to borrow the language of Sir Gerard Brennan) an unwritten or common law "matrix."[13] We would have to understand written constitutions from the perspective of a theory of *unwritten* constitutionalism.

Constitutionalism implies the subjection of state power, including legislative power, to law.[14] The idea of unwritten constitutionalism is controversial, especially where there is a written constitution, for at least two reasons. First, it may be said that the judicial imposition of unwritten constraints on legislatures represents the assertion of some sort of natural law, which is nothing more than the assertion by judges of (their own) morality over the decisions of elected lawmakers. The unwritten constitution is, from this perspective, "a mere legal fog bank" into which judges enter and return with theories of constitutional limitations of their own making.[15] Second, it may be said that many examples of unwritten constitutionalism are instances of structuralist analysis, a form of constitutional interpretation in which inferences are drawn from constitutional structures established by the written constitution. From this perspective, unwritten constitutionalism is not "unwritten" at all, but just a form of textual interpretation that fails to take the text seriously.

The naturalist and structuralist critiques mark the edges of a narrow path that the unmade constitution of legal decency must navigate. If the unwritten constitution strays to one side, it falls into unstructured moral reasoning and loses its claim to being law. If it strays the other way, it is caught in the

[11] *Reference re Secession of Quebec*, [1998] 2 S.C.R. 217 at paras. 49, 52, and 54 [*Quebec Secession Reference*].

[12] *Hanson v. Vernon*, 27 Iowa 28 (SC, 1869) at 73 (Beck J.). See Thomas Grey, "Do We Have an Unwritten Constitution?" 27 Stan. L. Rev. 703 (1975); Michael S. Moore, "Do We Have an Unwritten Constitution?" 63 S. Cal. L. Rev. 107 (1989); James R. Stoner, *Common-Law Liberty: Rethinking American Constitutionalism* (2003) at 9–10.

[13] *Theophanous v. The Herald & Weekly Times Ltd.* (1994), 182 C.L.R. 104 (HC) at 141.

[14] Thomas Grey, "Constitutionalism: An Analytic Framework," in J. Roland Pennock and John W. Chapman eds., *Constitutionalism, Nomos XX* (1979) at 189–209.

[15] *Campbell v. Jackman Bros.*, 118 N. W. 755 (Iowa SC, 1908) at 761 (Weaver J.).

branches of constitutional text and loses control over its own legal course. Finding the path of unwritten constitutionalism therefore involves finding a way to understand how law can be unwritten and still be law. To understand unwritten constitutionalism we need an appropriate theory of unwritten law. Only after we understand what unwritten constitutionalism is, or could be, within common law jurisdictions that have written constitutions, can we say what its merits are.[16] Only after we have found the path for unwritten constitutionalism between the naturalist and structuralist claims will we know if the path has been worth finding.

The obvious place to look for a theory of unwritten law capable of supporting a theory of unwritten constitutionalism in common law jurisdictions is, of course, the common law itself. In this chapter, I will, therefore, reconstruct a common law conception of unwritten law, one derived from a time before the unfortunate description of the common law as judicial legislation came to be understood literally, a time when the portrayal of the common law as *lex non scripta* was genuine. I will then examine the idea of unwritten constitutionalism in relation to three common law jurisdictions with written constitutions – the United States, Canada, and Australia – to see how the common law conception of unwritten law helps to answer the naturalist and structuralist claims. I will conclude by suggesting that the expressions "written law" and "unwritten law" are *both* (to adapt Bentham's phrase) paradoxical and unmeaning epithets, unless, that is, we recall that they are simply *metaphors* for two basic ideas about what law is – law-as-sovereign will and law-as-reason – both of which are essential for legitimate constitutional order.

THE COMMON LAW CONCEPTION OF UNWRITTEN LAW

The distinction between written and unwritten constitutions may be "old-fashioned," James Bryce wrote, but it is based upon an even older "rather confusing" distinction between "Written and Unwritten Law."[17] A full account of the history of that confusing distinction in the common law tradition would take us back to Roman theories of law and their influence upon early writing on the law of England.[18] For present purposes, however, it is sufficient to pick up the story at the beginning of the seventeenth century, when medieval notions

[16] David Mullan, "The Role for Underlying Constitutional Principles in a Bill of Rights World," [2004] N.Z. L. Rev. 9 at 32–8.

[17] James Bryce, *Studies in History and Jurisprudence*, vol. 1 (1901) at 126.

[18] E.g., J. W. Tubbs, The Common Law Mind: Medieval and Early Modern Conceptions (2000) at 1–21.

of English law as immemorial custom and/or the embodiment of natural law were giving way to modern notions of the common law as a body of judicially articulated case law.

We may begin, then, with Sir John Davies' account of the English common law as "*Ius non scriptum*" or "*unwritten* lawe."[19] The common law was not "made" by princes and "imposed" upon subjects, Davies argued, but rather it emerged from a time beyond memory and grew "to perfection" to fit the "nature & disposition" of the people, thus approximating "the lawe of *Nature*" and "farre excel[ling] our *written* lawes, namely our Statutes or Actes of Parliament." But Davies also sought a path for the common law between the normative ideal of natural law and the empirical fact of social custom. The common law, he continued, was really founded upon a "discourse of reason" in which judges, guided by the "*coherence*" or "*harmony of reason* in our lawe," applied "fixt & certeine" maxims to the "infinite diuersitie" of human affairs that they confronted. The modern common law thus emerged through a confluence of ancient custom, natural law and judicial reason.

Of course, the common law as a body of case law was increasingly the law of written case reports, and so it could not have been unwritten in the same sense that ancient custom or natural law were. Davies' claim, that case reports were "but Comments or interpretations vppon the Text of the *Common Law*: which Text was neuer originally written,"[20] only hints at reasons why the common law was still properly regarded as an unwritten law. What was needed was a theory of how law and writing related – something that Thomas Hobbes and Sir Matthew Hale struggled to articulate.

Hobbes divided law into two parts: "one part being written, is called Civill, the other unwritten, Naturall," and he defined civil law as "the will of him that commandeth" and natural law as the law that people know through their own faculties of reason rather than "other mens words."[21] But Hobbes conceded that his expressions were misleading. "By *written* law," he wrote, "I mean law which requires the voice or some other sign of the will of the legislator to become law"; the "requisite of *written law* is not *writing* but vocal expression, writing being merely a means "*to record law*."[22] To emphasize this point, Hobbes insisted that the laws of nonliterate people that were put into verse and transmitted through

[19] Sir John Davies, Le Primer Report des Cases & Matters en Ley resolues & adiudges en les Courts del Roy en Ireland (1615), Preface [no pagination].

[20] *Ibid.*

[21] Thomas Hobbes, Leviathan, Or The Matter, Forme, & Power of a Common-wealth Ecclesiasticall and Civill [1651], Richard Tuck ed. (1996), c. 26 at 185, 187, and 188 [Hobbes, *Leviathan*].

[22] Thomas Hobbes, *On the Citizen* [1641] Richard Tuck and Michael Silverthorne eds. (1998), c. 14, para. 14 at 161 [Hobbes, *On the Citizen*].

singing or recitation qualified as written laws.[23] *Written law*, then, was simply a *metaphor* used to signify a particular type of law.

Hobbes also acknowledged that unwritten law was sometimes written in form. The principles of natural law, he observed, were analysed in the books of philosophers and opinions of judges, but "they are not for that reason to be called written laws."[24] Hobbes accepted that in cases "overlooked by the *written laws*" judges applied natural law, natural reason, or natural equity.[25] The essence of this unwritten law was to "give equal to equals," but, over time, judicial customs would develop around the application of this principle, customs that would receive tacit approval from the sovereign.[26] At this point, Hobbes argued, laws that were unwritten became "properly accepted among the written laws," not because cases were reported in written form or because natural reason became legal reason, but because the judicial rulings were tacitly sanctioned by "the will of the sovereign."[27]

Like Hobbes, Hale divided law into two parts: English law was "*Lex Scripta*, the written Law" or "*Lex non Scripta*, the unwritten Law."[28] *Lex scripta* consisted of laws "formally drawn up in Writing" and enacted by Parliament, and *lex non scripta* was "binding" by virtue of "immemorial Usage" and included "the Common Law properly so called" as well as local customs.[29] But, again, these definitions were misleading.

Hale conceded that *lex non scripta* was not "simply an unwritten Custom . . . *Orally* deriv'd down from one Age to another," for it was evidenced by "Monuments in Writing," such as reports of judicial decisions.[30] Hale also observed that written laws might, over time, become unwritten. First, he concluded that statutes made before the time of legal memory (dated as 1189), whether extant or not, derived their authority from judicial custom and were "accounted Part of the *Lex non Scripta*, being as it were incorporated thereinto, and become a Part of the Common Law."[31] Second, statutes enacted *within* the time of legal memory, the written texts of which were still extant, might also be considered part of the unwritten law. Some of these statutes, he wrote, were "so ancient" and had been subjected to so many "Judicial Resolutions

[23] Hobbes, *Leviathan*, *supra* note 21 at 189 and *On the Citizen*, *ibid.* at 161.

[24] Hobbes, *On the Citizen*, *supra* note 22 at 161–2.

[25] *Ibid.* at 161, and Thomas Hobbes, *The Elements of Law, Moral & Politic* (1650) Pt. 2, Ch. 10, para. 10.

[26] Hobbes, *On the Citizen*, *supra* note 22 at paras. 161–2.

[27] Ibid. and Thomas Hobbes, A Dialogue Between a Philosopher and a Student of the Common Laws of England, Joseph Cropsey ed. (1971) at 61–3 and 67.

[28] Sir Matthew Hale, *The History of the Common Law of England*, 3rd edn. (1739) at 1.

[29] *Ibid.* at 2 and 22–3.

[30] *Ibid.* at 65 and 23.

[31] *Ibid.* at 3.

and Decisions" that the "old Statutes themselves" as well as the "Expositions and Decisions" were "incorporated into the very Common Law, and become a Part of it."[32] Third, Hale addressed the status of statutes made within legal memory the official texts of which were lost, statutes for which there was "no Record" and for which "written Evidence" was found only in books of pleadings and judicial decisions.[33] These statutes, concluded Hale, did *not* cease to be written laws merely because they were "not extant of Record."[34]

In other words, Hale thought that a statute, the written text of which still existed, might cease to count as a written law if the meaning of the text became, in essence, overwhelmed by a long history of judicial exposition, but that a statute for which the official written text no longer existed, and for which the only evidence was judicial approbation, did not, for that reason alone, cease to be a written law. How can these positions be reconciled?

Hale, like Hobbes, concluded that the real difference between written and unwritten law was not writing. Both Hale and Hobbes treated the expressions *written* and *unwritten* as metaphors for different types of law. Hale's discussion of old statutes suggests that he distinguished legal norms defined by canonical expressions of words adopted by a lawmaker from legal norms that emerged through judicial interpretation and judgment in individual cases in absence of canonical expressions of law. Hale did not provide a full explanation of the common law as case law, and Hobbes' conclusion, that the common law was a form of written law due to tacit royal sanction, was not accepted by common lawyers. For an account of the common law as unwritten judicial reason, then, we must look elsewhere, and in this respect there is no better place to look than the work of Sir John Doderidge.

Doderidge accepted that the common law was based upon immemorial custom and natural reason, but he insisted that it was, first and foremost, a "*discourse* of reason."[35] In developing this idea, Doderidge was influenced by Christopher St. German's *Doctor and Student*. St. German also thought English law was based on custom and natural reason, but he argued that most legal questions involved analysis of the "lawe of reason secundarye," a law of reason that identified the legal implications of rules or principles that were not founded directly upon primary or natural reason.[36] So, for example, the

[32] *Ibid.* at 9.

[33] *Ibid.* at 16.

[34] *Ibid.* at 15.

[35] Sir John Doderidge, *The English Lawyer, Describing A Method for the managing of the Lawes of this Land* (1631) at 37, 38, and 62 [emphasis added] [Doderidge, *The English Lawyer*].

[36] T.F.T. Plucknett and J.L. Barton eds., *St. German's Doctor and Student* (1974) at 33–9 [St. German, *Doctor and Student*]. See also Mark D. Walters, "St. German on Reason and Parliamentary Sovereignty," (2003) 62 Cambridge L.J. 335 at 339–41 [Walters, *St German on Reason*].

institution of property was not required or prohibited by natural reason, but once society recognized property rights it followed "not only upon reason" but also upon the "law or custom of property" that trespasses were wrong.[37] Legal propositions of this nature were not conclusions of natural reason, nor were they conclusions of positive law; they were propositions of law that followed from the law of secondary reason and thus there was "no need to have a written law on the point."[38]

Doderidge combined St. German's idea of secondary reason with humanist logic and rhetoric to produce a theory of common law method. He insisted that there was a "truth" about law that was not a matter of either history or metaphysics, but was discovered through "argument and disputation."[39] This discourse was informed by the liberal arts generally and "Morall Philosophy" in particular, but it represented a distinctively *legal* "Art of reasoning."[40] At the centre of this legal art was the ideal of coherence. Specific propositions of law were to be seen as part of a larger fabric of more abstract legal principle, and specific and abstract propositions alike were to be arranged "from the most ample and highest Generall, by many degrees of descent, as in a Pedigree or Genealogie, to the lowest speciall and particular" with all of the parts "combined together as it were in a consanguinity of blood and concordancie of nature."[41] We ought to see a "coherency" not just within "every title of the Law," insisted Doderidge, but throughout "the whole body thereof."[42]

Truth in law thus existed "in *concreto* as well as in *abstracto*," and the discourse of reason was an interpretive oscillation between concrete and abstract in search of what Ronald Dworkin later would call "reflective equilibrium."[43] Wrote Doderidge:

> ... mans understanding for the attaining of knowledge proceedeth from the effect to the cause, and againe from the cause to the effect; that is from the particular to the speciall, and from the speciall to the generall; and so to the more generall ... And so againe from such chiefe & primary Principles and propositions to more speciall and peculiar Assertions, descending even to every particular matter.[44]

[37] St. German, *Doctor and Student, supra* note 36 at 35.

[38] *Ibid.* at 35, 37.

[39] Doderidge, *The English Lawyer, supra* 35 at 62, 63, and 64.

[40] *Ibid.* at 37, 38, and 62.

[41] *Ibid.* at 258; also 64, 95, and 190.

[42] *Ibid.* at 190.

[43] *Ibid.* at 108. Dworkin's theory of law is largely built upon the idea of reflective equilibrium, which he attributes to John Rawls: Ronald Dworkin, *Taking Rights Seriously* (1977) at 155–68; Ronald Dworkin, *Law's Empire* (1986), 424 note 17 [Dworkin, *Law's Empire*]; Ronald Dworkin, *Justice in Robes* (2006) at 246.

[44] Doderidge, *The English Lawyer, supra* note 35 at 237.

The search for coherence through interpretive ascent and descent was the essence of "unwritten law" in England, a law ready to be identified through "discourse of reason" and "Iudiciall determination" when the occasion should require and not before.[45] Indeed, Doderidge insisted that unwritten law, as an accommodation of individual concerns in light of general principles, was more just than "positive Law" made in advance.[46] Even when general rules were made by positive law, Doderidge insisted that individuals affected unequally were excepted – an exception of the "Law of Reason" that St. German had argued was secured through judicial commitment to equity and "secretly understood in every generall Rule of every positive Law."[47] Written laws were to be read against the normative backdrop of unwritten law.

The true grounds of law, wrote Doderidge, were "not at all expressly published in words, but left neverthelesse implied and included in the cases so decided."[48] In new cases, there were legal answers waiting to be drawn from old cases, for the English lawyer is taught "that Cases different in circumstance, may be neverthelesse compared each to other in equality of Reason; so that of like Reason, like Law might be framed."[49] "[W]e perceive a coherence and likenesse between divers and sundry cases," he continued, and the law on any given matter thus emerges from "the unity of reason so found and considered in the said cases."[50] "It is not the Case ruled this way, nor that way, but the reason which maketh Law" – not abstract or natural reason but the secondary reason that emerges through a discourse aimed at the "equality of reason."[51]

From the work of St. German, Davies, Hale, and Doderidge, a common law conception of unwritten law can be seen to emerge. That conception may be summarized as follows.

Written law is a metaphor representing the sort of legal proposition that is set by a lawmaker using a linguistic formula that is to be taken as canonical by judges, and therefore as exhausting the relevant law for the matters to which it is held to apply. To interpret and apply written law, then, requires determining how the general and canonical language of a rule applies to specific situations.

Unwritten law is a metaphor representing the sort of legal proposition that is derived through a discourse of reason in which specific legal propositions directly or indirectly relevant to the matter under consideration are examined – not as canonical expressions of rules that exhaust the law on point, but as manifestations of more abstract principles of "secondary" reason from which, after

45 *Ibid.* at 241.
46 *Ibid.*
47 *Ibid.* at 210 (following St. German, *Doctor & Student*, *supra* note 36 at 97).
48 *Ibid.* at 243.
49 *Ibid.* at 244.
50 *Ibid.* at 265–6.
51 *Ibid.* at 268 and 270.

an interpretive oscillation between the specific propositions and the general principles they presuppose, and due consideration of the aspiration of "equality of reason," other specific legal propositions may be derived. Unwritten law is not simply historical custom or natural reason. It is a discourse of reason that seeks a "unity" of reason through an inductive ascent from particular manifestations of general principles to the general principles themselves, and then a descent back again to the level of specifics to articulate new rules or rights that cohere, in principle, with established rules and rights.

The common law view of law and writing recognized points of convergence between written and unwritten law. Written law only exhausts the law on point in a relative sense, for the meaning of general expressions of written law in individual cases is shaped by judicial commitment to equality (or a broad sense of equity) secured by the unwritten law of reason. The equality of reason is "secretly" a part of every written law. Also, a rule of law established through the canonical expression of a lawmaker might later be considered by judges as a mere reflection of more abstract legal principles from which other rules cohering in principle with the legislated rule may be identified. What was written law may, through judicial exposition, become unwritten law.

UNWRITTEN LAW AND CONSTITUTIONALISM

The claim that written constitutions in places like Australia, Canada, and the United States exist within the normative context of unwritten constitutionalism is a controversial one – but it is much less controversial when considered in light of the common law conception of unwritten law that I have just summarized. The principal insight to be derived from the common law theory of unwritten law and applied to constitutional law is that the expressions *written law* and *unwritten law* are not references to constitutional documents or their absence, but *metaphors* that symbolize distinctive approaches to constitutional interpretation. This assertion is, in one sense at least, hardly novel. In his famous book, *Introduction to the Study of the Law of the Constitution*, A.V. Dicey contrasted "unwritten" English constitutional law with written constitutions in countries like Belgium in the following way:

> There is in the English constitution an absence of those declarations or definitions of rights so dear to foreign constitutionalists.... [T]he difference... between the constitution of Belgium and the English constitution may be described by the statement that in Belgium individual rights are deductions drawn from the principles of the [written] constitution, whilst in England the so-called principles of the constitution are inductions or

> generalisations based upon particular decisions pronounced by the Courts as to the rights of given individuals.[52]

Dicey thus acknowledged that the important difference between written and unwritten constitutions is not so much the presence or absence of a written constitutional instrument, but the difference between a system in which judges give specific meaning to general propositions of constitutional law that are expressed in exhaustive and canonical form, and a system in which judges articulate constitutional law by inferring general principles from a nonexhaustive and noncanonical set of specific legal propositions. This distinction is analogous to the one implied by the written/unwritten metaphor at common law.

However, to recognize unwritten constitutional law, even in the metaphorical sense of the common law, is not necessarily to recognize the ideal of unwritten constitutionalism. The standard reading of Dicey – adopted by Jeffrey Goldsworthy, for example – is that he considered legislative power to be legally unlimited except where it had been constrained by the terms of a written constitution.[53] On this view, Dicey embraced what David Dyzenhaus calls "constitutional positivism"[54] – a position inconsistent with unwritten constitutionalism. But Dyzenhaus, like T.R.S. Allan, reads Dicey differently. Woven subtly into Dicey's account of the rule of law, they say, is a vision of legislative authority in which general statutory language is always shaped and limited in specific cases by the common law "spirit of legality."[55] In this reading of Dicey, then, we can see a connection between the common-law conception of unwritten law and the ideal of constitutionalism. The nature of that connection is revealed by distinguishing between the formal and substantive dimensions of the discourse of reason that lies at the heart of the common-law theory of unwritten law.

In its formal sense, the common-law discourse of reason is simply a technique or method of reasoning that will yield answers on points of law that could be

[52] A.V. Dicey, *Introduction to the Study of the Law of the Constitution*, 8th edn. (1908) at 192–3 [Dicey, *Law of the Constitution*].

[53] Jeffrey Goldsworthy, *The Sovereignty of Parliament: History and Philosophy* (1999) at 1–21 [Goldsworthy, *Sovereignty of Parliament*].

[54] On "constitutional positivism" see David Dyzenhaus, "The Incoherence of Constitutional Positivism," in this volume [Dyzenhaus, "Constitutional Positivism"]; David Dyzenhaus, *The Constitution of Law: Legality in a Time of Emergency* (2006) at 66–72 [Dyzenhaus, *Constitution of Law*]; David Dyzenhaus, "The Genealogy of Legal Positivism," (2004) 24 O.J.L.S. 39.

[55] Dicey, *Law of the Constitution*, *supra* note 52 at 409. See Dyzenhaus, Constitution of Law, *ibid.* at 71; T.R.S. Allan, *Constitutional Justice: A Liberal Theory of the Rule of Law* (2001) at 13–21 [Allan, *Constitutional Justice*].

highly technical or morally contingent. But the "equality of reason" that defines this technique implies a limited moral substance, too. The formal technique of common-law reasoning advances, to use Dworkin's language, the value of integrity, the value of treating individuals with equal concern and respect.[56] The interpretive oscillation between specific rules and the abstract principles that they presuppose in search of a "unity of reason" is a form of due process that respects individual equality through minimizing arbitrariness within state power. In its substantive dimension, then, the common-law conception of unwritten law is related to the value of legality or the rule of law that defines the minimal instantiations of equality and due process – what Allan calls the "unwritten principles of liberal constitutionalism" – that law must honour if it is to be *law*.[57] The common-law conception of unwritten law and the liberal conception of constitutionalism are intimately connected.

This is not to say that the relationship between unwritten law and constitutionalism has remained constant since the early seventeenth-century. English lawyers (not just Coke) thought that Acts of Parliament repugnant to reason were legally "void."[58] But it was never an established part of the English common law tradition for judges to strike down statutes on this ground. Focusing on this point, Goldsworthy rejects the historical argument for common law or unwritten constitutionalism.[59] In doing so, however, Goldsworthy overlooks the emergence of unwritten constitutionalism through more subtle or (to paraphrase St. German) "secret" interpretive methods. Ironically, it is in common law jurisdictions where written constitutions have been adopted that unwritten constitutionalism seems to have flourished in more overt ways.

For present purposes, however, the debate about the history of constitutionalism in the common-law tradition is one that can be left to the side. I wish to invoke the common-law conception of unwritten law in this essay not as historical support for a modern theory of judicial review of legislative power, but simply for the insights into the metaphors pertaining to writing and law that theory provides. The argument is simple: If we think about the distinction between unwritten and written constitutional law in a way that is roughly analogous to the way that common lawyers thought about the distinction

[56] Dworkin, *Law's Empire*, *supra* note 43.

[57] T.R.S. Allan, "Constitutional Justice and the Concept of Law," in this volume at 219 [Allan, "Constitutional Justice"].

[58] Walters, "St. German on Reason", *supra* note 36 and Mark D. Walters, "Common Law, Reason, and Sovereign Will," (2003) 53 U.T.L.J. 65.

[59] Goldsworthy, "Unwritten Constitutional Principles," in this volume [Goldsworthy, "Unwritten Constitutional Principles], and, in general, Goldsworthy, *Sovereignty of Parliament*, *supra* note 53.

between unwritten and written law, then a defensible theory of unwritten constitutionalism emerges.

Developing that theory fully is beyond the scope of this chapter. However, its broad outlines may be seen by considering the ways in which the common-law conception of unwritten law helps answer the naturalist and structuralist claims against the use of unwritten constitutional law in common law jurisdictions having written constitutions. I will now address each of these claims in turn.

The Naturalist Account

The naturalist account of unwritten constitutionalism may be considered on two levels. A first-order claim might be made that the judicial enforcement of unwritten constitutional principles against legislatures involves enforcing natural law or natural rights. A second-order claim might be made that the idea that written constitutions in common-law jurisdictions take effect within a larger context of unwritten constitutional law is premised upon natural law jurisprudence. These are slightly different claims, and one might accept one but deny the other.

One might deny the second-order claim by observing that one does not have to subscribe to natural law jurisprudence to accept the possibility of an unwritten constitution behind the written constitution, for that possibility is consistent with conceptual legal positivism, too. There is no reason why, the legal positivist might say, the rule of recognition for a system could not disclose a layer of higher unwritten law that defines the legal validity of the written constitution for that system. And the same legal positivist might adopt an inclusive positivist stance and accept the first-order claim: Natural law or natural rights may represent laws enforceable by judges against legislatures if that is what the rule of recognition for the system mandates. Conversely, one might accept the second order claim and say that unwritten constitutionalism is premised upon natural law jurisprudence, or some form of nonpositivist philosophy of law, but deny the first-order claim that unwritten constitutional laws are simply natural law or natural rights.

Although I think this second position is the right one, the status of second-order claims and their relationship to first-order claims raise jurisprudential issues that cannot be addressed here. I will, therefore, concentrate on the first-order "naturalist" claim, that by enforcing unwritten constitutional principles, judges enforce some sort of natural law or natural rights against legislatures. This characterization of unwritten constitutionalism is usually made by critics of the idea, and is followed quickly by the assertion that natural law is nothing more than personal preference about morality or justice or fairness. Thus, Justice Michael Kirby stated in the Australian case of *Durham Holdings Pty Ltd. v. New South Wales*, that the attempt to assert fundamental common law rights against legislative authority is an attempt to resurrect, in a new form, the ancient notion that "natural or divine law" binds Parliament, an argument that must be rejected; otherwise, the "judge's own notions of fundamental rights" will prevail over those of elected representatives.[60] In the colourful statement of one American judge, to invoke an unwritten constitution of natural rights is to enter a "cloudland" where no one can agree on anything.[61]

The common-law conception of unwritten law denies that unwritten law is simply natural reason, and the theory of unwritten constitutionalism based upon that conception does the same. Under this conception, unwritten law does not imply ascent into a constitutional cloudland; rather, it is a distinctly earthbound, or secondary, form of reason. However, convincing people of this point has never been easy, as the misunderstandings about the famous *obiter dictum* of Justice Samuel Chase from *Calder v. Bull* attest.[62]

In *Calder*, Justice Chase stated that the very purposes for which men "enter into society" – the promotion of general welfare, the securing of liberty, and the protection of persons and property from violence – establish the terms of the "social compact" and the proper objects of legislative power.[63] In the case of the United States, this meant that legislatures were bound by certain fundamental principles that "flow[ed] from the very nature of our free Republican governments."[64] There are, therefore, acts "which the Federal, or State, Legislature cannot do, without exceeding their authority," he insisted, for the "vital principles in our free Republican governments" will "over-rule" flagrant abuses of legislative power that purport to "authorize manifest injustice by positive law."[65] "An ACT of the Legislature (for I cannot call it a law) contrary to the great first principles of the social compact," he continued, "cannot be considered a rightful exercise of legislative authority."[66] There was no need for express constitutional provisions prohibiting laws that, for example, made acts unlawful retrospectively, or made a man judge in his own cause, or took property from A and gave it to B, for the "genius, the nature, and the spirit" of the republican governments established and "the general principles of law and reason" forbid them.[67]

[60] (2001) 205 C.L.R. 399 (HC) at 419–20, 427.
[61] *Campbell v. Jackman Bros.*, 118 N.W. 755 *per* Weaver J. at 761 (1908) (Iowa SC).
[62] *Calder v. Bull*, 3 U.S. 386 (1798) [*Calder*].
[63] *Ibid.* at 388.
[64] *Ibid.*
[65] *Ibid.*
[66] *Ibid.*
[67] *Ibid.*

It might be thought that Justice Chase invoked a standard liberal natural rights thesis, according to which the rights of individuals derive from a pre-political state of nature and are retained by them when they enter the social compact that establishes civil society, and these natural rights remain inviolable and may, therefore, be enforced by judges against legislatures.[68] If so, then Justice James Iredell would have been right to conclude in his reasons in the same case that Chase thought judges could review legislation on the grounds of "abstract principles of natural justice."[69]

But Justice Chase did not say that restrictions on legislative power came from pre-political natural rights. He said they were inherent in the very concept of law that obtained within a "free republican government," an entirely different theoretical proposition.[70] His views were informed by civic republicanism, not Lockean liberalism. As he explained on another occasion, the "republican form of government" implied a very particular conception of law, one based upon the protection of equality through adherence to (what we would now call) the rule of law.[71] People are free, argued Justice Chase, when "the same laws govern the whole society without any distinction," when "there is no power to dispense with the execution of the laws," and when justice is "impartially and speedily administered"; they are not free when law and its administration are "uncertain, partial or arbitrary, when "property is insecure," or when people are exposed to "insult and violence without redress by law."[72] He rejected the claim of "visionary and theoretical writers" that rights derived from a pre-political condition: The state of nature was a "creature of the imagination only."[73] For Justice Chase, all rights and liberties "spring out of civil society," and because rights are not "natural" but "social" in character, they may be defined and limited by society for the common good.[74] The republican value

[68] See *e.g.*, Kurt T. Lash, "The Lost Original Meaning of the Ninth Amendment," 83 Tex. L. Rev. 331 at 404–6 (2004). Most commentators assume that Chase presented a "natural law" argument: Edward B. Foley, "The Bicentennial of *Calder v. Bull*: In Defense of a Democratic Middle Ground," 59 Ohio St. L.J. 1599 at 1605 (1998); Raoul Berger, "Natural Law and Judicial Review: Reflections of an Earthbound Lawyer," 61 University of Cin. L. Rev. (1992) 5 at 19; Raoul Berger, "The Transfiguration of Samuel Chase: A Rebuttal," B.Y.U.L. Rev. 559 at 586–8 (1992).

[69] *Calder*, *supra* note 62 at 399.

[70] Morton J. Horwitz, "Republicanism and Liberalism in American Constitutional Thought," 29 Wm. & Mary L. Rev. 57 at 73–4 (1987); Rebecca L. Brown, "The Fragmented Liberty Clause," 41 Wm. & Mary L. Rev. 65 at 67–8 (1999).

[71] Judge Chase, Grand Jury charge, 2 May 1803, reprinted in Trial of Samuel Chase, An Associate Justice of the Supreme Court of the United States, Impeached by the House of Representatives, vol. 2 at v-vii (1805; reprint, 1970).

[72] *Ibid.* at vi.

[73] *Ibid.*

[74] *Ibid.* at viii.

of equality, however, disciplines the idea of law: The doctrine of "equal liberty and equal rights," properly understood, means that "every citizen, without respect to property or station, should enjoy an equal share of civil liberty; an equal protection from the laws, and an equal security for his person and property."[75] This idea – a conception of the rule of law premised upon the relatively restricted idea of republican equality – was the unwritten limitation on legislative power that Chase contemplated in *Calder*.

Of course, it might be thought that this reasoning is as much in constitutional cloudland as is abstract natural law reasoning. To be sure, it involves judicial reference to normative theories of law and political morality. But there is a significant difference between constructing a theory about pre-political rights that exist in opposition to civil society, and constructing a theory of legal rights that arises from the conception of what "law" is within a very particular form of civil society.

Justice Chase's position reflects some of the key ideas that we have described as the common-law conception of unwritten law. Far from requiring judicial inquiry into abstract reason, it is (as St. German would say) an inquiry into the implications for "secondary reason" of particular commitments made. Rather than reading the written constitution as a canonical and exhaustive expression of rights and powers, it represents the results of judicial reflection upon more abstract principles manifested by specific provisions of the constitution. And, finally, it may be said to embrace (as Doderidge would say) the aspiration of "equality of reason."

Other judges came to appreciate that this form of reasoning was not merely natural law reasoning. In *Loan Association v. Topeka*, for example, Justice Samuel Miller, writing for the U.S. Supreme Court, adopted Chase-like reasoning and concluded that legislatures are bound by "[i]mplied reservations of individual rights" that "grow out of the essential nature of all free governments," with the result that legislation directed at one class of people for the private benefit of another class "is not legislation" but "a decree under legislative forms" and therefore invalid.[76] Justice Nathan Clifford, in dissent, raised the usual objection that this reasoning amounted to limiting legislative power "according to natural justice," but he also tried to address the real essence of Justice Miller's argument by saying that judges should not nullify legislation "on the vague ground that they think it opposed to a general latent spirit

[75] *Ibid.*

[76] *Loan Association v. Topeka*, 87 U.S. 655 at 663 and 664 (1874) [*Loan Association*]. On the idea of "free government" and republican political theory, see Quentin Skinner, *Liberty Before Liberalism* (1998).

supposed to pervade or underlie the constitution . . . "[77] This characterization of Justice Miller's argument is still somewhat unfair; the limitation he invoked from the republican ideals of equality and the rule of law was not really vague. But at least Justice Clifford appreciated that what was invoked was a conception of law within a specific constitutional tradition rather than just abstract natural reason.

Unwritten constitutionalism, if properly conceived in a common-law jurisdiction, is not really about natural law or political morality in any indefinite or detached sense. It is not, as Goldsworthy argues, vague or abstract.[78] Rather, it is all about identifying the practical legal implications of the "spirit" of legality that pervades the forms of constitutionalism to which societies commit themselves. The approach taken by Justices Chase and Miller illustrate not only the technique or form of unwritten common-law reasoning, it manifests unwritten law in its substantive dimension, too: The discourse of reason about what "law" is for their society evidences commitment to the minimal standards of equality and due process that make law possible. Indeed, their assumption that rights to liberty and equality arise from the very notion of what law is within the republican tradition mirrors T.R.S. Allan's sense of what the liberal conception of the rule of law is.[79]

Engaging in a discourse of reason about the spirit of legality within a jurisdiction that has a written constitution requires that judges examine how this spirit relates to specific constitutional texts, and, as a result, the exercise, though invariably contentious, is not really "vague." Indeed, perhaps the real question is whether, given that the relationship between spirit and text is so close, describing the interpretive process as "unwritten" is really accurate. The structuralist account, to which attention is now turned, denies that it is.

The Structuralist Account

Nowadays, judicial reference to the latent spirit of the written constitution is often described as structuralist reasoning – "the method of inference," as Charles Black put it, "from the structures and relationships created by the [written] constitution . . . "[80] American and Australian judges insist that the resulting principles of constitutional law form part of the written constitution,

[77] *Loan Association*, *ibid.* at 668 and 669.

[78] Goldsworthy, "Unwritten Constitutional Principles," *supra* note 59.

[79] Allan, "Constitutional Justice," *supra* note 57 at 222.

[80] Charles L. Black, Jr., Structure and Relationship in Constitutional Law (1969) at 7 [Black, *Structure and Relationship*].

while in Canada they are described as unwritten; however, the approaches taken in all three jurisdictions are remarkably similar.

Structuralism is illustrated by the rationale given by Justice William Douglas for the right to privacy in *Griswold v. Connecticut*.[81] In that case, Douglas refused to locate the right to privacy within the more general concept of liberty in the Fourteenth Amendment.[82] Instead, he concluded that the "specific guarantees" in the U.S. Bill of Rights – such as the First Amendment guarantee of freedom of speech and assembly and the Third Amendment prohibition against quartering soldiers in houses during peace – were "facet[s]" of a more general right to privacy that was located within the "penumbra" of these other rights, and from that general right, a specific right to privacy in sexual relations between married couples could be deduced.[83] Justice Douglas did not state that the right of privacy was unwritten; on the contrary, he said that "the zone of privacy" had been "created" by the specific constitutional guarantees he mentioned.[84]

Another example is *Alden v. Maine*, in which a federal statute was struck down as violating the principle of state sovereign immunity – despite the fact that the Eleventh Amendment explicitly protects that principle in only a narrow range of instances, none of which was relevant to the facts of the case.[85] From "[v]arious textual provisions" addressing unrelated matters of constitutional detail, Justice Anthony Kennedy inferred a more general principle of state sovereignty from which the principle of state immunity from lawsuits was then deduced.[86] The principle was, he concluded, derived "from the structure of the original Constitution itself" and the narrower statement of the principle in the Eleventh Amendment was properly seen "as evidencing and exemplifying" the broader idea.[87] In response to Justice David Souter's claim that this conclusion was, in effect, based upon "a universally applicable proposition [about sovereignty] discoverable by reason" or "natural law,"[88] Justice Kennedy insisted that he was relying upon the "formal structure of federalism" as adopted by the framers of the Constitution, and he therefore appealed "to no higher authority than the Charter which they wrote ..."[89] For American judges, then, inferences from constitutional structure yield legal propositions that are part of the written constitution.

[81] *Griswold v. Connecticut*, 381 US 479 (1965).
[82] *Ibid.* at 481–2.
[83] *Ibid.* at 482, 483, and 484.
[84] *Ibid.* at 485.
[85] *Alden v. Maine*, 527 US 706 (1999).
[86] *Ibid.* at 713.
[87] *Ibid.* at 728 (quoting *Idaho v. Coeur d'Alene Tribe of Idaho*, 521 US 261 at 267–8 (1997)).
[88] *Ibid.* at 763.
[89] *Ibid.* at 758.

The same general approach to text and structure is apparent in Canadian and Australian judgments. Justice Ivan Rand concluded in the 1950s that the preamble to the *British North America Act, 1867*, which states that the Canadian constitution is "similar in principle" to the British constitution, identified a "political theory" that was elaborated by specific constitutional provisions establishing an "institutional apparatus" of parliamentary democracy, and from this "constitutional structure," certain political rights and freedoms – in particular, those relating to political expression – were, "by a necessary implication," protected from legislative violation.[90]

Similar logic was employed in Australia when a freedom of political communication was recognized in the early 1990s.[91] It was said that legislative authority is limited by "the fundamental implications of the doctrines of government" – including the doctrine of representative democracy – "upon which the Constitution as a whole is structured."[92] As Justice Rand had done in Canada, the Australian judges identified the general principle of representative democracy by inductive reasoning: From the specific provisions in the written constitution for an elected legislature, the more general principle of representative democracy was inferred. And then from this general principle, the specific freedom of political communication was deduced.[93] But the resulting principle was not seen as unwritten. As the Chief Justice, Sir Anthony Mason, observed, a constitutional implication is a concept that "inheres in the instrument and as such operates as part of the instrument."[94] Indeed, by the mid-1990s, the vertical interpretive ascent and descent illustrated by these cases had been replaced by a simple horizontal step from "text and structure" to the right or freedom at issue, perhaps foreclosing the possibility of articulating the freedom as "unwritten" in the formal sense.[95]

In Canada, the interpretive method adopted by Justice Rand has been applied to identify a series of underlying constitutional principles – including

[90] *Switzman v. Elbling*, [1957] S.C.R. 285 at 306–7, and *Saumur v. Quebec (City)*, [1953] 2 S.C.R. 299 at 331.

[91] *Nationwide News*, *supra* note 10 and *Australian Capital Television*, *supra* note 10.

[92] *Nationwide News*, *supra* note 10 at 69 (Deane and Toohey JJ.). For similar approaches, see *Australian Capital Television*, *supra* note 10 at 135 (Mason CJ.) and 208–9 (Gaudron J.).

[93] *Nationwide News*, *supra* note 10 at 70–3 (Deane and Toohey JJ.); *Australian Capital Television*, *supra* note 10 at 137–140 (Mason CJ.), and 209–10 and 211–12 (Gaudron J.).

[94] *Australian Capital Television*, *supra* note 10 at 135.

[95] *Ibid.* at 227, adopted in *Lange v. Australian Broadcasting Corporation* (1997), 189 C.L.R. 520 (HC) and *McGinty v. The State of Western Australia* (1996), 186 C.L.R. 140 (HC). See Adrienne Stone, "The Limits of Constitutional Text and Structure: Standards of Review and the Freedom of Political Communication," (1999) 23 Melbourne U.L.R. 668 at 673.

judicial independence, federalism, democracy, the rule of law, constitutionalism, parliamentary privileges, respect for minorities, human rights, and aboriginal self-government – from which more specific rules and principles may be derived.[96] However, unlike American and Australian judges, Canadian judges have concluded that these principles are *unwritten* constitutional laws. As the Supreme Court states: Written texts may occupy a "primary place" in determining constitutional law, but "they are not exhaustive" because the constitution "embraces unwritten, as well as written rules."[97]

The relationship between unwritten and written constitutional law in Canada may be conceived in different ways. At one point, Chief Justice Antonio Lamer observed that the role of unwritten principles is "to fill out gaps in the express terms of the constitutional scheme."[98] This statement might suggest that judges are just reading between the lines in order to make the text complete. Or, to use another metaphor, judges are constructing bridges over the waters that separate islands of constitutional text, creating a unified and useable surface.

But the gap-filling and bridge metaphors do not capture fully the theory of unwritten constitutionalism as it has developed in the Canadian cases. Chief Justice Lamer has also written that the specific provisions of the written constitution – the islands in our metaphor – "merely elaborate th[e] organizing principles in the institutional apparatus they create or contemplate."[99] Elsewhere, the Court states that the "unwritten" principles are the "postulates which form the very foundation of the Constitution of Canada,"[100] the "vital unstated assumptions upon which the text is based."[101] We must alter the bridge metaphor accordingly: The textual islands are merely the exposed parts of a vast seabed visible beneath the surrounding waters, and the bridges constructed by judges between these islands are actually causeways moulded from natural materials brought to the surface from this single underlying foundation. The

[96] See *Reference re Remuneration of Judges of the Provincial Court of Prince Edward Island*, [1997] 3 S.C.R. 3 (judicial independence) [*Provincial Judges Reference*]; *New Brunswick Broadcasting Co. v. Nova Scotia (Speaker of the House of Assembly)*, [1993] 1 S.C.R. 319 (parliamentary privilege); *Quebec Secession Reference, supra* note 11 (federalism, democracy, the rule of law, constitutionalism, respect for minorities); *R. v. Demers*, [2004] 2 S.C.R. 489 at para. 83 (human rights); and *Campbell v. British Columbia (Attorney General)* (2000), 189 D.L.R. (4th) 333 (BCSC) (aboriginal self-government).

[97] *Quebec Secession Reference, supra* note 11 at para. 32, citing *Provincial Judges Reference, supra* note 96 at para. 92.

[98] *Provincial Judges Reference, supra* note 96 at para. 95.

[99] *Ibid.* at paras. 97 and 95.

[100] *Reference re Manitoba Language Rights*, [1985] 1 S.C.R. 721 at 749–50.

[101] *Quebec Secession Reference, supra* note 11 at paras. 49 and 52.

constitutional text is not just supplemented by unwritten principles; it rests upon them.

Charles Black concluded that there is a "close and perpetual interworking" between textual and structural modes of reasoning, for the relevant structures are themselves "created by the text" and any inferences from them are "controlled by the text."[102] This conclusion is certainly consistent with the assumption of American and Australian judges that structural reasoning produces legal propositions that may be said to be part of, or implied by, the written constitution. But once we look at constitutional interpretation from the perspective of the common law conception of unwritten law, it is clear that courts in all three jurisdictions are engaged in the articulation of an unwritten constitution. In the cases examined, judges do not treat written constitutional provisions as canonical expressions of legal principle that exhaust legal meaning on the points to which they apply. Instead, they regard written constitutional provisions as manifestations of more abstract principles – as islands connected by a single seabed – from which propositions not expressly mentioned in the written constitution may be derived. The cases therefore reveal a discourse of secondary reason in which written law is regarded as but one source of unwritten law and judges seek a "unity" or "equality" of reason by oscillating between concrete and abstract propositions of law.

This point is made clearly by the Supreme Court of Canada. Constitutions, said the Court, must "endure over time" and must therefore contain a "comprehensive" and "exhaustive" set of fundamental laws, but because "problems or situations may arise which are not expressly dealt with by the text of the Constitution," reference to unwritten constitutional principles is "necessary."[103] The comprehensive and exhaustive nature of a constitution is a necessary value that is not dependent upon the choices made by the writers of the constitution; on the contrary, when the choices adopted by constitution writers result in written protections for an important constitutional principle that are not "uniform or consistent," the Court will conclude that the specific textual references are not an "exhaustive and definitive code" on the point, but are merely "elaborations of the underlying, unwritten [principle]."[104] This is a classic case of (to invoke Doderidge again) equal reason making equal law. So-called structural reasoning fits perfectly within the traditional common law conception of what unwritten law, in its formal dimension, is. And where that formal method identifies values intrinsic to a liberal conception of the rule of law, as it does in

[102] Black, *Structure and Relationship*, *supra* note 80 at 31.

[103] *Quebec Secession Reference*, *supra* note 11 at para. 32.

[104] *Provincial Judges Reference*, *supra* note 96 at paras. 85 and 107.

many of these cases, the substantive dimension of the discourse of unwritten reason is manifested in a particularly direct and forceful way.

The Scope of the Unwritten Constitution

The common-law theory of unwritten law, especially the idea that *written law* and *unwritten law* are to be understood as metaphors for distinctive styles of constitutional discourse, helps us to understand better what unwritten constitutionalism is and why the naturalist and structuralist claims against it are ineffective. But, it may be said, the cases I have examined in support of the theory all deal with judicial attempts to address problems arising from written constitutions that are less than comprehensive in their coverage; constitutions with "gaps." What if a written constitution is comprehensive and includes, for example, a bill of rights guaranteeing equality, liberty, due process, and other basic human rights? If our understanding of the unwritten constitution is shaped by the common law metaphors pertaining to writing and law, as I have suggested it should be, then does it not follow that a comprehensive written constitutional text will provide canonical expressions of law for all matters and further reference to the idea of unwritten constitutionalism will be unnecessary?

In my view, this conclusion does not follow. It is, however, a conclusion that finds at least superficial support in Dworkin's work. Dworkin argues that because the U.S. Bill of Rights "consists of broad and abstract principles of political morality, which together encompass, in exceptionally abstract form, all the dimensions of political morality that in our political culture can ground an individual constitutional right," it is "unintelligible" to speak of going "outside" the written text to articulate constitutional rights.[105] Dworkin is therefore critical of Thomas Grey's argument that when judges interpret abstract constitutional language they give effect to "values not articulated in the constitutional text" and thus articulate an "unwritten constitution."[106] In Dworkin's view, this line of reasoning misunderstands the nature of constitutional interpretation and contributes to the "crude popular mistake" that some judges obey the (written) Constitution and others do not.[107] When judges consider principles of political morality that underlie the written commitment to liberty and due process and conclude that these abstract concepts embrace a series of more specific rights, such as privacy, for example, they are, says Dworkin, interpreting the meaning

[105] Ronald Dworkin, *Freedom's Law: The Moral Reading of the American Constitution* (1996) at 78, 77, and 75.

[106] Thomas Grey, "Do We Have an Unwritten Constitution?" 27 Stan. L. Rev. 703 at 705 (1975).

[107] Dworkin, *Law's Empire*, *supra* note 43 at 359–60 and 450 note 5.

of the written constitution, not going outside the written constitution to an unwritten constitution.

Dworkin's argument is a powerful one. As Dyzenhaus observes, the idea of a separate unwritten constitution in these cases suggests that there is a moment when the abstract ideas expressed in the written constitution, in effect, run out and judges may articulate concrete rights based on other sources – a sure sign of constitutional positivism.[108] If we accept the basic insight of hermeneutics – that the meaning of any text is a product of complex relationships among the text and various interpretive contexts[109] – then reading abstract constitutional language in light of values of political morality is not, in itself, indicative of judicial abandonment of the written constitution for some unwritten constitution; it is, on the contrary, an inevitable aspect of *written* constitutionalism.

But it does not follow from this point that when written constitutional guarantees are expressed in relatively abstract terms that cover the field, so to speak, the idea of unwritten constitutionalism ceases to be relevant. Although the common-law metaphors of written law and unwritten law suggest that, in these instances, legal propositions will be expressed in canonical form and thus interpreted, in the formal sense at least, by judges as written rather than unwritten laws, the common-law conception of unwritten law contains two principles that suggest that ongoing reference to unwritten law may be appropriate, if not necessary, in these cases – though, as we shall see, the extension of these two principles to the constitutional context is not straightforward.

First, as Hale argued, the common law acknowledged the possibility that written law might, over time, become unwritten. How might this idea be applied in the modern constitutional context? It is frequently observed that important written constitutional provisions become "embedded" within a "thick tradition of precedent."[110] David Strauss argues that the result is a form of "common law constitutionalism," in which written constitutional provisions are reduced to notional starting points for inquiries into constitutional meaning that focus almost entirely upon judicial precedents and practices, or the "unwritten aspects of our constitutionalism."[111] This point thus echoes Hale's

[108] Dyzenhaus, "Constitutional Positivism", *supra* note 54 at 155–6.

[109] E.g., Hans-Georg Gadamer, *Truth and Method*, 2nd rev. edn., J. Weinsheimer and D.G. Marshall, trans. (2004).

[110] Laurence H. Tribe, "Taking Text and Structure Seriously: Reflections on Free-Form Method in Constitutional Interpretation," 108 Harv. L. Rev. 1221 at 1236 (1995).

[111] David A. Strauss, "Constitutions, Written and Otherwise," 19 Law & Phil. 451 at 464, 452 (2000). See also David A. Strauss, "Common Law Constitutional Interpretation," 63 U. Chicago L. Rev. 877 at 885, 888 (1996) and David A. Strauss, "Tragedies under the Common Law Constitution," in William N. Eskridge Jr. and Sanford Levinson eds., *Constitutional Stupidities, Constitutional Tragedies* (1998) at 236.

argument that old statutes subjected to sufficient amounts of judicial exposition were incorporated into the common law or *lex non scripta*.

There is, however, a potential difference that complicates the analogy. Hale was referring to statutes rather than constitutions, and so the canonical expressions of statute law that he had in mind may have been more detailed or concrete than the constitutional phrases with which we have become familiar. It is one thing to say that a detailed statutory expression can be transformed into unwritten law through judicial exposition, but perhaps another thing to say that an abstract constitutional expression can be transformed into unwritten law by the same method.

To see why, it may be helpful to consider a rare example of judges acknowledging explicitly such a written-to-unwritten transformation. Over many decades, two rather narrowly worded provisions in Canada's written constitution allocating to federal authorities the power of appointing provincial superior court judges and the duty of paying them came to be seen, through judicial exposition, as protecting the general principle of judicial independence from both provincial and federal legislatures. In 1997, a majority of the Supreme Court of Canada concluded that because the interpretation of these textual provisions had "come a long way from what th[ey] . . . actually say," it was appropriate to acknowledge that the written provisions were not the source of the principle of judicial independence, but were merely specific manifestations of "a deeper set of unwritten understandings" and that "judicial independence is at root an unwritten constitutional principle . . . "[112] The relevant provisions in the written constitution had thus ceased to operate as canonical expressions of law and had begun to operate, through judicial interpretation, as manifestations of more general unwritten principles.

But if this sort of change in judicial attitude toward written text is necessary before it can be said that a written constitutional principle has become unwritten, then it will be difficult to say that such a change is evident in the case law interpreting textual provisions that secure abstract ideals such as liberty or equality. Because these textual expressions are so abstract, it would be inaccurate to say that through judicial interpretation their meaning had moved a "long way from what th[ey] . . . actually say." The layers of judicial reasoning that give concrete meaning to general constitutional formulae betray important similarities with the common-law method, and may accurately be called a form of common law or unwritten constitutionalism; after all, the real meaning of the law will be found in the cases, not the text. But as long as judges respect the

[112] *Provincial Judges Reference*, *supra* note 96 at paras. 83 and 88–9.

written constitutional expressions that trigger lines of judicial interpretation as canonical, then, following Dworkin, we may conclude that it is unnecessarily confusing, even misleading, to say that judges have stopped interpreting the written constitution and are now giving effect to *another* constitution that is *unwritten*.

What Strauss' argument does, however, is challenge the assumption that a firm distinction between written and unwritten constitutional law is always sustainable. The second principle inherent within the common law conception of unwritten law relevant here is the idea that the boundaries between written and unwritten law are sometimes blurred. As St. German and Doderidge argued, the law of reason secured by judicial commitment to equity is "secretly understood in every generall Rule of every positive Law" – or, in other words, the general words of written laws must be interpreted in specific cases in light of the value of equality inherent within the unwritten or common-law rule of reason. Even within the common-law conception of unwritten law, then, the formal distinction between written and unwritten law is hardly absolute. What does this mean for modern constitutional law? The answer, I think, is found in T.R.S. Allan's theory of the rule of law.

Allan's work helps explain how the substantive values of legality or the rule of law – in particular, the value of equality – are manifested through adherence to the formal methods associated with the common-law metaphor of unwritten law. But Allan resists formalism and refuses to draw sharp distinctions between unwritten or common law on the one hand and statutes or written constitutional instruments on the other.[113] Allan insists that when judges in common-law jurisdictions committed to liberal democratic values interpret written constitutional guarantees of equality or liberty or other basic human rights, they engage in an interpretive activity that is, despite superficial differences, fundamentally the same as that which takes place within common-law jurisdictions that have not adopted written constitutional guarantees of this nature.[114] To interpret and apply a written constitutional provision on equality, for example, is, in Allan's view, to expound values that are intrinsic to the liberal conception of the rule of law, values that constitute an unwritten "rule of reason" that defines the very idea of valid "law" within liberal democratic societies, including those without written constitutions.[115] The "true meaning"

[113] T.R.S. Allan, "Constitutional Dialogue and the Justification of Judicial Review," (2003) 23 O.J.L.S. 563; T.R.S. Allan, "Legislative Supremacy and Legislative Intention: Interpretation, Meaning, and Authority," (2004) 63 Cambridge L.J. 685.

[114] Allan, *Constitutional Justice*, *supra* note 55 at 4–5, 153.

[115] *Ibid.* at 2 and 241.

of a constitutional text relating to human rights therefore "reflects our understanding of the requirements of the rule of law, articulated in particular cases by analysis and development of the common law."[116] Far from making the unwritten rule of reason redundant, the adoption of human rights protections in writing at best alters the ways in which common-law values pertaining to the rule of law are interpreted; Allan therefore argues that we should "question the degree to which the existence of a 'written' constitution truly alters the character of legal analysis at the most fundamental level."[117] Written constitutional law, at least in relation to the values intrinsic to the liberal conception of the rule of law, folds into unwritten constitutional law through judicial interpretation that seeks a coherent and justified vision of constitutional order. Formal distinctions between written and unwritten law are, in effect, overshadowed by the substantive connections between them.

Allan's analysis undermines the idea that written and unwritten law are wholly distinct forms of legal discourse. This is consistent with the traditional common law metaphors relating to law and writing: Written laws were to be read against the backdrop of an unwritten law of reason that produces "secret" or implicit exceptions of equity in every positive rule. But, once again, extending this idea to the constitutional context is not easy. In making their point, St. German and Doderidge likely had in mind situations in which detailed rules of positive law framed for general purposes were read in light of abstract values of reason to avoid injustice in individual cases. The same idea, extended to the modern constitutional context, cannot operate in quite the same way. What would it mean to say that an abstract statement of reason expressed in written form, say a constitutional guarantee of equality, must be read in light of an equivalent unwritten principle? The written and unwritten norms appear to be so similar that it may be best simply to follow Allan's lead and concede that the exercise in written and unwritten interpretation collapses in these cases and continued differentiation between them is significant only in a highly formal or technical sense.

Still, keeping this formal distinction in mind may be important for at least some purposes. In a common-law jurisdiction without a written constitutional provision guaranteeing equality, for example, judges will have to infer a general principle of equality through a discourse of reason that treats legal propositions as manifestations of more general principles, rather than as canonical statements of the law, before they can apply that general principle of equality to specific cases. In a common-law jurisdiction having a written constitutional

[116] *Ibid.* at 259.

[117] *Ibid.* at 204 and 243.

guarantee of equality, judges are saved the trouble of the first step in the interpretive process, the general principle having been given to them in a canonical form by the text, thus allowing them to proceed directly to the task of applying it to specific cases. The difference is practically and theoretically important, as the experience with equality in Australia and Canada suggests.

In Australia, there is no written constitutional guarantee of equality. In the 1992 case of *Leeth v. Commonwealth*, however, two Justices, Sir William Deane and John Toohey, examined the common-law doctrine of equality in light of written constitutional provisions establishing the judiciary, as well as "a number of specific [constitutional] provisions which reflect the doctrine of legal equality" (such as the guarantee of freedom of interstate trade and the guarantee of equality of voting rights), and they "discerned in the Constitution as a whole an assumption of the fundamental common law doctrine of legal equality which operates to confine the prima facie scope of the legislative powers which the Constitution vests in the Commonwealth."[118] This is classic unwritten constitutionalism, in both the formal and substantive senses.

In contrast, in Canada, where a written constitutional right to equality came into effect in 1985, judges have been spared the first step in the interpretive process and may proceed directly to, in the words of Justice Frank Iacobucci, "transform" the ideals and aspirations inherent in the "abstract" statement of equality found in the written text "into practice in a manner which is meaningful to Canadians..."[119] In formal terms, this is the interpretation of a canonical expression of constitutional law – it is written law. According to Allan's approach, however, Canadian judges will engage in an interpretive process that is substantively the same as that of Justices Deane and Toohey.

Politically, the difference is profound. In Canada, the judicial review of legislation against the constitutional standard of equality is universally accepted (though individual rulings are, of course, controversial). In Australia, however, Justices Deane and Toohey's attempt to do the same was described as "one of the most radical judgments – both in reasoning and result – seen to date in Australian constitutional jurisprudence,"[120] and it was seemingly rejected by other judges.[121]

Theoretical confusion helped produce this backlash. The claims against the reasoning used by Justices Deane and Toohey reasoning are familiar – they

[118] *Leeth v. Commonwealth of Australia* (1992), 174 C.L.R. 455 at 487 and 488 (HC).

[119] *Law v. Canada* (Minister of Employment and Immigration), [1999] 1 S.C.R. 497 at para. 2.

[120] Jeremy Kirk, "Constitutional Implications (II): Doctrines of Equality and Democracy," (2001) 25 Melbourne U.L.R. 24 at 24.

[121] *Kruger v. Commonwealth* (1997), 190 C.L.R. 1 (HC) [*Kruger*].

are the structuralist and naturalist claims we have already considered. Thus, Goldsworthy claims that the specific textual provisions that they relied upon to found a right to equality were "too flimsy to merit discussion"[122] – a valid point, but only if we assume that they were treating the constitution as a canonical source of law and trying to draw structural implications from it as such. Goldsworthy has also described the sort of reasoning they used as "unfettered practical reasoning that is ultimately governed by moral norms," a variation of the naturalist argument that fails to take seriously the sense in which interpretation may expound "secondary" reason, or a reason grounded in concrete legal propositions rather than just abstract or "primary" reason.[123]

The argument advanced by Justices Deane and Toohey, properly interpreted, was not a sorry attempt at textual interpretation or mere unstructured moral reasoning. It was a discourse of reason anchored in a sense of what law is, and what legality requires, within a very particular constitutional tradition, one committed to a liberal conception of the rule of law. When considered as an example of unwritten constitutionalism, as understood in light of the common-law conception of unwritten law, the naturalist and structuralist criticisms of their argument lose their force, for all of the reasons stated earlier in this chapter. But to see this point, it is, I think, necessary to appreciate the formal as well as the substantive dimensions of unwritten constitutionalism. Having a sense of unwritten legal reasoning in its formal dimension helps us to identify reasons why this form of reasoning may be legitimate, and why arguments against it may be misplaced, even if we accept, as we should, Allan's challenge to the value of emphasising formal distinctions between written and unwritten constitutional law on substantive grounds.

To return to the question of the unwritten constitution's scope, then, we may draw the following conclusions. In common-law jurisdictions with no written constitution or with a written constitution that fails to cover matters in a comprehensive manner, formal unwritten constitutionalism is inevitable. In fact, as Dyzenhaus argues, no common-law jurisdiction has managed the Benthamite aspiration of codifying in written form *all* of constitutional law. However, some written constitutions purport to cover the important rights of equality and due process that are intrinsic to a liberal conception of the rule of law. When a constitution is particularly comprehensive and abstract in this respect, its interpretation will be, in form, the sort of reasoning that, according to the common-law metaphors on law and writing, is symbolized by *written*

[122] Jeffrey Goldsworthy, "Implications in Language, Law and the Constitution," in Geoffrey Lindell ed., *Future Directions in Australian Constitutional Law* (1994) at 174.

[123] Jeffrey Goldsworthy, "Homogenising Constitutions," (2003) 23 O.J.L.S. 483 at 494.

law. In substance, however, this constitution can no more break loose from the *unwritten* constitution of legality that it exemplifies than an island can separate from the seabed that lies beneath the waters that surround it.

UNWRITTEN LAW, CONSTITUTIONAL HUMILITY, AND THE EQUALITY OF REASON

When judges invoke the unwritten constitution behind a written constitution they are not flying into a "cloudland" uncharted by law; nor are they simply interpreting the written constitution in a creative way. In these cases, judges engage in a form of interpretive analysis that replicates at the constitutional level the sort of discourse of reason represented by the metaphor "unwritten law" within the common-law tradition. Of course this conclusion does not, on its own, establish the rightness of unwritten constitutionalism. Just because Hale said long ago that judges considered ancient statutes as sources of unwritten law does not mean that judges today should treat the constitutional texts of their countries in the same way. When they do, it is appropriate to say that they articulate unwritten constitutional law. But should they do it? I have dismissed the naturalist and structuralist claims against the idea of unwritten constitutionalism as mischaracterizations of what the idea really is. But are there arguments to be made against unwritten constitutionalism, properly understood?

There are. It may be said that when judges treat the written constitution that a sovereign people has (to use Jay's words) "deliberately formed, maturely considered, and solemnly adopted"[124] as evidence of supreme law, rather than as a single canonical statement of supreme law, they may initiate developments in the law that move, even if incrementally, away from the choices adopted by the people who made the constitution. Written constitutions are made through "reflection and choice" rather than "accident and force," wrote Hamilton,[125] and those choices are to be honoured. In rejecting Justices Deane and Toohey's argument for equality in Australia, Sir Daryl Dawson J. stated: "Guarantees of equality before the law and due process were specifically rejected [by the drafters of the Constitution], not because they were already implicit and therefore unnecessary, but because they were not wanted."[126] If the people do not want a constitution founded upon equality, who are judges to stop them?

The obvious response to this argument is, of course, to point to the many ways in which written constitutions in the United States, Canada, and Australia were, in fact, shaped by "accident and force" rather than "reflection and choice,"

[124] *Henfield's Case, supra* note 7 at 58.
[125] "Federalist No. 1," *supra* note 5 at 1.
[126] *Kruger, supra* note 121 at 65.

or where the "choice" made by one set of people amounted to "force" against another set of people. In these areas of constitutional law at least, objections to judicial reliance upon implicit principles of justice behind the text seem to lose their edge. It is, perhaps, not by chance that the most explicit judicial support for unwritten constitutional principles from the three jurisdictions is the Supreme Court of Canada's decision in the *Quebec Secession Reference*,[127] a decision made against the background of claims by Quebec nationalists that the "choice" made to adopt the *Constitution Act 1982* over Quebec's objections deprived the Canadian Constitution of its legitimacy. In these circumstances, the Court's reliance upon unwritten constitutional principles gave its decision a degree of credibility in terms of political morality that simple reliance upon constitutional text would have lacked.

But this response is too narrowly focused. As seen, the rationale given by the Court in that case was not the need to address situations in which the (moral) legitimacy of written provisions is questioned. The primary rationale given for unwritten constitutional principles was the value of having a comprehensive and coherent constitutional order. Indeed, this rationale is, roughly speaking, the "equality of reason" that Doderidge used to defend the common-law conception of unwritten law. The question, then, is whether equality of reason represents an unwritten value of constitutionalism with sufficient weight to qualify, or in some sense inform, our understanding of the value that is attached in normative constitutional theory to the concept of *written* constitutionalism.

When considering this question, it may be helpful to reflect upon the value of written constitutions in general (aside from the obvious fact that they sometimes represent expressions of democratic will). The statements of Hamilton and Jay that celebrate written constitutions suggest that one important reason for the celebration is the one captured by Hart's notion of "rules of change": The act of writing law, including constitutional law, is one way, perhaps the best way, that people can deliberately make law something that it was not before. In other words, the very idea of *made-law*, to use Fuller's expression, may be said to have some inherent merit as a distinct human value.[128]

If the idea of made-law is a human value, however, it is a paradoxical one. Its virtue could not lie simply in the fact that it is something that can be made – after all, humans are good at making all sorts of things, not all of which are valuable or virtuous. The inherent virtue of made-law, then, must lie in the fact that the thing made is *law*. Conversely, made-law has no inherent virtue (indeed no existence) if the law-maker, in an effort to make law, fails and makes

[127] *Supra* note 11.

[128] Fuller, *The Anatomy of the Law*, *supra* note 9 at 63–99.

something else. In other words, the ideal of law, which made-law must at least approximate if it is to have any value as made-law, is not something over which the law-maker can have complete control; otherwise we would value made-law simply because it is something made rather than because what is made is *law*. The same can be said of constitutional law: There may be an inherent value in made-constitutions, as Hamilton and Jay argue, but only because what is made is a *constitution* as opposed to something else.

In developing these ideas, I am, of course, following Fuller's general lead. Fuller argued that made-law is impossible without the context provided by what he called implicit law.[129] In terms of constitutional law, Fuller argued that "a written constitution cannot dispense with the need for a resort to implicit or unwritten principles of legal decency..."[130] It was Fuller's view that the principles of legal decency – or the values of legality or the rule of law – are essential to the very existence of made-law as law, but, at the same time, they are impossible for the maker of constitutional law to capture fully in written form.

Something like this idea seems to have informed the arguments found in the old statements by Justices Chase and Miller, and, we might say, the arguments of theorists like Allan today – namely, that the very conception of law that is defined by the values and identity of the political community defines what counts as the sort of law that can be made within that community. One of the best sources of evidence on this point, of course, is the written constitution to which the community is committed. But the attempt to capture the ideal of legality in written form can never be seen as complete or exhaustive. The political value of constitutionalism should be seen to be based upon confidence in the ability of people to construct normative order through making laws and writing constitutions, but also upon a sense of humility that arises from the knowledge that no amount of law-making or constitution writing will produce all of the law the people need. If the value of made-law is dependent upon implicit-law, it must also be dependent upon an idea of *constitutional humility* that reveals the necessary connections between these types of law.[131]

For a liberal community, at least, this sense of constitutional humility, coupled with the normative requirement of equality, translates into an unwritten constitutional value that we can call the "equality of reason." The creative power of lawmakers and constitution writers will take the community a long way toward the ends of constitutional justice. But, as Doderidge observed,

[129] *Ibid.* at 64–5. [130] *Ibid.* at 94.

[131] See generally John D. Whyte, "Nations, Minorities and Authority," (1991) 40 U.N.B.L.J. 45 at 45–7.

"positive law" can never fully accommodate individual difference, and so the final determination of what the law is must wait until judicial assessment of how the general and the particular are reconciled within a "unity" of reason. This discourse of reason must be taken to the highest levels of law – to the supreme or constitutional laws of a community – if the sense of humility about made-law and the sense of commitment to liberal equality are both sincere. This is what the metaphor of unwritten constitutionalism represents.

11 Unwritten Constitutional Principles

Jeffrey Goldsworthy

INTRODUCTION

All of the constitutions I am familiar with have given rise to claims that they include or presuppose "unwritten" or "implied" principles.[1] These principles can be relatively specific, such as the implied freedom of political communication, first "discovered" by the High Court of Australia in 1992. Or they can be quite abstract, such as "the rule of law," which is regarded almost everywhere as a constitutional principle of some kind. They may concern individual rights or freedoms, governmental powers or immunities, or institutional safeguards such as the separation of judicial power. But all, in some way, qualify or override the authority of legislatures.

It is generally accepted that, whereas moral norms apply to us of their own force, whether or not we have adopted or subscribed to them, legal norms owe their existence to the practices of a particular time and place, whether by deliberate enactment or by the evolution of custom.[2] Even unwritten or implied constitutional principles can plausibly be thought to exist only if the legal system in question has, in some way, adopted or committed itself to them. But purported discoveries of such principles are often novel, in that the principles had previously gone unnoticed. For example, the implied freedom of political communication, "discovered" by the Australian High Court in 1992,

[1] There is much discussion in the American literature of "unenumerated" principles. But a written constitutional provision (such as, arguably, the Ninth Amendment of the U.S. Constitution) can refer to a class of principles without enumerating the members of the class. Although unenumerated, they are denoted by the written provision.

[2] I take this to be true even of Ronald Dworkin, who holds that legal norms are identified through the interpretation of such practices. Moral relativists might deny that there is any difference between legal and moral norms in this respect.

had not been noticed by lawyers and judges for the previous ninety years, except for one notoriously "activist" judge in the 1980s.[3]

This raises the question: How can a legal system incorporate unwritten principles – how can it have adopted or committed itself to them – without its most learned lawyers, judges, and scholars knowing about them? Some may be tempted to dismiss the very idea as make-believe, used to camouflage judicial inventiveness. But in principle, the idea can make good sense. We can distinguish between three different kinds of claims that have recently been made in Anglo-American legal systems on behalf of unwritten principles.

Conceptual Claims

Philosophical analysis can reveal that our concepts have contents that we do not fully or clearly grasp. By clarifying their contents, it can help us resolve uncertainties or disagreements about them. Working through our intuitive responses to actual or hypothetical examples and counter-examples, we may bring to the surface previously unconscious aspects of the mechanisms that have guided our previous applications of a concept. This might be described as an "interpretive" process that seeks to clarify the rationale underlying those applications.[4] For example, philosophers have long debated the content of the concept "knowledge": Does it mean "justified true belief," or something even more subtle? In doing so, they have concocted many ingenious hypothetical examples to test our intuitive applications of the concept. Natural lawyers attempt to use much the same strategy: By putting before us real or imaginary examples of wicked laws, they hope to persuade us that our concept of law, or related concepts such as legal authority or legal obligation, are infused with a moral content that legal positivists have struggled to suppress. If the natural lawyers are right, then our most basic legal concepts may incorporate unwritten moral norms that have not received due notice or acknowledgement. A similar strategy is used by those who seek to show that our concept of law embodies elements of the political ideal known as "the rule of law."

Common Law Claims

An increasingly popular claim is that the common law is the foundation of Anglo-American legal systems, and the ultimate source of all governmental

[3] I refer to Murphy J., whose views on this score were treated with disdain by his brethren.

[4] Ronald Dworkin describes what he calls "interpretive" concepts in something like this way; see his *Justice in Robes* (2006) at 10–12 and 223–6. But it could be argued that all concepts are "interpretive."

authority exercised within them, including the authority of our parliaments and, indeed, of our Constitutions. If this is so, and if Ronald Dworkin is right to insist that the common law rests on fundamental, unwritten principles that must sometimes be articulated through a process of "interpretation" involving moral judgment, then again, it must, in principle, be possible for us to discover unwritten constitutional principles that were previously obscure or unacknowledged. An alternative strategy is to claim that the interpretation of statutes, and constitutions, is governed by the common law, and therefore that their content is governed partly by unwritten principles. Theories of these kinds have attracted the label "common law constitutionalism."

Communicative Implication Claims

If a constitution, like other written laws, is an attempt to communicate legal norms, then its meaning is presumably affected by general principles of linguistic communication. One such principle is that the content of a communication is rarely, if ever, fully expressed by the words used to convey it. For example, when I order a hamburger, I do not bother to specify that it should not be poisonous or inedible. The possibility of being served such a hamburger would probably not even occur to me. Yet if I were served with one, I could plausibly claim that my order implicitly excluded it – that it was inconsistent with what I obviously meant when I placed my order. Meanings, along with intentions and other mental states, depend partly on an extensive network of background assumptions that are usually taken for granted. They may rise to the surface of consciousness only if they are unexpectedly contradicted or challenged.

Sometimes two, or even all, of these claims are combined. The Chief Justice of the Supreme Court of Canada, Beverley McLachlin, recently defended unwritten constitutional principles, seemingly (the argument is too thin and sketchy to be sure) on all three grounds: (a) "the nature of law itself"[5] (she labels herself a "modern natural law proponent"[6]); (b) the common law tradition of unwritten fundamental principles, identified by past usage;[7] and (c) the limited foresight of lawmakers and the consequent "incompleteness" of written laws.[8] T.R.S. Allan's work combines claims about the concept of the rule of law, which he takes to be intrinsic to the concept of law in modern western legal

[5] Chief Justice Beverley McLachlin, "Unwritten Constitutional Principles: What is Going On?" Remarks given at the 2005 Lord Cooke Lecture, Wellington, New Zealand, Dec. 1, 2005, online: The Supreme Court of Canada <http://www.scc-csc.gc.ca/aboutcourt/judges/speeches/Unwritten Principles_e_asp>.

[6] *Ibid.* at 11.

[7] *Ibid.* at 18.

[8] *Ibid.* at 16.

systems, with claims amounting to a version of common law constitutionalism. He seems to regard these claims as one and the same, because a commitment to the rule of law is fundamental to the common law. Mark Walters' contribution to this volume is similar in these respects, as is the work of David Dyzenhaus, although Dyzenhaus is more hesitant about claiming that the validity of statutes (as distinct from their interpretation) depends on their complying with the unwritten common law principles that constitute the rule of law.[9]

I will discuss all three kinds of claims on behalf of unwritten principles.

CONCEPTUAL CLAIMS

I am the last person to dismiss, out of hand, claims that our concept of "valid law" is best analyzed as requiring compliance with unwritten principles of justice, because I myself once published a lengthy argument to that effect.[10] My argument was based on H.L.A. Hart's concession that internal legal statements, which express the internal point of view, have a normative component that prevents them being reduced to statements of fact and, in particular, to statements concerning the elements of the Austinian theory – namely, commands backed by threats and habits of obedience. This is because internal legal statements use normative terms common to law and morality ("authority," "right," "obligation," *etc.*) to express acceptance that legal requirements are binding, to criticize others for failing to comply with them, and to justify the imposition upon them of legal sanctions for noncompliance.[11] I argued, against Hart, that the normative content of internal legal statements was best analysed in terms of moral commitment. Hart described his position as noncognitivist: as an interpretation of this normative content in terms of illocutionary or expressive force. But he offered no convincing reasons to distinguish the noncognitive attitudes and demands he believed to be expressed in internal legal statements from those expressed in moral statements, which might also be best understood in noncognitivist terms. If internal legal statements purport to publicly justify decisions imposing legal norms that have drastic effects on other people's lives, then it seems difficult to resist the conclusion that they express full-blooded moral commitment. "Purely legal" statements, with no moral content

[9] M. Walters, "Written Constitutions and Unwritten Constitutionalism," in this volume; D. Dyzenhaus, "The Juristic Force of Injustice," in M. Moran and D. Dyzenhaus, *Calling Power to Account: Law, Reparations and the Chinese Canadian Head Tax* (2005) [Dyzenhaus, *Calling Power to Account*].

[10] J. Goldsworthy, "The Self-Destruction of Legal Positivism," (1990) 10 O.J.L.S. 449 [Goldsworthy, "The Self-Destruction of Legal Positivism"].

[11] *Ibid.* at 454.

whatsoever, could not possibly justify, or reasonably be taken to justify, such decisions. My chain of reasoning then led from this premise, via Joseph Raz's analysis of the concept of validity, to the conclusion that the twin concepts of authority and validity in internal legal thought must also have an irreducible moral content, such that neither concept could be correctly applied to an egregiously unjust statute.

I still believe that the attitudes that characterise the internal point of view, as described by Hart, are moral attitudes. But I no longer believe that their expression forms part of the semantic content of terms, such as validity, that appear in internal legal statements. I did not pay sufficient attention to a possibility that I noted in a footnote, namely:

> There is doubt as to whether or not Hart believes that the non-cognitivist component is part of the semantic meaning of internal legal statements, or merely a normal implication of their being uttered by someone adopting the internal point of view. If the latter then, as G.P. Baker has pointed out, Hart's analysis of the meaning of those statements is reductionist, after all: see his 'Defeasibility and Meaning', in P.M.S. Hacker and J. Raz, (eds.), *Law, Morality and Society* (1977), 26, 41–2.[12]

Subsequently, Richard Holton – in an unjustly neglected analysis of the internal point of view – took up Baker's point.[13] Holton agreed with me that the internal point of view must be understood as expressing moral commitment. But he argued that this moral commitment is expressed by pragmatic implicature, rather than as part of semantic content. He explained how the groundbreaking work of H.P. Grice had shown that the phenomenon of implication is pervasive in our linguistic practices. Grice distinguished between what we *say* when we make some utterance, and what our saying so, in the circumstances, *implicates*:

> If I make a promise, what I do only makes sense against a background practice of promise making, and you can infer that I believe that there is such a practice and perhaps that I endorse it. But I have not strictly *said* so. Similarly, if the existence of a system of laws strictly requires that all the judges believe they are morally binding, then when a judge makes a judgment, we can infer that the judge thinks it is morally binding. But she has not strictly *said* that it is.[14]

[12] *Ibid.* at 454, n. 35.

[13] R. Holton, "Positivism and the Internal Point of View," (1998) 17 Law & Phil. 597 [Holton, "Positivism and Internal Point"].

[14] *Ibid.* at 611.

Grice's theory of implicature has proved so fruitful that it is now being deployed in the analysis of moral statements themselves, to clarify the relationship between their noncognitive (expressive or affective) components and their putatively cognitive (objective) elements.[15] In legal philosophy, it promises to resolve a number of problems that legal positivists have grappled with and, in particular, how to reconcile the normative (and apparently moral) component of internal legal statements with their basis in social fact. Both Hart and Raz, in different ways, struggled in this regard. Holton has confirmed my own diagnosis that Raz's legal positivism is in danger of self-destruction, due to a contradiction between his "sources thesis," which holds that all law is ultimately based on social facts, and his "semantic thesis," which holds that internal legal statements express commitment to the moral authority of law. Gricean analysis also offers a more plausible explanation of the relationship between internal and external legal statements, and of how someone can switch from one mode of speech to the other. If the two modes share the same semantic content – which is purely factual – and differ only in that the former conveys moral commitment by implicature, then it is easy to see how someone could cancel the implicature, and thereby shift smoothly from speaking "internally" to speaking "externally." For example, a judge who, for the first time, deemed a law to be so immoral as to lack any moral authority, could say so quite plainly, without contradicting any of the numerous statements he made previously that implicated his acceptance of the moral authority of the legal system he routinely helped enforce.

Of course, it may turn out that Gricean analysis fails to rescue Razian legal positivism from self-destruction. But it demands to be taken very seriously. It is no longer acceptable simply to assume that the "normativity" of internal legal statements forms part of their semantic content, and then quickly move to the conclusion that the validity (and therefore the existence) of law must – at least from the internal point of view – be governed partly by moral criteria.

Whether we should accept a Gricean analysis of internal legal discourse partly depends, as Holton pointed out, on the other parts of our theory of law.[16] If, in other respects, we have strong reasons to favour a positivist theory, then that, in itself, counts in favour of the Gricean analysis. I would argue that we do have strong reasons to do so. Here are some of them.

The perennial debate between positivists and natural lawyers is often conducted on a very abstract level, which overlooks the fact that some legal systems

[15] Stephen Barker, *Renewing Meaning: A speech-act theoretic analysis* (2004).
[16] Holton, *supra* note 13 at 613.

include fundamental constitutional doctrines, such as that of parliamentary sovereignty, which *positively assert* that even an extremely unjust law would be legally valid. Any analysis of the conceptual framework of legal thought in these systems should take this into account. This surely makes it more difficult to argue that normative legal concepts such as validity and authority should be analysed in natural law terms, because that would imply that experienced lawyers and judges have, perhaps for centuries, systematically misunderstood the nature and contents of their own legal concepts. Allan has argued that the doctrine of parliamentary sovereignty is "seriously confused," and I myself, in the article previously mentioned, maintained that the doctrine was a "misinterpretation" of the courts' traditional stance of deference to their parliaments.[17] But later, in writing a book devoted to the historical development and philosophical foundations of the doctrine, I became convinced that a perfectly sensible defence of it could be provided – indeed, that it could be found in the historical sources. The existence of that defence removes any perceived need to attribute conceptual confusion to orthodox British constitutional thought.

Political thinkers in earlier centuries were not fools: They had a hard-headed grasp of some practical imperatives of government, learned from bitter experience of insurrection and civil war, which they took to justify the doctrine. For example, in the eighteenth century, it was universally accepted that Parliament's authority was subject to limits, which could be enforced by popular resistance or, in the last resort, even revolution. But these limits, and that method of enforcing them, were deliberately classified as moral rather than as legal. It was considered undesirable for the law itself to acknowledge these limits to its own authority, or the right to enforce them through popular resistance, because that might encourage dissidents to invoke them too promiscuously. Moreover, given that the limits were abstract and vague, they might also be construed too broadly, promoting the incitement of unjustified resistance to legal authority, and the unravelling of social order. It was a question of balancing competing dangers, and for a variety of reasons, the danger of the law thereby corrupting or annulling its own authority was widely regarded as more to be feared than the danger of acquiescence in parliamentary tyranny.[18]

[17] T.R.S. Allan, *Constitutional Justice: A Liberal Theory of the Rule of Law* (2001) at 201 [Allan, *Constitutional Justice*]; Goldsworthy, "The Self-Destruction of Legal Positivism," *supra* note 10 at 482–3.

[18] Goldsworthy, *The Sovereignty of Parliament, History and Philosophy* (1999) at 178–8 [Goldsworthy, *The Sovereignty of Parliament*].

Although every individual must ultimately decide whether or not they ought morally to obey unjust laws, the obliteration of any distinction between moral and legal validity would tend to obscure the likely costs and benefits of such decisions. As Allan acknowledges, there are powerful reasons, concerning the maintenance of legal authority, why individuals often ought morally to obey laws they regard as morally wrong.[19] These reasons are likely to be obscured if a law that is deemed morally wrong is, for that reason, also deemed legally invalid. This is because disobeying legally invalid legislation does not directly challenge legal authority, and therefore does not obviously threaten its maintenance. The threat is more plainly apparent if the legislation in question is regarded as legally valid. To put this another way: Although it is clear that there can be good reasons for obeying legislation that is immoral but legally valid, it is not so clear that there can be good reasons for obeying legislation that is both immoral and legally invalid.

Today, we often think of judicial invalidation, rather than popular disobedience, as the principal remedy for unjust or oppressive laws. But structurally, the arguments for and against according legal recognition to vague, unwritten limits to legislative authority remain largely unchanged. It is still a question of balancing competing dangers. Allan and I agree that judges should disobey truly wicked legislation.[20] I suspect that we also agree that, in a modern, healthy democracy, outright disobedience is an extraordinary response – a remedy of last resort – that should be reserved for quite exceptional circumstances. We agree, in other words, that the judges' normal stance should be one of obedience, albeit tempered by strict interpretation of legislation impinging on common law rights.[21] But I conceive of judicial disobedience in exceptional circumstances as a moral obligation, which overrides the moral reasons that normally support compliance with their legal obligation, whereas Allan conceives of it as both a moral and legal obligation. I regard the distinction between legal and moral authority as a useful conceptual device that helps prevent the extraordinary response of disobedience being resorted to excessively, thereby eroding the normal judicial stance of obedience, and undermining democracy. Allan, on the other hand, is motivated by the opposite concern – that adherence to the distinction might deter judges from departing from their normal stance of obedience when necessary, leading to craven judicial acquiescence

[19] Allan, *Constitutional Justice*, *supra* note 17 at 76 and 221. The next few paragraphs are taken from my "Homogenizing Constitutions," (2003) 23 O.J.L.S. 483 [Goldsworthy, "Homogenizing Constitutions"].

[20] Goldsworthy, *The Sovereignty of Parliament*, *supra* note 18 at 261–70.

[21] See further discussion of this point at 299–304.

in egregious injustice. That is also a legitimate concern, but not necessarily the paramount one:

> The price that must be paid for giving judges authority to invalidate a few laws that are clearly unjust or undemocratic is that they must also be given authority to overrule the democratic process in a much larger number of cases where the requirements of justice or democracy are debatable. The danger of excessive judicial interference with democratic decision-making might be worse than that of parliamentary tyranny, given the relative probabilities of their actually occurring.[22]

This argument shows that, at the very least, Allan is wrong to claim that "it serve[s] no useful purpose, relevant to any question of practical governance, to attribute legal validity to a measure that wholly lack[s] moral legitimacy and ought, so far as possible, to be resolutely resisted."[23] The eighteenth century argument, which in an adapted form I have pressed into service, was, in effect, that "hard cases make bad laws" – or rather, that "hard cases make bad concepts of law." It is unwise to claim on behalf of the judiciary an authority that will undermine democratic decision-making in many cases that are certain to arise, in order to provide a remedy for extreme situations that are very unlikely to arise, and which would probably be useless if they did. (Why would a wicked government meekly submit to judicial admonishment?)

Note that even if the balance of competing dangers did favour legal recognition of unwritten principles of justice, that would not undermine my main point. We are not working with a blank slate, on which we can design from scratch a new conceptual framework for our legal practices. The question is how the balance was, in fact, struck by the statesmen, judges, and political theorists whose thinking, over many centuries, forged the conceptual framework that we have inherited. And the evidence overwhelmingly points to a framework that, in the case of statute law, is predominantly positivist in character, and accommodates the doctrine of parliamentary sovereignty. Those who disapprove of that doctrine are free to advocate constitutional reform to repudiate it.

Another conceptual claim is that our concept of law incorporates elements of the political ideal known as the rule of law. Allan, who has often advanced this claim, argues in his contribution to this volume that "there are moral constraints on the scope of law-making power that derive from our concept

[22] Goldsworthy, *The Sovereignty of Parliament*, *supra* note 18 at 269.

[23] Allan, *Constitutional Justice*, *supra* note 17 at 72.

of law, which is elucidated by reflection on the idea of the rule of law."[24] It is more surprising to find Jeremy Waldron appearing to agree:

> [W]e should not describe a system of governance as a system of law unless it does the sort of thing that the Rule of Law celebrates – for example, unless it... [uses] clear, general, stable norms, promulgated in advance so that they can be used as a basis on which individuals and firms can figure out what they owe to one another and to the state... On this account, directives emanating from a system that lacks that character cannot properly be described as laws, nor can their content properly be presented in statements of the form "It is the law that..." *The same is true of directives which emanate from a system that has that character for the most part, but which in themselves are not general, prospective etc.* No doubt the word "law" will continue to be used (wrongly but conveniently) in regard to such propositions. But... these degenerate uses... take advantage (as things stand) of the analytic talents of casual positivists to confer a spurious aura of juridical respectability on whatever directives happen to emanate from the centers of power.[25]

The italicized sentence suggests that putative laws cannot be regarded as genuine (valid) laws if they do not satisfy the core elements of the rule of law, such as that laws must be general in scope rather than aimed at particular persons, and prospective rather than retrospective. But, at least in Britain and the Commonwealth, the concept of law evolved in a constitutional tradition dominated by the doctrine of parliamentary sovereignty.[26] The British Parliament frequently exercised its unlimited legislative authority to enact "private statutes" that applied only to particular, named persons, and also statutes that operated retrospectively. Their validity – and status as genuine laws – was never seriously challenged. Given that our concept of law was shaped in the context of these largely unquestioned practices, over many centuries, it is unlikely that it could be incompatible with them.

"Private", and retrospective, statutes have not only been frequently enacted, but have often been legitimate. Even today, legislation that changes the legal rights or duties of particular legal persons is often justified, for example, to

[24] See T.R.S. Allan, "Constitutional Justice and the Concept of Law," in this volume at 233. For an earlier engagement with Allan's arguments, see my "Homogenizing Constitutions," *supra* note 19.

[25] J. Waldron, "The Concept and the Rule of Law" at 12–13, online: NYU School of Law <http://www.law.nyu.edu/clppt/program2006/readings/Concept%20and%20Rule%20of%20Law%20WALDRON.pdf>[internal footnotes omitted, emphasis added].

[26] J. Goldsworthy, *The Sovereignty of Parliament*, *supra* note 18, and J. Goldsworthy, "Legislative Sovereignty and the Rule of Law," in T. Campbell, K.D. Ewing, and A. Tomkins eds., *Sceptical Essays on Human Rights* (2001) 61, from which the following two paragraphs are adapted.

enable major public works or unique enterprises such as the staging of an Olympic Games, to proceed expeditiously, by conferring special legal powers or rights on their organizers. Sometimes, Acts of Indemnity or Amnesty, which relieve individuals or groups of liability for breaches of the law, are justified. Usually, such breaches have been inadvertent. But, as A.V. Dicey pointed out, in extraordinary situations of internal disorder or war, the executive government might have to break the law deliberately "for the sake of legality itself" – to uphold the rule of law – and then seek an Act of Indemnity.[27]

The requirement of prospectivity has never been regarded as absolute. Legislation that changes the law retrospectively can often be justified, sometimes by the rule of law itself. In rare cases, even retrospective changes to criminal laws can be justified. The strongest argument against retrospectivity is that it is unfair to upset expectations reasonably based on the state of the law at a particular time. But if expectations are based on mistaken, yet reasonable, beliefs about the state of the law, retrospective legislation may be justified to prevent them from being upset. In addition, some expectations, such as an expectation of legal immunity for grossly immoral conduct, are unworthy of respect, and the threat of subsequent retrospective legislation might help deter such conduct.[28] In other words, it might help to deter the exercise of arbitrary power. That is why "[t]he trial of the German leaders at Nuremberg by a law made *ex parte*, *ex post facto*, and *ad hoc* has been hailed as a vindication of the rule of law."[29] Recent legislation retrospectively made it a criminal offence under Australian law for persons in Europe during the Second World War, who may have had no connection with Australia at the time, to have committed "war crimes."[30] The legislation was justified, notwithstanding its retrospective operation. Moreover, even legitimate expectations can be outweighed by considerations of justice. It has been persuasively argued that the British Parliament in 1965 was entirely justified, by considerations of justice and equality, in enacting legislation that not only retrospectively abolished a legal right to compensation, but reversed a recent judicial decision awarding compensation to a particular party.[31] For

[27] A.V. Dicey, *Introduction to the Study of the Law of the Constitution*, 10th edn., (1959) at 411–13.

[28] For an excellent and thorough discussion of all these themes, see A. Palmer and C. Sampford, "Retrospective Legislation in Australia: Looking Back at the 1980s," (1994) 22 Federal Law Rev. 217 [Palmer and Sampford, "Retrospective Legislation"].

[29] F. Wormuth, "Aristotle on Law," in M.R. Konvitz and A.E. Murphy eds., *Essays in Political Theory Presented to George H. Sabine* (1948) 45 at 45.

[30] See *Polyukhovich v. Commonwealth*, (1991) 172 C.L.R 501.

[31] A.L. Goodhart, "The Burmah Oil Case and the War Damage Act 1965," (1966) 82 L.Q.R. 97, discussing the *War Damage Act* 1965 (U.K.), which retrospectively deprived the Burmah Oil Company of a right to compensation that had been upheld by the House of Lords in *Burmah Oil Co Ltd v. Lord Advocate*, [1965] A.C. 75.

similar reasons, judicial decisions altering the common law may justifiably have retrospective effects, even in criminal cases, which can no longer be concealed by resort to the old "fairy tale" that judges only declare what the law has always been, and do not really change it. A recent example involved the House of Lords in effect abolishing the common law immunity of a husband against being convicted for the rape of his wife, in the course of a case involving a husband charged with that offence.[32] German courts dealing with the prosecution of former East German border guards for shooting people attempting to enter West Berlin have felt justified in adopting novel interpretations of relevant East German laws that, in effect, amended them retrospectively.[33] The following conclusion to a thorough examination of retrospective legislation in Australia would, no doubt, be true of most countries:

> Retrospective law-making is neither particularly rare nor necessarily evil. It plays a more significant part in Australian legislation than most would imagine. Much of it can be justified. Some of it is very contentious and the justification should be subject to intensive and, hopefully, rigorous debate . . . However, the fact that the proposed statute is 'retrospective' should merely be the starting-point of that debate, not its conclusion.[34]

In the course of arguing that political disagreements, including disagreements about rights, should be resolved democratically rather than by unelected judges, Waldron once replied to the objection that, at the very least, the participatory rights that define democracy itself should be given constitutional protection and made judicially enforceable. He replied that the content of these abstract participatory rights, and their application in specific circumstances, are as much a subject of reasonable disagreements as the content and application of any other right, and these disagreements should be settled by "the people and their representatives, [because] it is an insult to say that the issues are too important or perhaps too formalistic for them (rather than the judges) to decide."[35] But the same is equally true of the abstract requirements of the rule of law. Like everything else in politics, their application in specific, complex circumstances, involving competing rights and interests, gives rise to reasonable disagreements concerning questions of priority and of degree – of more or less – that can be settled only by value judgments. It is uncharacteristic

[32] *R v. R*, [1992] A.C. 599.

[33] See J. Rivers, "The Interpretation and Invalidity of Unjust Laws," in D. Dyzenhaus ed., *Recrafting the Rule of Law: The Limits of Legal Order* (1999) 40.

[34] Palmer and Sampford, "Retrospective Legislation," *supra* note 28 at 277. For more detailed discussion, see C. Sampford, *Retrospectivity and the Rule of Law* (2006), especially at 65–8 on the concept of "law."

[35] J. Waldron, "A Right-Based Critique of Constitutional Rights," (1993) 13 O.J.L.S. 18 at 39.

of Waldron now to suggest that value judgments made by legislatures should be overridden by conceptual judgments made by judges.

COMMON LAW CLAIMS

The term "common law constitutionalism" is now widely used to denote a variety of theories that attribute some kind of constitutional status to the common law.[36] Strong common law constitutionalism holds that the common law is the ultimate source of the authority of statute law, and perhaps of written constitutions as well, and that therefore, either the common law already limits legislative authority, or it could be developed by the judiciary to do so. Weak common law constitutionalism holds that, although the common law does not limit the validity of statutes, it does control their interpretation, and also their "gravitational force."

Strong Common Law Constitutionalism

It is often claimed that Britain's "unwritten" constitution consists of common law principles, which are the source of all governmental authority, including Parliament's authority to enact statutes. As Allan puts it, "the common law is prior to legislative supremacy, which it defines and regulates."[37] Sometimes, this claim is extended to the authority of written constitutions, which is also held to derive from the common law. For example, it is argued that if a constitution was originally enacted as a statute by the British Parliament, its authority depended on Parliament's, and therefore derived indirectly from the same unwritten, supposedly common law, constitution.[38] Such arguments have been advanced in Australia and Canada.[39] Allan maintains that all the

[36] See, *e.g.*, Thomas Poole, "Back to the Future? Unearthing the Theory of Common Law Constitutionalism," (2003) 23 O.J.L.S. 435; Thomas Poole, "Questioning Common Law Constitutionalism," (2005) 25 Legal Studies 142.

[37] Allan, *Constitutional Justice, supra* note 17 at 271; see also 139, 225, 229, 240, and 243; T.R.S. Allan, "Text, Context, and Constitution: The Common Law as Public Reason," in Douglas E. Edlin ed., *Common Law Theory* (2007); T.R.S. Allan, "The Common Law as Constitution: Fundamental Rights and First Principles," in Cheryl Saunders ed., *Courts of Final Jurisdiction: The Mason Court in Australia* (1996) 146.

[38] Sir Owen Dixon, "The Common Law as an Ultimate Constitutional Foundation," in *Jesting Pilate* (1965), esp. 203, 206.

[39] Michael Wait, "The Slumbering Sovereign: Sir Owen Dixon's Common Law Constitution Revisited," (2001) 29 Federal Law Review 58; Mark D. Walters, "The Common Law Constitution in Canada: Return of the Lex Non Scripta as Fundamental Law," (2001) 51 U.T.L.J. 91 at 92 [Walters, "Return of the Lex Non Scripta"]; Mark D. Walters, "The Common Law Constitution and Legal Cosmopolitanism," in David Dyzenhaus ed., *The Unity of Public Law* (2004) 431.

constitutions in former Commonwealth countries are ultimately based on unwritten principles of constitutionalism and the rule of law, which lie at the heart of the common law tradition.[40]

At least three different versions of this kind of theory are possible, built around three different conceptions of the common law. There is, first, the legal positivist conception of the common law as a body of judicially posited rules and principles. Secondly, it is sometimes conceptualised as professional custom: "a body of practices observed and ideas received by a caste of lawyers . . . [and] used by them as providing guidance in what is conceived to be the rational determination of disputes . . . "[41] Thirdly, there is the Dworkinian conception of a body of norms based on abstract principles of political morality, which the judiciary has ultimate authority to enunciate, expound, and enforce.[42]

A fourth conception is also defensible, which depicts the common law – at least in constitutional matters – as customs or conventions of the community, or perhaps of legal officialdom in general, which the judiciary did not create and cannot unilaterally change. I will set aside this conception for the time being, because it undermines the main thrust of common law constitutionalism, which is that the unwritten constitution is "in the keeping of the judges," who have authority to change any part of it, or at least to develop it through creative reinterpretation.

According to the first two conceptions, Parliament owes its authority either to judicial law-making, or to judicial custom. According to the Dworkinian conception, its authority derives from, and is limited by, abstract principles of political morality, the identity and content of which are ultimately for the judges to authoritatively determine. These conceptions generate three versions of common law constitutionalism, all of which amount to a takeover bid. They all threaten – or promise – to replace legislative supremacy with judicial supremacy.[43] In Britain, instead of Parliament being the master of the constitution, with the ability to change any part of it (except, arguably, for the doctrine of parliamentary sovereignty itself), the judges turn out to be in charge. Parliament's authority is liable to be modified or curtailed as a result of either new judicial law-making, the evolution of judicial custom, or creative judicial re-interpretation of fundamental common law principles.

[40] See Allan, *Constitutional Justice*, *supra* note 17, *passim*.

[41] A.W.B. Simpson, "The Common Law and Legal Theory," in his *Legal Theory and Legal History, Essays on the Common Law* (1987) 359 at 376.

[42] I am using the term "Dworkinian" in a loose, generic sense. I am concerned with constitutional theorists who are heavily influenced by Dworkin, rather than with Dworkin himself.

[43] It is welcomed as a promise in M.D.J. Conaglen, "Judicial Supremacy: An Alternative Constitutional Theory," (1994) 7 Auckland U.L. Rev. 665.

Strong common law constitutionalism has been advanced on historical, as well as philosophical, grounds.[44] The historical argument is that England's unwritten constitution was always a matter of common law. The philosophical argument is that its present unwritten constitution is best analysed as a matter of common law. I have, elsewhere, subjected both the historical and philosophical arguments to critical scrutiny.[45]

As for history, there is no evidence of significant support for common law constitutionalism before the seventeenth century.[46] On the contrary, there is firm evidence that it was widely rejected. For much of that earlier period, the common law was regarded – as in the second conception discussed earlier – as the "common erudition" of the bench and bar.[47] The idea that the authority of the judges' superiors – the King who appointed and could dismiss them, and the High Court of Parliament that could overturn their decisions – was the product of the "erudition" expounded in their decisions, would have been dismissed out of hand as an absurdity. That is partly why, on several occasions, it was expressly and authoritatively denied that either the royal succession, or Parliament's privileges, was governed by the common law.[48] In the sixteenth century, the common law was often regarded as just one of a number of bodies of law, including civil, canon, and admiralty law. Even in the seventeenth century, sometimes depicted as the "classical age" of common law constitutionalism, that theory was fully embraced only by a few lawyers. Although Sir Edward Coke famously held that the King's prerogatives were derived from and controlled by the common law, he denied – at least sometimes – that the same was true of the royal succession and the privileges of Parliament. Sir John Davies, who shared Coke's conception of the nature of the common law, was a royalist who believed that the King, as the human source of all legal authority, retained prerogative powers that were "above" the common law. The King's power to make laws with the advice and consent of the two Houses of Parliament was the most "absolute" of those prerogatives. A great many lawyers, and

[44] For historical argument, see Walters, "The Return of the Lex Non Scripta," *supra* note 39 at 105–36.

[45] Goldsworthy, *The Sovereignty of Parliament*, *supra* note 18, *passim*, and "The Myth of the Common Law Constitution," in Douglas E. Edlin ed., *Common Law Theory* (2007) [Goldsworthy, "The Myth of the Common Law Constitution"].

[46] The next few paragraphs are adapted from "The Myth of the Common Law Constitution," *ibid.*

[47] J.W. Tubbs, *The Common Law Mind: Medieval and Early Modern Conceptions* (2000) at 2, 24–5, 45–52, 56–7, 65–6, 111, 114, 130, and 193–4. The common law as "common erudition" is also a principal theme in J.H. Baker, *The Law's Two Bodies: Some Evidential Problems in English Legal History* (2001), Lecture Three, esp. at 67–70, and 74–9.

[48] Goldsworthy, "The Myth of the Common Law Constitution," *supra* note 45 at 12–13.

other members of the ruling elite, agreed with Davies. Many others, such as Sir John Selden and Sir Matthew Hale, were contractualists, who believed that legal authority derived from the community as a whole, which had entered into a pact with the King that conferred and limited his powers. They regarded the common law as akin to statute law: Both were expressions of the will of the community. It should also be borne in mind that at that time, almost everyone accepted that the High Court of Parliament was the highest court in the realm, with ultimate authority to declare and interpret the common law itself.[49] Even those lawyers who accepted a version of common law constitutionalism did not subscribe to anything like the modern theory, which attributes ultimate authority to expound and develop the unwritten constitution to judges.

After the seventeenth century, the political theory of sovereignty, which maintained that there must be a sovereign lawmaker in every state who, by definition, stands above the law (including the common law), became ascendant. That theory was, of course, flawed, but it does not follow that common law constitutionalism was therefore the correct theory all along. The notion that the common law is the source of Parliament's authority seems to have been first propounded by constitutional writers such as Ivor Jennings in the 1930s. And they appear to have succumbed to the crude mistake of assuming that, because the source of Parliament's authority cannot be statute (as that would be bootstrapping), it must be the common law, which judges have authority to change or creatively reinterpret. This is a crude mistake because it overlooks the obvious retort that it cannot explain the authority of the judges, in developing the common law, without engaging in bootstrapping itself. If the common law is a body of law that the judges have made, or developed through creative interpretation, and if their authority to do so derives from the common law, then their authority rests on nothing more objective than their own say-so.

This is clearest in the case of the first two conceptions. If the judges' authority derives from the common law, and the common law consists of either judicially posited rules or judicial custom, then the judges have, in effect, conferred authority on themselves. But the argument is equally bootstrapping if the Dworkinian conception of the common law is adopted. Let us imagine, for example, that the House of Lords were to adopt a Dworkinian reinterpretation of Britain's unwritten constitution, and declare for the first time that it consists of fundamental principles of political morality that limit Parliament's authority. In the absence of a broader official consensus either as to the nature of the unwritten constitution or as to the judges' authority to reinterpret it in that way, their claim to possess such authority would, itself, be a product of their

[49] Goldsworthy, *The Sovereignty of Parliament*, *supra* note 18 at 110, 118–19, 153–4, and 156–7.

interpretation of it. Supposedly deriving from whatever principles of political morality they regard as morally justifying the legal system as a whole, their authority would ultimately rest on nothing more solid than their own assertion that it is morally compelling. This is hardly likely to persuade other legal officials – in Parliament, for example – who have a very different understanding of the nature of the unwritten constitution and its moral justification, and who could, with equal plausibility, claim the same authority for themselves.

As I have argued at length elsewhere, self-proclaimed moral authority – even if the proclamation is justified – is incapable, by itself, of sustaining law. Legal, in contrast to moral, authority depends on a widespread consensus that it exists, at least among the senior legal officials of the major branches of government.[50] For that reason, the thesis that the unwritten constitution is a matter of common law could be sustained only if the fourth conception of the common law were adopted, which portrays it as customs of legal officialdom in general, or of the community as a whole, which the judges did not create, and cannot change, unilaterally.[51]

Understanding the unwritten constitution in terms of the conventions of legal officialdom would be congruent with Hart's theory that the fundamental rules of recognition in any legal system are constituted by the practices of legal officials in general, and not just of the judiciary.[52] Such a conception of the common law was once popular, but is no longer regarded as plausible with respect to the vast tracts of ordinary common law, dealing with torts, contracts, property, and so on. This conception would, therefore, entail a bifurcated theory of the common law, its nature varying according to the subject-matter in question. That would be problematic. But in any event, it would undermine the central claim of common law constitutionalism, by establishing that the unwritten constitution is constituted by a consensus among senior legal officials in general, if not the community as a whole, and can change only if that consensus changes.

Weak Common Law Constitutionalism

According to David Dyzenhaus, the idea that the rule of law reflects an internal morality of the law is a modern version of an "ancient idea of the common law constitution – that positive law from whatever source is just evidence of the values of the law that have existed from time immemorial and that have their

[50] *Ibid.* at 254–6.

[51] See text above at 290.

[52] See H.L.A. Hart, *The Concept of Law* (1961), ch. 6, as explained in Goldsworthy, *The Sovereignty of Parliament*, *supra* note 18 at 240–1.

most explicit and main articulation in judicial reasoning about the application of the law in particular cases."[53] These values, of legality or the rule of law, possess "influential authority"[54] that guides the judges' reasoning in cases involving statutes as well as the common law as such. But common law values do not possess the "peremptory authority"[55] that would enable judges to declare statutes invalid. If the injustice in a statute is "absolutely explicit,"[56] the judges cannot withstand it; however, they can minimise injustice by giving the statute "the narrowest possible reading,"[57] and by confining its "gravitational"[58] or "juristic force."[59] They can confine a statute's force by not allowing it to have any influence on the interpretation of other statutes, or any continuing legal consequences after its repeal. "[T]he constitutional basis of their judgment . . . [is] that from their perspective the injustice is in principle limitable because it is a legal injustice, an affront to the rule of law."[60]

In what follows, I will ignore the question of a statute's "gravitational force" because it seldom arises, and Dyzanhaus's development of the idea seems quite novel, with little apparent support in the case law. As for statutory interpretation, on the other hand, his position is a popular one, and arguably has considerable precedential support. It is often suggested that, even if Parliament is supreme in making new law, the courts are supreme in interpreting it, and although a statute's validity is not dependent on the common law, its interpretation – and therefore its meaning – is. The courts have often interpreted statutory provisions restrictively, contrary to their literal meanings, in order to protect fundamental common law principles. Anything less than express words or necessary implication has been held not to alter or impinge upon those principles. An analogy has been drawn between the effect of interpretive presumptions, and the effect of constitutional, "manner and form" provisions that require express words or even a particular verbal formula in order to amend or repeal legislation of a certain kind.[61]

The orthodox justification for common law presumptions is entirely consistent with parliamentary supremacy. As the High Court of Australia has explained: "The rationale of all such rules lies in the assumption that the

[53] D. Dyzenhaus, "The Juristic Force of Injustice," in M. Moran and D. Dyzenhaus, *Calling Power to Account: Law, Reparations and the Chinese Canadian Head Tax* (2005) at 258–9 [Dyzenhaus, "The Juristic Force of Injustice"].

[54] *Ibid.* at 268

[55] *Ibid.*

[56] *Ibid.* at 274.

[57] *Ibid.* at 272.

[58] *Ibid.*

[59] *Ibid.* at 281.

[60] *Ibid.* at 281.

[61] For example, T.R.S. Allan, "Legislative Supremacy and the Rule of Law: Democracy and Constitutionalism," (1985) 44 Cambridge L.J. 111.

legislature would, if it intended to achieve the particular effect, have made its intention in that regard unambiguously clear."[62] Judges have, for centuries, accepted that this is the basis for the presumptions. Although Sir Edward Coke asserted that "the surest construction of a statute is by the rule and reason of the common law,"[63] he also said that "every statute ought to be expounded according to the intent of them that made it," and seems to have regarded this as the fundamental rule of interpretation.[64] It can be traced at least as far back as the fifteenth century: Chrimes reports that it was "certainly established by the second half of the fifteenth century," and by Henry VIII's reign, was "sufficiently established to be clearly stated several times from the bench."[65] Nonliteral, "equitable" interpretations of statutes were justified on that basis. "Equity is a construction made by the judges," Coke said, "that cases out of the letter of a statute, yet being within the same mischief... shall be within the same remedy... and the reason hereof is, for that the law-makers could not possibly set down all cases in express terms."[66] The same justification was given when cases within the letter of a statute were excepted out of it: "because the text is contrary to reason... therefore they took it that the intent of the maker of the statute could not be according to the letter."[67] The judges quite reasonably took the view that "injustice... is not to be presumed in a Parliament."[68]

Today, this kind of talk is often dismissed as an artificial rationalisation or polite fiction. In reality, it is said, courts have stubbornly protected the fundamental values of the common law from legislative interference, while acknowledging practical limits to their ability to do so.[69] It has been argued, for example, that the common law presumptions "no longer have anything to do with the

[62] *Bropho v. Western Australia* (1990) 171 C.L.R. 1 at para. 13.

[63] 1 Co Inst. 272b, quoted by T.R.S. Allan, *Law, Liberty and Justice: The Legal Foundations of British Constitutionalism* (1993) at ch. 1. n. 61 [Allan, *Law, Liberty and Justice*].

[64] 4 Co Inst. 330, discussed in R.A. MacKay, "Coke – Parliamentary Sovereignty or the Supremacy of the Law?" 22 Mich. L. Rev. 215 at 236–7 (1924).

[65] S.B. Chrimes, *English Constitutional Ideas in the Fifteenth Century* (1936) at 293–4. The rule was affirmed by Lord Chancellor Ellesmere, Plowden, and Selden, as well as Coke: On early English authorities, see R. Berger, "Original Intention in Historical Perspective," 54 Geo. Wash. L. Rev. 296 at 299–308 (1986), and R. Berger, "The Founders' Views – According to Jefferson Powell," 67 Tex. L. Rev. 1033 at 1059–65 (1989).

[66] 1 Co Inst. 24(b).

[67] *Fulmerston v. Steward* (1 & 2 Philip and Mary) 1 Plow. 101, 109–10; 75 E.R. 160, 172. See also *Earl of Leicester v. Heydon* (13 Eliz.) 1 Plow. 348, 398; 75 E.R. 582, 602–3; *Partridge v. Strange and Croker* (6 & 7 Ed. VI) 1 Plow. 77, 82; 75 E.R. 123, 130; and *Stradling v. Morgan* (2 Eliz.) 1 Plow. 199, 205; 75 E.R. 305, 315.

[68] *Hill v. Grange* (3 & 4 Philip and Mary) 1 Plow. 164, 175; 75 E.R. 253, 270. See also *Stowell v. Lord Zouche* (4 & 5 Eliz.) 1 Plow. 353, 361–5, 75 E.R. 536, 549–54.

[69] J. Burrows, "The Changing Approach to the Interpretation of Statutes," (2002) 33 V.U.W.L.R. 981, 982–3, 990–5 and 997–8.

intent of the legislature; they are a means of controlling that intent."[70] This leads to the claim that they "can be viewed as the courts' efforts to provide, in effect, a common law bill of rights – a protection for the civil liberties of the individual against invasion by the state."[71] Hence, Lord Browne-Wilkinson's argument in 1992 that Britain did not need a bill of rights because the rights protected by the common law, through presumptions in statutory interpretation, were no less extensive than those protected by the *European Convention on Human Rights*.[72] In the United States, presumptions used in statutory interpretation have been called "clear statement rules," and their creation described as "quasiconstitutional lawmaking."[73] I take Sir John Laws to mean something similar when he says that, even in Britain, "the common law has come to recognise that there exist rights which should properly be classified as constitutional or fundamental."[74]

It is undoubtedly true that judges have used common law presumptions to interpret legislation more narrowly than Parliament intended, resulting in the frustration of its purposes. This is notorious, for example, in relation to a good deal of legislation dealing with taxation and industrial relations, and attempting to restrict judicial review of administrative decisions. (The historical use of the presumptions by conservative judiciaries to thwart progressive legislation is not something that today's judges should be proud of. Instead of fearless, independent judges shielding vulnerable individuals from the tyranny of the state, they have, in these cases, prevented the state from protecting such individuals.) In many cases, then, judges did misapply the presumptions, by using them as a smokescreen or fig-leaf to conceal judicial disobedience of Parliament. But should these cases now be cited to support the proposition that the presumptions give effect to constitutional principles, which control statutes regardless of, and sometimes contrary to, Parliament's intentions?

We have two alternatives. The first is to endorse the orthodox understanding that the common law presumptions are justified by genuine uncertainty about

[70] L. Tremblay, "Section 7 of the Charter: Substantive Due Process," (1984) 18 U.B.C. L. Rev. 201 at 242.

[71] D.C. Pearce and R.S. Geddes, *Statutory Interpretation in Australia*, 5th edn. (2001) at 131.

[72] Rt Hon Lord Browne-Wilkinson, "The Infiltration of a Bill of Rights," [1992] P.L. 397 at 405.

[73] See W. Eskridge and P. Frickey, "Quasi-Constitutional Law: Clear Statement Rules as Constitutional Lawmaking," 45 Vanderbilt L. Rev. 593 (1992).

[74] *Thoburn v. Sunderland City Council*, [2003] Q.B. 151 *per* Laws L.J. at para. 62. See *R v. Secretary of State for the Home Department, Ex parte Simms*, [2000] 2 A.C.115 *per* Lord Hoffmann at 131 ("principles of constitutionality little different from those which exist in countries where the power of the legislature is expressly limited by a constitutional document"); D.L. Keir and F.H. Lawson, *Cases in Constitutional Law*, 4th edn. (1965) at 10; Lord Devlin "Judges as Lawmakers," (1976) 39 Modern L. Rev. 1 at 14; and R. Cross, *Statutory Interpretation*, 3rd edn. by J. Bell and G. Engle (1995) at 166.

legislative intentions.[75] This entails rejecting as wrongly decided those cases in which the presumptions have been used as a smokescreen to conceal judicial disobedience, in the form of de facto amendment or partial disapplication of legislation. The second alternative is to accept those cases as part of a stealthy, but ultimately successful, campaign by judges to acquire – more bluntly, to usurp – authority to protect "constitutional" values chosen by them.[76]

I will return to the choice between these alternatives after exploring the first of them in more depth. It makes a claim of the third kind, concerning communicative implications.

COMMUNICATIVE IMPLICATION CLAIMS

Implicit Assumptions

The meaning of almost everything we say depends on background assumptions that are taken for granted.[77] If they are not taken for granted, what we say is liable to be misunderstood in unpredictable and bizarre ways. Consider this example from Francis Leiber, writing in the nineteenth century:

> Suppose a housekeeper says to a domestic: 'fetch some soup-meat', accompanying the act with giving some money to the latter; he will be unable to execute the order without interpretation, however easy and, consequently, rapid the performance of the process may be. Common sense and good faith tell the domestic, that the housekeeper's meaning was this: 1. He should go immediately, or as soon as his other occupations are finished; or, if he be directed to do so in the evening, that he should go the next day at the *usual* hour; 2. that the money handed him by the housekeeper is intended to pay for

[75] This is subject to one possible qualification. To ensure that Parliament's intention to interfere with certain rights is known with sufficient certainty, it may be reasonable to adopt a rule that requires express words or necessary implication. But like other rules, this one might be overinclusive, if Parliament's intentions can sometimes be clearly established by means other than express words or necessary implication, such as statements made in parliamentary debates. The risks of error might be grounds for excluding such evidence where protected rights are at stake, even if it might sometimes be persuasive in such cases and is generally admitted in other cases. For a possible example, see *Re Bolton, ex parte Beane* (1987), 162 C.L.R. 514, discussed in J. Doyle and B. Wells "How Far Can the Common Law Go Towards Protecting Human Rights?" in P. Alston ed., *Promoting Human Rights Through Bills of Rights: Comparative Perspectives* (1999) at 57–8.

[76] See the comments of J. Evans, "Controlling the Use of Parliamentary History," (1998) 18 N.Z.U.L.R. 1 at 44.

[77] J. Goldsworthy, "Implications in Language, Law and the Constitution," in G. Lindell ed., *Future Directions in Australian Constitutional Law* (1994) 150 at 157–61, from which the following discussion is taken. See also W. Waluchow, *Inclusive Legal Positivism* (1994) at 244–5 and 257–8.

> the meat thus ordered, and not as a present to him; 3. that he should buy such meat and of such parts of the animal, as, to his knowledge, has commonly been used in the house he stays at, for making soup; 4. that he buy the best meat he can obtain, for a fair price; 5. that he go to that butcher who usually provides the family, with whom the domestic resides, with meat, or to some convenient stall, and not to any unnecessarily distant place; 6. that he return the rest of the money; 7. that he bring home the meat in good faith, neither adding anything disagreeable or injurious; 8. that he fetch the meat for the use of the family and not for himself. Suppose, on the other hand, the housekeeper, afraid of being misunderstood, had mentioned these eight specifications, she would not have obtained her object, if it were to exclude all *possibility* of misunderstanding. For, the various specifications would have required new ones. Where would be the end? We are constrained then, always, to leave a considerable part of our meaning to be found out by interpretation, which, in many cases must necessarily cause greater or less obscurity with regard to the exact meaning, which our words were intended to convey.[78]

More recently, the philosopher John Searle has argued, along very similar lines, that it is never possible for us to state exactly and literally what we mean or want, because no matter how many absurd possible misinterpretations we expressly rule out, there will always be others we have not thought of. This is because, first, many of the crucial background assumptions are "submerged in the unconscious and we don't quite know how to dredge them up,"[79] and secondly, for every assumption spelled out, others would spring up on which the meaning of the expanded utterance would depend.[80] Each assumption depends for its full meaning on others, which together constitute a vast and complex network of beliefs and values that are generally not consciously adverted to, let alone articulated in language. Even if it were possible to make all of this explicit, the result would be so prolix and convoluted that it would be very difficult to read, let alone to understand. It would be counterproductive to waste one's own time, and that of one's intended audience, by attempting to expressly state what should be obvious to all concerned.

This background network of assumptions may not be consciously adverted to by either the speaker or the hearer of an utterance. But it does not follow that the speaker's intentions are irrelevant. When we say that something is implicit in an

[78] F. Lieber, *Legal and Political Hermeneutics* (1839) at 28–30.

[79] J. Searle, *Intentionality: An Essay in the Philosophy of Mind* (1983) at 142 [Searle, *Intentionality*].

[80] J. Searle, "Literal Meaning," in his *Expression and Meaning* (1979) 117 at 126 [Searle, *Expression and Meaning*]; Searle, *Intentionality*, *ibid.* at 148; and "The Background of Meaning," in J. Searle, F. Kiefer, and M. Bierwisch eds., *Speech Act Theory and Pragmatics* (1980) at 228 [Searle, "The Background of Meaning"].

utterance in the sense that it is taken for granted, we are saying that the speaker took it for granted. But how can speakers have any intentions about matters that are not consciously in their minds? The answer seems to be that intentions, and other mental states such as beliefs and desires, depend just as much as meanings on a network of background assumptions. Searle, for example, describes what is necessarily assumed by anyone intending to run for President of the United States: that the United States is a republic, that it has a presidential form of government, that it has periodic elections, that these involve principally a contest between candidates of two major parties, the Republicans and the Democrats, that these candidates are chosen at nominating conventions, and so on indefinitely. Searle concludes that "[c]ertain fundamental ways of doing things and certain sorts of know-how about the way things work are presupposed by any such form of Intentionality."[81] Indeed, in his view, linguistic meaning depends on background assumptions precisely because language is a means of expressing our intentional states, such as our intentions, beliefs, and desires.[82] It is because those intentional states depend on a network of background assumptions that their expression in language does too.[83]

This is why, in our original example, Leiber plausibly describes his complex interpretation of "fetch some soup-meat" as "the housekeeper's meaning," although it is unlikely that much of it passed through her conscious mind. In conveying an intention, belief, or desire, an utterance conveys something which, itself, depends on background assumptions that are taken for granted, and if this is not understood, the utterance is not properly understood. Our understanding of meanings is, in this respect, analogous to the way in which our understanding of what we see when we focus on something depends on its surroundings, which our peripheral vision registers even when we are only dimly aware of them, or do not consciously notice them at all.[84]

Implicit Assumptions in Statutes

Those who draft legal documents generally attempt to express themselves as explicitly as possible, rather than to rely on implication. Generally speaking, what is implied is more likely to be misunderstood, or even overlooked, than what is expressed.[85] This is especially true when communication is restricted to

[81] Searle, *Intentionality, supra* note 80 at 20; see also Searle, *Expression and Meaning, ibid.* at 141.
[82] Searle, *Expression and Meaning, supra* note 80 at 5 and 176–9.
[83] Searle, "The Background of Meaning," *supra* note 80 at 231–2.
[84] R. Dickerson, *The Interpretation and Application of Statutes* (1975) at 104 [Dickerson, *Interpretation and Application*].
[85] See M. Dascal, *Pragmatics and the Philosophy of Mind I* (1983) at 159 and esp. note 117.

writing, without the assistance of cues used in face-to-face conversation, such as stress, pitch, pause, facial expression, and gesture, and is aimed at a large and diverse audience rather than a single person. Participants in everyday conversation know more about one another, and the context in which they are speaking, than does a legislature and its audience. In conversation, people take much more for granted, and also more risks in doing so, because of the opportunity for feedback and the immediate correction of misunderstandings.[86]

Nevertheless, full comprehension of written laws also depends on implicit assumptions. These include what courts take to be simple common sense.[87] But they also include pre-existing legal principles. As Francis Bennion explains, it is impossible for a drafter to explicitly restate all the ancillary legal considerations that may be necessary for the operation of an Act. "The Act relies for its effectiveness on [an] implied importation of surrounding legal principles and rules."[88] Indeed, he goes so far as to claim that "virtually the whole body of the law is imported, by one enactment or another, as implied ancillary rules."[89]

This is why *mens rea* is usually held to be implicit in statutes creating new criminal offences that include no express reference to it. Justice Stephen said that it is simply assumed.[90] It is also why Lord Denning once held that the *British North America Act* 1867 (U.K.) did not disturb a pre-existing royal proclamation, which was "an unwritten provision which went without saying."[91] All the common law presumptions used in statutory interpretation can arguably be justified on this ground, the context provided by the general law implicitly limiting language that, read literally, would be overinclusive.[92] They include the presumption that statutes are not intended to extend beyond territorial limits, to be retrospective, or to override fundamental common law principles. Judges are therefore often justified in claiming that by interpreting statutory language restrictively, so that it does not disturb common law principles, they are giving effect to Parliament's implicit intention. Even in the case of unusual and unanticipated situations that fall within the literal meaning

[86] See F. Bowers, *Linguistic Aspects of Legislative Expression* (1989) at 25–6.

[87] F. Bennion, *Statutory Interpretation*, 2nd edn. (1992) at 407 [Bennion, *Statutory Interpretation*].

[88] *Ibid.*, 727. See also Dickerson, *Interpretation and Application*, *supra* note 84 at 29, and as to the drafting and interpretation of criminal laws, the words of Lord Diplock in *R v. Miller*, [1983] 2 A.C. 161 at 174.

[89] Bennion, *supra* note 87 at 728.

[90] *R v. Tolson* (1889), 23 Q.B.D. 168 at 187. See also Lord Diplock in *Sweet v. Parsley*, [1970] A.C. 132 at 162–3.

[91] *R v. Secretary of State for Foreign and Commonwealth Affairs, ex parte Indian Association of Alberta*, [1982] Q.B. 892 at 914.

[92] For many examples, see Bennion, *supra* note 87, Parts XVI, XVII, XXIII, and XXIV.

of a provision, and with respect to which the legislature had no conscious intention at all, it can make sense to say that it did not intend the provision to apply.

Hence the decision in the celebrated American case of *Riggs v. Palmer*.[93] There, a statute requiring the enforcement of wills according to their terms was held not to do so if the testator had been murdered by his beneficiary. The decision is best justified by the "tacit general legal assumption" that wrongdoers should not profit from their wrongs.[94] Dworkin himself now accepts something like this explanation of the decision. In *Law's Empire*, he rejected what he called the "speaker's meaning" explanation of the decision, based on the idea "that those who adopted the statute did not intend murderers to inherit."[95] But he now says this:

> I continue to think that the majority reached the right decision, in *Riggs v. Palmer*, in holding that, according to the better interpretive reconstruction, those who created the State of Wills did not intend to say something that allowed a murderer to inherit from his victim... It is a perfectly familiar speech practice not to include, even in quite specific instructions, all the qualifications one would accept or insist on: all the qualifications, as one might put it, that 'go without saying'.[96]

In a similar English case, the High Court held that a statutory provision granting widows a pension did not benefit a widow convicted of the manslaughter of her husband. Lord Lane C.J. said that the lack of any specific provision to that effect was "merely an indication... that the draftsman realised perfectly well that he was drawing this Act against the background of the law as it stood at the time."[97] Even Allan has endorsed this understanding of the phenomenon. After explaining why general rules are necessarily insensitive to morally relevant circumstances in some individual cases, he observes that in applying legislation, the courts

> should seek to limit adverse consequences, incidental to the statutory purpose. Quite apart from overriding constitutional limitations, it is usually reasonable to assume that a general rule was not intended to cause serious harm to individuals without any (or sufficient) countervailing benefit to the public

93 (1889) 115 note Y. 506, 22 note E. 188.

94 Dickerson, *Interpretation and Application*, *supra* note 84 at 108 note 14; Bennion, *supra* note 87 at 532–3.

95 R. Dworkin, *Law's Empire* (1986) at 351–2.

96 R. Dworkin, "Reflections on Fidelity," (1997) 65 Fordham L. Rev. 1799 at 1816.

97 *R v. Chief National Insurance Commissioner, ex parte Connor*, [1981] Q.B. 758 at 165. See also *Re Sidgworth*, [1935] ch. 89, and *Re Royse*, [1985] ch.22 *per* Ackner L.J. at 27.

> good. The discovery of such *implicit* qualifications . . . is none the less entailed by an intelligent construction of the 'statutory meaning': such assumptions show proper respect for the legislators' general good faith and moral integrity.[98]

Elsewhere, I have explained presumptions of legislative intention in terms of protecting the legislature's "standing commitments." The legislature is deemed not to have abandoned its standing commitment to a fundamental legal principle unless and until it clearly repudiates it.[99] I also pointed out that a legislature's standing commitments need not be confined to those implicit in past practice: A legislature can make them explicit, and even subscribe to new ones. The British Parliament did this when it enacted the *Human Rights Act*, which requires courts to interpret legislation, whenever possible, as compatible with enumerated rights.

We can now return to the two alternatives described at the end of the previous section: Should we abandon the traditional and still orthodox justification of the common law presumptions in terms of legislative intention, and concede that they are really constitutional principles that the judges use to control the exercise of legislative authority irrespective of legislative intention? I suggest there are good reasons to refuse to do so.

The first is that the orthodox interpretation is the traditional one. Dyzenhaus continually identifies his own theory of common law constitutionalism with an "ancient" common law tradition,[100] but I have seen little evidence that the theory really does have deep historical roots. Relatively recent (post-1960) judicial innovations in the field of administrative law do not constitute such evidence. Nor does a handful of earlier but eccentric dicta, such as that of Coke C.J. in *Dr Bonham's* case.[101]

The second reason is that to reject the orthodox interpretation is implicitly to accuse many judges in the past of lying about the true reasons for their decisions – of concealing defiance of Parliament behind spurious claims about Parliament's intentions. Admittedly, some of them probably have lied, but I would argue that such cases are relatively rare. Some claim that the decision in the famous *Anisminic* case is an example of a court, in effect, refusing to obey Parliament's plain denial of its jurisdiction to review the decisions of a

98 Allan, *Constitutional Justice*, *supra* note 17 at 127–8, emphasis in original.

99 J. Goldsworthy, "Parliamentary Sovereignty and Statutory Interpretation," in R. Bigwood ed., *The Statute, Making and Meaning* (2004).

100 Dyzenhaus, The Juristic Force of Injustice," *supra* note 53 at 258.

101 (1610) 77 Eng. Rep. 646.

statutory authority.[102] Yet even Allan, no friend of parliamentary sovereignty, once justified that decision on the orthodox ground of presumed legislative intention. He said:

> [i]t is quite as reasonable to suppose that Parliament intended the courts to superintend the Foreign Compensation Commission, as regards the extent of its jurisdiction, as to suppose the contrary. Far more reasonable – it would seem almost absurd to think that Parliament intended the Commission's activities to be free from all legal control . . .[103]

David Dyzenhaus has also endorsed the orthodox understanding of the judicial treatment of privative clauses:

> [S]ince judges operate on the assumption that government under the rule of law aspires to realize the values of the common law model, they will interpret legislation on the basis that it shares that aspiration unless they are forced by very explicit language to abandon that assumption. . . . In the common law world, courts have come to accept the position that a privative clause is largely redundant, since a legislature cannot seriously intend that a tribunal be delegated legally unlimited authority . . .[104]

(To be fair to Allan and Dyzenhaus, in other places they appear to repudiate this orthodox understanding.[105]) It might be added that, even when judges do seem to have lied, the fact that they felt it necessary to do so – rather than to boldly claim authority to rewrite statutes – indicates that they themselves realised that their disobedience was, legally speaking, illicit.

A third reason for resisting the suggested change is that the new theory of common law presumptions may prove difficult to confine. In other words, the weak version of common law constitutionalism may be unstable and prone to collapse into the strong version. When judges interpret provisions nonliterally

[102] For example, H.W.R. Wade and C.F. Forsyth, *Administrative Law*, 7th edn., (1994) at 737; Justice E.W. Thomas, "The Relationship Between Parliament and the Courts: A Tentative Thought or Two for the New Millenium," (2000) 31 V.U.W.L.R. 5 at 27.

[103] T.R.S. Allan "Legislative Supremacy and the Rule of Law: Democracy and Constitutionalism," (1995) 44 Cambridge L.J. 111 at 127. Allan does not seem to have subsequently changed his mind: See Allan, *Constitutional Justice*, *supra* note 17 at 211–12.

[104] D. Dyzenhaus, "The Juristic Force of Injustice," *supra* note 53 at 278. Elsewhere, he describes the courts having to choose between Parliament's "particular intention" in enacting a privative clause, and its "abstract intention" in prescribing a necessarily limited mandate to executive agencies: D. Dyzenhaus, *The Constitution of Law: Legality in a Time of Emergency* (2006) at 104 [Dyzenhaus, *Constitution of Law*].

[105] *E.g.*, Dyzenhaus, *The Constitution of Law*, *ibid.* at 72 ("judges are entitled to uphold the aspirational conception whatever the facts about legislative intention.").

because they presume that the legislature remains committed to common law principles, they still act as the legislature's faithful agents. If that justification were jettisoned as a disingenuous rationalistion, it would be more difficult both to defend and to limit a judicial power of nonliteral interpretation. It would look much more like a power of amendment, or even partial disapplication, than genuine interpretation. And if judges were openly to claim authority to amend or partially disapply legislation in these cases, why not go all the way, and claim a comprehensive authority to amend or disapply statutes in order to enhance justice? Why not, in a case of extreme statutory injustice, disapply the statute completely – which is to say, invalidate it? Allan would reply: why not indeed? He has consistently argued that the power of invalidation is implicit in the power of partial disapplication through restrictive interpretation: The former is just an extreme version of the latter.[106] If Allan is right, then Dyzenhaus's denial that the judiciary possesses the former power may be subverted by his apparent claim that they possess the latter.[107] Moreover, if the common law confers on judges a power of amendment or partial disapplication, exercisable irrespective of Parliament's intentions, the common law must be superior to statute law. If so, then even if the common law does not yet recognise that judges can invalidate statutes, the judges could change the common law and repudiate any self-imposed limit to their power of disapplication. They would possess effective supremacy over statute law, because they would always have the last word at the point of application of the law.

Implicit Assumptions in Written Constitutions

There can be no doubt that implications can properly be drawn from a written constitution. Indeed, written constitutions arguably rely more on implication than most other legal documents, because they must be "expressed in general propositions wide enough to be capable of flexible application to changing circumstances."[108] Their method "is rather to outline principles than to engrave details."[109] Justice Gaudron of the Australian High Court remarked that some fundamental doctrines are not expressed "either because they are assumed by the Constitution, or because what they entail is taken to be so obvious that

[106] Allan, *Law, Liberty and Justice*, *supra* note 63 at 267.

[107] See *supra* note 53.

[108] *Australian National Airways v. Commonwealth* (1945), 71 C.L.R. 29 *per* Dixon C.J. at 81.

[109] *Tasmania v. Commonwealth and Victoria* (1904), 1 C.L.R. 329 *per* Barton J at 348; see also *ibid. per* Griffith C.J. at 338 and *Jumbunna Coal Mine No Liability v. Victorian Coal Miners' Association* (1908), 6 C.L.R. 309 *per* Barton J. at 343.

detailed specification is unnecessary."[110] The best Australian example is the power of judicial review itself. Many lawyers have puzzled over the failure of the drafters, who undoubtedly intended the courts to possess the power, to confer it by express provision.[111] But as Sir Owen Dixon insisted, the Constitution was born not in a vacuum, but in a pre-existing legal system in which the acts of colonial governments and legislatures were governed by the principle of *ultra vires*.[112] Therefore "to the framers of the Commonwealth Constitution the thesis of *Marbury v Madison* was obvious."[113] So obvious, indeed, that they apparently took it for granted and expected others to do likewise.

Two Australian judges once argued that legislative power under the Australian Constitution is limited by implications that "flow from the fundamental rights and principles recognised by the common law at the time the Constitution was adopted as the compact of the Federation."[114] One of them, Toohey J., suggested that this argument was supported by the principle, previously discussed, that statutes are enacted against a background including the common law. Given that the Constitution was enacted in a British statute, it should be presumed, in the absence of clear evidence to the contrary, not to have been intended to disturb fundamental common law principles.[115] But this principle of interpretation provides the argument with no support whatsoever. A constitutional provision conferring a power that includes the capacity to disturb fundamental common law principles does not, itself, disturb those principles. Quite the contrary: The most fundamental principle recognised by British courts throughout the nineteenth century was that of the sovereignty of the Imperial Parliament, and by the end of that century, colonial legislatures were deemed to possess a similar sovereignty within the limits to their powers imposed by the written instruments governing them. Within those limits, their powers were considered to be of the same nature, and as absolute and plenary, as the sovereign powers of the Imperial Parliament itself.[116] As the

[110] *Australian Capital Television Pty Ltd v. Commonwealth* (1992), 108 C.L.R. 577 at 650, footnote omitted.

[111] See G. Lindell, "The Justiciability of Political Questions: Recent Developments," in H.P. Lee and G. Winterton eds., *Australian Constitutional Perspectives* (1992) 180 at 223–8 and other sources listed there.

[112] *Ibid.* at 43.

[113] *Ibid.* at 174; see also R. Garran, *Prosper the Commonwealth* (1958) at 171, and Sir A. Mason, "The Role of a Constitutional Court in a Federation," (1986) 16 Fed. L. Rev. 1 at 6.

[114] *Nationwide News v. Wills* (1992), 108 A.L.R. 681 *per* Deane and Toohey J.J. at 721.

[115] Justice John Toohey AC, "A Government of Laws, and Not of Men?" (1993) 4 Public L. Rev. 158 at 170.

[116] See the cases cited in *Union Steamship Co of Australia Pty Ltd v. King* (1988), 166 C.L.R. 1 at 9–10.

Privy Council said in 1885, power to make laws "for the peace, order and good government" of a colony, the words used to confer legislative power on the Australian Parliament, conferred "the utmost discretion of enactment."[117]

This position was well established by the final decade of the nineteenth century, and well known to those who drafted the Australian Constitution. Indeed, section 3 of the *Colonial Laws Validity Act* 1865 (U.K.) had been enacted specifically to put an end, once and for all, to assertions by some colonial judges of the power to invalidate colonial legislation on the ground of repugnance to fundamental principles of English law, including common law.[118] Section 3 provided that no colonial law should be deemed void or inoperative for repugnancy to "the law of England" (which included the common law), except in cases of repugnancy to an Act of the Imperial Parliament or an Order or Regulation having the force and effect of such an Act. In speaking of "the limits on power arising from fundamental common law liberties," Toohey J. was therefore attempting to revive virtually the same doctrine as the one that section 3 was designed to abolish. By attributing those limits to an implication within the Constitution, he was suggesting that this implication, in effect, amended section 3 of the *Colonial Laws Validity Act*. This did not, I am sure, occur to any of the experienced lawyers in Australia or the British Colonial Office at the time. Thus, the Australian Constitution is not based on an implicit assumption that limits the ability of legislatures to override common law principles, even principles of "legality." Presumably the same is true of the Canadian Constitution.

What is implicit in or implied by a constitution is very difficult to explain except in terms of original intent. Most implications are not expressed by a constitution's words, and it is rare for legal implications to be logically entailed by express words.[119] Most legal implications therefore depend on some ingredient in addition to the words of the text, and this is usually taken to be their purpose. Strictly speaking, words do not have purposes: only the people who use them do. And it is natural to think that where a constitution is concerned, the relevant people are those who founded it. For this reason, the orthodox view is that a constitution is based on or embodies "unwritten" or "structural" principles, such as representative democracy, federalism, the rule of law, and the separation of powers, only if and insofar as its provisions were intended by the founders to implement those principles.

[117] *Riel v. R.* (1885), 10 App. Cas. 675 at 678.

[118] D.B. Swinfen, "The Genesis of the Colonial Laws Validity Act," [1967] Juridical Review 29 at 32, 39, 54–6.

[119] Some "conventional" implications are expressed by words.

It is sometimes suggested that so-called "structural" implications are derived from specific provisions by inductive, as opposed to deductive, logic.[120] The idea is that if a number of specific provisions appear to be instances of a general principle, they might be evidence that the principle itself is part of the constitution. I have no objection in principle to this. The question is how we should understand the nature of such inductive arguments, and of the implications they are used to reveal. Inductive arguments are inferences to the best explanation of some observed phenomena: they seek to explain the observed in terms of the unobserved. When used in science, for example, an inductive argument might take observed regularities to be evidence of an underlying causal relationship. In the constitutional context, what is the nature of this unobserved thing – the counterpart of the causal relationship? Legal provisions are the products, not of mindless natural processes governed by causal laws, but of intentional human action. The legal equivalent of the underlying causal relationship revealed by scientific induction is therefore the lawmaker's intention. In other words, an inductive argument is persuasive only if constitutional provisions that instantiate some general principle are evidence that the founders intended the principle itself, and not just the particular provisions, to be judicially enforceable. An implication is justified when there is sufficient evidence of the existence of such an intention. The catch, of course, is that if this is what the inductive argument points to, then other evidence that such an intention could not have existed will defeat the argument. Inductive arguments are defeasible, not conclusive: They constitute evidence of something, but can be defeated by stronger counter-evidence.

This orthodox view is contested by those who argue that the purposes of a constitution are determined not by those who founded it, who are long gone, but by those who continue to accept it for their governance today – by contemporary values and expectations, rather than the "dead hand of the past." But this argument is fraught with danger, if it is alleged that the purposes of a constitution have changed as a result of changes in these values and expectations, and that the meaning and effect of the constitution has thereby been altered. Implications are often justified by the argument that they are practically necessary for the constitution to achieve one of its purposes (although I will question his argument shortly). But, in combination with a non-originalist theory of what those purposes are, this would give judges a virtually boundless power to change the constitution. If judges could "discover" in the constitution whatever is practically necessary for it to achieve certain purposes, and

[120] *E.g.*, Mark Walters, "Written Constitutions and Unwritten Constitutionalism," in this volume at 263.

these purposes could themselves change according to the judges' perceptions of contemporary values or expectations, then in effect the judges could add to the constitution anything they believe to be practically necessary to satisfy contemporary values or expectations – without any formal amendment being required![121] That surely cannot be right. If today's citizens really do want their constitution to serve some new purpose, or to pursue an old purpose by new means, they should agitate for formal amendment by whatever democratic process the constitution itself prescribes.

But the "practical necessity" argument can be used to rationalise judicial amendment even if judges purport to be guided by the founders' original purposes or intentions. Consider the following form of argument:

1. The founders intended the constitution to achieve *x*;
2. The founders did not expressly include *y* in the constitution, because they believed that *y* is unnecessary to achieve *x*;
3. The founders were wrong: *y* is necessary to achieve *x*;
4. A legal instrument includes by implication any norm that is practically necessary for it to fulfil one of its intended purposes;
5. Therefore, the constitution includes *y* by implication.

This form of argument, in practice, may be open to various objections. One is that the necessity alleged in step 3 may be false. It is all too easy for judges to attribute necessity to a norm that is, at best, arguably desirable. In Australia, for example, an implied freedom of political speech was held to be implicit in the Constitution on the ground that it is "necessary" to ensure that voters are able to make a genuine choice in electing members of Parliament, as required by the Constitution.[122] But there is no necessity here at all, as is obvious from the existence of many flourishing democracies that have had no judicially enforceable right to free speech. Freedom of speech, sufficiently ample to enable genuine electoral choices to be made, has been effectively protected by cultural traditions and by the democratic process itself. That is why the implied freedom escaped the notice of Australian lawyers and judges for the previous ninety years, even though they argued and decided cases in which it would have been decisive had it been noticed.[123] It would undoubtedly be legitimate for a court, in enforcing express provisions requiring that the people choose their representatives, to invalidate legislation restricting political communication

[121] See J. Goldsworthy, "Interpreting the *Constitution* in its Second Century," (2000) 24 Melbourne U.L. Rev. 677 at 690.

[122] *Australian Capital Television Pty Ltd v. Commonwealth* (1992), 177 C.L.R. 106.

[123] Most notably *Australian Communist Party v. Commonwealth* (1951), 83 C.L.R. 1.

so severely that it prevents them from making a genuine choice. But there is no necessity to go one step further, and derive from those provisions an implied freedom that is then applied independently of them, to invalidate any laws deemed to infringe the freedom, whether or not they prevent genuine electoral choices.

A second objection is that, even if step 3 is granted, step 4 is false, and therefore so is the conclusion in step 5. The founders' supposed error is taken to show, not that the constitution needs to be amended to correct a deficiency, but that it already includes something that was deliberately excluded from it, because it ought to have been included in order to achieve the founders' objectives. If this reasoning is sound, then again, almost anything could in principle be added to a constitution, particularly if the founders' objectives are pitched at a very abstract level (such as "the founders intended the Constitution to achieve democracy, or justice, or good government"). Judges are surely bound not only by the founders' ends, but by the means they chose to achieve those ends. Otherwise a constitution is just a set of abstract objectives, which the judges can choose to implement in any way they think fit. That is why it has been said that a constitution's deliberate omissions are entitled to just as much respect as its positive provisions.[124] Judges are not permitted to delete a positive provision from a constitution on the ground that its inclusion was a mistake. How, then, could they be justified in adding a provision to a constitution on the ground that its omission was a mistake? Judges are not supposed to be "statesmen," appointed to fill the shoes of the founders and continue the task of constitution-making as an on-going enterprise, correcting mistakes and omissions wherever they see them.

Step 4, the proposition that a legal instrument includes by implication any norm that is practically necessary for it to fulfil one of its intended purposes, is false because the drafters of the instrument may simply have made a mistake. If they decided not to include that norm, because they did not think it necessary to achieve their objectives, it hardly seems plausible to regard it as an implicit assumption or any other kind of implication.[125] The usual requirement that

[124] The Hon. M. Gleeson, *The Rule of Law and the Constitution* (2000) at 70.

[125] It might be argued, to the contrary, that the founders can be assumed to have had an overarching intention that any norm subsequently thought to be practically necessary for the fulfilment of any of their other intentions should be held to be part of the Constitution, even if they themselves did not believe and probably would not agree that the norm is practically necessary. But this is extremely implausible: It would amount to the founders intending to give the judges a blank cheque to add to the Constitution whatever the latter might happen to believe is necessary for its effective operation, regardless of whether or not the founders themselves believed or would have agreed that it is.

an ad hoc implication should be recognised only if it is "necessary" should therefore be understood as concerned with a kind of psychological rather than practical necessity. Instead of asking whether the alleged implication is practically necessary for the instrument to operate effectively, we should ask whether or not interpreters are, as it were, compelled to acknowledge the implication, because it is so obvious as to be undeniable. In contract law, the question has sometimes been said to be whether the court is "necessarily driven" to the conclusion that some term is implied.[126] The term "necessity" is used loosely here: what is really required is not that the implication cannot *possibly* be denied, but that it cannot *reasonably* be denied. In a case involving statutory interpretation, Isaacs, Barton and Rich JJ. said that "necessary intendment only means that the force of the language in its surroundings carries such strength of impression in one direction, that to entertain the opposite view appears wholly unreasonable."[127]

A third possible objection to the form of argument in question is that step 1 may misstate the founders' intention. They may have intended the constitution to achieve *x* – such as to implement some constitutional principle – only to a partial or qualified extent, because they wanted to accommodate some competing principle or objective. Such accommodations should be respected, even if judges today believe them be regrettable. This is the main objection to Mark Walters' argument in his contribution to this volume. He asserts that unwritten constitutional principles are "not dependent upon the choices made by the writers of the constitution," because if those choices "result in written protections for an important constitutional principle that are not 'uniform or consistent,'" the judges may resort to a common law practice of "equal reason" and conclude that the principle should be given comprehensive protection.[128] Walters apparently believes that any constitution lacking a bill of rights is "less than comprehensive," in which case the judges' resort to "unwritten constitutionalism is inevitable."[129] For example, if the constitution lacks a written provision guaranteeing equality, judges "will *have to* infer a general principle of equality through a discourse of reason."[130] He therefore approves of the reasoning of two judges who held that the Australian Constitution includes a doctrine of legal equality, which limits legislative power, even though the

[126] *Hamlyn v. Wood* (1891), 2 Q.B. 488 *per* Kay L.J. at 494, quoted with approval by Lord Atkinson, speaking for the Judicial Committee of the Privy Council, in *Douglas v. Baynes*, [1908] A.C. 477 at 482. See also *Nelson v. Walker* (1910), 10 C.L.R. 560 *per* Isaacs J at 586. See also H. Lucke, "Ad Hoc Implications in Written Contracts," (1973) 5 Adel. L. Rev. 32 at 34.

[127] *Worrall v. Commercial Banking Co of Sydney Ltd* (1917), 24 C.L.R. 28 at 32.

[128] Walters, "Written Constitutions and Unwritten Constitutionalism," in this volume at 265.

[129] *Ibid.* at 29 and 38–9.

[130] *Ibid.* at 36 [emphasis added].

Constitution's founders considered and rejected a proposal to include just such a provision.[131] I find it ironic that Walters ascribes this approach to "a sense of humility,"[132] because it would be extraordinarily arrogant for judges to presume to correct what they perceive to be a lack of "uniformity or consistency" in the founders' decision to provide only partial or qualified provision for particular principles. Even if their decision were in some sense wrong, surely it should be corrected by the democratic institutions in which the Constitution itself has vested the power of formal amendment.[133]

All this is subject to a proviso. Elsewhere, I have acknowledged that the difficulty of amending constitutions might be regarded as a reason for judges to be more creative when interpreting them, compared with other laws.[134] Consider the extent to which judges should remedy failures on the part of the constitution's founders to expressly provide for problems. They may have failed to anticipate the problem because it was very unlikely to arise, or because they were too busy, or insufficiently astute, to do so. When interpreting statutes, judges are often reluctant to rectify failures of that kind, preferring to leave it to the legislature to do so. But when dealing with a constitution, it is arguable that they should be more willing to provide a solution. If, because of the founders' oversight, a constitution might fail to achieve one of its main purposes, the potential consequences are grave. They include the danger of constitutional powers being abused, of the democratic process or the federal system being subverted, of human rights being egregiously violated, and so on. If the constitution is extremely difficult to amend formally, or if amendment requires action by the very politicians who pose the threat that needs to be checked, there may be good moral reasons for the judges to act. Many judicial decisions recognising implied intergovernmental immunities have been reached in cases of this kind. On the other hand, there is an obvious risk of this reasoning justifying extensive rewriting of the constitution, especially if the founders' purposes are pitched at a very abstract level.

But whether or not the judges should rectify a legal instrument, by in effect inserting some norm into it, is a different question from whether or not the norm can plausibly be regarded as already implicit in it. If judges decide to rectify a legal instrument, they should frankly acknowledge what they are doing, and not hide behind make-believe implications – unless they are morally justified

[131] *Ibid.* at 36–8 and 40 note 125.

[132] *Ibid.* at 43.

[133] To the extent that Walters' argument is based on the notion that certain principles of "legality" form part of the concept of "law" that is presupposed by the Constitution, it is vulnerable to objections made in the text above at 285–9.

[134] This passage is taken from J. Goldsworthy, "Conclusions," in J. Goldsworthy ed., *Interpreting Constitutions: a Comparative Study* (2006) 321 at 324.

by extraordinary circumstances in lying about what they are doing. It is notable that lawyers often feel compelled to speak, eccentrically, of some term being "implied into" a legal instrument by a court. This is eccentric because in ordinary parlance, an implication is not inserted into a text by an interpreter, but found to be already within it. It is implied by the text, from which it is inferred by the interpreter, and not "implied into" the text by the interpreter. Note the similar eccentricity of the notion of a term being "read into" an instrument by judges. Such terminology is euphemistic: it shows that even when lawyers are aware that judges are really inserting terms into legal texts, they are reluctant to admit it openly.

CONCLUSION

I have discussed three kinds of claims on behalf of unwritten or implied constitutional principles: claims that they are inherent in our concept of law; claims that they are inherent in a "common law constitution" that supposedly underpins our written constitutions; and claims that they are implied or presupposed by particular, written constitutions. I have argued that claims of the first two kinds are refuted once we take into account the doctrine of parliamentary sovereignty. This is the elephant in the room that is usually overlooked or ignored by those who seek to aggrandize our "ancient tradition" of "legality." The doctrine's predominance within Britain's *actual* constitutional tradition (as opposed to mythical ones concocted by wishful thinking) – inherited by countries such as Canada and Australia – is inconsistent both with the proffered analysis of our concept of law, and with the pretensions of common law constitutionalism. Claims of the third kind may in some cases be persuasive, but that depends on there being sufficient evidence that the constitution's founders had the requisite law-making intentions.

Index

For EU product safety concerns, contact us at Calle de José Abascal, 56–1°, 28003 Madrid, Spain or eugpsr@cambridge.org.

www.ingramcontent.com/pod-product-compliance
Lightning Source LLC
LaVergne TN
LVHW090309210926
848480LV00001B/184
* 9 7 8 0 5 2 1 1 7 3 3 4 6 *